LAW IN ENVIRONMENTAL DECISION-MAKING

Law in Environmental Decision-Making

National, European, and International Perspectives

TIM JEWELL

and

JENNY STEELE

University of Southampton

CLARENDON PRESS · OXFORD
1998

Oxford University Press, Great Clarendon Street, Oxford OX2 6DP
Oxford New York
Athens Auckland Bangkok Bogota Bombay Buenos Aires
Calcutta Cape Town Dar es Salaam Delhi Florence Hong Kong Istanbul
Karachi Kuala Lumpur Madras Madrid Melbourne Mexico City
Nairobi Paris Singapore Taipei Tokyo Toronto Warsaw
and associated companies in
Berlin Ibadan

Oxford is a registered trade mark of Oxford University Press

Published in the United States
by Oxford University Press Inc., New York

First published 1998

British Library Cataloguing in Publication Data
Data available

Library of Congress Cataloging in Publication Data
Law in environmental decision-making / [edited by] Tim Jewell and Jenny Steele.
p. cm.
Includes bibliographical references and index.
1. Environmental law—Great Britain. 2. Environmental law, International. 3. Environmental protection—Decision making. I. Jewell, Tim. II. Steele, Jenny.
KD3372.L39 1998
344.41′046—dc21 98–12334

ISBN 0–19–826077–6 ✓

1 3 5 7 9 10 8 6 4 2

Typeset by Graphicraft Typesetters Ltd., Hong Kong
Printed in Great Britain
on acid-free paper by
Bookcraft Ltd., Midsomer Norton, Somerset

Notes on Contributors

Christine Chinkin is Professor of International Law at the London School of Economics. Her research interests are in public international law, alternative dispute resolution, and feminism and the law. She is author of *Third Parties in International Law* (Oxford, 1993) and co-author (with Hilary Astor) of *Dispute Resolution in Australia* (Sydney, 1992).

Tony Evans is a Lecturer in Politics and International Relations at the University of Southampton. His research interests are in international political theory and the political economy of human rights. He is author of *US Hegemony and the Project of Universal Human Rights* (Basingstoke, 1996), and editor of *Human Rights Fifty Years On: A Reappraisal* (Manchester, 1998).

Tim Jewell is a Lecturer in Environmental Law at the University of Southampton, where he is also Director of the Centre for Environmental Law. His interests include environmental enforcement policy and practice, the regulation of mineral exploitation, and power sharing in environmental management. He is co-author of Waite and Jewell, *Environmental Law in Property Transactions* (London, 1997), and Managing Editor of the journal, *Environmental Law and Management.*

Clíona Kimber is a Lecturer in Law at the University of Aberdeen, and Director of the University of Aberdeen Centre for Environmental Law and Policy. Her research interests include European environmental law and environmental regulation. She has recently completed a study, together with Meropi Voytazi and Maria de la Torre, of implementation of the European Directive on Access to Environmental Information.

David Robinson worked as a solicitor with the Environmental Defender's Office (Sydney) from 1989–1992, and was a visiting tutor and researcher in environmental law at the University of Southampton and the Institute of Advanced Legal Studies, London, from 1992–94. He is currently a legal officer with the Environment Protection Authority, New South Wales. He is co-editor of *Environmental Responsibilities Law Service* (New South Wales) and of Robinson and Dunkley, *Public Interest Perspectives in Environmental Law* (Chichester, 1995).

Han Somsen is a Lecturer in Law at the Catholic University of Nijmegen, the Netherlands, and was formerly at the University of Warwick. He is editor of

Protecting the European Environment (London, 1996), and editor-in-chief of the *Yearbook of European Environmental Law* (Oxford).

Jenny Steele is a Lecturer in Law at the University of Southampton. She has published a number of articles on the development of common law responses to environmental problems, on environmental liability more generally, and on environmental policy.

Contents

Preface ix
Table of Cases xi
Table of Legislation xvii
Table of Abbreviations xxix

1. Law in Environmental Decision-Making 1
   Jenny Steele and Tim Jewell
2. Regulatory Evolution in Pollution Control 29
   David Robinson
3. Public Law and the Environment: The Prospects for Decision-Making 73
   Tim Jewell
4. Assessing the Past: Tort Law and Environmental Risk 107
   Jenny Steele
5. Understanding Access to Environmental Information: the European Experience 139
   Clíona Kimber
6. Dynamics, Process, and Instruments of Environmental Decision-Making in the European Union 161
   Han Somsen
7. International Environmental Law and the Challenge of Globalization 207
   Tony Evans
8. International Environmental Law in Evolution 229
   Christine Chinkin

Bibliography 267
Index 285

Preface

At the time when we first formed the idea for this collection of essays, it seemed to us that environmental law had matured beyond the stage where it was struggling for recognition as a distinctive subject, and that it was appropriate to consider not so much how it might be distinguished from other areas of law, but how it might influence and be influenced by those other areas. During the writing of this collection, a number of factors—including the emerging centrality of 'sustainable development' in the language of environmental policy, and the emphasis on new legal styles to replace or at least qualify the traditional 'command-and-control' techniques of this area of law—have persuaded us that our initial approach is increasingly pertinent, and that it is related to a broad issue concerning the role of environmental concerns among other policy goals. Our contributors have thus been able to draw on a broad range of recent developments in environmental law in the course of their arguments, though it should be emphasised that this collection makes no claim to exhaustiveness on this account. The contributions were substantially completed by October 1997.

Since the collection has been evolving for a number of years, we have accumulated a very large debt of gratitude to a considerable number of people. We would like to thank Richard Hart for his very important early interest in and support of this project, and our editor, Myf Milton, for seeing it through to completion with such patience. Early versions of most of the papers were presented at the SLSA conference in Southampton in 1996, and we would like to thank the participants at the relevant sessions for their contributions, especially Neil Gunningham and Annemarie Sprokkereef. Later drafts of certain chapters have greatly benefited from the comments and criticisms of Michael Purdue, Brian Thompson, Martin Loughlin, Andrew Halpin, Colin Reid, Ben Pontin, Laurence Lustgarten, and Kit Barker. Heartfelt thanks to all of these, although as usual they should not be taken to be in any way responsible for the contents. Parts of the opening chapter were also 'aired' at a meeting of the SPTL Environment Section in Manchester in 1997, and the comments of participants were much appreciated. At one time or another, we have also benefited from the excellent research assistance of Ben Pontin (again), Dave Carter, and Lucy Arnott. General thanks are owed to all our colleagues in the Law Faculty at Southampton, for contributing to the unusually warm and supportive environment to be found there. We also acknowledge with thanks the assistance of the ESRC. Work conducted on the funded research project, 'The Financial Implications of Environmental Legislation' (Project No. L320253226), has greatly influenced the first chapter of this book, in particular.

Finally, and above all, Jenny would like to say 'thank you' to Adrian and to her parents, and Tim would like to thank Kay, Sylvia, Simon, Emily, Lucy, Tayla, and of course Martin. We would also like to welcome to the world both Ben Robinson and Seth Evans, who arrived during the time spent finishing this collection.

Southampton,
March 1998

Tim Jewell
Jenny Steele

Table of Cases

Australia

Commonwealth of Australia v State of Tasmania (1983) 158 CLR 1, High Ct 264
Environment Protection Authority v Caltex Refining Co. Pty. Ltd. (1993) 68 ALJR 127 48
He Kaw Teh (1985) 157 CLR 523 48
Olson v CSR Ltd. and Midalco Ltd., Dust Diseases Tribunal of New South Wales, 24 December 1994 128

Canada

R v City of Sault Ste Marie (1978) 85 DLR 161 48

European Union

Numerical List

Case 26/62: Van Gend en Loos [1963] ECR 1 ....178, 199
Case 34/73: Variola v Italian Finance Administration [1973] ECR 981 189
Case 33/76: Rewe-Zentralfinanz v Landwirtschaftkammer [1976] ECR 1989 202
Case 45/76: Comet v Produktschap [1976] ECR 2043 202
Case 106/77: Amministrazione delle Finanze dello Stato v Simmenthal [1978] ECR 629 202
Case 120/78: Rewe-Zentrale v Bundesmonopolverwaltung für Branttwein [1979] ECR 649 ....173, 191
Joined Cases 91 and 92/79: Commission v Italy [1980] ECR 1099 ....182, 199
Case 102/79: Commission v Belgium [1980] ECR 1473 199
Case 171/80: Commission v Italy [1981] ECR 203 198
Case 71/81: Commission v Belgium [1982] ECR 175 199
Case 96/81: Commission v Netherlands [1982] ECR 1791 197
Case 97/81: Commission v Netherlands [1982] ECR 1819 ....197, 199
Case 301/81: Commission v Belgium [1983] ECR 467 198

Case 14/83: Von Colson and Kamann v Land Nordrhein Westfalen [1984] ECR 1891 202
Case 240/83: Procureur de la République v Association de Défense des Brûleurs d'Huiles Usagées [1985] ECR 531 182
Case 294/83: Parti Ecologiste 'Les Verts' v Parliament [1986] ECR 1339 ... 185
Case 291/84: Commission v Netherlands [1987] ECR 3483 198
Case 236/85: Commission v Netherlands [1987] ECR 3989 .... 196, 197
Case 247/85: Commission v Belgium [1987] ECR 3029 196
Case 252/85: Commission v France [1988] ECR 2243 196
Case 262/85: Commission v Italy [1987] ECR 3073 196
Case 412/85: Commission v Germany [1987] ECR 3503 .... 196, 197
Case 1/86: Commission v Belgium [1987] ECR 2797 199
Case 68/86: Commission v United Kingdom [1988] ECR 855 185
Case 131/86: United Kingdom v Council [1988] ECR 905 185
Case C–131/87: Commission v Council [1989] ECR 3743 185
Case C–339/87: Commission v Netherlands [1990] ECR I–851 196
Case 380/87: Cinisello Balsamo [1989] ECR 2491 .... 197, 198
Case C–131/88: Commission v Germany [1991] ECR I–825 199
Case C–322/88: Grimaldi v Fonds des Maladies Professionelles [1989] ECR I–4407 190
Case C–361/88: Commission v Germany [1991] ECR I–2567 197
Case C–57/89: Commission v Italy [1991] ECR I–57 196
Case C–59/89: Commission v Germany [1991] ECR I–2607 197
Case C–213/89: R v. Secretary of State for Transport, ex parte Factortame [1990] ECR I–2433 202
Case C–300/89: Commission v Council [1991] ECR I–2867 .... 177, 185–7
Case C–2/90: Commission v Belgium [1992] ECR I–4431 186
Joined Cases C–6/90 and C–9/90: Francovich and Bonifaci v Italy [1990] ECR I–5357 202
Case C–190/90: Commission v Netherlands [1991] ECR I–3265 197
Case C–355/90: Commission v Spain [1993] ECR I–4221 200
Case C–155/91: Commission v Council [1993] ECR I–939 186
Case C–392/93: R v HM Treasury, ex parte British Telecommunications [1996] ECR I–1631 202
Case T–585/93: Greenpeace International and Others v Commission of the European Communities [1995] ECR II–2205 150
Case C–5/94: R v Ministry of Agriculture, Fisheries and Food, ex parte Hedley Lomas [1996] ECR I–2553 202
Case C–179/94: Dillenkofer v Germany [1996] ECR I–4845 202
Case C–194/94: CIA Security International v Signalson SA and Securitel SPRL [1995] ECR I–180 198
Case T–105/95: WWF (UK) v Commission of the European Communities [1997] ECR II–313 149

Alphabetical List

Amministrazione delle Finanze dello Stato v Simmenthal (Case 106/77) [1978] ECR 629 202
Cassis de Dijon. *See* Case 120/78: Rewe-Zentrale 202
CIA Security International v Signalson SA and Securitel SPRL (Case C–194/94) [1995] ECR I–180 198
Cinisello Balsamo (Case 380/87) [1989] ECR 2491 ....197, 198
Comet v Produktschap (Case 45/76) [1976] ECR 2043 202
Commission v Belgium (Case 102/79) [1980] ECR 1473 199
Commission v Belgium (Case 71/81) [1982] ECR 175 199
Commission v Belgium (Case 301/81) [1983] ECR 467 198
Commission v Belgium (Case 247/85) [1987] ECR 3023 196
Commission v Belgium (Case 1/86) [1987] ECR 2797 199
Commission v Belgium (Case C–2/90) [1992] ECR I–4431 186
Commission v Council (Case C–131/87) [1989] ECR 3743 185
Commission v Council (Case C–300/89) [1991] ECR I–2867 ....177, 185–7
Commission v Council (Case C–155/91) [1993] ECR I–939 186
Commission v France (Case 252/85) [1988] ECR 2243 196
Commission v Germany (Case 412/85) [1987] ECR 3503 ....196, 197
Commission v Germany (Case C–131/88) [1991] ECR I–825 199
Commission v Germany (Case C–361/88) [1991] ECR I–2567 197
Commission v Germany (Case C–59/89) [1991] ECR I–2607 197
Commission v Italy (Joined Cases 91 and 92/79) [1980] ECR 1099 ....182, 199
Commission v Italy (Case 171/80) [1981] ECR 203 198
Commission v Italy (Case 262/85) [1987] ECR 3073 196
Commission v Italy (Case C–57/89) [1991] ECR I–57 196
Commission v Netherlands (Case 96/81) [1982] ECR 1791 197
Commission v Netherlands (Case 97/81) [1982] ECR 1819 ....197, 199
Commission v Netherlands (Case 291/84) [1987] ECR 3483 198
Commission v Netherlands (Case 236/85) [1987] ECR 3989 ....196, 197
Commission v Netherlands (Case C–339/87) [1990] ECR I–851 196
Commission v Netherlands (Case C–190/90) [1991] ECR I–3265 197
Commission v Spain (Case C–355/90) [1993] ECR I–4221 200
Commission v United Kingdom (Case 68/86) [1988] ECR 855 185
Dillenkofer v Germany (Case C–179/94) [1996] ECR I–4845 202
Francovich and Bonifaci v Italy (Joined Cases C–6/90 and C–9/90) [1990] ECR I–5357 202
Greenpeace International and Others v Commission of the European Communities (Case T–585/93) [1995] ECR II–2205 150
Grimaldi v Fonds Maladies Professionelles (Case C–322/88) [1989] ECR I–4407 190
Marisma de Santona. *See* Case C–355/90: Commission v Spain

Parti Ecologiste 'Les Verts' v Parliament (Case 294/83) [1986] ECR 1339 185
Procureur de la République v Association de Défense des Brûleurs d'Huiles Usagées (Case 240/83) [1985] ECR 531 182
R v HM Treasury, ex parte British Telecommunications (Case C–392/93) [1996] ECR I–1631 202
R v Ministry of Agriculture, Fisheries and Food, ex parte Hedley Lomas (Case C–5/94) [1996] ECR I–2553 202
R v Secretary of State for Transport, ex parte Factortame (Case C–213/89) [1990] ECR I–2433 202
Rewe-Zentrale v Bundesmonopolverwaltung für Branttwein (Case 120/78) [1979] ECR 649 ....173, 191
Rewe-Zentralfinanz v Landwirtschaftkammer (Case 33/76) [1976] ECR 1989 202
Simmenthal (Case 106/77) [1978] ECR 629 202
Titanium Dioxide. *See* Case C–300/89: Commission v Council
United Kingdom v Council (Case 131/86) [1988] ECR 905 185
Van Gend en Loos (Case 26/62) [1963] ECR 1 ....178, 199
Variola v Italian Finance Administration (Case 34/73) [1973] ECR 981 189
Von Colson and Kamann v Land Nordrhein Westfalen (Case 14/83) [1984] ECR 1891 202
WWF (UK) v Commission of the European Communities (Case T–105/95) [1997] ECR II–313 149

International

Australia-Republic of Nauru: Settlement of the Case in the International Court of Justice Concerning Certain Phosphate Lands in Nauru (10 August 1993) Rep. 32 ILM 1471 (1993) 257
Barcelona Traction Light and Power Company Case (Belgium v Spain) New Application 1970 ICJ Rep. 3, 32 (Order of 5 February) 255
Certain Phosphate Lands in Nauru (Nauru v Australia) Preliminary Objections 1992 ICJ Rep. 240 (judgment of 26 June) 255–7
Continental Shelf (Libya Arab Jamahiriya/Malta), Case Concerning, *Application by Italy to Intervene* [1984] ICJ Rep. 3 (judgment of 21 March) 253, 258
Continental Shelf (Tunisia/Libya Arab Jamahiriya), Case Concerning, *Application by Malta to Intervene* 1981 ICJ Rep. 3 (judgment of 14 April) 253
Corfu Channel Case (United Kingdom v Albania) Merits 1949 ICJ Rep. 4 (judgment of 9 April) 233, 250, 258, 262
East Timor (Portugal v Australia) 1995 ICJ Rep. 90 (judgment of 30 June) 257, 258
Factory at Chorzów (Germany v Poland) Merits 1928 PCIJ Ser. A No. 17 233

Gabcíkovo-Nagymaros Project (Hungary-Slovakia), Case Concerning 1997 ICJ Rep. (judgment of 25 September) 243, 251, 252
Lac Lanoux Arbitration (France v Spain) 24 ILR 101 250
Land, Island and Maritime Frontier Dispute (El Salvador/Honduras) *Application by Nicaragua to Intervene* 1990 ICJ Rep. 92 (judgment of 13 September) 253
Legality of the Threat or Use of Nuclear Weapons 1996 ICJ Rep. (Adv. Op. 8 July) Rep. 35 ILM 809 (1996) 235, 238, 260–2
Legality of the Use by a State of Nuclear Weapons in Armed Conflict 1996 ICJ Rep. (Adv. Op. 8 July) 259, 261
Military and Paramilitary Activities in and against Nicaragua (Nicaragua v United States) *Declaration of Intervention* 1984 ICJ Rep. 215 (Order of 4 October) 253
Monetary Gold Removed from Rome in 1943, Case of (Italy v France, United Kingdom and United States) Preliminary Question 1954 ICJ Rep. 32 (Order of 15 June) 256, 257
New Zealand's Request for an Examination of the Situation in accordance with Paragraph 63 of the Court's 1974 Judgment concerning Nuclear Tests (New Zealand v France) 1995 ICJ Rep. 306 254
Nuclear Tests *Application by Fiji for Permission to Intervene* 1974 ICJ Rep. 530; 1974 ICJ Rep. 535 (Order of 20 December) 253, 254
Nuclear Tests (Australia v France) 1974 ICJ Rep. 253 ....234, 235, 253–5, 263
Nuclear Tests (New Zealand v France) 1974 ICJ Rep. 457 ....234, 235, 253, 254, 263
Nuclear Tests (New Zealand v France) 1995 ICJ Rep. 306 (Order of 22 September) 253–6, 263
Reparation for Injuries Suffered in the Service of the United Nations 1949 ICJ Rep. 174 (Adv. Op. 11 April) 236
South West Africa Cases (Ethiopia v South Africa; Liberia v South Africa) Second Phase 1966 ICJ Rep. 4 (judgment of 18 July) 254–6
Trail Smelter Arbitration (United States v Canada) 3 RIAA (1941) 1907 ....233, 250
United States Restrictions on Imports of Tuna (EEC and the Netherlands v United States) Rep. 33 ILM 839 (1994) 241
United States Restrictions on Imports of Tuna (Mexico v United States) Rep. 30 ILM 1598 (1991) 241

United Kingdom

Alphacell v Woodward [1972] AC 824 48
Anns v Merton [1978] 1 AC 728 134
Bushell v Secretary of State for the Environment [1981] AC 75 95

Cambridge Water Co. Ltd. v Eastern Counties Leather plc [1994] 2 AC 264 ....9, 127, 130, 131, 133
Caparo Industries Ltd. v Dickman plc [1990] 2 AC 605....126
Gillingham v Medway (Chatham) Dock Co. Ltd. [1992] 2 WLR 449....137
Graham and Graham v ReChem International Ltd. [1996] Env LR 158 ....130, 131
Hunter v Canary Wharf Ltd.; sub nom Hunter v London Docklands Development Corporation [1997] 2 WLR 684, HL; [1996] 2 WLR 348, CA....130, 132–7
Khorasandjian v Bush [1993] QB 727, CA....133
Margereson v JW Roberts Ltd.; Hancock v JW Roberts Ltd. (judgment of 27 October 1995, High Ct.); appeal dismissed by judgment of 2 April 1996, CA....125–30
Merlin v BNF [1990] 3 WLR 383....130
Pride of Derby v British Celanese [1953] 1 All ER 179....107
R v Beck, ex parte Daily Telegraph plc [1993] 2 All ER 177....156
R v Secretary of State for Trade and Industry, ex parte Duddridge (1995) 7 Journal of Environmental Law 224....8
Reay and Hope v BNF [1994] 5 Medical LR 1....130
Rylands v Fletcher (1868) LR 3 HL 330....130–2
Wheeler v Saunders [1995] 2 All ER 697....137

United States of America

Environmental Defense Fund v Environmental Protection Agency, 489 F.2nd 1247 (D.C. Cir. 1973)....35
Natural Resources Defense Council v Train DDC, 1976; 8 ERC 2120....45
US v Fleet Factors Corp, 901 F.2nd 1550 (11th Cir. 1990)....23

Table of Legislation

Australia

Commonwealth

Resource Assessment Commission Act 1989 61

New South Wales

Clean Air Act 1961 34
Clean Waters Act 1970 .... 34, 36, 45
s. 11 35
Environmental Offences and Penalties Act 1989 48
Environmental Planning and Assessment Act 1997 46
Environmentally Hazardous Chemicals Act 1985 34
Fisheries Management Act 1994 51
Freedom of Information Act 1989 56
Noise Control Act 1975 44
Pesticides Act 1978 46
s. 37 46
Protection of the Environment Administration Act 1991
s. 6 51
s. 11 53
Protection of the Environment Operations Act 1997 44–6
Threatened Species Act 1995 51
Waste Disposal Act 1970 34

Victoria

Environment Protection Act 1970 51
ss. 19D–19G 70
ss. 26A–26E 64

Canada

Coastal Fisheries Protection Act 1985 234

European Union

Treaties

Single European Act 165, 167, 171, 173, 175, 181, 182, 185
Treaty of Amsterdam............................4, 163, 164, 165, 169, 204
Treaty of Rome (EC Treaty) 170, 176, 177, 179
art. 2............................163, 170, 178, 181–3
art. 3 ....163, 164, 170, 178, 181, 183
art. 3b 183, 187–9, 194
(2), (3) 189
new art 3d 4, 164
art. 4............................170, 172, 181
art. 5 ....190, 194
arts. 30–34............................166
art. 30............................186
art. 36............................166
art. 43 ....177, 185
art. 75............................177
art. 93............................173
art. 100 ....166–8, 182, 185
art. 100a............................176, 182, 183, 185, 186
(1) 169, 204
(3)............................164, 166, 185
(4) 164, 169, 173, 183, 203
art. 100r 163
(2) 164
arts. 100s, 100t 163
arts. 113, 129a............................177
art 130............................4
art. 130r 166, 182, 184, 185, 204
(1)............................182, 183, 204
(2) 185
(3) 204
art. 130s 166, 175, 176, 182–6, 194, 204
(1), (2) 184
(3)............................180, 181
art. 130t............................166, 169, 182, 183
art. 155............................197
art. 164............................196
art. 169 ....173, 174, 182, 196, 201
art. 170............................201
art. 171(2)............................200

art. 173 .... 170, 185, 204
art. 175 .... 170, 181
art. 177 .... 170, 196, 201, 202
art. 186 200
art. 189 189
arts. 189b, 189c 175
art. 228 177
(6) 170
art. 235 .... 166, 167, 181
art. 236 181
Treaty on European Union (Maastricht Treaty) 8, 165, 169, 174–7, 180, 183, 185–7
art. B 183
art. C.1 183
art. L 177
art. N 181

Regulations

Regulation 1210/90/EEC (OJ 1990 L120) 192
Regulation 880/92/EEC (OJ 1992 L99) 79, 147
Regulation 1836/93/EEC (OJ 1993 L168) 64, 82
art. 1 64

Decisions

Decision 93/731/EC (OJ 1993 L340) 147

Directives

Directive 75/442/EEC (OJ 1975 L194)
art. 3(2) 197, 198
Directive 76/160/EEC (OJ 1976 L31) 86, 167
art. 1(2)(a) 195
Directive 76/464/EEC (OJ 1976 L129/33) 166, 193
Directive 79/409/EEC (OJ 1979 L103) 167, 169, 196, 197
Directive 82/501/EEC (OJ 1982 L230) 176
Directive 83/129/EEC (OJ 1983 L91) 176
Directive 83/189/EEC (OJ 1983 L109)
arts. 8, 9 198
Directive 85/337/EEC (OJ 1985 L175) 147, 203
recital (2) 168

Directive 84/631/EEC (OJ 1985 L326)....176
Directive 89/428 EEC (OJ 1989 L201)....185
Directive 90/313/EEC (OJ 1990 L15)....15, 17, 96, 139, 144, 146–60
recital (3)....142
art. 2....148
art. 3....148, 153
art. 4....151
art. 8....139
art. 9....153
Directive 91/156/EEC (OJ 1991 L78)....186
Directive 94/62/EC (OJ 1994 L365)....79
Directive 96/61/EC (OJ 1996 L257)....50
Proposed Directive on Ecological Quality of Water (OJ 1994 C222)
art. 6....86

Rules of Procedure

rr. 63, 121....175

Germany

Gesetz zur Umsetzung der Richtlinie 90/313/EWG des Rates vom 7.6.1990 über den freien Zugang zu Information über die Umwelt vom 8 Juli 1994, BGBI I 1994, p1490 (UIG)....153
§ 7(1), (2)....156
§ 8.II(1)....157
Reichsnaturschutzgesetz 1935....161

International Agreements

African Charter on Human Rights and Peoples Rights (27 June 1981) Rep. 21 ILM 58 (1982)
art. 22....238
art. 24....236
African Nuclear Weapon Free Zone Treaty (Addis Ababa, 21–23 June 1995) Rep. 35 ILM 698 (1996)....263
Agenda 21 (Earth Summit, Rio de Janeiro, 1992) UN Doc. A/Conf. 151/PC/100/Add. 1 (1992)....214, 229
Chapter 2....240
Chapter 8....79

Agreement for the Implementation of the Provisions of the UN Convention on the Law of the Sea of 10 December 1982 Relating to the Conservation and Management of Straddling Fish Stocks and Highly Migratory Species (4 August 1995) Rep. 34 ILM 1542 (1995) 234
Agreement Relating to the Implementation of Part XI of the UN Convention on the Law of the Sea Rep. 33 ILM 1309 (1994)
Annex, s. 5(1)(a) 242
American Convention on Human Rights (22 November 1969) OAS TS No. 36
arts. 33, 44 237
Biodiversity Convention Rep. 31 ILM 818 (1992) 211, 244
arts. 23, 25 248
art. 27 263
Budapest Treaty (16 September 1977) 251
arts. 15, 19, 20 ....251, 252
Comprehensive Nuclear Test Ban Treaty (September 1996) 262
Convention for the Protection of World Cultural and Natural Heritage (23 November 1972) 1037 UNTS 151 ....256, 259
Convention on Early Notification of a Nuclear Accident (Vienna 1986) Rep. 25 ILM 1370 (1986) 244
Covenant of the League of Nations 1919
art. 22 257
European Convention for the Protection of Human Rights and Fundamental Freedoms (4 November 1950) ETS No. 5
arts. 19–66 237
Protocol No. 11 (11 May 1994) Rep. ILM 943 (1994)
art. 1 237
European Social Charter (1961) 529 UNTS 89
art. 11 236
General Agreement on Tariffs and Trade 63, 241, 243
art. XX(b), (g) 240
Geneva Convention on the High Seas (1958) 450 UNTS 82
art. 2 234
Hague Declaration on the Environment (1989) Rep. 28 ILM 1308 (1989) 245
Instrument for the Establishment of the Restructured Global Environment Facility (1994) Rep. 33 ILM 1273 (1994) 232
Inter American Convention on Human Rights
Additional Protocol 1989 Rep. 28 ILM 156 (1989)
art. 11 236
International Covenant on Civil and Political Rights (16 December 1966) 999 UNTS 171
art. 1 238
art. 25 239
art. 28 237
First Optional Protocol 237

International Covenant on Economic, Social and Cultural Rights (16 December 1966) 993 UNTS 3
arts. 1, 11 238
Montreal Protocol on Substances that Deplete the Ozone Layer Rep. 26 ILM 1550 (1987) 211, 244
art. 2(5) 232
arts. 8, 11 248
North American Agreement on Environmental Cooperation (Washington, Ottawa and Mexico City, September 1993) Rep. 32 ILM 1480 (1993)
art. 1(d) 242
arts. 8–16 242
North American Free Trade Agreement (Washington, Ottawa and Mexico City, December 1992) Rep. 32 ILM 289 (1993)
Preamble 242
Pacific Security Treaty (ANZUS Treaty) (1 September 1951) 131 UNTS 83 235
Protocol on Environmental Protection to Antarctica (1991) Rep. 30 ILM 1455 (1991) 247
Rio Declaration (Declaration on Environment and Development, Rio de Janeiro, 1992) Rep. 31 ILM 876 (1992) 231, 245, 246
Principle 1 .... 231, 239
Principle 2 246
Principle 3 238
Principle 4 .... 9, 239
Principle 11 232
Principle 12 .... 240, 241
Principle 15 232
Principles 20–22 163
Principle 24 236
Principle 27 246
art. 10 163
South Pacific Convention for the Protection of the Natural Resources and Environment of the South Pacific Region, Noumea, Protocol for the Protection of Pollution of the South Pacific Region by Dumping and Protocol Concerning Co-operation in Combating Pollution Emergencies in the South Pacific Region Rep. 26 ILM 38 (1987) 248, 254, 256
art. 16 254
South Pacific Nuclear Free Zone Treaty (Raratonga, Cook Islands, 6 August 1985) 263
Annex 4 248
Statute of the International Court of Justice
art. 27 251
art. 34 252

art. 36 .... 249, 256
(2) 234, 235, 256, 257, 263
(a) 262
art. 38(1) 243
(c) 262
art. 50 258
art. 59 262
art. 62 .... 252, 253
art. 63 252–4
art. 66(2) 261
Stockholm Declaration on the Human Environment UN Doc. A/Conf.48/14 and Corr. 1 (1972) Rep. 11 ILM 1416 (1972) 229, 231, 245
Principle 1 .... 236, 238
Principle 21 246
Timor Gap Treaty (Treaty between Australia and the Republic of Indonesia on the Zone of Co-operation in an Area between the Indonesian Province of East Timor and Northern Australia, Timor Sea) (11 December 1989) Aust. TS No. 9, 1991 .... 257, 258
Treaty for the Prohibition of Nuclear Weapons in Latin America (Tlatelolco, 1967) 634 UNTS 281 263
Treaty on the South East Asia Nuclear Weapon Free Zone (15 December 1995) Rep. 35 ILM 635 (1996) 263
UN Charter 249
art. 2(3) 249
(4) 260
(7) 234
art. 13 245
art. 33 249
art. 39 235
art. 51 261
art. 92 262
art. 96 259
Chapter VII 235
UN Convention on the Law of the Sea (Montego Bay, 10 December 1982) Rep. 21 ILM 1261 (1982) 243, 244
art. 87 234
art. 144 242
art. 283 263
Pt. XI 242
Pt. XV 263
Annexes VII, VIII 263
UN Draft Code on Conduct of Transnational Corporations Rep. 23 ILM 626 (1984) 233

UN Framework Convention on Climate Change Rep. 31 ILM 851 (1992) 211, 231, 244
arts. 7, 9, 10 248
art. 14....263
UN General Assembly Resolutions—
GA Res. 217 A (III), 10 December 1948 264
GA Res. 2997, 1972 244
GA Res. 3281 1974 (XXIX) 242
GA Res. 41/128, 4 December 1986 238
GA Res. 45/94, 1990 236
GA Res. 47/37, 25 November 1992....236
UN Security Council Resolutions—
SC Res. 678, 28 November 1990....235
SC Res. 687, 3 April 1991 236
UNECE Draft Convention
recitals 142, 143
Vienna Convention for the Protection of the Ozone Layer (22 March 1985) Rep. 26 ILM 1529 (1987)....244, 263
Vienna Convention on the Law of Treaties (23 May 1969) 1155 UNTS 331 68
art. 2....246
art. 26....233
art. 31(1)....178
art. 34....244
arts. 53, 64....238
World Charter for Nature (1982) Rep. 23 ILM 455 (1983)....245

Republic of Ireland

Statutes

Freedom of Information Act (21 April 1997)....152

Statutory Instruments

Access to Information on the Environment Regulations 1993 (SI 1993 No. 133)....153
Access to Information on the Environment Regulations 1996 (SI 1996 No. 185)....153

Spain

Ley 38/1996, de 12 diciembre, sobre el derecho de accesso a la información en materia de medio ambiente 153
art. 3.1(e) 156

United Kingdom

Statutes

Alkali Act 1863 161
Clean Air Act 1956 .... 6, 85
Clean Air Act 1968 .... 6, 85
Clean Air Act 1993 .... 6, 85
Control of Pollution Act 1974
s. 41 93
Environment Act 1995 .... 8, 10, 78, 87, 100, 104, 128, 131, 132
s. 4(1) 7
s. 12 97
s. 31 7
ss. 41, 42 99
Pt. II (ss. 57–60) 6
s. 57 .... 86, 94
s. 78R 94
Pt. IV (ss. 80–91) 5
s. 80 87
(1) 95
s. 81 .... 87, 88
ss. 84, 92 87
ss. 93–95 82
Sched. 22, para. 170 94
Environmental Protection Act 1990 .... 6, 11, 50, 78, 85, 87
Pt. I (ss. 1–28) 5
s. 3 85
(5), (7) 95
s. 7(4) 8
s. 20 93
(1)(g) 56
s. 21 94
s. 22 .... 56, 94
Pt. II (ss. 29–78) 82

s. 36 ... 94
s. 52 ... 100
s. 64 ... 92, 94
ss. 65, 66 ... 94
Pt. IIA (ss. 78A–78YC) ... 6, 86
s. 143 ... 78
Sched. 1, Pt. I ... 94
Finance Act 1987
s. 1 ... 100
Finance Act 1996
ss. 39–71 ... 100
Hydrocarbon Oil Duties Act 1979
s. 13A ... 100
Nuclear Installations Act 1965 ... 122
Planning and Compensation Act 1991
s. 27 ... 87
Sched. 4 ... 87
Public Health Act 1875 ... 161
Rivers Pollution Prevention Act 1863 ... 161
Rivers (Prevention of Pollution) Act 1951
s. 7 ... 93
Smoke Nuisances (Metropolis) Act 1853
s. 1 ... 8
Town and Country Planning Act 1990
ss. 31–35C ... 86
s. 31(6) ... 86
ss. 39–48 ... 86
s. 54A ... 87
ss. 65, 69, 188 ... 93
Water Act 1989
ss. 104–106 ... 85
Water Industry Act 1991
s. 196 ... 93
Water Resources Act 1991
s. 37 ... 94
ss. 82–84 ... 85, 95
s. 88 ... 94
s. 189 ... 93
s. 190 ... 92, 93
s. 191 ... 93
s. 191A ... 94
Sched. 10 ... 94
para. 1(5) ... 94

Statutory Instruments

Air Quality Standards Regulations 1989 (SI 1989 No. 317) 85
Asbestos Industry Regulations 1931 (SI 1931 No. 1140)....127, 128
Control of Industrial Air Pollution (Registration of Works) Regulations 1989 (SI 1989 No. 318) 93
Control of Noise (Measurement and Registers) Regulations 1976 (SI 1976 No. 37)....93
Control of Pollution (Applications, Appeals and Registers) Regulations 1996 (SI 1996 No. 2971) 93
reg. 4....94
Controlled Waste (Registration of Carriers and Seizure of Vehicles) Regulations 1991 (SI 1991 No. 1624) 94
Environmental Information Regulations 1992 (SI 1992 No. 3240) ...96, 97, 153
reg. 3(1)....96
reg. 4(2)(b) 156
Environmental Protection (Applications, Appeals and Registers) Regulations 1991 (SI 1991 No. 507)....93
regs. 4, 5....94
Environmental Protection (Waste Recycling Payments) Regulations 1992 (SI 1992 No. 462) 100
Health and Safety (Emissions into the Atmosphere) Regulations 1983 (SI 1983 No. 943)....93
Landfill Tax Regulations 1996 (SI 1996 No. 1527)....100
Nitrate Sensitive Areas Regulations 1994 (SI 1994 No. 1729) 100
Set Aside Regulations 1988 (SI 1988 No. 1352) 100
Town and Country Planning (General Development Procedure) Order 1995 (SI 1995 No. 419)
arts. 6, 8, 25, 26 93
Town and Country Planning (Development Plan) Regulations 1991 (SI 1991 No. 2794)....86
Waste Management Licensing Regulations 1994 (SI 1994 No. 1056)
reg. 10 ....92, 94
Water Resources (Licences) Regulations 1965 (SI 1965 No. 574) 93

United States of America

Administrative Procedure Act 1946 10
Clean Air Act 32, 35, 47
Comprehensive Environmental Response, Compensation and Liability Act 1980 10

Emergency Planning and Community Right to Know Act 42 U.S.C.
§§ 11001–11050 .... 144, 154
Federal Water Pollution Control Act 35, 45
s. 101a(1), (5) 45
Marine Mammal Protection Act 1972 241
National Environment Protection Act 46

Table of Abbreviations

AJIL	*American Journal of International Law*
Aust TS	*Australian Treaty Series*
BAT	Best available control technology
BATNEEC	Best available techniques not entailing excessive cost
BNF	British Nuclear Fuels plc
BPM	Best practicable means
BSE	Bovine spongiform-encephalopathy
CEO	Chief executive officer
CERCLA	Comprehensive Environmental Response, Compensation and Liability Act 1980 (US)
CFCs	Chlorofluorocarbons
DDT	Dichlorodiphenyltrichloroethane
DG	Directorate General
Duke JCIL	*Duke Journal of Comparative and International Law*
EA 1995	Environment Act 1995 (UK)
EC	European Community
ECJ	European Court of Justice
ECR	European Court Reports
ELM	*Environmental Law and Management*
EMAS	Eco-management and audit scheme
EMS	Environmental management system
ENFO	Environmental information
Env LR	*Environmental Law Reports*
EPA	Environmental Protection Agency (US)
EPA (NSW)	Environment Protection Authority of New South Wales
EPA 1990	Environmental Protection Act 1990 (UK)
ESD	Ecologically sustainable development
ESRC	Economic and Social Research Council (UK)
ETS	*European Treaty Series*
EU	European Union
G7	Group of Seven
GIS	Geographical information system
Hague Recueil	*Recueil des Cours de l'Académie de droit international*
Harv ILJ	*Harvard International Law Journal*
HL	House of Lords
ICI	Imperial Chemical Industries
ICJ	International Court of Justice
ICJ Rep	*International Court of Justice Reports*

ICLQ	*International and Comparative Law Quarterly*
ILC	International Law Commission
ILM	*International Legal Materials*
ILR	*International Law Reports*
IPC	Integrated pollution control
IPPC	Integrated pollution prevention and control
ISO	International Organisation for Standardisation
JPL	*Journal of Planning and Environment Law*
LDDC	London Docklands Development Corporation
LQR	*Law Quarterly Review*
Medical LR	*Medical Law Reports*
MEP	Member of the European Parliament
Mich JIL	*Michigan Journal of International Law*
MLR	*Modern Law Review*
MNC	Multinational corporation
NAFTA	North American Free Trade Agreement
Neths YBIL	*Netherlands Yearbook of International Law*
NGO	Nongovernmental organization
NIEO	New International Economic Order
NIMBY	Not in my backyard
NSW	New South Wales
OAS TS	*Organisation of African States Treaty Series*
OECD	Organisation for Economic Co-operation and Development
OJ	Official Journal of the European Communities
OJLS	*Oxford Journal of Legal Studies*
PCIJ	Permanent Court of International Justice
PCIJ Ser. A	*Permanent Court of International Justice Reports*, Series A—Judgments
PIG	Public Interest Group
R&D	Research and development
RAC	Resource Assessment Commission
RIAA	*Reports of International Arbitral Awards*
SEA	Single European Act
TCPA 1990	Town and Country Planning Act 1990
TEU	Treaty on European Union
TNC	Transnational corporation
UNCED	United Nations Conference on Environment and Development
UNCLOS	United Nations Convention on the Law of the Sea
UNEP	United Nations Environment Programme
UNTS	*United Nations Treaty Series*
VJIL	*Virginia Journal of International Law*
WHO	World Health Organisation

WRA 1991	Water Resources Act 1991
WTO	World Trade Organisation
WWF	World Wide Fund for Nature
YBICJ	*Yearbook of the International Court of Justice*
YBIEL	*Yearbook of International Environmental Law*

1

Law in Environmental Decision-Making

JENNY STEELE AND TIM JEWELL

This book does not aim to deal with an exhaustive series of legal issues in respect of the environment. Instead, its chapters are concerned with a range of legal frameworks, and a number of sources of environmental law. Included here are elements of national law; of the law and policy of the European Union; and of international law. In respect of these different sources, the chapters address aspects of one broad question: to what extent is law—in a variety of forms—able to play a positive role in decisions having an environmental impact? This question is taken not only to include issues of law-making and legal decision-making on the part of legislatures, courts, or agencies; but also to take in issues about the application of law, and the way it is received by other actors.

Although the perspectives represented here are diverse, some common sources of concern can be identified. In particular, environmental issues are thought to pose a number of challenges for some familiar forms of law. Such challenges are traced for example to the nature of much environmental harm, including its unpredictability and its ability to cross boundaries both legal and national;[1] to the existence of an increasingly important debate between rival perceptions of democracy, and especially the emergence of new roles for participatory as opposed to representative democracy;[2] and to the changing role of the state associated in particular with privatization and globalization.[3] All of these factors are treated as having significant implications for the types of legal response which environmental issues are likely to prompt, and for their likely success.

There is therefore a general sense in this collection that environmental issues ought to be of concern to a range of different legal disciplines,[4] and a number of contributors explore the links between environmental issues, and existing legal categories. Tim Jewell, for example, provides an analysis of existing and emerging environmental decision-making processes and their legal framework, from a perspective informed by traditional public law concerns of accountability and transparency; while Jenny Steele explores the uses of tort law by individuals and groups who challenge the effects of past decisions, against a regulatory background which has been dominated by forward-planning and managed risk. These two chapters

[1] See especially the chapters by Christine Chinkin, Tony Evans, and Han Somsen.

[2] David Robinson, Clíona Kimber, Jenny Steele.

[3] Tim Jewell, Jenny Steele, Tony Evans.

[4] It will be explained in the course of this introductory chapter that this also implies a reciprocal interest: environmental law ought to be concerned with the resources of a range of legal disciplines.

concentrate on domestic law, and consider the often problematic relationship between newly emerging environmental issues, and established frameworks of legal thinking.

Further contributions broaden the inquiry to include observation of European and international legal frameworks. Han Somsen explores the dynamics and processes of law-making within the European Union, and studies institutional factors which affect the development of European environmental law. At the international level, chapters by Christine Chinkin and Tony Evans investigate from quite different starting points the increasing involvement of international law with environmental issues, and the factors which inhibit effective responses to such issues through international law. In each case, it is the structure of international law itself (whether in terms of its law-making or dispute-resolving processes, or in terms of those interests which it recognizes or allows to be represented) which is the focus of critical attention. So, Christine Chinkin assesses various efforts to accommodate environmental issues within the processes of international law, and explores the points of contact and of conflict between such issues, and other evolving or more established elements of international law, such as rights to development, or international trade. Writing from an International Relations perspective, Tony Evans provides valuable and challenging insights into the relationship between law and the causes of environmental damage, in the particular context of globalization. Significant points of contact between this account, and some of the issues which preoccupy domestic environmental lawyers, are explored in the course of this introductory chapter.

These contributions are complemented by essays from David Robinson and Clíona Kimber, which assess the emergence and evolution of new approaches to pollution control, and of European legislation on access to environmental information respectively. These chapters are to some extent concerned with the development of specific techniques of environmental protection, but in their assessment of contemporary developments they share many of the broader themes of the other contributions. In particular, their authors seek to investigate not only the possibilities for improving environmental protection, but also the apparently shifting balance of decision-making functions as between governments, citizens, and enterprises, which is bound up with the development of new legal 'techniques'.

These two contributions also suggest the existence of broad trends which are not isolated to individual jurisdictions, and take in not only UK developments but also developments in other European Union ('EU') member states, in Australia, and elsewhere. Although some solutions to the challenge of effective environmental law are domestic or even local, many of the problems are shared. This is not simply because environmental problems are recognized as crossing national boundaries, though this is certainly the case. Indeed, this factor can easily give rise not to a sense of shared purpose, but to divisions between states with rival national interests. Such divisions underlie much of the analysis in Christine Chinkin's chapter, where they are argued to have undermined, in the context of specific disputes, the apparent progress towards a sense of shared purpose in establishing global environmental security.

This introductory chapter has two general aims. We intend both to sketch out some key shared themes of the diverse chapters, and to suggest the relationship between the collection as a whole, and current developments in environmental law. In particular, some such current developments would seem to pull towards a more 'integrated' approach to the subject, and to suggest the development of environmental law as a distinctive field with distinctive subject-matter. From such a point of view, the type of analysis adopted in this collection—which emphasizes the specific qualities of particular (perhaps even traditional) legal frameworks and sources—will require some explanation. If the current emphasis is on a distinctive series of 'environmental' problems to be solved, then it would seem that 'component' categories of law would need to be amended, or even transcended, in order to achieve such goals. On the other hand, questions of environmental law are intimately associated with questions of legal technique, and even innovative techniques have both a practical and an academic history and setting. In addition, it will be suggested that it is in the nature of current developments in environmental law to invite consideration of environmental issues as part of other concerns, and as connected with other bodies of law.

Therefore, whilst it is possible to see the recent history of environmental law as being concerned in part with the development and gradual recognition of a distinctive set of environmental law issues, we would argue that environmental law—and current approaches to it—raise issues which have edged it towards a more prominent role in broader debates concerning the possibilities and patterns of legal control. This relationship—between a distinctive field of environmental law and environmental problems, and a much broader series of issues in which many of these problems might be seen as central—is a shared theme of many of the contributors to this volume.

1. Environmental Law: 'Integration' and 'Diffusion'?

An initial focus on domestic environmental law may be helpful in drawing out some issues for more general development. This section therefore begins with UK environmental law, and introduces the idea of 'integration' within that body of law. However, we will also explain how more recent developments suggest a rather different process, which might be referred to as a 'diffusion' of environmental law, for example through development of the concept of sustainability. Such diffusion is important to this collection, where it is explained as raising issues relating to the nature of the legal and non-legal processes and instruments employed in the pursuit of environmental goals (explored for example in the chapters by David Robinson and Tim Jewell), and also relating to the status of environmental considerations in comparison with others (Christine Chinkin and Han Somsen).

Against this background, this section will trace some integrating trends within the UK's domestic environmental law—specifically, in terms of controls, principles of action, and agency structure. However, it will also introduce the connections between these integrating trends, and the broader 'diffusion' whose nature and implications are developed in the volume as a whole.

Integration and Diffusion: Some Observations

The word 'integration' is encountered quite frequently in contemporary environmental law and policy, and some of the occasions on which it is used are explored by various contributors to this book. However, this use of a common term can lead to confusion between a number of different ideas associated, perhaps, with 'stages' of development in environmental law. For example, the Treaty of Amsterdam is expected to insert a new Article 3d into the Treaty of Rome, which would enshrine the idea of integration of environmental protection requirements into the implementation of other Community policies.[5] This is not at all the same form of integration which is implied by, say, 'integrated pollution control' in UK law. Because of our concern with different styles and sources of law, these different uses are important to this collection.

As explained above, the aim here is not to argue that internal integration is the most important current trend even in domestic law, but to describe some such processes of integration—associated with seeing and responding to environmental law as a distinctive field of problems and solutions with something in common—as precursors to a rather different process, which might be referred to as a diffusion of environmental law into a range of different legal and other contexts.

As Han Somsen notes, it is still not universally acknowledged that there is 'a' body of environmental law. However, we would distinguish between those respects in which relevant legal responses are not yet perceived as connected to a general body of environmental law as a whole; and those respects in which problems are indeed recognized as environmental problems, yet they are thought to require recognition within a variety of forms of legal and indeed other types of response. Both issues are important here, the former issue having particular practical significance for example in respect of adjudication by the International Court of Justice. Here, a specialist Chamber has been established for environmental disputes but, as Christine Chinkin reports, it remains little-used. This is due largely to fears on the part of states parties that to recognize a dispute as involving 'environmental' elements will have unwelcome consequences. In particular, such recognition may tend to legitimate the involvement of third parties, and thereby threaten the essentially bilateral nature of the adjudicative process. Most disputes are therefore presented as turning on narrower points of recognized

[5] This builds on and makes more explicit the existing requirements of Art. 130.

legal principle, more consistent with established notions of (in particular) states' territorial integrity and sovereignty. Nevertheless, it is the second process referred to above—the integration of environmental law into a variety of other contexts—which is identified by most of the contributors as being at the heart of current developments, including developments in other aspects of international law.

This latter type of approach can be identified for example in David Robinson's description of pollution control systems in terms of an integration *of* law, *with* other factors and determinants of action. Integration in regulatory policy on his account involves not only legal but also extra-legal elements, and this is captured in the notion of 'holistic' regulatory policy. As he puts it, environmental policy should dictate the style and content of environmental law, and not the other way around. This has parallels with the more specifically 'legal' integration described in Han Somsen's chapter, in respect of environmental decision-making within the European Union. As he explains, there are tensions between the aspiration towards an autonomous environmental law and policy, and the 'horizontal' nature of that policy: the effect is an assimilation of environmental protection into the definition and implementation of other policy spheres.

These are two examples, but it is more generally implied by the contributors to this book that the connection between environmental and 'other' contemporary problems is likely to increase, and the boundaries of the subject to blur, as understanding of the causes of environmental harm is further generalized. Multiple uses of the term 'integration' are perhaps to be expected in that integrating trends *within* environmental law are still themselves regarded as a relatively recent phenomenon.

'Integration' in UK Environmental Law

Identifying integration within the body of environmental law is therefore only a first step. From a UK perspective, the most obvious forms of integration are the recent domestic and European legislative reforms which have brought about an explicit integration of controls to co-ordinate polluting emissions to the environment as a whole, rather than to individual environmental media.[6] Such developments therefore treat together the impacts of some types of pollution on the three environmental media of air, land, and water. This is an integration in the subject-matter of pollution control. Subsequently, legislative provisions have effected a further collection—of atmospheric controls in particular—within national and local plans,[7] illustrating an increasingly strategic approach to the problems of pollution and of legal responses to it. This is a somewhat different, geographical integration, but together these developments perhaps indicate that pollution is

[6] Environmental Protection Act 1990 ('EPA 1990'), Part I. See M. Purdue, 'Integrated Pollution Control in the Environmental Protection Act 1990: A Coming of Age of Environmental Law?' (1991) 54 *MLR* 534–51.

[7] e.g., Environment Act 1995 ('EA 1995'), Part IV.

increasingly perceived as 'a' problem, rather than a series of individual problems; and that this has implications for the way in which it should be tackled.

The point was made above that such developments carry with them the likelihood of a further and very different integration. Having identified pollution, for example, as one problem, not a series of individual ones, this general problem may then be increasingly perceived as one aspect of much broader phenomena, going well beyond the traditional boundaries of environmental law. As explained below, the concept of 'sustainable development' tends to reflect a recognition of this further 'integration' or (as it was expressed above) diffusion. But the law has only relatively recently taken the step of treating pollution as something other than a series of individual, fragmented problems. Diffusion of the type observed in this collection depends to some extent on such an integration in understanding and response.

So, the emergence of 'integrated pollution control' can be seen as part of a broader and earlier trend, gathering together previously fragmented laws whose origins predate the recognition of a category of 'environmental' law as such. It is well recognized that such historic regimes continue to exert an influence on the contemporary law, and to some extent remain an important component of it. A variety of controls originating in the protection of public health, including statutory nuisances, provide an example: in the UK, powers to control statutory nuisances were incorporated into the Environmental Protection Act 1990, and are now widely thought to have provided the model for the new regime for the remediation of contaminated land.[8]

Similarly, a degree of co-ordination has also arisen without deliberate legislative intervention. For example, even prior to the explicit integration referred to above, controls relating to atmospheric pollution had largely been placed in the hands of local authorities, and had emerged in practice as more co-ordinated than might have been suggested by their fragmented basis in a combination of statutory nuisance and specific controls such as the Clean Air Acts. A glance at the original edition of the first general textbook on environmental law in the UK will illustrate the degree of integration which has occurred in the last ten to fifteen years, since the innovative framework for that textbook was provided by the gathering together of apparently 'discrete' controls over different environmental media.[9]

However, it would take more than the collection of a series of previously disparate legal responses under an 'environmental' banner, together with some integration of pollution controls, before UK environmental law could be described as a distinctive subject. In the light of this, is it possible to specify factors which indicate some more general shifts?

One such factor is organizational integration, and its implications. New unified 'Environment Agencies' for England and Wales and for Scotland have recently

[8] EA 1995, Pt. II, introducing a new Pt. IIA into EPA 1990 (following Pt. II: Statutory Nuisance): *Official Report*, HL Vol 562, cols. 1054–5, 20 March 1995, Viscount Ullswater.

[9] D. Hughes, *Environmental Law* (1st ed., London, 1986).

been created, in place of the previous range of separate agencies with control over specific environmental media. To some extent, this has also resulted in the merging of pollution control with other functions.[10] This is a functional integration, which genuinely suggests that, say, pollution control and conservation have something in common, whatever the tensions between them.[11] Apart from the symbolic importance of this merging of functions, the resulting institutional integration can also be expected to encourage a degree of practical co-ordination, and in this way to provide a more unified approach to 'environmental' responses.[12] Like the co-ordination of atmospheric pollution controls in local authority hands referred to above, this could therefore be described as a case of potential spontaneous co-ordination, effected on this occasion by institutional change. Unlike that example, such co-ordination is an intended outcome of the new agency structure.[13]

Diffusion: The Emergence of Sustainable Development

The legislation which established the UK agencies also took the step of outlining the general guiding aims and principles of action to which those agencies are subject. In particular, their overarching aim in the exercise of all their functions is to make an appropriate contribution to the attainment of 'sustainable development'.[14] In this way, a general policy goal has been given a key role as a matter of statutory definition. It should be noted that in form, this specification of an overriding aim acts as a control on the scope of the agencies' action: not only is their role in protection of the environment defined in terms of (and not separately from) the pursuit of sustainable development, it is also defined according to the contribution thought appropriate by relevant Ministers. As a more general point, the inclusion of this statement in the Act is interesting because it enshrines in legal form, for one particular but influential purpose, the principal organizing concept of recent UK environmental policy; and this concept implies a particular type of relationship between 'environmental' and other goals.

Each of these points emphasizes the degree to which UK environmental law is controlled by the legislature. But the pre-eminence of sustainable development also raises the whole issue of how environmental and 'other' policy fields are related. It also remains to consider the relationship between 'sustainable development', and a number of other 'principles' or guiding concepts.

[10] See T. Jewell and J. Steele, 'UK Regulatory Reform and the Pursuit of "Sustainable Development": The Environment Act 1995' (1996) 8 *Journal of Environmental Law* 283–300.

[11] As between pollution control and conservation, these tensions derive in part from the key role of pollution licensing as a strategy of pollution control.

[12] Particularly relevant here perhaps are the general advisory functions of the Agencies.

[13] Department of the Environment, *Improving Environmental Quality: The Government's Proposals for a New, Independent Environment Agency* (October 1991), at 1.

[14] EA 1995, s. 4(1). The Scottish Agency is subject to the same guiding aim, and similar guidance: EA 1995, s. 31.

To start with the latter issue, the Environment Act 1995 also specified, along with the priority of sustainable development, key roles for both cost-benefit analysis, and risk assessment. Both of these techniques might be regarded as aspects of—or as closely associated with—the notion of 'sustainable development' itself, at least as it is currently understood in domestic environmental policy. Statutory reference to 'techniques' to assist in decision-making are a familiar part of UK environmental law: a well-known example is the obligation on most major industrial polluters to employ the 'best available techniques not entailing excessive cost' ('BATNEEC') to eliminate or minimize polluting emissions, or to render them harmless.[15] This in turn is a modernization of the older 'best practicable means' ('BPM') requirement, which is of long standing.[16] Cost-benefit analysis and risk assessment are (arguably) rather different. They expressly relate not just to practical pollution control measures as such, which were and are the sole focus of BPM and BATNEEC, and they are therefore broader in their application. In addition, the new techniques do not have the same narrow focus on scientific-technical expertise. They perhaps represent a new kind of 'technique', in which susceptibility to changing policy priorities is more evident.

Further, parallels may be drawn and distinctions made between the statutory incorporation of 'sustainable development', and the earlier emergence of environmental 'principles' (the preventive principle, the precautionary principle, the polluter-pays principle)[17] in European environmental law and policy at the end of the last decade. The direct impact of such principles in UK domestic law has been limited,[18] though at a policy level they have at least formed a potential nucleus for the development of common themes linking separate issues and aspects of environmental law.[19] The High Court, for example, has concluded that the version of the precautionary principle found in the Treaty on European Union has no binding legal effect in UK law over the exercise of certain statutory powers, although it may comprise an uncertain part of a backdrop of 'relevant considerations'.[20] Equally, the existence of rapidly developing environmental legislation has even acted to constrain the development of the common law in an environmental

[15] EPA 1990, s. 7(4). [16] Smoke Nuisances (Metropolis) Act 1853 (c. 128), s. 1.

[17] This list is not exhaustive. To it might be added a more recent notion of 'shared responsibility': see for example the European Commission's Green Paper, *Remedying Environmental Damage* (1993), COM(93) 47 final. This raises the possibility that not all of the various 'principles' are easily reconcilable.

[18] The experience of some other European jurisdictions is a little different: see for example K. von Moltke, *The Vorsorgeprinzip in West German Environmental Policy* (London, 1987).

[19] Purdue, op. cit., suggested a 'coming of age' for environmental law in the UK at the time of the EPA 1990. This view was based partly on the statutory development of an integrated approach to pollution control, but partly also on the emerging recognition of a range of environmental law 'principles' derived predominantly from EC legislation. These did not include sustainable development, which is discussed here as a broad policy goal, not as a 'principle'.

[20] *R v Secretary of State for Trade and Industry, ex parte Duddridge* (1995) 7 *Journal of Environmental Law* 224.

context,[21] when principles of environmental protection might otherwise have operated to encourage the distribution of environmental liabilities.

In comparison with these 'principles', 'sustainable development' represents a rather broad goal or end rather than a specific principle of action. Perhaps this is part of the reason why it has been so enthusiastically embraced by recent UK governments. It leaves greater scope for legislative as opposed to judicial influence, and for domestic legislative independence, because of its very generality and its expression in terms of a goal rather than a technique. Nevertheless, the key concept though broad is not without substance. It is likely to have a very considerable influence for example on the domestic interpretation of existing concepts such as 'polluter pays'.[22] It will therefore be important to consider the substance of 'sustainable development'.

'Sustainable development' can be taken to imply at least a balance, and possibly also a reconciliation, between the potentially conflicting goals of environmental protection, and development. It is significant that the notion of 'sustainable development' is by its very nature linked to the process of 'diffusion' with which we are concerned in this volume. It implies that all development should be considered from the point of view of environmental effects; but it also implies that environmental policy in turn cannot be considered separately from the economic necessities of development and growth. This is indeed explicitly stated to be the significance of sustainable development in international environmental law, as explained in Principle 4 of the Rio Declaration.[23] The concept is central to the functions of the UK's new agencies and to much else in environmental law, but it cannot be seen as a concept belonging purely to the environmental field. The nature of this particular goal therefore has important implications, which will be further explored in section 2 of this chapter. In particular, links will be made between the key concept of 'sustainable development', and the evolutions in legal form exemplified by contemporary developments in intervention and control.

Styles of 'Control'

So far, we have briefly sketched the development of environmental law from a series of controls, towards a more co-ordinated system or systems of control, with perhaps a number of incipient guiding goals or (as appropriate) 'principles'.

[21] e.g., in *Cambridge Water Co Ltd v Eastern Counties Leather plc* [1994] 2 AC 264, per Lord Goff.

[22] The relationship between 'sustainable development' and principles such as 'polluter pays' and the precautionary principle, is investigated by Jewell and Steele, op. cit., at 292–3.

[23] Environmental protection 'shall constitute an integral part of the development process and cannot be considered in isolation from it', Declaration on Environment and Development, Rio de Janeiro, 1992. The implications of this for international environmental protection in the light of an emerging 'right to development' are explored by Christine Chinkin, in Chapter 8, below.

A further and equally significant trend is towards different approaches to, or styles of, control. Here too there is an interplay between integration, and diffusion. The development of new regulatory styles may well have been eased by the recognition of environmental law as a subject, since this has encouraged some evolution of recognized common problems, but has also assisted with the recognition of common causes. This does not necessarily mean however that overarching principles offer the best solution, and indeed many of the emerging environmental law techniques suggest a need for flexibility and subtlety of response, and also of responsiveness to particular contexts.

Comparisons can be made between this account of UK developments and the experience of other jurisdictions, as is indicated by the contributions here from David Robinson (Australia) and Clíona Kimber (EU member states). The United States is also a fruitful source of comparisons and distinctions for UK lawyers. In the US, an Environmental Protection Agency ('EPA') was created at a far earlier date than the UK equivalent.[24] The nature of the legal framework within which the US Agency operates is quite different from—and in many ways more elaborate than—that with which UK public lawyers are familiar. In particular, the US EPA has a significant role in drafting detailed regulations, and must also be prepared for legal challenges to those regulations. This has been explained as flowing from the particular separation between legislature and executive in the United States, which (it has been suggested) means that the legislature has little incentive to ensure that legislation is coherent and comprehensive, but a strong incentive to ensure that its execution is reviewed, and therefore to encourage review of agency procedures by courts and interested parties. Not only is the process of formal rule-making by federal agencies subject to standards imposed by the Administrative Procedure Act 1946, but regulations are also subject to frequent judicial review, including pre-enforcement review by parties who will be affected by them. Again, it has been argued that this militates against a co-operative approach to policy-formation, with the parties being inclined to treat the rule-making process as a means of gathering evidence for launching, or defending, a subsequent review by a court.[25]

This particular legal context of challenge and of policy articulation ensures that environmental law has at least appeared to be permeated by broader general principles than our own domestic version, from an earlier stage. There are distinct differences of substance between the general aims set out in UK and US legislation,[26] but in addition the more diffuse, less direct influence of the US

[24] In 1970, through an administrative reorganization under President Nixon.

[25] See generally S. Rose-Ackerman, *Controlling Environmental Policy: The Limits of Public Law in Germany and the United States* (New Haven, 1995), and esp. at 13–16 and 133–7.

[26] Compare in particular the duty imposed on the US EPA by the Comprehensive Environmental Response, Compensation and Liability Act 1980 ('CERCLA') to protect human health and the environment, with the duties on the UK agencies under the EA 1995 to make a relevant contribution to sustainable development.

legislature in the evolution of agency practice,[27] and more frequent intervention by the courts, also invites a distinction of form between the guiding principles of UK and US environmental law, with the US version appearing to take a more distinctively legal (or on some accounts, judicialized) form. Nevertheless, there is some evidence that despite significant differences in the language and structures of control over environmental law and policy with which lawyers in the two jurisdictions will have been occupied, recent interest has focused in a similar fashion on innovation in styles of environmental regulation.

This may be illustrated by taking as an example the growth of 'integrated' controls cited above. Although 'integrated pollution control' in the UK and indeed in many other European jurisdictions can still be described as a recent development, the form which it took in the Environmental Protection Act 1990 was relatively familiar and traditional. Despite being 'integrated', and to this extent innovative, such controls still in essence represent a form of 'command-and-control' regulation. Many US scholars have argued for less traditional methods of 'control', as (increasingly) have others around the world. Most interestingly though, in some instances this has been seen specifically as a stage in an historical evolution, from the development of centralized (largely federal) control over specific risks, to the realisation of endemic risks, which are said to require greater flexibility in the style of their management.[28]

Arguably, this latter diagnosis has significant points of contact with the emerging centrality of 'sustainable development' as a key concept in the domestic environmental and economic policy of some nations, and in international decision-making. Indeed, the priority of sustainable development may in some senses, despite the points made above about its political role as a policy aim, lead to an increasing convergence in the discussion of environmental legal technique, relatively divorced from the specific legal structures of different nations or perhaps of substantive environmental standards. Whether or not this is the case, the academic discussion of new legal techniques for environmental control has—like the idea of unified environmental protection agencies—developed rather more quickly in the United States than in the United Kingdom, and experimentation with some variants of new legal technique (particularly economic instruments) has progressed further.

To summarise, it may be possible to trace an integration in UK domestic environmental law in terms of controls, principles of action, and agency structure. However, the emergence of common policy goals and guiding concepts or principles, whether legal or extra-legal, itself requires further analysis, because of the particular nature of those policy goals and principles, and because of the

[27] See the general account of differences in legislative influence in C. Graham and T. Prosser, *Privatizing Public Enterprises: Constitutions, the State, and Regulation in Comparative Perspective* (Oxford, 1991).

[28] B. A. Ackerman and R. B. Stewart, 'Reforming Environmental Law: The Democratic Case for Market Incentives' (1988) 13 *Columbia Journal of Environmental Law* 171–99.

particular types of transformation being brought about in environmental law. In addition, the story of development in environmental legal responses runs parallel to generalization in understanding of the sources of environmental harm. As explained above, this in itself has led not only to integration, but also to a potential diffusion of environmental law into a broader variety of legal forms and responses. Moreover, this process is enhanced by the priority of sustainable development, which consciously brings consideration of environmental issues into other contexts, and is not 'just' an environmental law concept.

2. Innovation: Emerging Variety in Legal Instruments

A current trend which is traced throughout the contributions to this book is one towards 'innovation'. The need for innovation in environmental law appears to have become a matter of widespread agreement. In part, this is mirrored by similar moves in other aspects of regulation, outside the environmental context, and in particular a general decline in commitment to simple command-and-control models.

Simply put, command-and-control regulation is based on the prohibition of defined behaviour and enforcement through the criminal law. It therefore usually relies on a criminal prohibition, often with associated 'licensed' exceptions, and more complex provisions for setting limits or standards to acceptable behaviour.[29] Despite their historical resilience, unmodified command-and-control regimes are increasingly perceived as being old-fashioned in some respects. Whilst growing concern for environmental problems has prompted—even very recently—the establishment of new command-and-control systems such as the integrated pollution control regimes described above, the limitations of such techniques are now a matter for widespread discussion.

A formidable catalogue of problems with 'early' or unmodified command-and-control regimes is provided here by David Robinson. For example, he refers to the perverse cost effects of such approaches (cleaner industry is rendered more costly to run by 'end-of-pipe' approaches, when less adversarial, more responsive approaches might reveal ways of producing cleaner industry which is also less costly); to their predisposition for shifting rather than reducing pollution as a whole; and to the over-use of criminal law in contexts where, he argues, welfare rather than culpability might have provided a more appropriate and effective analysis. Interestingly, some of the developments beyond command-and-control are described by Jenny Steele in this collection as potentially signalling a decline in decisive and prospective judgements as to welfare, and she associates this with changing attitudes to the role of private law. David Robinson's point is a very

[29] A. Ogus, *Regulation: Legal Form and Economic Theory* (Oxford, 1994), ch. 5.

useful indication that the form adopted by traditional regulation may itself have been on many occasions incompatible with its 'welfare' goals.

Nevertheless, it is important not to understate how much has been achieved by innovation within command-and-control structures, and (equally) not to dismiss them as ineffective without asking serious questions above their successes and potential for improvement, as well as about their limitations. David Robinson for example also points to the outright prohibition of DDT in the United States (and later in other countries) as exemplifying one of the simplest, but also one of the most effective, legal interventions into the causes of environmental harm —the product ban. Changes are now occurring within command-and-control systems which themselves perhaps reflect significant cultural shifts in environmental decision-making. The suggested extension of such systems in some jurisdictions to include 'third parties' (such as affected communities or environmental pressure groups) in the negotiation and monitoring of licences themselves (described as 'co-regulation') is one example of such a culture-shift. This implies an opening-up to wider influences of what in practice have often been quite closed and exclusionary systems.[30]

On this theme, David Robinson suggests how a combination of improved access to 'better' environmental information and greater reliance on industrial self-regulation and reporting could address many of the criticisms levelled at command-and-control licensing systems, and produce a more 'organic' involvement of environmental issues in decision-making by potential polluters. In a sense, these examples emphasize that legal form is not the ultimate determinant of the ways in which law is able or unable to guide behaviour. They also illustrate that a realization of the range of factors influencing the outcomes of decisions in which legal rules and actors play a part can itself be a fruitful step in prompting subtle and innovative responses to regulatory problems. Not all such innovations need to operate outside command-and-control structures. Instead, modified self-regulation is referred to as a 'third generation' policy instrument in the development of command-and-control. Hierarchical command-and-control is the first generation, followed by negotiated initiatives which have perhaps reasonably been regarded as 'compromising' the rule of law through the nature of their involvement with the regulated sector. The new form of participatory regulation combines an element of negotiation or (as David Robinson puts it) 'communicative informality',[31] with new types of legal instrument.

Nevertheless, the developments suggested by David Robinson and those authors on whom he draws represent a significant reorientation of command-and-control

[30] N. Gunningham, 'Environment, Self-Regulation, and the Chemical Industry: Assessing Responsible Care' (1995) 17 *Law and Policy* 57–109.

[31] He derives this term from I. Koppen, 'Ecological Covenants: Regulatory Informality in Dutch Waste Reduction Policy', in G. Teubner, L. Farmer, and D. Murphy (eds.), *Environmental Law and Ecological Responsibility: The Concept and Practice of Ecological Self-Organization* (Chichester, 1994).

structures, in at least two ways. One is that they recognize the need to incorporate other voices more effectively into the regulatory process, including its enforcement aspect. They would thus mark a shift in the culture of 'control', which has been (and in large part remains) outside the competence of elected local bodies or community groups, whose influence has often been by-passed whether through agency or direct legislative action.[32]

The other way in which these developments mark a significant reorientation in command-and-control systems forms a link with approaches which seek to transcend existing models more thoroughly. This feature of newer approaches concerns the perceived need to move from an 'external' legal voice, to a style of regulation which places the regulator in a close—even an intimate[33]—relationship with the regulated party. The goal is not only to improve enforcement (in which context the problems of negotiated rules and under-enforcement are well-recognized), but also to develop the possibility of legal interventions which are less heavy-handed, and more responsive to the demands and possibilities of their context. The promise of this style of regulation is therefore of greater effectiveness; the threat however is that it would reduce opportunities for holding the parties to that regulation to account and, as such, the introduction of third party voices is an important—but not necessarily a sufficient—innovation. A particular tension can be perceived between the need for any 'improvements' which might be provided by improving sensitivity to the immediate environment of the decision, and the need for representation of and participation by citizens or specific interested and affected groups in both law-making and decision-making in general. So, the two types of trend (toward broader participation, and toward 'closeness' to the regulated party) are related, but their precise connections are not easy to identify.

An important part of the tension here relates to the need for legitimacy in law, whether this is thought to be delivered through the legislative process, or through recognizable and defensible legal principle. Some approaches take the view that participation by citizens is in itself a means of achieving better (in the sense of *more effective*) environmental regulation. This form of instrumental approach to citizen participation, which explores the substance of regulatory powers and sees participation in this broad sense largely as a regulatory strategy, is taken up by David Robinson in this volume. The broad question of the connection between effectiveness and participation is also explored by Clíona

[32] The susceptibility to variation of centralized environmental standards has long been a distinctive characteristic of UK environmental law, but so too has the practice of setting site-specific standards within the relationship between the regulator and regulated. The evolution of enforcement practice provides similar examples: K. Hawkins, *Environment and Enforcement: Regulation and the Social Definition of Pollution* (Oxford, 1984).

[33] The reference to 'intimacy' here is intended to capture a deep-rooted sense that the core of commercial decision-making is a private realm, divorced from the 'public' business of regulation. As such, approaches like this should not be too quickly dismissed as overly 'comfortable' for regulated parties, since they involve a kind of intrusion which end-of-pipe approaches did not.

Kimber in her study of European legislation providing rights of access to environmental information.[34] However, this chapter illustrates the resistance of certain member states to more open access to state-held information. Such resistance has narrowed the potential scope of the Directive, and this in turn suggests that citizen participation is not seen simply as a means of supporting regulatory action, at least by certain governments.

In a different context, participation and legitimacy come together as underlying concerns in Jenny Steele's account of the challenges brought through tort law by members of the public, and their relationship with prospective regulation. A range of different approaches to 'participation' in environmental law is outlined in that chapter, and a distinction is drawn between those approaches which link the decline of command-and-control with a form of democratization in itself (the removal of an external, authoritative legal voice), and those which regard third party or public participation as a separate issue—generally, a necessary addition or qualification to privatization strategies in regulatory technique.

Innovation Beyond Command-and-Control

Having explained some of the contemporary evolution of command-and-control systems, we have also made a link between innovations in such systems, and broad questions about the nature of decision-making and identity of decision-makers; and linked this to discussions in various contributions to this book. To a large extent, innovation has started or first been felt within command-and-control structures. But innovation also has broader implications, either through its introduction into command-and-control structures of legal techniques which have not generally been associated with them in the past, or (conversely) because it tends to give rise to a diffusion of environmental law into less familiar locations. Here we aim to consider some aspects of such innovation. Again, our aim in doing so is not to classify regulatory structures—to determine, for example, whether they are or are not still command-and-control structures—but rather to pick up some significant implications for contemporary environmental decision-making.

Importantly for the general approach adopted in this collection, certain innovatory trends imply that 'other' legal techniques (not usually associated with classic, interventionist environmental law) are being employed or considered. In pollution control, for example, we can observe the emergence of civil liabilities within regulatory regimes requiring the remediation of historic contamination. These liabilities have different implications from those normally suggested by law in the command-and-control form, in that they are not triggered by failure to abide by prohibitions or stay within licensed exceptions, but relate to sums required for clean-up or compensation without necessary reference to any pre-defined

[34] Directive 90/313/EEC (OJ L158/56, 23.6.90).

prohibition at all. In principle, this runs counter to the familiar emphasis on prospective control.

The justification for employing liability-type mechanisms which are independent of prospective prohibition, can sometimes be found in economic thinking. Such thinking has to some extent permeated discussion of common law actions, such as nuisance, for many years,[35] and aspects of the statutory liability regimes referred to above also appear to 'fit' some basic tenets of the law and economics approaches. In particular, liability does not take the form of externally-derived 'fines' for breach of prohibitions, but appears to attach to the effects of the activities of private parties. At first glance, this seems to leave more to private decision-makers, largely because the possibility of damage is internalised as part of a risk calculation by the private actors who may ultimately bear liability. This image is misleading in many ways however, not least because the liabilities in question are triggered by contamination (a state which gives rise to a risk of damage) rather than by damage as such; and because 'contamination' therefore needs to be discovered and defined.

Nevertheless, law and economics studies have focused on the incentive effects of different patterns of liability within such regimes, where there is indeed an interesting blend of public and private responsibilities at work: an amended version of a private law technique is pressed into service as part of an administrative regime, for the satisfaction of welfare goals.[36] Classically, economics approaches have their own conclusions on the relationship between public goals and private activity. The variety of instruments being developed in environmental law suggests that the same issue may need to be considered from other perspectives too.

Here, Tim Jewell and David Robinson consider the impact of some 'economic' instruments, including tradeable permits. Clearly, these are rather different from the new forms of civil liability referred to above, in that they are a form of prospective licensing, rather than a retrospective allocation of costs. However, they once again combine a public process of standard-setting with private decision-making processes. The reasons for this form part of the broader trends discussed below. At this stage, however, it is important to note that there is a shift in understandings of how law 'controls', and the nature of its 'commands', and that this invites analysis of the roles occupied by public agencies and private parties. Equally, it is important to note that some traditional legal concerns with process and

[35] See, e.g., G. Calabresi and A. D. Melamed, 'Property Rules, Liability Rules and Inalienability: One View of the Cathedral' (1972) 85 *Harvard Law Review* 1089–1128; A. Ogus and G. Richardson, 'Economics and the Environment—A Study of Private Nuisance' (1977) 36 *Cambridge Law Journal* 284–325.

[36] See, e.g., with particular emphasis on the potential role of lenders, D. Balkenborg, 'Bargaining Power and the Impact of Lender Liability for Environmental Damages', Southampton Discussion Paper in Economics and Econometrics No. 9709 (1997). This draws on, e.g., M. Boyer and J.-J. Laffont, 'Environmental Risks and Bank Liability', paper presented to the Workshop on Designing Environmental Policy for Management of Natural Resources and the Environment, Crete, 1994; and R. Pitchford, 'How Liable Should a Lender Be? The Case of Judgement-Proof Firms and Environmental Risk' (1995) 85 *American Economic Review* 1171–85.

fairness might contribute in important ways to the debate about public and private responsibilities which surrounds the emergence of these instruments.

A further trend which may be observed in contemporary environmental law is towards access and participation. The extent of this development is debateable, as emerges in part from Clíona Kimber's analysis of the European Directive on access to environmental information, and its implementation in a number of member states. Part of the analysis in that chapter queries the rationale for the development of such legislation. If it is true that more information will lead to better enforcement, what are the limits to the availability of information, and why will citizens be a useful complement to government agencies in employing it? There are questions here about whether citizens are regarded as likely to make up for government failure, and whether they are expected to work alongside governments, or (on the other hand) to challenge government decisions. Beyond the effects on interested individuals, what is the expected outcome of arming public interest groups with such information? Once again, these questions point to complications in the traditional division between private pollution and public control; but also suggest that easy analyses (for example, an assumption that the public's involvement will improve effectiveness without disrupting enforcement policy) may be misplaced.

3. Supranational and International Developments: Finding Space for Environmental Law

Analysis from a legal perspective properly brings with it other preoccupations concerning the status of environmental law. For EU member states, there are particular considerations concerning the constitutional place of environmental law within the Union. In this connection, Han Somsen considers the significance of enshrining environmental protection at a European constitutional level alongside the economic goal of market integration, and the impact of this on law-making in particular. This may be perceived as an issue of constitutional innovation, and it also throws up problems concerning the relationship between economic and environmental goals which clearly mirror many issues in domestic (and also international) law. As can be seen from his analysis, the elevation of environmental protection to a position of constitutional importance has brought with it significant, and sometimes unexpected, consequences for the identity of decision-makers and for the scope and content of European law.

Han Somsen deals with two particular concerns. One is that the autonomy of European environmental law will be compromised by its need to support the dominant aim of market integration, particularly given the requirement that environmental considerations be integrated into the implementation of other policies. The second is that states will, if given the chance, engage in a 'race-to-the-bottom'—a competition to get away with the least environmental protection. Both of these suggestions are rejected on the basis of experience to date, and situations are pointed out in which the devolution of decision-making may, though it appears intuitively unlikely, have environmental benefits. This point is developed further below.

The differences between European and international law experiences are very marked. This is no doubt partly due to the distinction between international and supranational law, and the ability of European institutions to produce binding law through qualified majority voting. So, Han Somsen addresses the relative contributions of the European Commission, Parliament, and Court of Justice in producing and enforcing environmental law, and also considers the role of member states. It might particularly be noted here that the proactive role of the European Court of Justice in developing environmental law is partly made possible by the widespread perception that it deals with specifically legal issues. This may be a strength rather than an impediment because, as Han Somsen explains, the Court is widely regarded as dealing with largely technical issues, and this can act as a cloak for some fairly free, 'contextual' approaches to interpretation. Furthermore, there are institutional factors at work. As Christine Chinkin explains, there has been no specific environmental agency within the UN to push for a positive environmental agenda in international law. This contrasts both with the development of environmental law within the European Union, where Han Somsen describes institutional dynamics as playing a large part in promoting and shaping the emerging law, and with the development of human rights law within the international system.

In respect of all the European institutions examined, the contrast with international law is clearly evident. Christine Chinkin for example describes the international legal system as decentralized and lacking in legislative authority, while both she and Tony Evans emphasize the limiting effect of a legal system whose subjects are states. But part of the explanation also no doubt lies in political differences: within the smaller and more homogeneous group of states which makes up the European Union, it may be easier to isolate a reluctant party and to exert effective political pressure.[37]

On the face of it, many international treaties give the same kind of prominence to environmental issues as is reflected in their position within the EU. Here, Christine Chinkin explores significant obstacles to the effective incorporation of such concerns in respect of each of the processes of international law development considered, beginning with treaty formation but with particular emphasis on the resolution of specific disputes, and attempted innovations in dealing with disputes which have an environmental element. Her investigation highlights

[37] See, e.g., the UK's recent decision to end its opt-out on dumping of nuclear waste at sea, reported as being at least partly in response to pressure from other EU member states: *The Guardian*, 3 September 1997, at 6. However, isolation within the Union (a threat of refusal to ratify core Treaties for example) can also be used as a weapon, to win concessions on more 'peripheral' issues; and Han Somsen considers some examples of this.

particular instances of a general problem: although in principle the need for environmental protection is recognized within the international system, in practice such arguments are in regular conflict with states' interests. In this sense, the international legal framework acts as a constraint on the development of effective environmental law. The recognition of environmental issues as influencing the very stability of the international legal order emerges as a significant challenge to that order as it is currently understood, but so far there are relatively few signs that the existing order has been fundamentally altered by this recognition.

Though the conflict of states' interests and environmental interests has its mirror in environmental law at any level, it might appear that the international legal order suffers from particular problems. This perception should however be balanced by some of the details of Tony Evans' analysis. Although this too is concerned with international law, the key problem identified is not simply a matter of conflicts within and between states' interests. Rather, there is an emphasis on the resilience to legal control of powerful non-state actors. An inconsistency is observed between the subjects of the law on the one hand, and the causes of environmental degradation on the other.

In a sense, this is the very discontinuity which some of the new 'techniques' of environmental regulation seek to overcome, since they diagnose a failure on the part of traditional regulation to reach to the root of commercial decisions. Tony Evans however does not point to technical improvements in legal instruments as the solution, nor does he share the perception that the private sector—or some revision in understanding of the relationship between public and private sectors, and members of the public—may hold the answer. Rather, he points beyond the law, to social and political transformation.

In exploring the implications of innovation then, the contributors emphasize the implications of specific legal contexts, which influence the way in which new 'solutions' operate. In some instances, this is because a sensitivity to the nature of the legal instruments themselves will illuminate some implications of the intended solution—this is so in respect of the discussion of civil liability and economic instruments referred to above. In other instances, the legal framework has implications for the ability of environmental issues to be heard, and for there to be an effective response to them: this is particularly so in respect of the contributions relating to international and European law.

4. The Environment in Contemporary Legal Development: Connection and Assimilation?

On the whole, the significant factor in driving innovation in environmental law has been the need for 'effectiveness'. Previous legal interventions undoubtedly contributed to slowing decline in environmental quality and prompted positive improvements. For example, the impact of industrialization on the health of some classes in the UK was enormous, and these highly visible effects were eventually combated by a number of health and safety measures. In some respects, the developments charted immediately above embody a process of recognizing and responding to general, rather than specific problems and causes, and thereby continue the 'integrating' trend initially described as a starting point.

But there have also been gradual changes in our understanding of the nature of the damage and risks created by human activity. Environmental damage itself is now recognized as displaying features which separate it from the risks of early industrialization: contemporary risks may be less localized, less visible, and less limited to specific media or specific population groups. Climate change and the effects of deforestation—examples of dwindling global environmental resources—also present particular challenges for law, and for international law in particular. Not only can problems be traced to structural causes, rather than specific errors, but there is also an extra element of uncertainty: the nature of human development is such that we have created and continue to create environmental problems the effects of which are unknown. This, in turn, contributes to the sense that environmental lawyers need to be innovative beyond the limits of existing legal methods of control.

This picture might seem to continue the process of isolating the subject from others; and perhaps—quite contrary to our intentions—to separate its study from that of other areas of law. It would certainly suggest that there are some reasons particular to the nature of environmental problems (or at least, particular to the development of environmental policy) which necessitate the innovations assessed in various chapters of this book, for example, those relating to the creation and assessment of environmental risk. However, the directions currently being taken by environmental law suggest not separation from, but connection with, general trends and associated general controversies.

In parts of the collection, this is associated with the current diffusion of environmental issues into a diversity of contexts. But in another sense, there is nothing new about the connection of environmental law with more general controversies. Much early academic work on environmental regulation was done by scholars of regulation in general, rather than by those who would characterize themselves as specialist environmental lawyers. Most influential have been those studies which have explored the ways in which dominant forms of regulation operate, and which have exposed the tensions between 'formal' law and its implementation or enforcement.[38] Whilst sensitive to their context, these are studies in the operation of law rather than an assessment of whether environmental law achieves environmental goals. Similarly, Neil Gunningham's *Pollution, Social Interest and the*

[38] e.g., B. Hutter, *The Reasonable Arm of the Law? The Law Enforcement Procedures of Environmental Health Officers* (Oxford, 1988); K. Hawkins, op. cit.; and G. Richardson, A. Ogus, and P. Burrows, *Policing Pollution: A Study of Regulation and Enforcement* (Oxford, 1982).

Law[39] considered what aspects of the law-making process could act as obstructions to the realization of 'social interests', but was less concerned with the definition of where the social interest lies when development and environmental protection are at odds.

A fuller understanding of environmental law developments has therefore always had to be sought outside the details of specific cases and statutory materials, gathered together to form the body of environmental law. But the authors of such work have undoubtedly been partly prompted by the emergence of environmental issues: it is no coincidence that their subject-matter is environmental control. There is perhaps a symbiotic relationship here. Legal responses to perceived environmental problems build on or employ established legal techniques, and can be illuminated by controversies which are recognized (and can perhaps be understood) within different legal 'disciplines' or modes of legal thought. Some of these we have alluded to already (tort law, human rights law or public law, for example), but the disciplines in question might also include property law, contract and insurance law, or criminal law. At the same time, environmental issues combine a sense of urgency with some particular problematic features, such as (commonly) the lack of obvious human victim or recognized protected interest (at least, until it is too late) and the dependence on slowly-developing scientific opinion for an assessment of damage and risk,[40] which implies a retrospective element in legal understanding. This has meant that the relationship cuts both ways: the experience of environmental issues has been and will be difficult and also instructive for many legal disciplines, yet it also poses problems and challenges to these 'other' (or perhaps component) disciplines. To some extent, environmental issues may therefore be a catalyst for more general changes in perceptions.

The approach taken here is therefore linked to some extent with observation of an 'assimilating' stage in environmental law. This has been described by Gerd Winter as a stage in which 'all law should become environmental law'.[41] This tends to reinforce the view that environmental lawyers should engage with the concerns of a range of legal disciplines, as well as the rather more obvious vice versa: existing disciplines need to adapt to environmental challenges. It also reflects the fact that the process of generalization referred to above has not ceased with the emergence of a 'discipline' called environmental law, nor with the apparent emergence of a body of law adopting an integrated or distinctive approach to environmental issues. In a further stage of development, environmental law is regarded as permeating and influencing other branches of law. What should not be missed, we would add, is that environmental law is thus *in turn* deeply influenced by the 'instruments' which it seeks to employ.

[39] London, 1974. [40] e.g., in respect of chemical or ecological interactions.

[41] G. Winter, 'Perspectives for Environmental Law—Entering the Fourth Phase' (1989) 1 *Journal of Environmental Law* 38–47, at 46.

So as well as the 'integrating' trend, we can make out a trend to use or consider an array of other legal instruments. It is important not to analyse these purely in terms of instrumental effectiveness. Of course, questions of effectiveness are crucial. But it is also clear that patterns of legal thought have a role in *defining* problems. Other, non-legal patterns may be even more powerful in this respect (for example, distinctive imperatives may emerge both from economic logic and from commercial concerns), and this will have an impact on the nature and extent of legal interventions themselves. A starting point for many of the contributors to this book, then, is that legal tools are problem-defining as well as problem-solving. It is therefore important to consider how law in a variety of forms 'understands' environmental problems, and how environmental policy-makers and other actors understand the potential of various legal instruments.

Perhaps the most important point of 'connection' putting environmental law at the centre of more general developments, can be clarified by emphasising the *nature* of the innovations which are being explored in this field. Changing conceptions of state and economy, and changes in the style of state intervention, coincide with the perceived decline of command-and-control described above, and also a perception of 'government' as well as 'market' failure.[42] A highly significant set of connections between innovation in environmental law, and shifts in law-making strategies more generally, lies in the combination between pursuit of social goals, and 'privatization' in one form or another. The decline of 'command-and-control' solutions in environmental law is thus not isolated, but forms part of a general shift. To define the exact nature of new directions in regulation is to take part in a broader discussion about the role of the private sector.

Social Goals, Privatization, and Environmental Law

It was suggested above that the sorts of development described in this chapter have been presented in environmental law (and elsewhere) as wholly or at least predominantly concerned with instrumentality, or a search for effective tools. In environmental law, this naturally tends to mean effective tools for environmental protection. For example, at a technical level the view may be that industry has the best understanding of its own production processes, and is thus best placed to assess practicable changes for the pursuit of environmental goals. Where this shift of decision-making to the private sector is a development from command-and-control regulation, it can be described as a form of privatization: in substance it may bear many of the hallmarks of self-regulation, although its genesis in more 'public' control is likely to have particular implications for the

[42] The former phrase is a counter to the notion of market failure, which has been familiar in literature concerning environmental issues and the market. The phrase 'government failure' is employed for example by J. Rowan-Robinson, C. Theron, and A. Ross, 'Policing the Environment: Private Regulation and the Role of Lenders' [1996] *Environmental Liability* 114–18, at 118.

form it might take.[43] In these cases, it is more likely that there will be provision for externally-imposed, public penalties, than in new self-regulatory systems which have emerged organically, or (as perhaps with financial services) where government has never been closely involved.

It is sometimes implied that privatization of one sort or another, together with the decline or qualification of traditional attempts at legal intervention, is an inevitable trend—a 'fact' to which law must respond, not a choice. As explained above, David Robinson provides a catalogue of ways in which classic command-and-control interventions have indeed been regarded as defective. But there is a philosophical, as well as a practical aspect to such debates, which he encapsulates to some extent in the various 'idioms of analysis' which have been applied to environmental law. Elsewhere in this volume, the philosophical aspect of changing styles of legal regulation is taken up by a number of other contributors.

Han Somsen for example describes the liberal philosophies of the Enlightenment as having encouraged the development of a body of law whose main aim and effect was to allow the full exploitation of nature by human beings, and he identifies the current decline in command-and-control as resulting from the rise of neo-liberal philosophies. Similarly, Tony Evans attributes some of the failures of international environmental law to the continuing influence of liberal philosophy in the same sense. And a similar theme is continued in Jenny Steele's chapter, which includes investigation of a range of approaches to environmental decision-making.

Nowhere is the philosophical element of existing debates more apparent than in respect of environmental liabilities. From a UK perspective, the retrospective liabilities imposed by US legislation in the 1980s, and most especially the activities of the US courts in pursuing deep pockets,[44] can be and have been seen as an attempt to make up for a deficit in public, prospective control. On one view, this could simply reflect a belated recognition that a potential problem exists, rather than a preference for private over public law mechanisms. This would seem particularly to explain the imposition of true 'deep pockets' liability, with no genuine likelihood of positive incentive effects. But this kind of 'mistake' is itself symptomatic of an individualist philosophy, which prioritizes the completion of individual projects, whilst neglecting strategic reflection on their broader, collective effects.

More generally, it has also been argued that tort liability as a whole, with its attribution of individual blame, appeals in any event to certain styles of right-

[43] This has in some cases been characterized as 'enforced self-regulation': J. Braithwaite, 'Enforced Self Regulation: A New Strategy for Corporate Crime Control' (1982) 80 *Michigan Law Review* 1466–1587, cited in N. Gunningham, 'Environment, Self-Regulation, and the Chemical Industry: Assessing Responsible Care' (1995) 17 *Law & Policy* 57–109.

[44] In respect of lenders, see especially *US v Fleet Factors Corp*, 901 F. 2nd 1550 (11th Cir 1990). Insurers were also subject to 'deep pocket chasing' decisions by US courts. For a general, non-specialist discussion of the way in which the insurance cases affected British insurers, see A. Raphael, *Ultimate Risk* (London, 1994).

wing thought, even though the reality of the tort system can only be grasped by attention to the distributive effects of insurance.[45] There is thus an ideological resistance to analysis of the distributive aspects of tort law and this, on Patrick Atiyah's account for example, is why third party insurance continues to be preferred over first party insurance as a means of compensating for accidents. It might be noted that an emphasis on either form of insurance would amount to the employment of 'private law' in solving the problem of compensation, but (to put it crudely) one turns on tort law, the other on contract. Clearly neither version would operate entirely without state intervention.

Privatization Beyond National Boundaries: Globalization and Legal Development

It follows from the comments above that for many of the contributors to this book, it is important to identify the broader sources of supposed regulatory failure, beyond the identification of technical defect. Is the failure of governments (via law) to control pollution and other forms of environmental harm related to the causes of such harm? In some cases, the causes of environmental harm seem able to evade the control of states, and in a sense to be more influential than states. In Tony Evans' chapter, this effect is attributed to globalization, and he argues that the impotence of states to control the interests which create pollution renders unlikely any major success for international environmental law. It is important to stress again that the impact of 'globalization' is not confined to international law, but is also felt domestically. Tony Evans points to some potential obstacles to legal solutions with clear implications for domestic, as well as international, law. For example, multinational corporations may on his account simply relocate their operations in order to avoid unwelcome and costly state interventions in the form of environmental regulation.

This analysis is not entirely supported by Han Somsen's exploration of European environmental law. Here, the incentives on states might be assumed to be towards the lowest possible environmental standards, but observation of European environmental law-making suggests that this is not necessarily the case. Instead, states might be argued to compete in their provision of public goods and regulation, and devolution of decision-making therefore does not necessarily promote a 'race-to-the-bottom', but may even instigate a 'race-to-the-top'.

These latter observations are prompted in Han Somsen's chapter by a rather different issue, in that they are concerned with the likely effects of European harmonization or (alternatively) devolution in the making of environmental law. Tony Evans on the other hand is emphatically not concerned with law-making, but with law's effectiveness. Nevertheless, Han Somsen's reflections on this

[45] P. Atiyah, 'Personal Injuries in the Twenty First Century: Thinking the Unthinkable', in P. Birks (ed.), *Wrongs and Remedies in the Twenty-First Century* (Oxford, 1996).

particular issue suggest the possibility of a positive development, leading from Tony Evans' concern that environmental goods and even life forms have been 'commodified' (a circumstance which, he argues, enhances the likelihood of ecological degradation, and further weakens the ability of states to control such degradation through law). In other words, environmental quality may itself be a commodity over which nations compete.

Clearly, there is a potential problem with this. There may be a distinction between what will be regarded as desirable by potential citizens in a Europe with free movement, and what will be regarded as desirable by large corporations seeking an appropriate venue for their operations. Of course, this is a controversy which surrounds the whole social element of European integration, not just environmental policy. In this sense, we seem to be some way from finding the elusive 'win-win' situation prefigured in the notion of sustainable development and sustainable growth. But a partial mediation may perhaps be sought in David Robinson's suggestion—offered in a slightly different context—that clean or 'green' technologies are not necessarily more costly. In other words, we could take seriously the potential marketability of newer forms of environmental regulation as such, even among the 'regulated' target group. This is illustrated by the dual, 'regulatory' and 'market', justifications for internationally-recognized environmental management systems.[46] Such an approach would once again raise issues about the traditional division between economic and social roles.

The essence of these disagreements can perhaps be captured as follows. When translated into a domestic law setting, the observation of 'government failure' and the decline of interventionist law, though generally used for quite different purposes, would appear to support a general conclusion about the impotence of the state which is shared by theorists of globalization. Whether looked at internationally or domestically, the question is whether current forms of 'innovation' in law-making are likely to succeed in addressing the possibility of impotence, or whether the 'assimilation' of environmental decision-making to the very patterns of thought which have given rise to environmental problems is no more than an admission of defeat.

David Robinson's analysis, like Clíona Kimber's, suggests some positive benefits associated in particular with information-based strategies. For David Robinson, the advantages of information-based strategies include the possibility of building consensus in cases where risks need to be traded off against benefits, and this possibility is considered to outweigh the possibility of regulatory inefficiency. Clíona Kimber adds some salutary warnings concerning the detailed requirements of rights to information: these cannot be expected to provide desired benefits if they do not take into account the needs and capabilities of users, for example. Han Somsen's analysis of EC environmental law suggests that here too, there are ways of overcoming the perceived likelihood of a deficit in environmental

[46] See Chapter 2 below.

protection. But there are also notes of caution throughout this volume, and in particular there are attempts to scrutinize the legitimacy and openness of new and evolving techniques.

To summarise, 'privatization' affects environmental law in a range of ways. At the simplest level, the urgency of sometimes newly-discovered environmental problems has coincided with an era of restrictions in public sector expenditure. Most obviously, this has implications for environmental goals which involve immediate costs, such as clean-up or compensation, where the temptation (exemplified as explained above in certain cases in the US) has been to target the deepest (private) pockets. More subtly however, the shift toward the private sphere is not only about footing a bill for environmental damage that has already been done. Rather, it is about seeking to anticipate future damage and the acceptability—and distribution—of its likely costs.

Much environmental damage is an inevitable part of ongoing desired activities, and environmental law is still most frequently concerned with mitigating, rather than prohibiting, continuing environmental harm, and slowing the use of resources rather than reversing the trend to their eventual exhaustion. Although in some cases 'sustainability' in resource-use genuinely implies the replacement of those resources, in others (for example the use of fossil fuels) sustainability means (at a maximum) that the needs of future generations to employ the same resource will be taken fairly into account. Environmental law cannot for the most part be seen in terms of absolute prevention, and must be seen as being bound up with the assessment, and taking, of 'risks'. 'Sustainable development' suggests reconciliation of competing goals, rather than outright prohibition, in most cases; and environmental law continues to regard risks as possessing a positive as well as a negative aspect. The trends set out above therefore illustrate the role of the traditional private sector not just in paying for damage, but in decision-making and, crucially, in making decisions as to risk.

Environmental Law and Public Law

It is important to balance this discussion by noting the relationship between some of the general trends outlined so far, and the character of environmental law as an aspect of public law. As explained by Tim Jewell in this collection, public lawyers in particular have been very much concerned with process, sometimes even at the expense of substance. This has perhaps not been so obviously the case in respect of many aspects of environmental law, which have (as we observe above) been predominantly concerned with effectiveness. And yet, environmental law offers significant examples of statutorily-defined decision-making processes and methods. Clearest among these perhaps is the example of land use planning, which involves its own interplay between process, and substance.

The essence of Tim Jewell's chapter is to suggest that some general directions in contemporary public law thinking may usefully be pursued by environmental lawyers. Most notable in this respect is the extension of discussions of accountability and transparency from a narrow focus on Parliament, toward the development of a broader range of modern democratic institutions. At the same time, and for the same reasons (the relative neglect of general public law principles within the study of environmental law), the example of environmental law and policy has perhaps been under-employed as a potential source in informing these broader academic developments. When the evolving public law understandings of, for example, accountability are applied to contexts influenced by privatization and innovation, a new set of challenges may be said to emerge. Environmental law may, as explained above, be regarded as centrally involved with exactly these developments. As a result, there are particular lessons for established processes such as planning, which must now incorporate the concept of sustainable development and all that it implies; and the exercise may also open the door to some interesting analyses of new decision-making methods, such as risk assessment.

Some Closing Remarks

Environmental risks cannot easily be defined, but they have been recognized in many contexts as distinctive. They raise in a stark fashion notions of uncertainty and of subjective evaluation (and thereby critically of the identity of the party or parties who evaluate them), and they are often surrounded by a sense of urgency. Lawyers can differ over whether either facet—the problem of 'control', or the problem of environmental degradation—presents us with a 'crisis' or merely a 'challenge', and it is noticeable that the two chapters here which deal with global aspects of environmental change (including deforestation, the threat to biodiversity, climate change, and exhaustion of natural resources) are most inclined to express such issues in fundamental terms of 'survival'. This may reflect the nature of the most pressing environmental problems as being those that cross national boundaries; but it may also reflect a long-standing perception that international law and international relations are centrally concerned with fundamental issues of 'security'. As Christine Chinkin notes, the multiplication of international laws has been of limited effectiveness, but this multiplication suggests a recognition that environmental issues are issues of survival. As Tony Evans reiterates, part of the problem in the international system is to encourage a shift in thinking from national survival, in terms dictated by states, to global survival.

Whatever the language employed, our summary of the developments explored in this book should perhaps include an account of one particular dilemma. This is the tension between (on the one hand) the priority of technical and process-oriented approaches, which has not been diluted but is possibly intensified by recent trends in regulatory development; and (on the other) the shadow of 'crisis', or at least of urgency. Although much debate in environmental law takes place against the background of such a sense of urgency, the supposed failures of traditional command-and-control almost inevitably imply flexible, responsive, and process-oriented responses.

As an example, David Robinson explains that one of the problems with command-and-control approaches to the regulation of pollution in particular has been that they are analogous to a 'cage', containing some end-of-pipe pollution, but leaving the sources of pollution untouched, and constantly lagging behind in the recognition of new sources. Though many emerging approaches to law and the environment emphasize flexibility and responsiveness in order to avoid just this type of problem, the line between responsiveness and mere reactiveness is sometimes a very fine one. Further, as Jenny Steele argues, the process of attempting simultaneously to achieve both regulatory effectiveness, and significant participation, poses considerable challenges for law.

It is tempting to conclude that more than ever, the causes of environmental harm are more potent than the legal solutions offered. The contributions to this book could be regarded as exploring exactly this sort of boundary between improved effectiveness, and the fundamental limits of law. Their authors share a sense of environmental law's distinctiveness and importance, but they also describe from their various perspectives its increasingly obvious dependence on a diversity of legal and political contexts.

2

Regulatory Evolution in Pollution Control

DAVID ROBINSON[1]

Commentaries on environmental law often refer to the relative novelty of the subject. In the case of pollution control, however, law has been central for a number of decades. The law has achieved some success in controlling gross emissions. However, problems associated with economic and population growth—such as natural resource depletion, declining water quality, cumulative impacts, diffuse source pollution, and the build-up of hazardous wastes—suggest the limitations of law, at least of the prescriptive 'command-and-control' type still dominant in the pollution control systems of many industrialized countries.

This chapter characterizes that law, describes its limitations from the point of view of four perspectives, or 'idioms of analysis', and indicates alternative approaches for the future. Of these, information-based strategies are argued to be the most important. This is because regulatory, economic, and policy means of controlling pollution are ultimately only as effective as the public wants them to be, and the degree to which information is available and understood is a major influence on public opinion.

1. 'Holistic' Regulatory Policy

Before analysing the 1970s 'command-and-control' approaches to pollution, this section will introduce the concept of integrated or holistic regulatory policy with respect to pollution, in contrast to a predominantly legal approach. Of course, the desire to consider pollution control holistically is not new, and the 'process', 'systems', and 'institutional' approaches in law, political science, and management are recognized as having integrating themes of this sort. The section concludes with the observation that the role of law in pollution control is by no means fixed, and suggests that the central issue for pollution control is understanding the nature of and relationships between all components of the system, not just law. For example, a 'command-and-control' legal approach tends to favour quantitative limits on emissions because they can be enforced more easily. However,

[1] The views expressed in this chapter are personal to the author, and are not necessarily those of the Environment Protection Authority of New South Wales. The author acknowledges the assistance of Tim Jewell and Jenny Steele in commenting on drafts of this chapter, and the support of the Centre for Environmental Law, University of Southampton, and EPA (NSW) enabling attendance at the 1996 Conference of the Socio-Legal Studies Association held in Southampton, at which an earlier draft of this paper was presented.

enforceability is but one of many necessary considerations. In some cases less black letter law may be the better approach overall, taking into account economic investment, regional, attitudinal, and technical considerations. Stated differently, this chapter argues that environmental policy should dictate the content of environmental law, not vice versa.[2]

Holistic regulatory policy seeks to use and co-ordinate a number of regulatory instruments, not just law. Table 1 describes the range of instruments which it is sought to integrate. The relative emphasis to place on alternative policy instruments is a controversial matter reflecting political and value judgments. In some cases it may be consistent to 'bet both ways', for example seeking to educate regarding correct waste disposal practices, and backing that up with more surveillance and prosecutions. In others, dissipation of regulatory resources and confusion can result from pursuing multiple, concurrent approaches. For example, modified self-regulatory approaches may be set up for industry as an alternative to government regulation. However, the cost and complexity of running parallel regulatory streams may be considerable. On balance, it may be that concurrent use of a number of instruments to achieve behavioural change obtains better environmental outcomes, even if it is inefficient. This suggestion is further discussed in section 3, below.

In the UK, 'integrated pollution control' refers to cross-media pollution control in a single statute, and administered by agencies in a co-ordinated manner. While this constitutes some legal and administrative integration of two traditional foci for reform, this chapter searches for integration and development of other policy instruments as well, and thereby takes the argument beyond purely 'legal' integration. The search for integrated approaches to control of pollution is common to 'process', 'systems', and 'institutional' policy analyses. These analyses are described in the following three paragraphs.

Under the 'process' approach to law, the interest is more in the actual operation of law in society than in the content of the regulatory provisions themselves. The process approach recognizes that ethical, information, economic, moral, administrative, and enforcement factors affect behaviour, as well as law.[3] A 'process' perspective seeks to consider legislation, court decisions, and attitudes of the

[2] In the United States, law and litigation play a major role in determining environmental policy. Pollution laws limit the scope of the Environmental Protection Agency's discretion, contain Agency-forcing provisions requiring actions to be taken by a certain time or in mandatory ways, offer extended administrative review processes of a judicial or quasi-judicial nature, and allow any person to bring proceedings to enforce the law. However, in countries where litigation is less frequent, mimicking American laws as a means of developing environmental policy may be inappropriate. The weighting and nature of factors which affect behaviour vary from country to country, and the pre-eminence of law in US environmental policy provides little reason for other countries to follow suit.

[3] M. S. McDougal, 'Law as a Process of Decision: A Policy-Oriented Approach to Legal Study' (1956) 1 *Natural Law Forum* 53–72, discussed in P. Finkle, 'Canadian Environmental Law in the Eighties: Problems and Perspectives' (1983) 7 *Dalhousie Law Journal* 257–76, at 271–3; abstracted in D. Chappell and R. D. Moore, *The Use of Criminal Penalties for Pollution of the Environment: A Selective and Annotated Bibliography of the Literature*, Studies in Regulation and Compliance, Department of Justice, Canada, 1988.

TABLE 1: *Regulatory Instruments for Integrated Pollution Control*[†]

WAYS OF CONTROLLING POLLUTION
Improving Knowledge through Monitoring, and Research and Development (R&D) Monitoring: environmental conditions and impact of policies. R&D: biophysical, technological, social and economic.
Improving Communication Partnership building at both inter and intra-jurisdictional levels: individuals, firms, non-government organizations, researchers, agencies. Mechanisms include: state of the environment reporting; natural accounting; pollutant inventories; project and cumulative environmental impact assessment; agency and industry performance reporting. Public participation: policy formulation and enforcement; community-based monitoring; informal and ongoing (as well as in formal consultation periods); consultation and negotiation.
Education Public and targeted. General (schools and universities) and vocational (job skills training).
Law Civil (for example orders to stop polluting, to clean-up or to report; individual and collective liability rules for ecological damage; common law). Criminal (orders backed by threat of fine, imprisonment or other sentencing options). International and inter-jurisdictional agreements.
Modified Self-Organization By firms of sectors, with external accountability checks. Environmental management systems involving standards, codes of practice, auditing and environmental performance review; exclusion rules for non-complying members.
Market (Economic) Mechanisms Pollution and product charges; tradeable permits or use quotas; environmental taxes and allowable deductions; deposit refunds; performance bonds; product labelling.
Cross-Sectoral Policy Accommodation Removal or adjustment of distorting policy settings and institutional barriers across all areas of government.

[†] Adapting Dovers: S. Dovers, 'Information, Sustainability and Policy' (1995) 2 Australian *Journal of Environmental Management* 142–56, at 150. Environment Protection Authority (NSW), *A New Approach to Environmental Education in New South Wales* (1996), at 18.

public, industry, and government for the purpose of more realistic evaluation of the political problems of administration and enforcement. Negotiation, bargaining, and compromise are recognised as inherent in command-and-control systems, if not in pollution control generally.[4]

The search for integrated environmental policy has also been described as a 'systems' approach. For example, one American lawyer has explained the regulatory failure of the Clean Air Act in terms of the 'systematic limitations on legislative control of administrative behaviour'.[5] At the international level a 'systems approach' by states for the protection of the commons of the biosphere has been advocated.[6] Most importantly, environmental management systems ('EMSs'), involving particularly the adoption of international and national standards, are now proposed as a tool for improving the environmental performance of industry. These seek holistic management approaches within enterprises, partly to satisfy external regulatory requirements to control pollution. These are discussed further below, under 'Modified Self-Organization'.

The theme of integration also underlies the 'institutional' analyses of political scientists. In this respect, it should be noted that processes of societal organization, not model institutions (for example, environment protection agencies), are intended by the term 'institutions'.[7] One 'institutional' analysis of command-and-control pollution control systems is discussed below.[8] In response to Hardin's 'Tragedy of the Commons' dilemma,[9] Ostram has proposed a model for a sustainable common pool, including common, but finite, resource systems such as those relating to fisheries, to traditional commons for grazing, and water extraction.[10] While developed for different purposes, the model suggests some of the characteristics of integrated pollution control, such as clear rules; rules appropriate to local conditions; the ability of affected persons to participate to change rules; monitoring; graduated sanctions; and conflict resolution mechanisms.[11]

While recognizing that each country must develop its own approach to pollution control in response to its geographic, industrial, cultural, and constitutional

[4] Finkle, op. cit.; M. Rankin and P. Finkle, 'The Enforcement of Environmental Law: Taking the Environment Seriously' (1983) 17 *University of British Colombia Law Review* 35–7; K. Hawkins, *Environment and Enforcement: Regulation and the Social Definition of Pollution* (Oxford, 1984); G. Richardson, 'Policing Pollution: The Enforcement Process' (1982/3) 11 *Policy Studies Journal* 153–64; all abstracted in Chappell and Moore, op. cit.

[5] H. Latin, 'Regulatory Failure, Administrative Incentives, and the New Clean Air Act' (1991) 21 *Environmental Law* 1647–720, at 1650.

[6] United Nations/World Commission on Environment, 'Proposals for International Environmental Law—Developments Towards the Year 2000' (1986) 16 *Environmental Policy and Law* 90–6.

[7] '"Institutions" can be defined as sets of working rules that are used to determine who is eligible to make decisions in some arena, what actions are allowed or constrained, what aggregation rules will be used, what procedures must be followed, what information must or must not be provided, and what pay-offs will be assigned to individuals dependent on their actions.': E. Ostrom, *Governing the Commons: The Evolution of Institutions for Collective Action* (Cambridge, 1991), at 51.

[8] See 'Idioms of Analysis', below.

[9] G. Hardin, 'The Tragedy of the Commons' (1968) 162 *Science* 1243–8.

[10] Ostram, op. cit. [11] Ibid., at 90.

circumstances, there is nonetheless a global dimension. The biosphere is a common, and transboundary pollution is of increasing concern. Further, much pollution is generated in standard ways, for example, emissions from automobiles and fuel-burning power stations. Often the technologies involved are the result of international market penetration of products and technologies, suggesting the need for international approaches to pollution control. However, the determinant should be whether the proposed system will work in the country in question. An organic approach is therefore warranted. One part of the organism may look weak, but proper assessment can only be made of the system as a whole.

For example, the pollution control laws of Japan cannot be meaningfully assessed by comparing them to the characteristics of the pollution control laws of the United States without recourse to the broader factors indicated above. This is because law plays different roles in Japanese and American society. In Japan it would appear that criminal law operates by threat more than enforcement: civil laws attract bigger penalties; and behaviour, in any event, is more conditioned by cultural factors such as fear of loss of reputation. Industry as a whole supported stringent pollution controls to prevent any firm from gaining a competitive market edge in the wake of the Big Four toxic pollution cases.[12] These differences illustrate that whilst the components of pollution control systems may be the same internationally (in this example civil laws, criminal laws, psychological factors, and corporate influences), the relative weighting of each may vary from country to country. As a result, there can be no international checklist or blueprint for good pollution control law.

The implications of integrated analysis for the comparative study of pollution control law are daunting. Comparative legal study will be worthwhile only if immersed in a broader analysis of the role of every other policy instrument, and of the instruments, legal and non-legal, in each system. Exclusive attention to any single pollution control instrument is of limited value, as other factors which affect behaviour will be neglected. For example, the common reaction of governments to reports about increased pollution is to create new offences or increase the penalties for existing ones. Whether these measures will have a deterrent effect in practice may well be influenced by economic, corporate, and attitudinal factors which tougher sanctions do not address.

2. Command-and-Control Responses to Pollution in the 1960s and 1970s

It was not until the late 1960s and early 1970s that governments systematically sought to control pollution other than where human health was directly

[12] J. O. Haley, 'Sheathing the Sword of Justice in Japan: An Essay on Law Without Sanctions' (1982) 8 *Journal of Japanese Studies* 265–81; M. Peterson and L. Wade, 'Environmental Pollution Policy in Japan: A Public Choice Hypothesis', in A. Groth and L. Wade (eds.), *Public Policy Across Nations: Social Welfare in Industrial Settings* (Greenwich, 1985), at 71.

threatened.[13] A combination of factors aroused the interest of governments. One simple factor was that pollution was largely a new problem, being a by-product of economic and population growth and new technologies in industrialized countries after 1945 (for example the transformation of agriculture through increased use of chemical fertilizers, herbicides, and pesticides). Other factors contributing to the interest in pollution during this period include rising educational standards, and the maturing of a generation in Western countries concerned about quality of life in a period of general material prosperity.

One study has traced the responses of seven governments in Europe and North America.[14] An initial response was for governments to set up independent expert groups to advise them on environmental matters (median date 1970). At about the same time, environmental bureaucracies were established, and air and water pollution laws were made. Toxic chemicals laws followed (median date 1976), then waste disposal laws. The chronology is roughly the same in some other jurisdictions, for example New South Wales ('NSW').[15]

The chairperson of one regulatory agency has characterized traditional environmental regulation as:

> . . . based on a mosaic 'Thou shalt not' concept known as command-and-control. This has had a number of important consequences. It has:
> — resulted in the abatement of gross industrial pollution;
> — produced an end-of-pipe culture where pollution control costs were regarded as overheads (with no hope of return on investment);
> — produced a minimum compliance culture which stifled innovation;
> — ensured that the environment remained an externality;
> — produced a new criminal class and required established legal norms to be overturned;
> — focused attention on corporate behaviour at the expense of individual behaviour; and
> — ignored cumulative impacts.[16]

The regulatory responses of the 1970s typically required permits from industry with regard to air and water pollutants. They were media-specific. In the USA, uniform water effluent limits were placed on 500 different industries.[17] They were based on best available control technology so long as the costs would not shut

[13] For accounts of earlier regulatory approaches to pollution, see D. Hughes, *Environmental Law* (3rd ed., London, 1996); H. Bradby (ed.), *Dirty Words: Writings on the History and Culture of Pollution* (London, 1990).

[14] A. Weale, *The New Politics of Pollution* (Manchester, 1992).

[15] The State Pollution Control Commission (NSW) was established in 1970. The major enactments were the Clean Air Act 1961, the Clean Waters Act 1970, the Waste Disposal Act 1970, and the Environmentally Hazardous Chemicals Act 1985.

[16] B. Robinson, Chairperson, Environment Protection Authority (Victoria), 'ISO 14000: Eagle or Albatross', Paper delivered to 'ISO 14000—Regulation, Trade and Environment', Conference of the Australian Centre for Environmental Law, Australian National University, Canberra, 2 July 1996.

[17] B. A. Ackerman and R. B. Stewart, 'Reforming Environmental Law: The Democratic Case for Market Incentives' (1988) 13 *Columbia Journal of Environmental Law* 171–99, at 173.

down the relevant plant or industry ('BAT').[18] A similar approach was, in practice, adopted in setting standards for new sources of air pollution.[19] In the UK, fewer substances were made subject to quantitative emission controls, and a generic requirement that pollution be controlled using the 'best practicable means' ('BPM') was favoured.

Some attempts at establishing ambient standards or quality objectives were made.[20] However the complexity, scientific uncertainty, and enormity of the task of determining these across various media and broad geographic areas, and then issuing or adjusting the permits at individual facilities accordingly, proved too great a task. As a result, the earlier permitting systems were not based upon ambient or environmental quality plans or objectives for the catchments or airsheds to which they related.[21] Rather, the systems imposed immediate limits on particular, widespread pollutants emitted from the most obviously polluting industries.

The ideas behind pollution control were pragmatic, involving end-of-pipe filters and scrubbers, better diffusion (such as through taller chimneys for power stations and sewerage discharge further out to sea) and, in the case of toxic by-products, isolation (for example, of nuclear wastes).

Criminal laws underpinned the earlier, command-and-control permitting systems. They were complemented in the USA and Germany with civil penalties and procedures, and in the UK and Sweden with controls imposed administratively.[22] Within industry itself, so long as a level of compliance sufficient to prevent prosecution was achieved, pollution control 'was left largely to those marked "unsuitable for senior posts" to manage, a low priority for [Chief Executive Officers] and remote from consideration of the Board'.[23]

Having characterized command-and-control approaches as 1970s in inspiration, it would be wrong to regard them as superseded. In fact they remain the foundation of many pollution control systems. There will always be a place for commands backed by threats with regard to the control of certain substances. For example product bans, such as the DDT ban imposed in America in 1972[24]

[18] Latin, op. cit., at 1661. Technology-based control was the centrepiece of the 1972 amendments to the Federal Water Pollution Control Act.

[19] Ackerman and Stewart, op. cit., at 173.

[20] e.g., s. 11 of the Clean Waters Act 1970 (NSW) enables waterways to be classified in categories ranging from 'specially protected' (into which no wastes can be discharged) to 'ocean outfall' (into which a large number and quantity of wastes can be discharged). Similarly, the Clean Air Act (USA) sought to apply uniform federal air quality standards to regulate existing industrial sources of certain widespread pollutants: Ackerman and Stewart, op. cit., at 173.

[21] With reference to the two examples cited in n. 20, in NSW only thirteen per cent of the State's rivers were classified (State Pollution Control Commission, *Annual Report 1990–91*) and in the USA, where the federal air quality regional standards are not achieved, in practice the technological fall-back control (reasonably available control measures) applies (Ackerman and Stewart, op. cit.).

[22] Weale, op. cit., at 16–17.

[23] B. Robinson, op. cit., at 3.

[24] *Environmental Defense Fund v Environmental Protection Agency*, 489 F.2d 1247 (D.C. Cir. 1973), upholding a 1972 cancellation of registration of most uses of DDT. Discussed in J. L. Anderson, 'The Environment Revolution at Twenty-Five' (1995) 26 *Rutgers Law Journal* 395–430, at 420.

and subsequently in other countries, is command-and-control law at its simplest and, arguably, its best. The government simply commands that an activity, for example the sale or manufacture of a product, shall cease, under threat of legal sanction.

However, most pollution problems are less clear than the need to stop DDT from entering the food chain. Compromise of economic and environmental outcomes may be needed. Technical solutions may not be clear-cut or available without research and investment. In the face of uncertainty, the command-and-control approach has been questioned. The 'implementation deficit'—the failure of the first round of command-and-control laws to achieve all that they set out to do—is therefore of continuing relevance.

Implementation Deficit

In addition to product bans, command-and-control approaches have had other successes in controlling certain pollutants from major factories and sources.[25] However, economic growth, associated natural resource depletion, and diffuse source pollution have outstripped the modest gains made by command-and-control laws. Emission control laws, for example, may reduce the emissions of individual vehicles, but these gains may be outstripped by increases in vehicle numbers and general use.

The term 'implementation deficit' suggests that legislatively mandated pollution controls may not be applied in practice. If so, better enforcement would be the obvious solution. Examples abound of poorly resourced enforcement agencies and of regulatory cultures favouring compromise, warnings, and bargaining with industry rather than strict application of the letter of the law. However a task of this chapter, indeed of this book, is to question more fundamentally the role of law in environmental decision-making. Giving more resources to regulators, and a tougher approach to enforcement, is only part of the solution to pollution. The development of different types of law, of non-legal environmental instruments, and of ways of ensuring that these complement each other, will also be proposed as elements of the solution.

[25] Sulphur dioxide, particulates, and ambient lead reductions have been achieved: Organisation for Economic Co-operation and Development, *Reducing Environmental Pollution: Looking Back, Thinking Ahead. An Examination of OECD Member Country Progress, Trends and Opportunities for Accelerated Pollution Reduction in the 1990s and Beyond* (Paris, 1994), at 7. See also D. Kee, 'Sooty Skies and Burning Rivers No Longer Dragons to Slay' (1995) *Environmental Manager* 19–21. Point-source controls imposed under the Clean Waters Act 1970 resulted in a reduction of ninety per cent of the dry weather pollution load on the Parramatta River by 1975. Sydney's photochemical smog and oxidants emissions were contained by more stringent controls on car emissions in the early 1980s (unleaded petrol and catalytic converters on new cars): State Pollution Control Commission, *Annual Report 1990–91*, at 13–15.

Idioms of Analysis

The task of this and the following section is to explore the inadequacies of the 1970s command-and-control approach in more detail. The task is easy to state, but difficult to undertake. Different analyses highlight different reasons for the failure. This section describes the work of Weale in grouping the analyses of prescriptive pollution control law into four types, termed 'idioms of analysis' because their concepts and foundations are loose and idiomatic. Weale's idioms are explored because they help with an understanding both of the regulatory systems which they analyse, and of the beliefs and priorities of their exponents. In reviewing each of the idioms, elements of critique of command-and-control are introduced. This critique is developed further in the following section, 'Limitations of the Initial Command-and-Control Approach'.

Rational Choice Idiom

In a 'rational choice' or 'public choice' idiom the role of pollution policy is regarded as being to implement the polluter pays or user pays principle. In other words, policy must result in industry internalizing, through market mechanisms, the external costs of air, water, and soil degradation. The focus of analysis is on self-interested individuals. Accordingly, as environment does not affect the incomes of voters, it is characteristically a peripheral political issue, manifesting itself most strongly through 'not-in-my-backyard' ('NIMBY') and symbolic environmental concern. Politicians will tend to be pragmatic about the environment rather than following principled commitments. Bureaucrats seek power and, as the opportunities for salary increase are limited in public life, they fulfil their ambitions by building pollution control empires larger than needed for the public good. Alternatively, they can achieve salary increase and higher social status by switching to the private sector. They thus tend to foster good working relationships with industry to keep career doors open for themselves. The 'public choice' literature is sceptical of the notion that pollution agency staff are public-spirited.[26] Industry, the strongest lobby, will tend to exploit opportunities to weaken the impact of environmental regulation. No-one has an incentive to estimate the costs and benefits of regulation. The polluter is considered as an amoral, calculating type who will pollute if the profits from the illegal emission exceed the punishment costs, duly discounted according to the likelihood of being caught. Industry will comply with pollution law minimally in order to keep the regulator at bay, and to the extent that a corporate image of social responsibility is good for business.[27]

[26] 'The "public choice" literature is characterized by claims that legislation and regulation are normally produced by "rent-seekers" intent on maximizing their own returns from public service.': Latin, op. cit., at 168.

[27] P. Downing and J. Kimball, 'Enforcing Pollution Control Laws in the US: Introduction to the Issues' (1982/3) 11 *Policy Studies Journal* 55–65, abstracted in Chappell and Moore, op. cit., at 28.

Political Economics Idiom

In contrast to the micro analysis of rational choice idiom, in which the behaviour of individuals is paramount, a 'macro' analysis characterizes the 'political economics' or 'systems' idiom. Neo-Marxist analyses adopt this idiom. For writers such as Yeager,[28] the need to expand the forces of production and accumulate capital are seen to conflict with the state's need to satisfy the democratic and environmental amenity aspirations of its citizens. The state faces the internal contradiction of needing to spend to provide social and environmental amenity for citizens, but also needing not to burden industry with taxes. The state will attempt to solve the problems of pollution by regulation (and over-regulation), however the social system must be changed to solve the externalities problem. There is a tendency in the capitalist system to turn problems of political values into problems of technical rationality. The bounds of pollution control are set 'by the systemic needs of the political economic system of capitalist democracies'.[29] The shortcomings of planned economies in protecting the environment, for example in allowing gross industrial pollution to continue in Eastern Europe, might also be explained in political economics idiom (as well as others), as constructing reasons of a systemic nature for the environmental failings of communism.

Policy Discourse Idiom

Eco-philosophically inspired appraisals of pollution control systems illustrate the third idiom of analysis identified by Weale, namely 'policy discourse'. To the deep green, the failure of the law adequately to protect the environment is a reflection of core beliefs, understandings, and value systems. Pollution control can only be achieved as part of a broader and deeply-rooted eco-philosophy in which material and non-material values are weighted differently.

Institutional Idiom

Finally, the 'institutional' idiom analyses pollution control by focusing on the characteristics and practices of the groups of people involved. For example, Vogel has explained the survival of discretionary law in the UK, in contrast to black letter and prescriptive pollution control law of the USA, in terms of institutional differences.[30] The British civil service was respected, its business community was expected to defer to public authority, and the public was not unduly suspicious of industry. The early command-and-control laws were limited by a commonly

[28] P. C. Yeager, *The Limits of Law: The Public Regulation of Private Pollution* (Cambridge, Mass., 1991).

[29] Ibid.

[30] D. Vogel, *National Styles of Regulation: Environmental Policy in Great Britain and the United States* (Ithaca, 1986).

held zero sum concept, namely that more environment meant less development. As development and growth are the dominant societal goals, there was thus only limited room for pollution control.

In political systems in which negotiated outcomes play an important role, command-and-control fails because governments favour specific benefits (such as economic growth) over diffuse, collective benefits (such as environmental protection). Organizations will tend to use old procedures to solve new problems, partly because of the slow rate of assimilation of knowledge in large organizations. Environmental policy is analysed in terms of the interactions of policy communities, each informed by different expertise and values. For example, allegiances of scientific experts, civil servants, and politicians may create different environmental policies than allegiances which include trade unions or environmental organizations.

A variation of this is Latin's explanation of the failures of the US EPA in terms of the disciplinary biases of its administrators, which prevail over statutory goals. He cites examples of a science-based EPA failing to respond early enough to community concerns such as when Rachel Carson's *Silent Spring* drew attention to toxic chemicals. Latin has characterized other regulatory failures in institutional terms. For example, in conflicts between political considerations and technocratic requirements, he says that politics usually prevails. The EPA is too weak and the political expediency of allocating funds, for example to clean up contaminated land or to build public-owned sewerage treatment plants, upon a political rather than an environmental needs basis is too great. In analysing pollution control, institutional idiom theorists emphasize the compromises and bargaining which result when vague laws are sought to be applied and enforced in practice.[31]

Table 2 compares the approach taken by the above idioms to the concept of sustainable development, and the problems of vehicle emissions and declining water quality. While the political economics and policy discourse idioms have almost opposite foundations (materialism versus idealism), they both advocate radical and fundamental change, and have been grouped together in the table for simplicity.

Limitations of the Initial Command-and-Control Approach

The above idioms of analysis attribute the relative failure of the 1970s command-and-control approach to a variety of causes. The lack of consensus as to cause might suggest that a more detailed, technical review of command-and-control will be fraught with value judgments which could not possibly satisfy the concerns of the exponents of all idioms. However, common elements do exist across the idioms. This section attempts to identify these elements, developing a theme that

[31] Hawkins, op. cit. and Richardson, op. cit.

TABLE 2: *Different Characterizations of Pollution*

IDIOM OR PERSPECTIVE	KEY ISSUE	TOOLS	ATTITUDE TO SUSTAINABLE DEVELOPMENT	HOW TO IMPROVE VEHICLE EMISSIONS	HOW TO IMPROVE WATER QUALITY
Rational choice.	Internalize external environmental costs through free and regulated market mechanisms.	Technical (e.g., economic instruments).	Achievable and underway.	More stringent emission limits on manufacturers. Financial incentives (e.g., tax on leaded petrol) for increased environmental efficiency of vehicles. Better emission detection technology in order to identify and prosecute grossly polluting vehicles.	Increase charges (for consumption of clean water and for pollution emissions). Bigger criminal law sanctions and hard-line prosecutorial focus (polluters will emit what they can get away with).
Political economics; policy discourse.	Growth, absence of eco-philosophy.	Macro-political, ethical.	Self-contradictory.	State control of vehicle production, distribution and usage. Better public transport. Reduce the need for vehicles by promoting small, self-sufficient communities in which work-places are situated near homes.	More social control of polluting industry, for example by measuring and rewarding production in terms of environmental outcomes as well as profits. Educational and ethical focus on the inherent value of clean water and healthy aquatic ecosystems.

					Planning initiatives to reduce diffuse source pollution from urban sprawl e.g. through medium density housing and shared open space.
Institutional.	Compromise through political accommodation.	Participation and policy change.	Possible, but presently economics outweighs environment.	Awareness-building of the power exerted by vehicle manufacturers, oil companies and road building interests in transport planning. Encouraging alternative interest groups and policy communities to balance the power of the motor industry lobby. Gamekeeper/poacher separation in government (e.g. road builders approving their own proposals).	Address agency 'capture' by increasing accountability and enabling public participation in water planning and extraction and discharge licensing More stringent control of gross polluters e.g. sewerage utilities. Grass-roots awareness development e.g. community monitoring and involvement in catchment management.

command-and-control systems can have only limited success, because they seek to control pollution mechanically, not organically.[32]

Command-and-control approaches can be likened to a cage built around the most obvious sources of pollution long after the industrial, combustion, and urban processes which generate the pollution commenced operation. The sources remain, and the cage sometimes works to contain some of the pollution, and sometimes fails, but in any event the relevance of the cage diminishes as additional, uncaged sources of pollution proliferate. The cage, or end-of-pipe solution, can thus be characterized as a mechanical approach. Permits and filters do not fundamentally change existing production systems, let alone deal with inherent enforcement limitations. The symptoms of production, not the underlying causes in productive processes, are addressed. Added to this, however, are further limitations of early command-and-control approaches.

1. Expense

As filters and scrubbers are additional rather than integrated plant, the more they control pollution, the greater is the resulting cost of production. This notion is conveyed in Figure 1, relating to waste management attitudes in the twentieth century. End-of-pipe treatment of waste is characterized as having increasing costs over time, as standards and disposal costs rise and volumes of waste increase. In contrast, waste prevention approaches, while initially requiring greater design and capital investment in whole-of-cycle production processes, can be expected to decrease the cost to society of handling waste, for example as valuable raw materials are retrieved from the waste stream, and re-use and recycling reduces the quantity of waste for disposal.

2. Pollution Shift, Not Reduction

Media-specific laws and consequent multi-permitting schemes failed to take into account total pollutant loads. For example, sulphuric acid works might have separate licences under air pollution and water pollution laws. This left open the possibility of avoiding restrictions placed on one medium by converting them into emissions to the medium where less restrictive controls existed. A similar pollution shift (as opposed to reduction) occurred in NSW in the 1970s and 1980s regarding the emission of toxic substances into waterways. The regulatory authority encouraged the clean-up of creeks and estuaries by enabling factories to emit into the sewerage system. Rather than pollution reduction at source, the toxics problem was moved to the sewerage processing plants and ocean discharge points.[33]

3. Distortion Resulting from the Size of Enterprises

Regulatory controls are more costly, in proportion to total costs, for small industrial concerns. Tougher pollution controls make it more difficult for small indus-

[32] Matthew Arnold coined the term 'mechanical' reform: Weale, op. cit., at 27.
[33] S. Beder, *Toxic Fish and Sewer Surfing* (Sydney, 1989).

FIGURE 1: *Waste Management Paradigm Shifts*†

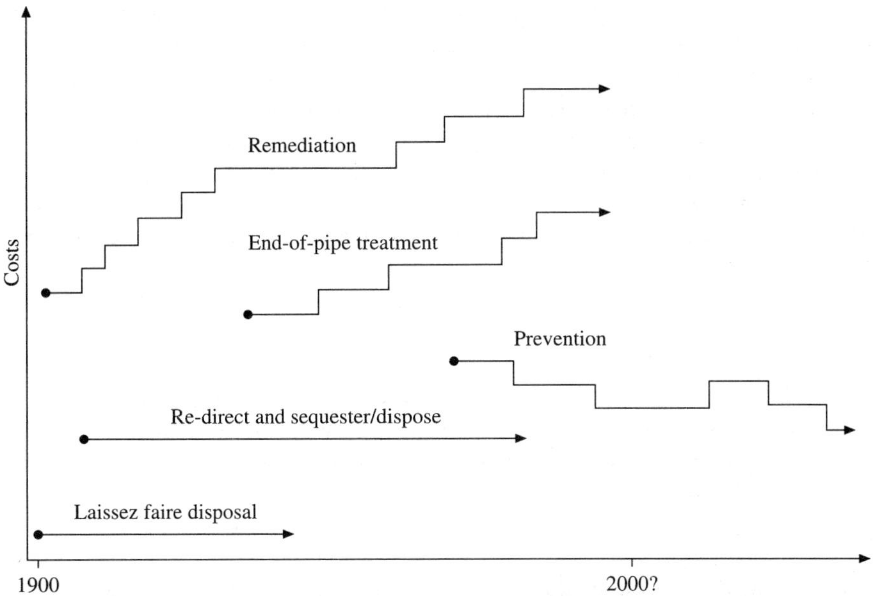

† Reprinted with permission from J. Hirschorn, T. Jackson, and L. Baas, 'Towards Prevention – The Emerging Environmental Management Paradigm', in T. Jackson (ed.), *Clean Production Strategies: Developing Preventive Environmental Management in the Industrial Economy* (Stockholm, 1993), at 126. Copyright Lewis Publishers, an imprint of CRC Press, Boca Raton, Florida. © 1993.

tries to compete with larger ones. On the other hand, in some systems only larger industry is caught by permitting or quantitative discharge standards, with qualitative (for example 'best practicable means') control theoretically imposed on smaller emitters. In practice, 'qualitative controls' have often translated into no control at all, as the regulatory system is poorly suited to the control of small but widespread sources, even though cumulatively they cause considerable pollution. The common element of these two phenomena—regulation which has a disproportionate impact on small industry, and regulators who focus on large industry—is that of pollution control distortion: the system does not treat polluters equally.

4. Reactive Nature

Command-and-control approaches are driven by notorious incidents and waves of public environmental concern. Legislation is passed and sought to be enforced during the wave of concern. Because control is external to the productive system, once the public attention wanes there is little capacity or incentive for regulatory bodies to measure the effectiveness of legislation, or for industry to raise standards over time or to audit its environmental performance.

5. Dependence on Regulatory Authority

Command-and-control systems assume the existence of an omniscient, ever-present regulatory authority. That authority must identify the substances for control, then set standards. This demands technical expertise across a daunting array of substances and environments. The number of substances to be controlled, and the time and resources involved in setting controls on each one, let alone enforcing them, is substantial. In addition, earlier command-and-control approaches specified operating controls for particular items of plant, not just emission limits or performance standards. Involvement in both means and ends created even more demand for regulatory resources.

Administrative law in some countries requires public consultation and negotiation at each stage of regulatory intervention. It is no coincidence, therefore, that the EPA in the United States became one of the largest federal bureaucracies, quite apart from the additional resource requirements of parallel State EPAs. An army of staff was needed to issue permits; to write and review laws, regulations, and guidelines; and to detect or investigate, and adequately respond to all pollution incidents.

Except in the USA,[34] the role of the citizen in early command-and-control systems was merely to inform the agency of possible breaches. Pollution control was viewed as a specialist matter for the expert agency. This is in contrast to the broader potential role of third parties, which is advocated both in this chapter and elsewhere in this book.

As permits were the focus of control, considerable resources of regulatory authorities were dedicated to issuing and renewing them. The requirement to hold a permit was not always linked to effective assessment of the environmental risk posed by a particular industry or facility. For example, in NSW industrial activities carried out on premises of more than 400 square metres require a Noise Control Act 1975 licence, even though land area is a patently inappropriate indicator of whether the activity is sufficiently noisy to warrant the imposition of site-specific controls.[35]

6. Static Nature

Under the 1970s approach, standards were set at achievable discharge levels taking into account the age of plant. Once a standard was set, there was no incentive for industry gradually to reduce pollution below that standard. As a result, there was little incentive to invest in better pollution control technologies or plant. The setting of lower environmental performance standards for older plant

[34] See D. H. Robbins, 'Public Interest Environmental Litigation in the United States', in D. Robinson and J. Dunkley (eds.), *Public Interest Perspectives in Environmental Law* (Chichester, 1995), and D. Robinson, 'Public Interest Environmental Law Firms in the United States', in Robinson and Dunkley (eds.), op. cit., ch. 2.

[35] The Protection of the Environment Operations Act 1997 (New South Wales) removes the anomaly of land area of premises being a criterion for whether a pollution control licence is required.

constituted a disincentive to upgrade, as by prolonging the life of old plant, the need to meet the more stringent emission controls applicable to new plant could be postponed.

7. Complexity

While the idea of controlling major pollutants from major facilities is conceptually simple, refining the system procedurally, adding new substances for control, and extending the controls over facilities not originally caught results in voluminous, complex laws. For example, in NSW logging operations were not, in practice, caught by the Clean Waters Act 1970. Concern about loss of topsoil, scouring, and waterway turbidity from logging operations, including access road work, resulted in the Environment Protection Authority (NSW) issuing generic water pollution licences to the forestry agency in 1992. These were made increasingly specific over time, in order to control water pollution more effectively. The forestry water pollution licences became complicated and time-consuming to administer. By 1997 the logging licences were still considered to be a trial programme, and proposals to complement the licences with guidelines to suggest ways in which pollution could be minimized in logging operations were being considered.[36]

8. Legislative Duplicity

In some countries, particularly the USA, ambitious objectives for environmental improvement were included in pollution control legislation.[37] While such objectives may have a civic, educative function, they can also be criticized as rhetorical, and as creating unrealistic expectations in the minds of citizens. Behind the rhetoric, the legislation contained tensions or ambiguities as to fundamental issues which the parliament failed to resolve. For example, the Federal Water Pollution Control Act (USA) gave the Environmental Protection Agency duties to list and stringently control toxic pollutants (those causing death, disease, or genetic mutation). The simple legislative mandate to list substances on the basis of toxic effects glossed over great uncertainty and controversy as to safe levels of exposure. As a result the EPA failed to meet the legislative timetable for listing. Notorious citizen suits ensued, and the resulting judgments directed the EPA away from absolutist toxic effects considerations towards listing toxins, almost twenty years after the legislation was enacted, through an approach which took into account existing technological and cost factors.[38]

[36] Environment Protection Authority (NSW), Protection of the Environment Operations Bill 1996, *Impact Analysis of the Draft Schedule of EPA-Licensed Activities*, 1996, at 74.

[37] The Federal Water Pollution Control Act, for example, had a statutory objective to eliminate the pollution of navigable waters by 1985, and to prohibit the discharge of toxic pollutants in toxic amounts: s. 101(a)(1) and (5).

[38] See *Natural Resources Defense Council v Train* DDC 1976; 8 ERC 2120 (the 'Flannery Decree'). Aspects of the Flannery Decree were incorporated into the 1977 amendments to the legislation. The timetable was modified in court eight times between 1979 and 1987. See D. Robinson, 'Public Interest Environmental Law Firms in the United States', op. cit., at 57–8.

In some cases the legislation was incapable of enforcement. For example, failure to observe instructions is a major cause of water pollution from pesticide run-off or air pollution from spray drift. The Pesticides Act 1978 (NSW) created offences for the misuse of pesticides, and successive governments employed a number of pesticide field inspectors with an apparent enforcement, as well as educative, role. However, the important offences required proof of harmful intent.[39] As this was usually impossible, few prosecutions resulted. The result was self-contradictory regulatory policy. The government appeased conservationists by pointing to the existence of the inspectors, but kept farmers on-side by providing the inspectors with law which was practically unenforceable.

9. Administrative Fragmentation

With the notable exception of the National Environment Protection Act (USA) and environmental impact assessment laws inspired by it (for example, the Environmental Planning and Assessment Act 1979 (NSW)), 1970s pollution control laws were discrete, and little integrated with other laws or regulatory policy areas such as land-use planning, transport, industry, energy or taxation. The creation of separate environmental agencies to implement the new laws, with little change being made to existing agencies, illustrates the 'external' nature of the first laws. More than an oversight, this was a reflection of the political reality that pollution control could not be allowed to disrupt industry or economic growth except in symbolic ways, such as through the creation of environmental ministries or agencies.

For example, in NSW there have been few instances of outright rejection of applications for pollution permits. The pollution regulator has historically sought to accommodate development approvals under the separate, land-use planning system by issuing the necessary pollution permit. While opportunities existed for the EPA to comment on pollution-generating developments at the planning stage, and while the EPA did so regarding certain high-impact projects, the planning and pollution laws and administrations, dating from the 1970s, were not integrated.[40]

10. Jurisdictional Tension

In both unitary and federal countries, command-and-control laws encountered geo-political obstacles. Lower levels of government were disrespected. Federal

[39] Section 37, for example, creates an offence of causing a risk of personal injury or property damage by a pesticide, but only if it can be proven that the action was both wilful and without reasonable cause.

[40] Greater integration of planning consents with pollution licences has been achieved with the Environmental Planning and Assessment Amendment Act 1997 and the Protection of the Environment Operations Act 1997 (both NSW). Local councils must incorporate as conditions on development consents any pollution licensing requirements of the EPA. The EPA can only vary those licence conditions following the first licence review, of which public notice must be given, and which must take place within three years.

agencies were reluctant to submit to state pollution laws.[41] The pollution policies of central governments reached local governments late or only in part. Disputes between governments resulted in implementation deficits as federal, regional, and local government levels compromised and negotiated pollution controls.[42] The relative failure of the states to implement the US Clean Air Act is an example of this.[43] A final element of jurisdictional tension, particularly in North America and Europe, was the reliance upon the nation-state as the principal source of law, with only a small role for international law.

11. Undue Reliance on the Criminal Law

Legal responses in the 1970s satisfied populist demand that there ought to be a law against gross acts of pollution, such as clandestine dumping of waste. Criminal law was the natural choice, as imprisonment and criminal fines indicated society's concern for environmental damage. However, pollution control is considerably more complicated than having tough sanctions available to punish environmental vandals. This is because most pollution is not caused by a small number of criminal stereotypes, but by 'respectable' industries, and is also 'the by-product of our own consumer lifestyles and, therefore, something in which everybody is implicated to varying degrees'.[44]

In dealing with respectable polluters, the moral judgments of regulators influence enforcement, and this militates against the application of criminal law, for example when a 'decent', employment-creating company commits a strict liability pollution offence. The reality of pollution control is that it is negotiated, and law is a last resort.[45] In practice, 'just deserts' is seen as an insufficient reason for prosecution if the industry has taken remedial or preventive action.[46] In the USA, where unrealistic air and water clean-up goals were set, it was not politically feasible to prosecute for non-attainment of those goals.[47]

As for diffuse, 'lifestyle' pollution, such as from urban and farming run-off, poor waste management, and vehicle emissions, the criminal law plays an awkward

[41] e.g., in Australia the Commonwealth telecommunications and defence bodies have long resisted compliance with the environmental laws of the states in which they operate, citing the lack of uniformity between state laws as a concern.

[42] P. Downing, 'Cross-National Comparisons in Environmental Protection: Introduction to the Issues' (1982–3) 11 *Policy Studies Journal* 39–43, abstracted in Chappell and Moore, op. cit., at 71.

[43] State Implementation Plans under the US Clean Air Act proved largely ineffective, with states delaying making plans, or making inadequate ones, and the EPA remaining reluctant to undertake politically perilous and costly litigation to force the states to take adequate action: Anderson, op. cit., at 417. See also Latin, op. cit.

[44] D. Farrier, 'In Search of Real Criminal Law', in T. Bonyhady (ed.), *Environmental Protection and Legal Change* (Sydney, 1992), at 117.

[45] Hawkins, op. cit. and Richardson, op. cit.

[46] Richardson, op. cit.

[47] 'The original Clean Air Act, passed in 1970, ordered that air quality in cities meet EPA standards by 1987. By 1989, ninety-six cities still failed to comply. But what could the EPA do? Whenever it tried to impose penalties with real consequences, congressional representatives from the afflicted cities raised a storm': D. Osborne and T. Gaebler, *Reinventing Government: How the Entrepreneurial Spirit is Transforming the Public Sector* (Reading, 1992), at 300.

role. Even where offences have been created, the effort and evidence involved in proving particular cases beyond reasonable doubt exceed the deterrent or punitive effect where a sea of other breaches are not prosecuted and, more importantly, where the lifestyle or underlying causes remain unchanged.

A further problem with the way that criminal sanctions were imposed in the earlier command-and-control systems was the absence of attention to the gradations of polluting activities and to varying public attitudes to those activities. In addition to the inappropriateness of prosecution as a response to minor offences, insufficient attention was given to the mental element for the new environmental offences.

In 'real' criminal law, such as murder, the prosecution must prove that the defendant had a guilty mind in committing the act. In exceptional cases of criminal law, absolute liability may be imposed, for example for breach of nuclear waste management rules, where no excuses for non-observance of the rules are allowed.

Generally, however, pollution fits in to a third category of public welfare offences to which strict liability applies. Thus, failure to obtain a permit, to observe the conditions imposed on a permit or, where a permit is not required, to observe control standards set by regulation, are offences regardless of the state of mind or awareness of the accused. All that the prosecution need prove is the doing of the act, although (as an exception to this) the defence of reasonable mistake applies.

The three categories (guilty mind, absolute, and strict criminal liability) have had a long evolution in case law, in the absence of statutory direction as to the precise ingredients of environmental offences, and they continue to be debated.[48] For example, do offences involving recklessness or intention require the additional element of knowledge that serious environmental harm will result from the polluting conduct to be proved? Similarly, the pollution cases continue to deal with criminal law issues such as vicarious and contractor liability; the respective liability of corporations, directors, and managers; whether the privilege against self-incrimination should extend to corporations;[49] and defences and double jeopardy. Many of these issues are direct consequences of trying to mould 'real' criminal law in dealing with arguably non-criminal, welfare issues.

The result of failing to categorize pollution offences was that the criminal enforcement process was applied to all manner of pollution breaches, not just where it

[48] *Alphacell v Woodward* [1972] AC 824; *R v City of Sault Ste Marie* (1978) 85 DLR 161; *He Kaw Teh* (1985) 157 CLR 523; discussed in Farrier, op. cit., at 82–5. N. Franklin, 'Environmental Pollution Control: The Limits of Criminal Law' (1990) 2 *Current Issues in Criminal Justice* 81–94. Law Reform Commission (Canada), Report, *Our Criminal Law*, 1976; Working Paper 44, *Crimes Against the Environment*, 1985; Report 31, *Recodifying Criminal Law*, 1987. See also Z. Lipman and L. Roots, 'Protecting the Environment through Criminal Sanctions: The Environmental Offences and Penalties Act 1989 (NSW)' (1995) 12 *Environmental and Planning Law Journal* 16–36; A. Hutchinson, 'Sault Ste Marie, *Mens Rea* and the Halfway House: Public Welfare Offences Get a Home of Their Own' (1979) 17 *Osgoode Hall Law Journal* 415–44, abstracted in Chappell and Moore, op. cit.

[49] *Environment Protection Authority v Caltex Refining Co. Pty. Ltd.* (1993) 68 ALJR 127.

could play the important role of value-underlining to punish and deter gross acts. As for other acts of pollution, where public values as to the stigma, guilt or financial or social responsibility which should be attached are far less clear, the criminal law has been a blunt tool, and the negotiated, compromised application of it by regulators is partly a reflection of societal uncertainty about 'every-day' pollution and the inappropriateness of criminal law to deal with it.

3. Improved Legal and Alternative Strategies

It would be reassuring if, in this section, each of the deficiencies of the initial command-and-control approach outlined could be dealt with in turn, creating a neat 'then' and 'now' contrast, and showing the environmental management improvements by industrial countries in the war against environmental degradation. Many confounding factors prevent such an analysis, however. First, it is not clear whether industrial countries are in fact making overall progress, despite improvements in discrete areas. Secondly, the command-and-control approach described as '1970s' in inspiration remains, as already noted, the dominant model of regulatory policy. It is easy to call 'for environmentalists to stop celebrating the statutory revolution of the 1970s',[50] but difficult to find the best combination of legal, educative, economic, and policy approaches to replace the initial command-and-control laws. Thirdly, and most difficult of all, some of the failures identified may be inherent problems in all pollution control strategies, rather than peculiar to command-and-control models.

Thus prescriptive command-and-control pollution law has a continuing role. However, alternative legal and non-legal approaches are needed. The scene for reform is described in the following two paragraphs, then some examples of the changing focus of concern are offered by way of example. The remainder of this chapter deals with the initiatives themselves under four general headings: information-based strategies; economic instruments; modified self-organization (including systems-based approaches); and innovative law and enforcement approaches.

In the late 1980s and early 1990s a new wave of environmental concern led to reappraisal of the pollution control system. The concept of sustainable development gained momentum after the Brundtland Report and was a central theme of the 1992 Earth Summit in Rio de Janeiro. The 'nil gain' idea that environmental benefits could only be achieved with economic sacrifice lost popularity. Associated with this 'ecological modernization'[51] was a broader acceptance of the win-win view, for example regarding reduced vehicle emissions (both saving fuel bills and improving air quality), or improved materials recovery (reducing raw material costs through re-use and recycling as well as the volume of waste

[50] Ackerman and Stewart, op. cit., at 199.

[51] M. A. Hajer, '"Verinnerlijking" (Internalisation): The Limits to a Positive Management Approach', in G. Teubner, L. Farmer, and D. Murphy (eds.), *Environmental Law and Ecological Responsibility: The Concept and Practice of Ecological Self-Organisation* (Chichester, 1994), ch. 8.

sent to landfill). External costs to the environment caused by development began to be given greater recognition, suggesting that conservation and pollution control could be a prerequisite of long term economic and social welfare, rather than being inconsistent with it.

Integration became a key concept in pollution strategies. Integrated pollution prevention and control become the aspiration of OECD countries in the 1990s.[52] The focus moved to consideration of risk of harm to the environment as a whole, not just to air, water or soil considered independently.

Additional focuses for an integrated approach were sources (including industrial processes, products, and economic sectors), and geographical regions. Further, integration of environmental factors was sought with areas such as planning, energy, transport, agriculture, forestry, development aid, and taxes. This takes us closer to integration of the 'holistic' sort examined here. Such an approach requires a more inter-disciplinary approach to environmental management, involving (for example) politics and sociology to complement economics and science-based approaches. Cradle-to-grave consideration of products and substances, not just at the point of emission to the environment, was advocated. Waste minimization replaced disposal as a primary purpose of regulation. Effects-oriented measures, such as environmental quality objectives, began to influence the setting of emission limits. Where complete information was lacking, a precautionary approach was advocated to mitigate the risk of harm to the environment. The role of the public in contributing to environmental policy and decision-making was acknowledged, necessitating change to the expertise model of decision-making in many countries.

In addition to achieving better environmental outcomes, an objective was to reduce the inefficiencies resulting from fragmentation of responsibilities across government departments. 'Seamless regulation' involves a single system of permitting and accountability across related areas, such as land use planning, occupational health and safety, dangerous goods control, and environmental protection.[53] Explicit compliance and enforcement policies and integrated inspection and enforcement authorities were encouraged, as was the issuing of single permits covering all releases and processes. Greater use of inventories of releases at the national level, and monitoring of emissions at all levels were other aspects of integrated pollution control. In some jurisdictions, including the UK, the theme of integration resulted in new pollution legislation which integrated the former media-specific laws and rationalized the regulatory agencies.[54] The new legislation also sought to highlight the need to integrate economic and environmental

[52] Organisation for Economic Co-operation and Development, 'Recommendation of the Council on Integrated Pollution Control', C(90)164 final, 31 January 1991. See also F. H. Irwin, 'An Integrated Framework for Preventing Pollution and Protecting the Environment' (1991) 22 *Environmental Law* 1–76.

[53] B. Robinson, op. cit., at 7.

[54] e.g., Environmental Protection Act 1990 (UK); EC Directive 96/61 on Integrated Pollution Prevention and Control, OJ 1996 L257.

TABLE 3: *Changing Paradigms in Pollution Control 1970–2000*†

OLD PARADIGM	NEW PARADIGM
Control	Prevention
End of pipe	Cleaner production
Prescription	Outcome focus
Command	Co-operation
Community concern	Public involvement
Point source discharges	Catchment and airshed management
Separate controls on each environmental medium	Integrated holistic management
Controls on disposal	Cradle to grave care
Administrative fees and penalties	User and polluter pays
Local focus	Global focus
Short term outlook	Inter-generational equity

† Environment Protection Authority (Victoria), *The Environment Protection Act 1970: 25 Years of Making a Difference* (Melbourne, 1996), at 7.

considerations through 'sustainable development' objects clauses.[55] There was therefore an integration both within pollution control laws, and of such laws with other considerations.

The developments in environmental thinking have been summarised by the Victorian EPA in terms of changing paradigms (Table 3). Particular examples of the change of focus and perception of pollution are listed in Table 4. The changing focus (third column) is additional to, not a substitute for, the initial focus of pollution control systems (second column). Without doubt, the additional concerns are more difficult to deal with, more complex, and more complicated than the initial ones. This is not surprising, as any regulatory system will target the easier, more visible problems first.

[55] The Protection of the Environment Administration Act 1991 (NSW) established an EPA with a statutory objective (s. 6) of maintaining ecologically sustainable development ('ESD') through implementation of the precautionary principle, inter-generational equity, conservation of biological diversity, and improved valuation and pricing of environmental resources. The Fisheries Management Act 1994, the Threatened Species Act 1995, and various enactments corporatizing water and energy utilities in New South Wales also contain ESD objects clauses.

TABLE 4: *Changing Perceptions of Pollution*

EXAMPLE PROBLEMS	INITIAL FOCUS	ADDITIONAL CONCERNS FOR INTEGRATED POLLUTION CONTROL
Water pollution	Factories	Urban runoff
Chemicals	Acute effects of single chemicals	Chronic, long-term effects, including combinations of chemicals
Environmental impact assessment	Single projects at proposal stage	Ongoing, cumulative effects of projects collectively, as well as of single projects
Haze/photochemical smog	Stringency of vehicle emission standards imposed on manufacturers	Transport infrastructure; ways to reduce the rate of vehicle distance travelled per capita

Information-Based Strategies

Information about the feasibility of achieving certain pollution standards is often lacking. Resource constraints result in regulators relying on information provided by the regulated. The result is that negotiation and compromise are inherent components of command-and-control systems.[56] Industry seeks to reduce or exploit uncertainty to its own advantage.[57] Thus more recent strategies for pollution control have emphasized the need to improve the environmental knowledge base.

Deeper and more widely shared knowledge is a prerequisite to better pollution control. This is particularly important as the focus for pollution expands, as illustrated in Table 4, to include diffuse, cumulative, and more synergistic aspects. For example, transboundary air pollution, ozone layer depletion, and vehicle emissions are more complicated to comprehend and deal with than gross, point-source emissions. To develop awareness and take appropriate action, strong information gathering and sharing is required. Attempts to respond to the problem of environmental decision-making without full knowledge include the attempt to encourage regulators to adopt a precautionary approach, and industry to focus on emission prevention and minimization.

In the following paragraphs various information-based initiatives to manage pollution are considered. Some involve gathering technical, specialist information, whilst others involve developing public awareness. Information acquisition

[56] Rankin and Finkle, op. cit.

[57] A. Ullmann, 'The Implementation of Air Pollution Control in German Industry' (1982–3) 11 *Policy Studies Journal* 141–52, abstracted in Chappell and Moore, op. cit., at 90.

is considered first, followed by initiatives aimed at better reviewing and disseminating that information.

Gathering Environmental Information

Given the 'pervasive uncertainty' surrounding environmental decision-making, we need a profound increase in ecological research and monitoring, and stronger statutory and informational bases for gathering, co-ordinating, and communicating information.[58] Many countries, including the UK,[59] now publish substantial periodic environmental reports.

In NSW, biannual State of the Environment reporting is a statutory obligation of the EPA.[60] At present reports are published on paper and on the internet, however some progress is being made to developing a more comprehensive approach, comprising a relational database management system and a geographic information system ('GIS'). The role of 'state of environment reports' in measuring the effectiveness of regulatory policy is further considered in 'Policy and Regulatory Impact Auditing', below.

Sharing Environmental Information and Decision-Making

Increasing public scrutiny and accountability are part of information-based strategies. Technical, 'neutral' information is not the only type needing better gathering and dissemination however. Information about what regulators and governments are doing in response is just as desirable. If citizens are dissatisfied, they should have avenues open to them to seek policy changes and, where appropriate, to take action themselves to enforce environmental law. As citizens are a part of the pollution problem, information should be shared with them, and a greater role accorded to them in generating solutions.[61]

There is a tension in employing the law to provide citizens with rights to information, for example through Freedom of Information and Ombudsman legislation, through more extensive environmental reporting, and through legal rights to influence policy formation and decision-making with regard to particular permit applications. Against this technique, it could be said that openness and frank exchange between the regulator, the regulated, and the public would be better promoted in a co-operative, administrative setting, rather than one driven by such formal legal rights and obligations. On the other hand, the law can serve as a backstop to guarantee the provision of information to the citizen when co-operative approaches

[58] Dovers, op. cit.

[59] See *Sustainable Development: The UK Strategy* (1990) and the subsequent *This Common Inheritance* reports, London, HMSO (published annually).

[60] Protection of the Environment Administration Act 1991, s. 11 (NSW) requires EPA to provide 'state of the environment' reports to the Minister, for tabling in Parliament, every two years.

[61] D. Robinson, 'Public Participation in Environmental Decision-Making' (1993) 10 *Environmental and Planning Law Journal* 320–40; Robinson and Dunkley (eds.), op. cit.; World Bank Participation Sourcebook at http://www.worldbank.org/html/edi/sourcebook/sbhome.html.

merely prolong an unsustainable status quo. On balance, law can usefully complement and give credibility to strategies to foster co-operative relationships.

While public participation rights pose a threat to closed, technocratic pollution agencies, they can also act as a shield. Bureaucrats are conditioned by the manipulative tactics of regulated parties.[62] By keeping the public and interested groups informed and involved in policy, regulatory reform, and enforcement issues, the support of other stakeholders can help decision-making which one interest group opposes but which is desirable in the public interest.

In many jurisdictions there exists a degree of public participation in pollution policy development, although approaches taken vary. Participation does not fit easily into the Diceyan model of representative (rather than participatory) democracy which persists for historic, rather than constitutional, reasons in countries such as Australia.[63] In the representative model, bureaucrats are considered to be technical experts charged with executing the commands of ministers. The bureaucrats may not have been chosen for their public consultation skills. Subsequently–imposed requirements to consult and discuss proposals with the public can be perceived as anomalous, and in fact crude approaches to participation have this characteristic: they are not an organic part of decision-making. Thus the policy is formulated first, and the public meeting or other consultation is largely a public relations exercise, added to the process of government (and thus likely to be criticized as a cause of delay), rather than being integrated both formally and informally within the process. A public consultation period for a draft policy may be allowed, for example, but little attempt is made to discuss proposals informally as they develop. To the contrary, the bureaucrats are secretive about work-in-progress, and often cite confidentiality and the potential for draft documents to be misunderstood as decided policy, as reasons for not discussing their work with affected stakeholders.

More open approaches are emerging, however. For example, in 1996 the UK Department of the Environment issued a number of working drafts of its proposed Guidance on Contaminated Land prior to proceeding with the formal consultation process. Interested stakeholders could thus express views on work in progress as it developed. Ongoing and informal participation is far more likely to result in informed comment from the public, as stronger relationships can develop between bureaucrats and the public, and the public has time to learn about and comment on proposals as ideas are evolving, rather than after the event. The efficiency arguments raised by the 'information-only', lower rung approach to the ladder of participation[64] need to be balanced with the equity arguments of the advocates of greater participation.

[62] Latin, op. cit.

[63] D. Robinson, 'Public Participation in Environmental Decision-Making', op. cit., at 321.

[64] S. Arnstein, 'A Ladder of Citizen Participation' (1969) 35 *Journal of the American Institute of Planners* 216–24.

To the extent that public values and risk perception underpin pollution regulation, pollution regulators should tend to offer higher levels of participation. Through participation, openness, and responsiveness to criticism, public confidence and support for regulatory initiatives can develop.[65] Participation is particularly valuable where value judgement, not technical rationality, is at stake. The Asarco smelter case (considered under 'Education', below) is an example of the former situation.

It may also be that the way we consult, teach, debate, and research in some cases presents an obstacle to more effective communication. In the institutional idiom, we are conditioned by policy allegiances or communities. Particular circles of scientists, regulators, and governments may develop working relationships which effectively exclude input from others. Hierarchies can prevent cross-sectoral or cross-institutional exchange. For example, academic analysts tend to publish their research broadly, whereas bureaucrats tend only to report internally on research undertaken, as political and other factors inhibit floating ideas outside their agencies. The shame of this is that parallel streams of research do not inform each other as well as they deserve to. Typical results can be that the bureaucrats regard academics as over-critical and out of touch with practical constraints, and academics regard bureaucrats as paralysed by procedural constraints and gagged by Ministers.

A precondition to better sharing of environmental information and decision-making is the desire to improve relationships between stakeholders in pollution problems. With a respect for the legitimacy of alternative perspectives and idioms, relationship integrity can develop. The ability to communicate informally, and for confidentiality to be observed where appropriate, is one characteristic of relationship integrity. One Dutch writer has described this as the need to retain 'communicative informality' without compromising formal legal requirements.[66] 'Tripartism' suggests the new paradigm for such relationships. The old paradigm was regulatory 'control' of enterprises. The new paradigm acknowledges the role of industry groups, non-governmental organizations, and the public collectively as a third stakeholder in decision-making. Industry and regulatory initiatives to share information can add to credibility, even if the information is bad. In September 1996, for example, ICI publicly released an analysis indicating the contamination of groundwater under an industrial estate in Sydney where it has a factory. Greenpeace praised ICI for releasing the report. Such openness enables any hazards to be rationally addressed by reducing the possibility for community suspicion or misunderstanding.

[65] See, e.g., the work in risk communication in the US of Peter Sandman, creator of the 'Risk = Hazard + Outrage' concept.

[66] I. Koppen, 'Ecological Covenants: Regulatory Informality in Dutch Waste Reduction Policy', in Teubner, et al, op. cit., ch. 9.

Improved Information Dissemination and Opinion Research

This section contains four examples of how the mass media and market surveys can help understand and influence attitudes to pollution. The examples are the publicizing of monitoring results, publicizing of prosecutions, market survey-based awareness campaigns, and environmental behaviour research, again using market survey techniques.

Monitoring information required under pollution permits is increasingly available for public scrutiny. For example in the UK, it must be provided on public registers,[67] while in NSW the public can obtain it under access to information legislation applicable to all government agencies.[68] A worthwhile aspect of US permitting reform proposals relates to greater publicity being given to monitoring data,[69] so that the public relations implications of poor or good compliance act as an incentive to perform. Proposals include greater access to monitoring results, increased obligations to provide plain-English interpretation of the results, and the requirement that offenders publicize their conduct in newspapers. With regard to problematic facilities, such as sewerage treatment plants near bathing or recreational waterways, additional reporting of plant failure not just to the regulatory authority but also to the public has been mooted in Sydney. The water authority would be required to inform the mass media when sewerage over-flowed to waterways, and to draw attention to problem points. This could increase public awareness of the stormwater and sewerage treatment problem, and place pressure on the water authority to take remedial action.

One reason to prosecute illegal polluters is to deter others. However, the deterrent effect can only result if the cases are well-publicized at every stage. In order to protect civil liberties, or to avoid prejudicing pending legal proceedings, or for fear that journalists will mis-describe allegations of pollution breaches as court judgments, in some jurisdictions there has been considerable reluctance to publicize prosecutions initiated by regulators. Broader publication of legal proceedings against polluters is beginning to occur, while still respecting the pre-eminent need for accuracy, and for enhancing appropriate relationships with all stakeholders.

This liberalization is of itself an example of integrated approaches being adopted by regulatory authorities. The earlier model of action would be that inspectors would brief lawyers, lawyers would prosecute, and the media would then make what they could of the stories after the news was old (namely, when the court judgments were delivered). In the EPA (NSW), the three now work concurrently as a team, resulting in greater notoriety being attached to enforcement processes.

[67] The Environmental Protection Act 1990 (UK) provides that information required to be kept by the conditions of an authorization (which in practice should include monitoring results) must be kept on a public register (s. 20(1)(g)), subject to a commercial confidentiality exclusion (s. 22).

[68] Freedom of Information Act 1989 (NSW); Protection of the Environment Operations Act 1997, s. 320.

[69] Environmental Protection Agency (USA), *Permits Improvement Team Concept Paper on Environmental Permitting and Task Force Recommendations—Draft*, May 1996.

Use of the media in public education campaigns, for example to prevent littering and to promote voluntary recycling, has long been an approach of regulatory authorities to develop public awareness and encourage public action to prevent pollution. The quality of these campaigns has been variable. A more recent effort to improve quality and effectiveness has been to use market research techniques to measure community attitudes and the effect of media campaigns. For example, the EPA (NSW) conducted a benchmark study on environmental attitudes, skills, and behaviour in 1994–5. The study ranked environmental concerns in comparison with other issues for government such as unemployment and law-and-order. It also indicated public priorities and awareness regarding particular pollution problems. Following up this study a television and bill-board media campaign, 'Solutions to Pollution', focused on practical actions which the public could take with respect to stormwater pollution and household waste. Effectiveness was measured through focus groups and telephone surveys before the launch, midway through the campaign and, to measure retentiveness of the message, after the campaign. The market research indicated a doubling of awareness of actions that can prevent stormwater pollution, but a need to broaden the focus of people's attention from recycling alone to include activities that reduce waste generation in the first place.[70]

In 1996 the EPA (NSW) also co-commissioned a psycho-graphic study of attitudes to 'green' products and activities, for example consumer attitudes to recycling, and to products sold in refillable containers, to non-phosphorus detergents and preferences for energy efficient household appliances. As a result of 1200 interviews of people in three regions, the study segmented the Australian public according to attitudes, ranging from the 'living green' segment, comprising people who cared for, knew a lot about and did a lot for the environment, to 'brown bombers', who knew a little about the environment, but did not care or do anything about it. The study characterized the segments in terms such as income, education, age, gender, religious belief, and neighbourhood type. It also challenged the notion that, in all cases, empowerment prompts behavioural change. The 'lip service greens' are empowered in the sense that they say they care about the environment, and individuals realize that their actions will make a difference, yet they do little about it. On the other hand, 'grudging greens' may be sceptical of whether their actions can do much to save the environment, yet despite this they do quite a lot.

The study highlighted the need to target awareness campaigns. For example, if the campaign is seeking to encourage new and possibly onerous behaviour, such as the sorting and recycling of an additional type of waste, the substantive content of the campaign can be high. This is because it will only be the greener segments who will respond, and these tend to comprise better educated people who may be interested in more than a slogan. If, on the other hand, the campaign

[70] EPA (NSW), *Annual Report 1994–95*, at 34.

is oriented towards behavioural change by browner segments, for example to reduce littering, the campaign emphasis should be on distinctiveness, with minimal content, as for beer or soft drink advertising.

Finally the study highlighted the inappropriateness of 'gunshot' awareness campaigns. For the segments of the community who care little for the environment, or who say they care but do little, awareness campaigns may be less effective than regulation or economic approaches. In browner segments, which are unlikely to be affected by awareness campaigns, implementation of waste minimization policy, for example, may be better achieved by regulating the size of garbage bins, or by increasing disposal charges.

One appraisal of an EPA has identified four criteria for measuring the agency's performance: responsiveness to the public, fidelity to the technical merits, civic education, and capacity building.[71] The above studies are aimed at the first criterion. They use community surveys and awareness to better understand and respond to public attitudes and behaviour, and illustrate an evolving information-based attempt of government to choose the alternative tools of education, regulation, or economic instruments on a more informed basis.

Education

Education should play a central role in information-based approaches to pollution control. Education is desirable across all ages and sectors regarding the nature, extent, sources of, and prevention and minimization of pollution. An obstacle to pursuing this self-evident objective rigorously is that education tends to be dealt with as a soft issue, or even a non-issue. As education is a diffuse objective, being long-term and with many contributing factors and institutions, the tendency for pollution regulators has been to do little.

In the USA, the failure of the EPA to educate the public has been criticized as its single greatest shortcoming.[72] The EPA has encouraged the public to think that problems are simple, for example by ignoring economic impacts, and by emphasizing technical rather than political and underlying value aspects of decision-making. It has treated safety as if it were a scientific notion definable by experts, and has failed to convey the idea of acceptable risk, of shades between safety and harm, and of variable factors to be taken into account in every case. Public dissatisfaction with the EPA in the United States in recent years might well be attributable in part to the survival of unrealistic public expectations that the EPA's role was to return the nation to a pristine state. Congress was partly to blame. Some US pollution legislation, as discussed, encouraged over-simplification by setting ambitious clean-up goals without reference to cost.

[71] M. K. Landy, M. J. Roberts, and S. R. Thomas, *The Environmental Protection Agency: Asking the Wrong Questions from Nixon to Clinton* (New York, 1994), ch. 1.

[72] Ibid.

Regulatory agencies must promote better public understanding of the relativity of risk and safety. Agencies must address the tendency to simplify complex situations, for example to regard a chemical as either 'safe' or 'hazardous', neglecting gradations, combinations, chronic versus acute exposure considerations, and environmental variables. They must address the 'availability heuristic'[73] in which dramatic, unusual events, such as explosions and spills, are regarded as more environmentally significant than diffuse and cumulative problems, such as vehicle emissions and declining water quality. The role of environmental agencies is to act as guardians of decision-making processes in the face of considerable environmental uncertainty. Where administrative decisions reflect social values, not just technical judgments, public education and deliberation is essential.

An example of a worthwhile public education strategy was the manner in which the US EPA dealt with the Asarco copper smelter in Tacoma, Washington. Faced with predictions of the number of lung cancers which would be contracted in the town each year according to variously stringent new controls on Asarco's arsenic emissions on one hand, and cost constraints on the other, the EPA conducted a series of public workshops for the people of the town to debate the issue. The case received national press coverage, and there was criticism that the EPA was asking the impossible of the Tacomans—asking them, that is, whether to trade the economic survival of the town for human lives. The Administrator of the EPA defended the public deliberation approach, arguing that at least a handful of Tacomans learned from the exercise that there was no 'right' answer, but a need for the community to decide its own future.[74]

Education of regulatory staff is also important. Technical training needs to be complemented with methodological development, for example in early stage consultation with stakeholders and through encouraging problem-oriented, rather than rule-oriented, approaches.

Policy and Regulatory Impact Auditing

A final aspect of newer information-based approaches relates to auditing and monitoring. In this section, the need to audit the effectiveness of government initiatives to control pollution is discussed. The issue of auditing by industry, for example pursuant to environmental management systems, is considered in 'Innovative Law and Enforcement Approaches', below.

The processes of law—of developing and enacting policy and of implementation, enforcement, and further reform—can lag behind environmental needs and do not always achieve the intended environmental outcomes. Traditional regulation

[73] P. L. Stenzel, 'Right-to-Know Provisions of California's Proposition 65: The Naivete of the Delaney Clause Revisited' (1991) 15 *Harvard Environmental Law Review* 493–527, at 514.

[74] R. B. Reich, 'Public Administration and Public Deliberation: An Interpretive Essay' (1985) 94 *Yale Law Journal* 1617–40, at 1632–40.

has often lacked mechanisms for review and adaptation, with the result that inappropriate processes are repeated without learning from the earlier failures.

Only recently has regulatory policy incorporated systematic effectiveness checking. Mandated audit mechanisms, for example, may be desirable in the effort to sustain a funding commitment to policy review and associated empirical study. The 'State of the Environment' reports in NSW must be prepared biannually whereas in Victoria and at the Australian Commonwealth level their frequency and content has been the victim of changing governments and political expediency. Statutory obligations to report on how policy is working can help reduce the temptation of government to cut funds on environmental reporting.[75]

Evaluation of public participation strategy is another area in which policy auditing can increase the quality of pollution control administration. There is emerging in the field of risk management with, for example, greater recognition of the need to deal with public perception ('outrage'), and not just the physical and objective hazard.[76] In the UK, a recent government report has developed effectiveness criteria so that participation strategy can move from an *ad hoc* to an integrated, planned, and evaluated component of environmental policy development.[77]

An interesting about-face appears to be occurring in the USA regarding audit of the EPA's performance. Congress feared agency hostility to its ambitious environmental laws of the 1970s. It thus inserted 'agency forcing' provisions into the enactments. These required the EPA to do certain things by a stated deadline, for example to specify the criteria which would be adopted for evaluating certain chemicals, or requiring the EPA to prepare a plan or rule by a certain date. Citizens could pursue administrative and ultimately legal procedures to keep the EPA on target.[78] Despite some successful outcomes in environmental terms,[79] the agency forcing provisions have lost favour with some commentators, on the basis that tying the EPA's hands through stringent mandates, restrictions, and timetables does not necessarily advance the achievement of substantive goals.[80]

Political Commitment

Full implementation of the information-based initiatives discussed above can occur only with informed, robust political support. If viewed as apolitical, 'soft' options for government, the likelihood is that information initiatives will be merely

[75] Dovers, op. cit., at 155. [76] Sandman, op. cit.

[77] Department of the Environment (UK), Planning Research Programme, *Community Involvement in Planning and Development Processes* (1995); noted at (1995) 7 *Environmental Law and Management* 70–2.

[78] D. Robinson, 'Public Interest Environmental Law Firms in the United States', op. cit.

[79] The Natural Resources Defense Council successfully brought proceedings to register and control sixty-five priority toxic substances: see n. 38.

[80] EPA's first Administrator William Ruckelshaus, 'Stopping the Pendulum', Address to the Environmental Law Institute, Washington D. C., 18 August 1995 on the occasion of the US EPA's 25th Anniversary.

symbolic. Better collection, analysis, and dissemination of environmental information can result in exposure of the political nature of decision-making. Bureaucrats may have to take stakeholders' views more seriously into account, and their ability to mould government decisions can be reduced. These can be seen as either a threat or an opportunity, as illustrated by the following two examples from Australia's vexed forestry industry policy.

By the Resource Assessment Commission Act 1989, the Commonwealth established a Resource Assessment Commission ('RAC') to inquire into the future use of Australia's natural resources, upon references from the government. It gathered information and generated policy options regarding matters such as forestry, coastal management, and uranium mining.[81] Politicians and bureaucrats were unhappy about the transparency of the political process. Given the preference for hiding behind the cloak of expert advice, the government surprised few when it decided in the 1993–94 Budget round to abolish the RAC. The Commission's 'crime' was to use a rational and visible process, thus exposing the nature of the decision to the public gaze.

Whereas the federal government buckled to the pressures generated by its RAC, and responded by killing the messenger, more recently a state government has attempted to utilize these pressures to iron out a forests settlement with full involvement of stakeholders in structured, formalized, and government facilitated negotiations. The NSW government initiated an 'Interim Forest Assessment Process' to identify all the areas of public native forest likely to be needed for a comprehensive, adequate, and representative reserve system, long promised by both federal and state governments. Government information, in part generated from RAC and RAC-type investigation and research, was made available to industry, unions, and conservationists. Much of this was graphically accessible through GIS. Over a four week period, representatives of the stakeholders discussed conservation options for each forest in round-table negotiations co-ordinated by the government and utilizing the GIS to provide background, factual information. A draft Interim Forestry Assessment Report identified the implications of a range of forestry options in particular regions, ranging from the national forest conservation target (fifteen per cent of original forests), through to options favouring the timber industry view. More informed debate has resulted from detailed and accessible information being made available by government. More acceptable and reasoned compromise is likely to result, and ultimately better environmental and political outcomes, from this investment in information gathering and sharing, and structured negotiation.[82]

[81] I. Lowe, 'Implementing the Precautionary Principle', in R. Harding and L. Fischer, *Proceedings of Precautionary Principle Conference* (University of New South Wales, 1993), cited in D. Stewart and G. McColl, 'The Resource Assessment Commission: An Inside Assessment' (1994) 1 *Australian Journal of Environmental Management* 12–23, at 23.

[82] See Resource and Conservation Assessment Council (NSW), *Draft Interim Forest Assessment Report*, June 1996.

The above approaches are aimed at better acquiring, co-ordinating, and disseminating information about pollution, and sit comfortably within policy discourse and institutional idioms of analysis. However, they do not satisfy the perspectives of public choice analysis. It will be recalled that this idiom views the aim of environmental policy as being internalization of the costs of pollution. The use of economic tools to this end is thus the subject of the next section.

Economic Instruments

Among the better-known types of economic instruments are pollution charges and tradeable permits. Other economic instruments include environmental taxes, product charges, deposit refunds, and performance bonds. Despite debate in the 1970s and 1980s about the potential use of economic instruments for environmental protection, it seems that in many countries their use remains tentative and experimental. Nevertheless, a review of the use of such instruments for environmental protection was published by the OECD in 1989. The study found more than 150 examples of applications of economic instruments within the fourteen countries surveyed.[83] This section illustrates the use of pollution charges, and tradeable pollution permits.

Pollution Charges

By charging for emissions and effluent, pollution reduction can become a means of reducing production costs. However, the incentive effect will be only slight if pollution costs do not represent a large proportion of total costs. In this case the economic instrument can still serve to raise revenue, and exist as a redistributive device, but will not modify behaviour.

Whether such environmental taxes, for example tollways, ultimately serve an environmental (as distinct from revenue-raising) purpose will be determined by how the revenue is hypothecated towards other environmental expenditure. For example, when Sydney's surfing beaches became polluted by increasing sewerage discharges from ocean outfalls, the NSW Government imposed an annual $80 environmental levy on all Sydney property owners. For some years, the proceeds were used to finance new sewerage infrastructure to reduce the beach pollution. However, the Government subsequently appropriated the proceeds under the guise of an 'efficiency dividend' which the water authority was required to make to consolidated revenue, with the result that the economic instrument ceased to have an environmental purpose.

[83] Organisation for Economic Cooperation and Development, *The Distributive Effects of Economic Instruments for Environmental Policy* (Paris, 1994). This Report is considered, along with related issues, by Tim Jewell in Chapter 3, below.

Tradeable Pollution Permits

In the case of tradeable pollution permits, a control authority sets a maximum total allowable discharge load for a catchment or airshed, and polluters compete to purchase these rights to discharge to the environment. For example, in NSW a salinity credit scheme is used regarding discharges from coal mines into the Hunter River catchment. The scheme has encouraged miners to plan the discharge of saline tailings water only when the river is high, and water quality is less likely to be affected. This will encourage miners to invest in more adequate retention ponds in order to avoid the high cost of having to purchase salinity discharge rights from other operators who, because they have bigger retention ponds, do not need to discharge saline water in dry periods.

Permit reform along rather different lines is in operation for sewerage treatment plants on the Hawkesbury River, also in NSW. A single or 'bubble' licence is issued for all the plants, and the utility is thus able to arrange the upgrade and operation of the individual facilities in order to achieve the total emission conditions set in the licence most cost-effectively.

In terms of effectiveness in achieving environmental objectives, efficiency gains, ongoing incentives, equity aspects, community acceptance, and administrative feasibility and cost, various advantages and limitations of using economic instruments have been identified.[84] In practice regulatory instruments often support economic instruments, so that the choice is between regulatory instruments alone, or regulatory and economic instruments together.

Modified Self-Organization

The limitations of command-and-control, whether through regulation or economic instruments such as tradeable emission schemes, both of which depend upon informed and continuing intervention and supervision by regulatory authorities, have prompted a search for more efficient, organic means of controlling pollution. Self-regulation is such an alternative, but long-standing doubts about its effectiveness exist. Self-regulation, for example in the form of chemical industry codes of practice, has often been bundled with the simplistic deregulatory policies of the 1980s. However, some modified self-regulatory approaches do take into account the admitted impossibility, if external control mechanisms do not exist, of asking poachers to become gamekeepers .

The cost of devising, updating, implementing, and enforcing increasingly voluminous command-and-control laws has been cited as one reason why governments have looked for alternatives. Another pressure has been the pre-eminence of competition policy internationally, culminating in the General Agreement on

[84] Ibid.

Tariffs and Trade. Pollution control laws have the potential to be used as non-tariff barriers to trade. As a result, international standards for environmental management systems (EMSs) have been developed to complement national pollution control laws. Additional factors contributing to the interest of industry in EMSs have been increasing public pressure to improve environmental performance, and recognition that cleaner production need not constitute a cost with no return on investment. Cleaner production could have positive effects on shareholders, the public, and workforce morale, and in some cases could even save money.

Hence EMSs are emerging long after systems approaches were applied to other factors of production. The British Standard specification for environmental management systems (BS 7750), dating from 1992, was adopted subsequently by a number of other countries.[85] In 1995 the Eco-Management and Audit Scheme (EMAS) Regulation 1836/93 of the European Union came into force. The object of EMAS is to allow voluntary participation by companies in a scheme to promote continuing improvement in environmental performance. EMAS provides for the establishment of EMSs; for the systematic, objective, and periodic evaluation of their performance by accredited, independent evaluators; and for the provision of performance information to the public.[86] Member states must provide infrastructure for EMAS sites to be listed on a national EMAS register, and to accredit EMAS evaluators. The International Organization for Standardisation has introduced standards concerning environmental management systems (referred to as 'ISO 14001'). These include elements relating to performance evaluation, auditing, life-cycle assessment, and labelling.

Both market and regulatory forces are driving the adoption of EMSs. The market force is the desire to differentiate products by EMS certification. A contrasting 'regulatory' influence is the ability for companies to show environmental due diligence in any prosecutions brought, through the adoption and observance of an EMS. There is also the possibility of reduced reporting requirements for companies with accredited EMSs. For example, the Victorian EPA has established an accredited licensing scheme.[87] Under the scheme, licensees who meet certain criteria can obtain a five year (rather than the usual annual) licence over an entire facility without detailed regulatory prescription and with the licence fee reduced by twenty-five per cent. A record of good environmental performance, an EMS, an environmental audit program (preferably involving an accredited environmental auditor), and an environmental improvement plan involving the local community are the major prerequisites for companies wishing to participate in the accredited licensing scheme.

[85] The Netherlands, Denmark, Israel, Ireland, France, and South Africa: C. Sheldon, 'BS 7750 and Certification—A Developmental History', in P. Sharratt (ed.), *Environmental Management Systems* (Rugby, 1995), ch. 4.

[86] Art. 1.

[87] See ss. 26A–26E of the Environment Protection Act 1970 (Victoria), introduced in 1994.

There are drawbacks. EMSs set process-related, not environmental performance or outcome standards. Provided that it is meeting its own goals, a company may therefore have an accredited EMS, yet still cause a lot of pollution. Another fear is that ISO 14001, like the Quality Assurance ISO 9000 series, may tend to become a paper exercise only. ISO 14001 is considerably weaker than BS 7750 and EMAS with regard to external auditing, public disclosure, and reporting requirements. The weaknesses in ISO 14001 are largely the result of successful lobbying by the USA.[88]

As EMSs have developed, so too have proposals for 'responsive' environmental regulation. If a company has an EMS, the law should prescribe environmental performance outcomes. The law should also ensure that third party checking exists, for example, by external compliance-auditors and through public reporting of performance results.[89] On the vexed question of confidentiality of voluntary audit results, one suggestion is that audits themselves should not be able to be used to incriminate a company, but that the conclusions of audits should be required to be submitted to the regulator, triggering investigation if the legally mandated performance outcomes are not met.

A focus for regulation is increasingly to set directions and performance requirements for industry, and to provide safety nets if systems fail. If systems are working, there is no need for regulation to stipulate the means to achieve the ends. In this way, the notions of 'co-regulation', 'reflexive law', and 'modified self-regulation' have entered the lexicon. 'Co-regulation' refers to industry sectors establishing their own pollution control rules to complement those set by governments. 'Reflexive law', in this context, is law which seeks to provide direction for industry without prescribing means to achieve required outcomes, and which is capable of rapid reform in reflex-like response to the actual effects of its implementation in practice.[90]

'Modified self-regulation' is another way of describing the changing roles of industry, government, and the general public in pollution control. Public guarantees are added to self-regulatory arrangements through externally-imposed reporting and performance standards. Modified self-regulatory approaches such as covenants between stakeholders in waste management could be a third generation of policy instrument. The first generation was the hierarchical command-and-control regulation. The second was characterized by negotiated decision-making and participatory initiatives, but here the rule of law was sometimes compromised. For example, prosecutions would not be brought for breaches of laws or permit conditions where the polluter could convince the regulator, in private negotiations, that it had taken remedial or preventative action. In the third generation, the participation of stakeholders continues to provide communicative informality,

[88] N. Gunningham, 'From Adversarialism to Partnership? ISO 14000 and Regulation', Paper delivered at Australian Centre for Environmental Law, Australian National University conference, 'ISO 14000: Regulation, Trade and Environment', Canberra, 2 July 1996.

[89] Ibid. [90] Teubner, et al, op. cit.

but new legal rules, for example covenants between all stakeholders, operate as well.

The three generations can be illustrated by evolving approaches to litter control in NSW. In the first approach, the Government simply made littering an offence, with limited effect. In the second, the Government entered into a contract with soft drink and food packaging manufacturers to fund a 'Do the Right Thing' publicity campaign aimed at developing a greater sense of individual and civic responsibility not to litter. This resulted in a most successful media campaign. The television and print media advertisement imparted the basic message with such impact that the slogan 'Do the Right Thing' became synonymous with 'Put rubbish in garbage bins'.

On the other hand, the pollution regulator[91] agreed not to reintroduce beverage container deposit regulations in return for the industry funding. Non-government organizations cited the agreement as evidence of regulatory capture (the Government agreeing not to require bottles to be reused if industry encouraged people to dispose of them responsibly). The contract with industry was not renewed and the campaign's budget, now without private sector funding, was slashed. Whilst to date there is no third generation response in this example, it might be constituted by a new contract, but this time between all major stakeholders, not just industry. For example, environmental or consumer groups, as well as industry or government, could seek compromise in such a way that feasible regulatory approaches to litter control could be pursued, as well as accepting funding from industry for worthwhile media campaigns.

Ecological covenants, joint ventures or quasi-contracts may play a role where preliminary, environmentally favourable agreement can precede regulation, or where a covenant could supplement or tighten regulation. The absence of traditional regulatory controls, and of guarantees for parties not party to the covenant, are admitted problems with covenants. Their use in the Netherlands is exploratory. For example after protracted negotiations with all stakeholders regarding waste reduction, the Dutch Government broke off multilateral negotiations and entered into a bilateral covenant with the packaging industry regarding recycling targets. Whilst bilateral, the covenant contained stronger environmental provisions than the recycling targets set by government as an initial proposal, indicating the value of including third parties in the negotiations. Despite doubt as to the enforceability of the covenant, the negotiation process may itself have created a high level of commitment from industry, particularly given the broad public awareness of the circumstances and the final agreement.

Modified self-regulatory approaches, combining economic, regulatory, and participation tools, continue to be experimented with. Self-regulation has clear limitations, but the involvement of industry, government, and the community in

[91] The regulator was the State Pollution Control Commission (NSW), now replaced by the Environment Protection Authority.

industry proposals to control pollution is attractive, if only for the cost, delay, and ineffectiveness of the command-and-control alternative.

A problem with 'modified self-regulation' is that it has to be so dramatically transformed from its voluntary starting point in order to be effective. What starts out as a red-tape cutting exercise can finish up with as much policy and rule statement as the regulation it seeks to replace. For example, the prerequisites under the Victorian accredited licensing scheme, outlined above, are so onerous that only five licensees had been accredited under the new scheme in its first three years of operation (1994–97).

Modified self-regulation is also inefficient because it requires parallel regulatory streams (internal management of pollution, but safeguards to resort to command-and-control if internal management fails). However it may still have some complementary role to traditional incentives through legal norms and economic instruments, because the predictive capacity of norm-incentive or market-incentive models is limited. Casting a wider net, with pollution controls imposed externally by government as well as internally by industry, may make the achievement of environmental objectives more likely.[92]

Innovative Law and Enforcement Approaches

In this final section a number of directions for more effective pollution laws are discussed.

Appropriate Levels of Discretion

While accountability and clarity of purpose remain important criteria for legislative reform, the high level of prescription which has characterized the US approach to pollution control is currently being questioned. It has been suggested that Congress should set policy more clearly, and allow the EPA more discretion to implement that policy, moving away from the ambitious legislation of the 1970s, and the fetters placed on the EPA regarding timetables, stringent mandates, and restrictions.[93]

Jurisdictional Integration

Another general direction for improved pollution control is that of better integrating approaches between the international, regional, national, and local levels. The quality, and certainly the quantity of international pollution conventions is increasing, and can provide an impetus and framework for action at other

[92] See the discussion of reflexive law in Teubner, et al, op. cit., and discussed in the final paragraph of 'Innovative Law and Enforcement Approaches', below. Other aspects of 'reflexive law' are discussed by Jenny Steele, in Chapter 4, below.

[93] Ruckelshaus, op. cit.

levels. The international success in containing the emission of ozone-depleting substances is a case in point.[94]

Simpler Law

A superficially attractive suggestion is to make greater use of simpler rules, such as product bans and emission caps.[95] While simplicity is a valid criterion for evaluating environmental instruments, it appears that pollution is so embedded within complex industrial processes and lifestyles, that there is little practical scope for greater reliance on simpler rules.

More Appropriate Criminal Law

In a number of jurisdictions the criminal law is being extended and adapted to try to overcome the considerable shortcomings of a simple command-and-control approach towards behavioural change. One trend is towards clarification of the requisite mental element, if any, of pollution 'welfare' offences. Another is the extension of liability to managers, directors, and contractors in cases of corporate offences. A third development in Australia is the use of hybrid penalties to respond to minor offences not warranting criminal prosecution. For a number of littering, waste, noise, air, and water pollution offences, the regulatory agencies can choose to proceed by way of penalty infringement notices. These are 'on-the-spot' fines for which the recipient can choose to pay and attract no criminal record, or take to a local court for prosecution in the traditional way. Penalty infringement notices are efficient and fast regulatory responses. In some cases it appears that the deterrent effect is greater, because they are issued within a few days of the offence, than when higher penalties are ordered by a court, months or years later. Finally, a broader range of sentencing options is being made available for environmental offences, such as community service orders, adverse publicity, and environmental restoration orders.[96]

Collective Liability

A further field of investigation for pollution control law regards the development of collective forms of liability for ecological damage. It is often difficult to establish causal links between individual actions and ecological damage. Rather than overtly introducing collective responsibility, the law has expanded individual liability through such measures as deeming provisions, enhanced application of the

[94] United Nations Environment Programme—Industry and Environment, 'Vienna Plus Ten. The Vienna Convention—10 Years of Achievement', November 1995, *OzoneAction Special Supplement*; W. W. Gibbs, 'The Treaty that Worked—Almost', September 1995, *Scientific American* 18–20; D. MacKenzie, 'Ozone's Future is Up in the Air', 16 December 1995, *New Scientist* 14–15.

[95] Anderson, op. cit.

[96] Lipman and Roots, op. cit., at 30–2.

notion of *res ipsa loquitur*, piercing the corporate veil to fix liability on parent corporations, reversing the burden of proof, probabilistic causation, joint and several liability in multiple causation, enterprise liability, market share liability, extended notions of causation under Superfund, and individual liability for corporate wrongs. One proposal for explicit collective liability is to define relevant risk groups opportunistically, according to the suitability of members to manage risk collectively. For example industry itself, rather than individual manufacturers, would be liable for ecological risk from hazardous products.

Collective liability law would encourage collective, preventive action by members of risk groups. The risk pool would be strictly liable to victims. Within the pool, negligence would govern respective shares, or, if this is not possible, in order of application of liability tests such as individual risk contribution, pollution, or market share.[97]

Adaptive Management

The above innovations concern the substantive content of law. However the *process* of law needs reform as well, so that law can become a tool for adaptive management. As uncertainty pervades ecological processes, environmental management should be more dynamic, experimental, and oriented towards continual learning. Regulatory agencies should experiment with different tools, recognizing that the right mix for a particular industry, region, or time will constantly change. So too should industries adapt EMSs to their particular needs. Legal institutionalization of agencies and their approaches can assist adaptive strategies if accountability and transparency measures exist to encourage continuing dialogue of the agencies with stakeholders.

Legal institutionalization of environmental management approaches can prevent adaptation, however, where top-down, centralized management structures prevail. The prevailing interpretation of an environmental problem at a particular time tends to be encoded in the regulatory framework.[98] If it is not out of date by the time it is enacted, it may well be by the time it is understood and applied by inspectors lower down the management hierarchy. Because of the investment in a particular approach, both the agency and industry may be loathe to adapt it. Hierarchical control results in 'rule-book' approaches poorly suited to adaptive management and flexibility. Mid-level regulators may be more appropriate decision-makers, to avoid losing programs in the multiple responsibilities imposed on the highest agency officials.[99]

Environmental law and policy often fail to factor uncertainty into decision-making. If a pollution licence is up for renewal, and some doubt exists about the adequacy of conditions, the status quo will be likely to continue until the level

[97] G. Teubner, 'The Invisible Cupola: From Causal to Collective Attribution in Ecological Liability', in Teubner, et al, op. cit., ch. 2.

[98] Iles, op. cit., at 298.

[99] Latin, op. cit., at 1719.

of certainty that new conditions are justified is very high. This is due in part to the effect on bureaucrats of conservative science.[100] Bureaucrats are also conditioned by negative feedback from active decisions (issuing a licence with controversial conditions) even though passive management (allowing the status quo to continue) may produce worse environmental outcomes. What is needed is policy which encourages experimentation together with stakeholders, (perhaps) through the piloting of small-scale projects, and which makes sure that reviews of these initiatives are systematically publicized and employed in policy-adaptation. Regulation should provide for such adaptation and experimentation by exemption from the normal regulatory processes where accountability can be maintained. For example, in Victoria premises otherwise requiring works approvals regarding pollution-generating industry can instead undertake research, development, and demonstration approvals for relevant projects instead.[101]

There are other factors in addition to hierarchical control and the inhibitive effect of criticism on bureaucrats which mitigate against complete implementation of pollution law and the reluctance of bureaucrats to take innovative management initiatives. Institutional, professional, and personal incentives for regulators to so act may be lacking. Bureaucrats face criticism if implementation of pollution control law could cause economic dislocation. Negative feedback needs to be counterbalanced. Latin has suggested that this could be done, for example, by enabling under-represented groups to participate more in decision-making, and by rotating agency staff to different areas or offices in order to increase their independence and guard against 'sweetheart' deals.[102] Overlapping institutional responsibilities and multiple compliance strategies should be avoided. Better results may be achieved if a single regulatory body decides policy, and implements this through a single primary strategy or mechanism. Theoretical responsiveness to local situations may be lost in adopting a single implementation approach, however these may be outweighed by lower implementation costs and fewer opportunities for strategic avoidance.

4. Summary and Conclusion

The integrated pollution control approaches reflected in the OECD Council recommendation outlined above[103] and discussed in this chapter draw upon a number of value systems. 'Polluter pays' is the catchcry of the dominant rational choice idiom. Radical change is advocated in political economics and policy discourse. Participation and policy change are key factors in the institutional analysis of liberals.

[100] Latin, op. cit. Latin suggests that two 'laws' regulating administrative behaviour are that 'agencies avoid resolving disputed issues unless they can render scientifically credible judgements' and 'regulators are influenced by disciplinary norms that may conflict with statutory mandates'.

[101] Environment Protection Act 1970, ss. 19D-G (Victoria).

[102] Latin, op. cit.

[103] See 'Improved Legal and Alternative Strategies', above.

Information-based initiatives, economic instruments, modified self-organization, and innovative law and enforcement approaches describe many of the contemporary reform directions in pollution control. For example, in the USA a public performance-based permitting program is being investigated by the EPA.[104] The elements of the program are increased public participation and disclosure of performance in pollution permitting, together with improvement of permitting performance in three respects.

The first key feature of the proposal is increased ambient monitoring as a permit condition in selected permits in order to improve measurement of environmental effects. The second is better–targeted facility compliance reporting. This may involve less prescription for facilities with good compliance records (for example, longer licence periods, less regular reporting requirements, multimedia permits, and eliminating the need to obtain permission for plant modifications except if more pollution will result). Also under consideration are alternatives to site-specific, individual permits, such as general permits for standard facilities such as stormwater discharges, and conditional exemptions from permitting if certain performance standards are met. The third proposal for improving permitting performance refers to the regulator's performance. Indicators of this include the number and quality of permits processed and reviewed, and greater public reporting of these.

An integrated, 'holistic' approach does not favour lists of characteristics which should be present in more effective pollution control laws because other variables must be taken into account, such as the nature of the pollution, the nature of the receiving environment, the traditions, attitudes, and cultures of communities affected, and the relative roles of complementary ways to combat pollution, such as EMSs, information-based strategies, and economic approaches. However, bearing in mind the interdependence of all tools to reduce pollution, this chapter suggests that the following questions might be asked in pollution law reform:

1. Will the collection and dissemination of environmental performance information be enhanced?
2. Are partnerships between stakeholders encouraged?
3. Will the proposal contribute to awareness-building and education?
4. Does the law incorporate an audit mechanism to review the practical effect of its implementation?
5. Are the regulatory and environmental costs recoverable in accordance with the polluter and user pays principle?
6. Is there incentive for co-regulatory initiative by industry, for example through the adoption of environmental management systems or collective liability mechanisms?

[104] EPA, *Permits Improvement Team Concept Paper on Environmental Permitting and Task Force Recommendations—Draft*, May 1996.

7. What overall assessment can be made in terms of the simplicity, efficiency, fairness, and efficacy of the law?
8. Is any criminal law proposal appropriate to regulate the particular pollution problem?
9. Does the law promote adaptive management, and address existing regulatory and behavioural disincentives which inhibit adaptive management?
10. Is the outcome best achieved by regulation?
11. If regulation is only part of the answer, does the proposal modify and involve other tools to complement the regulatory initiative?

From the account which opened this chapter, it may be concluded that the effectiveness of command-and-control pollution regulation in industrial societies was limited at the outset as growth, not pollution control, was the overriding societal goal. Perhaps the most compelling of all the approaches now being used to complement law in the search for sustainability through integration are the information-based initiatives. With better and more widely understood information about pollution and its effects, participatory democracies can set environment and development priorities with greater awareness of the costs and benefits. However, in the last analysis, the choice of which tools we use for pollution prevention and control is secondary to the level of political and financial commitment there exists to preventing and controlling it in the first place.

All the tools described have weaknesses and strengths, and all of these can be addressed if a well-informed electorate really wants them and is willing to pay for them. While other approaches may increase the efficiency with which pollution policy is implemented, information-based initiatives can strengthen the policy itself, as this flows directly from public attitudes. Regulatory agencies must be and be seen to be open in the decision-making process. Openness to all stakeholders is a key to securing continuing public support for environmental improvement programs. With that support, the public has reason to allow greater discretion to the agencies, which in turn can be exercised for more adaptive management.

3

Public Law and the Environment: The Prospects for Decision-Making

TIM JEWELL

In this chapter, I will explore some of the processes provided by statute for making decisions with a direct environmental impact. In this way I hope to draw out some of the tensions which arise between issues of legal form or process, and substantive environmental protection. This is not, then, a thorough exploration of contemporary environmental regulation,[1] but rather an examination of some of the ways in which process and substance interrelate in UK environmental regulation, and the implications of that relationship. The first step in addressing these questions is to identify those features of statutorily-defined environmental decision-making processes with which I will be concerned, and to place them in a broader public law context.

1. The Public Law Context

At its most general, 'public law' is concerned with the allocation of governmental power and the means of constraining that power—or at least this is how the subject matter of 'administrative law' has been described.[2] More specifically, it is possible to characterize a principal task of public law as being to provide a legal framework within which essentially non-legal (or political) battles are fought; a characterization which represents a distinction between matters of process and matters of substance which is very familiar to public lawyers. This is what I mean by the phrase 'process orientation'. The process in question is most frequently defined by statute.

This distinction between process and substance results, at least in part, from the dominating procedural character of public law. Certainly when considering how public law powers are exercised, the lawyer's concern for procedural propriety frequently (if not exclusively) takes formal priority over any overt concern with substantive goals. Even if it is substantive disagreement which in reality provides the motivation for raising procedural objections (a view that a wrong decision has been made), those objections will often be framed in procedural terms

[1] Some central issues are considered in Chapter 1, and developments in the particular area of pollution control are David Robinson's focus in Chapter 2, above.

[2] A. I. Ogus, *Regulation: Legal Form and Economic Theory* (Oxford, 1994), at 99.

(that is, that a decision has been made wrongly). A central concern for public lawyers is therefore that how decisions are made is often seen as more susceptible to legal challenge than what decisions are made. This description goes some way to explaining the prominence of judicial review as the principal remedy in UK administrative law, and its increasing use in environment-related cases.[3]

This characterization is, of course, not complete. In particular, it emphasizes the role of public law in providing processes for decision-making, or conferring powers to make decisions, amongst them decisions having some environmental impact. Clearly this is not the only perspective from which public law can be explored. The articulation of legal processes through statute is just one part of a more complex web of policy and law-making.

For example, law provides complex statutory systems for licensing environmentally harmful behaviour, and public law makes provision to ensure that those licensing powers are exercised appropriately. Those systems would be meaningless if certain sorts of activity were not first prohibited, and if powers were not created to define the circumstances in which pollution is in fact permitted, and perhaps to what extent. The existence of such licensing processes therefore derives from certain substantive judgments having already been made as a matter of public policy.

A broader understanding of public law would therefore be informed by the relationship between the public and private sectors, the extent of the public interest in influencing private behaviour, and how that influence is to be effected. This would be a massive task, especially given that there is no longer, if there ever was, a strict division between the public and private sectors;[4] that the UK lacks clear and entrenched constitutional values or principles; and that it has arguably witnessed the cumulative 'disintegration' of the established model of representative and accountable government.[5] These factors are considered in much of the recent writing on public law in the UK.

My starting point is rather more limited. Once public policy has found expression through recognition of the need to create a decision-making process, the real issue may be the priority which is then given to environmental implications within that process. In this sense, the mere fact that environmental considerations are increasingly considered in statutorily constituted processes of decision-making is less significant than the details of the process for assessing them, and especially for assessing their relative importance, against other substantive goals. This is important in a public law context in which the substance of decisions is often not susceptible to challenge, whereas the manner in which statutory powers are exercised is so susceptible. In considering the balance between process and

[3] C. Reid, 'Judicial Review and the Environment', in B. Hadfield (ed.), *Judicial Review: A Thematic Approach* (Dublin, 1995).

[4] N. Lewis, 'Regulating Non-Government Bodies: Privatization, Accountability, and the Public-Private Divide', in J. Jowell and D. Oliver (eds.), *The Changing Constitution* (2nd ed., Oxford, 1989).

[5] N. Johnson, 'Accountability, Control and Complexity: Moving Beyond Ministerial Responsibility', in A. Barker (ed.), *Quangos in Britain* (London, 1982), cited in Lewis, op. cit., at 220, n. 3.

substance, it is therefore important to understand the desirable features of decision-making processes derived from public law, before looking at how those processes now accommodate or reflect environmental concerns.

'Good' Features of Statutory Decision-Making Processes

The absence of entrenched constitutional standards against which to judge decision-making processes does not mean that certain values or principles of 'good' decision-making cannot be identified in constitutional terms. There are disagreements about the meaning of 'public law'. However, if public law is to have any useful meaning or impact it must represent aspirations towards constitutional goals: aspirations which could be expressed through systems created to make administrative decisions. In this chapter, I therefore take a 'constitutional' view of public law, which can be contrasted with a narrowly 'administrative' view.

In general terms, environmental decision-making of the sort being considered here operates within a theoretical context concerned with constitutional principles of fairness and legitimacy. The most direct impact of this is in the extent to which such principles transcend individual decisions or decision-making processes: in other words, the extent to which normative principles of law precede legislation, rather than 'just' emanate from it.[6] An important implication of this is the potential it creates for tension between views of what 'fair process' should be, and goals of contemporary environmental policy. This tension lies at the heart of the relationship between process and substance in environmental decision-making. Legislation might be seen in very instrumental terms as the mechanism for implementing the priorities of government: in this sense, descriptions of law as a tool or technique take on a very real significance. The tension emerges however in considering the extent to which high-profile environmental priorities should be influenced by or accommodate principles of public law which go beyond individual statutory contexts.

Principles of constitutional concern or importance most obviously relate to the powers of Parliament, the Courts, and the Crown, and to the relationship between them. As such they would seem to be most relevant to types of decisions which are not directly relevant to this chapter. However, the impact of principles of this sort extends throughout the whole of public law. In particular, discussions of the unwritten principles of the UK constitution demonstrate the central importance of 'procedural fairness' to UK public law. Descriptions of the Rule of Law, for example, and its 'disabling function' in respect of the theoretically unlimited sovereignty of Parliament, emphasize notions of legal certainty, limitation of administrative discretion, and procedural fairness.[7]

[6] The distinction between the former 'normativist' style of public law and the latter 'functionalist' style is pivotal to Martin Loughlin's analysis in *Public Law and Political Theory* (Oxford, 1992), see especially ch. 4.

[7] J. Jowell, 'The Rule of Law Today', in J. Jowell and D. Oliver (eds.), *The Changing Constitution* (3rd ed., Oxford, 1994), at 72. See also Loughlin, op. cit., ch. 4.

This focus on procedural fairness is sharpened by commentators who suggest that an important measure in public law of the legitimacy of decision-making is the extent to which it accommodates principles of openness and accountability. This derives in part from the view that recipients of public power should be obliged to explain and justify their actions.[8] Although they are as uncertain as many other so-called 'principles' of UK public or constitutional law, these 'essentially procedural principles' of openness and accountability do at least provide a rough frame of reference against which to assess contemporary decision-making under statute in the context of the environment.[9]

Yet it is clearly difficult to know what these principles mean in practice, or how they relate to different substantive contexts. At a basic level, for example, a principle of openness would suggest wide access to information not only as to the fact that decisions are to be or have been made, but also as to the reasons for those decisions—in fact, a basic level of access to decision-making. Although even this sort of openness might be subject to exceptions (based on commercial confidentiality or national security for example), more complex is the 'opening' of decision-making to diverse influence other than that of institutional decision-makers and the persons seeking decisions (such as applicants for licences).[10] This represents a more extended understanding of 'openness', although certainly not an unusual one. It also illustrates how openness may become transformed into a form of 'accountability', albeit at a relatively low level. Indeed, openness of this sort can be described as a form of *ex ante* accountability.

As with openness, the meaning of 'accountability' cannot be taken for granted. It might, for example, operate differently at different levels of a given decision-making hierarchy: notions of ministerial accountability clearly have a very particular meaning, and one which is rather different to the accountability of, say, local councillors. Equally, there will often be a tension between procedural and substantive accountability. The sort of accountability represented by opportunities to challenge decisions after they have been made will depend on the balance struck between rights to challenge the process, and rights to challenge substantive conclusions. A predominance of the latter would represent the high-water mark of ideas of open access to decision-making. Given the associated practical complications, it must also represent something of an ideal.[11] Discussions of account-

[8] C. Graham, 'Self Regulation', in G. Richardson and H. Genn (eds.), *Administrative Law and Government Action* (Oxford, 1994).

[9] A general recognition of the role of openness and accountability in this context can be seen in the reports of the Royal Commission on Environmental Pollution, e.g., in its Twelfth Report, *Best Practicable Environmental Option* (Cm. 310, London, 1988), at para. 1.13.

[10] The term 'institutions' is a broad one for the purposes of this chapter. It extends beyond agencies through which governmental power is exercised to include systems of rules or practices defined by public law, or operating under them, by which decisions may be made.

[11] This procedural/substantive distinction is, of course, only a starting point. Other forms of accountability might also be considered. Ogus, for example, adds financial accountability to the procedural and substantive: op. cit., at 111. See also Her Majesty's Treasury, *Spending Public Money: Governance and Audit Issues* (Cm. 3179, London, 1996). Financial accountability is not a principal focus here, but in any event clearly falls within the bounds of the general description.

ability often concentrate on *ex post* accountability of this sort. However, and as has been suggested, the general notion of accountability is more fluid than that concentration might suggest.

Openness and accountability are therefore best understood as operating across a continuum, starting from knowledge that a decision is to be made, moving through the process of decision-making itself, to rights of recourse after conclusions have been reached. Some issues might arise throughout that continuum (access to information for example), others only at particular points (such as third party rights of appeal). In assessing the extent to which a given decision-making process is open or provides for accountability, we must recognize that a balance must be struck between different parts of that continuum. Early and effective involvement in decision-making may offset the need for extensive rights of recourse once a decision has been made, whilst *ex post* rights of substantive challenge may compensate to some extent for an opaque decision-making process. But what does emerge from a central concern with openness and accountability is the importance not just of the identity of decision-makers, but of the contributors to a particular decision-making process and the opportunities they have truly to influence decisions.[12]

One of my concerns here is to illustrate the transposition of general principles, such as accountability, to particular environmental situations. This is a more specific concern than the sort of work which has observed the preoccupation of UK public law with the accountability of Parliament, and of Ministers to Parliament. My approach might be seen as a specific version of Prosser's suggestion that the democratization of public law demands new forms of accountability beyond this relatively narrow focus on Parliament, and in particular the development of a more modern range of democratic institutions.[13]

With this context in mind, and putting aside any search for absolutes, it can be seen that one role for public lawyers must be to examine new or adapted decision-making processes in order to assess whether they are more or less open, or provide for more or less accountability than existing processes. Further than this, such questions as these must be part of any inquiry into what makes a 'good' environmental decision: decisions are 'better' from a public law point of view if they demonstrate those characteristics. This sort of assessment takes on a new urgency in view of the contemporary dominance of statutory decision-making processes in UK environmental law. It does emphasize the procedural rather than the substantive however, and whilst procedural matters clearly have substantive implications (some of these, relating to the effective locus of decision-making for example, are considered below), the substantive environmental context is important too. The public lawyer's concern must therefore be instrumentalist as well,

[12] Some commentators make more of this point than others. Prosser, for example, places far higher priority on participation than Graham does: T. Prosser, 'Democratisation, Accountability and Institutional Design: Reflections on Public Law', in P. McAuslan and J. McEldowney, *Law, Legitimacy and the Constitution* (London, 1985) and Graham, op. cit.

[13] Op. cit., at 170.

in that public law must also be concerned with making better *environmental* decisions. Some issues relating to the latter point will therefore be considered now.

Towards Better 'Environmental' Decisions

As a grouping of laws relating to one particular substantive area, legislative responses to environmental problems quite predictably bear many of the hallmarks of approaches or techniques already very familiar to public lawyers. For example, the favoured method of environmental regulation is still the 'command-and-control' licensing system under the guidance of a regulatory authority: a basic model which is long-standing, and has been applied in substantive contexts more varied than those which might be described as 'environmental'. Questions relating to the structure of such licensing systems and how they operate therefore go well beyond questions of environmental licensing.

Equally, whatever the relative roles of specialist statutory environmental agencies and local authorities with environmental functions, the exercise by those bodies of powers conferred by statute raises issues which cut across substantive areas of governmental or quasi-governmental activity. Those issues relate to the distribution of powers between different decision-makers and the form their powers take, as well as to the manner of their exercise. They also extend beyond *de novo* decision-making to opportunities for appeal or challenge, and include questions as to the appropriate fora for resolution of environmental disputes (as witness the continuing debate in connection with calls for a specialist environmental court or tribunal).[14] The sort of analysis adopted here therefore goes beyond purely environmental legal interest, to provide fertile ground for considering the state of contemporary public law itself.

There are also indications of how public law has responded to growing environmental concern however. The creation of specific statutory systems for the regulation of environmental impacts has already been mentioned, and is an important (if crude) indicator of the political priority given to environmental protection.[15] But to these environmental measures can be added other more sophisticated developments. These include the assimilation of environmental considerations within existing decision-making systems; changes to the scope of licensing systems in order better to reflect the nature of environmental problems (a trend towards the 'integration' of environmental management); and a restructuring of the agencies responsible for environmental regulation. Such developments would suggest that familiar public law processes of decision-making can be tailored to the particular

[14] e.g., G. McLeod, 'Do We Need an Environmental Court in Britain?', in D. Robinson and J. Dunkley (eds.), *Public Interest Perspectives in Environmental Law* (Chichester, 1995).

[15] Most recently see the Environmental Protection Act 1990 ('EPA 1990') and the Environment Act 1995 ('EA 1995'), although legislative responses sometimes reveal a less than mature policy position: e.g., the controversy surrounding the (now repealed) s. 143 of EPA 1990. See R. Lewis, 'Contaminated Land: The New Regime of the Environment Act 1995' [1995] *JPL* 1087–96.

demands of environmental 'protection', and thus provide environmentally better decisions.

Assimilation

There are now many examples of the assimilation or, as it is sometimes described, 'integration' of environmental concerns into established legal decision-making processes. This use of the words 'assimilation' and 'integration' suggests that they are synonymous, or at least similar. A more precise usage is preferred here, consistent with the explanation provided in Chapter 1: 'assimilation' is taken, for these purposes, to refer to the incorporation of environmental considerations within wider, often existing, decision-making systems; 'integration', by contrast, is used to refer to the bringing together of disparate controls into less fragmented controls over environmental harm. To this extent it represents significant legal change, but this is still change within a relatively narrow body of recognized 'environmental' law.

An obvious illustration of assimilation is in planning controls, where there are very clear signs of a reorientation of planning controls towards environmental protection even without marked legislative change.[16] Other examples include waste policy and moves towards eco-labelling, although in these cases some more marked legislative reform has been undertaken.[17] More broadly, however, expressions of policy make it clear that a general 'greening' of all forms of decision-making is considered to be a desirable feature of modern government.[18] This starts at the top of the policy-making hierarchy with policy-making systems,[19] but clearly extends to the furtherance of 'greened' policy through legal mechanisms.

This process of assimilation has been praised by many, and clearly has advantages, both from an administrative point of view and an environmental one. It has been argued forcefully, for example, that the environmental consequences of human behaviour must be addressed at every opportunity if effective long term solutions are to be secured. In the sense that assimilation means making environmental

[16] Compare D. Millichap, 'Sustainability: A Long-Established Concern of Planning' [1993] JPL 1111–19, with T. Jewell, 'Planning Regulation and Environmental Consciousness: Some Lessons from Minerals?' [1995] *JPL* 482–98.

[17] e.g., Directive on Packaging and Packaging Waste (94/62/EC, OJ 1994 L365) and Regulation on Community Eco-label Award Scheme (880/92/EEC, OJ 1992 L99).

[18] Department of the Environment, *Sustainable Development: The UK Strategy* (Cm. 2426, London, 1994) affirms that 'the Government has long been committed to the integration of environmental concerns in its decision-making at all levels' (para. 29.2) and places heavy emphasis on the international context provided by Agenda 21 (agreed at the Earth Summit in Rio de Janeiro in 1992). Chapter 8 of Agenda 21 is concerned with the 'integration of environment and development in decision-making', see: N. Robinson (ed.), *Agenda 21: Earth's Action Plan* (1993), at 115–36.

[19] For illustrations of this approach see the Department of the Environment's *Policy Appraisal and the Environment: A Guide for Government Departments* (1991) and *Environmental Appraisal in Government Departments* (1994). The latter expressly seeks to ensure that environmental considerations 'are integrated into the general appraisal of policy in a systematic way' (para. 1.5, using 'integrated' to mean 'assimilated' in the sense described above).

concern one more factor for consideration in established decision-making processes, this is also one illustration of how environmental decision-making fits into the general approach of public law described above.

Assimilation in this sense does have its limitations however. Not least amongst these is the administrative complexity of assimilating environmental considerations into all aspects of decision-making and implementation.[20] Recent efforts towards assimilation in this respect have certainly been strongly criticized.[21] More fundamental reservations have been expressed by groups such as Friends of the Earth and the Green Alliance, which argue that the assimilation of environmental concern should mean consistently favouring the environment, rather than merely taking account of environmental considerations as one of many competing priorities. The latter view is the one which the government, for example, has so far preferred.[22] As these groups understand assimilation, it is concerned at a general level with the 'totality of human welfare and quality of life, with fundamental consequences for social, economic and cultural policy' and at a specific level with prioritizing environmental protection above competing policy goals. If the traditional role of public law has been accurately described here, assimilation in the focused sense of prioritizing environmental considerations above other policy goals as a matter of law is a remote prospect.

Integration

The 'integration' of regulatory functions, particularly in traditional command-and-control models of environmental licensing, owes its origins to the perceived environmental benefits of adopting a less fragmented approach to environmental control. This approach is part of a wider, and international, trend towards the integration of environmental management in general, and of pollution controls in particular.[23]

The most obvious example of this sort of integration is the co-ordination of controls over pollution of different environmental media to have regard to the

[20] This helps to explain the government's rejection in 1995 of an amendment to the then Environment Bill during its House of Lords Committee Stage which would have required all ministers, public bodies, statutory undertakers, and persons holding public office to integrate requirements for environmental protection into the definition of their policies and plans, and into the performance of their functions under any enactment (*Official Report*, cols. 1586–92, 2 March 1995). See also cl. 2 of the unsuccessful *Environment Protection Bill* (HL Bill 6, Session 1989–90) which would have imposed a duty on all employers and self-employed persons to 'ensure, as far as reasonably practicable, the protection of the Environment'.

[21] As 'not remotely successful' and as merely 'a cosmetic change': House of Lords, *Report from the Select Committee on Sustainable Development, Session 1994–95* (HL Paper 72), para. 6.12. The Committee concluded that 'a clear and prompt re-statement of the functions and purpose of the Government's own internal integrating mechanisms would be welcome' (para. 6.15).

[22] Ibid., at paras. 6.5–6.7. The prospect of change under the current government is uncertain, although the obstacles would be many, not least because of the entrenchment of the developments considered in Part 2, below.

[23] N. Haigh and F. Irwin (eds.), *Integrated Pollution Control in Europe and North America* (Washington D. C., 1990).

effects of pollution on the environment as a whole. This was an important part of changes made in 1990 to the structure of pollution control in the UK. These saw the establishment of the 'integrated pollution control' system, central to which is consideration in licensing decisions of the 'best practicable environmental option'. This aims to ensure that any pollution which is authorized has the least effect on the environment as a whole, rather than concentrating on its effect on an individual environmental medium.[24]

A number of arguments have been put in favour of the integration of pollution controls. Most start from the point that environmental problems demand 'integrated' solutions, that is, solutions that consider the potential long-term aggregated effects of pollution. This, commentators have suggested, enables pollution problems to be solved rather than transferred from one part of the environment to another, improves the ability to set priorities and to improve the efficiency of controls, enables co-operation between policy sectors, and simplifies the administration of pollution control.[25] However, as discussed in Chapter 1, extension of the idea of integration beyond pollution control is more problematic. Whilst the establishment of unified agencies is pinpointed there as a possible step in a broadly integrating direction, various factors are also isolated which give rise to instability in the process of integration. Such factors suggest that 'integration' of this sort is only an intermediate stage.

Among the key factors which could be discussed as giving rise to a further process of diffusion or assimilation in environmental law is the emergence of key concepts such as 'sustainable development' and 'environmental stewardship'.[26] For example, the new agency structure referred to above is also accompanied by statements of general policy direction; and the general policy goals have in this way become part of the agencies' 'institutional terms of reference'.

The Importance of Environmental Standards

It is all very well having a more effective institutional structure, guided by express statements of agencies' goals, but certainly from the point of view of some observers, those institutions can only be as effective as the standards in which they result. An important part of any inquiry into the ability of statutory powers

[24] Royal Commission on Environmental Pollution, Twelfth Report, *Best Practicable Environmental Option* (Cm. 310, London, 1988); J. Gibson, 'The Integration of Pollution Control', in R. Churchill, L. Warren, and J. Gibson (eds.), *Law, Policy and the Environment* (1991) *Journal of Law and Society*, Special Issue, 18–31.

[25] Haigh and Irwin, op. cit., at 7–9.

[26] The emergence of these is charted in Chapter 1, although it is interesting to note in addition that the Environment White Paper, *This Common Inheritance* (Cm. 1200, London, 1990), asserted that the ethical imperative of 'stewardship' was the foundation of the Government's environmental policy. That is, 'a moral duty to look after our planet and to hand it on in good order to future generations' (para. 1.14; cited in J. Rowan-Robinson, A. Ross, W. Walton, and J. Rothnie, 'Public Access to Environmental Information: A Means to What End?' (1996) 8 *Journal of Environmental Law* 18–42, at 18).

based in public law to solve environmental problems must therefore relate to environmental standards. Although this issue involves a complex debate even at a relatively general level, there are problems with some types of environmental standards. For example, it cannot be assumed that the scientific basis for standards or their technical 'measurability' are unproblematic, nor that they live up to the appearance of technical (and, by implication, objectively justifiable) rationality suggested by their prominence in environmental law in the UK and elsewhere.

These problems are well known to environmental lawyers, who are even more familiar with their incidence in respect of quasi-technical standards such as 'best practicable means', 'best available techniques not entailing excessive cost', or 'wholesomeness'. The difference is, first, that the problems with standards are often overlooked in relation to numerical standards and, secondly, that quasi-technical standards have frequently been implemented in practice by providing them with technically or numerically-based meanings. Other problems arise too on a more practical level, where standards come to be applied in varied geographical conditions. Indeed, it is a characteristic of UK environmental standards that they are adaptable to the circumstances of individual cases.

Environmental Self-Regulation

Partly as a consequence of the limitations of formal standards-based approaches there is a growing tendency in environmental law to design systems for the delivery of best environmental practice, rather than to elaborate the detailed objectives of environmental regulation through numerical standards. This new 'systems' approach is described by David Robinson in Chapter 2, above. For present purposes, such an approach can be regarded as distinct from the process orientation of public law considered above (although it forms part of it), and as representing a form of environmental self-regulation over which external regulators exercise general, but limited, day-to-day supervision. Examples include the recently established 'environmental management systems' described by David Robinson, as well as an almost universal commitment to processes of 'risk assessment' in place of detailed regulatory prescription of environmental standards or regulators' requirements in individual cases.[27]

Other related developments towards self-regulation include ideas such as 'producer responsibility' in the management of waste[28] and, even more recently, discussions of 'co-regulation'. The latter is a qualified form of self-regulation

[27] Regulation for an Eco-Management and Audit Scheme (1836/93/EC), Department of the Environment Circular 2/91 (noted at (1995) 7 *Environmental Law and Management* 111), and *British Standard on Environment Management Systems* (BS 7750, see also ISO 14001); and Department of the Environment, *Guide to Risk Assessment and Risk Management for Environmental Protection* (London, 1995). The first of these is described by David Robinson in Chapter 2.

[28] EPA 1990, Pt. II; EA 1995, ss. 93–5.

proposed in jurisdictions other than the UK which seeks to address some of the most fundamental criticisms of self-regulation (criticisms based in part on the public law concerns at issue here).[29] Some commentators also propose the assimilation of environmental considerations into commercial decision-making as an improvement on attempts to coerce organizations into desired behaviour through formal legal interventions.[30] This would potentially be the most marked example of the reaction against the limitations of established mechanisms for articulating environmental standards.

On one level, these self-regulatory trends are consistent with a general deregulatory policy emphasis which seeks to dovetail economic efficiency arguments with a reduction of traditional forms of regulation.[31] The substitution of incentive mechanisms for crude and commercially intrusive regulation is presented as having general regulatory advantages, no less so in the pursuit of environmental policy than other policy goals. Arguably, this approach presents better prospects for addressing environmental problems than some existing forms of regulation; one apparent paradox being that governments might better implement environmental policy by doing less, but differently. It does, of course, bring its own problems too.[32]

Summary

What this selective discussion of contemporary developments in UK environmental law shows is how distinctively environmental considerations are emerging to influence the development of statutory responses to environmental problems. In many ways these have resulted in changes which are of interest to public lawyers: reorganization of the agencies of governmental control, and trends towards self-regulation being amongst them. The assimilation or integration of environmental concerns is more obviously environmentally distinctive, but here too familiar issues arise. For example, we might consider how competing priorities could be weighed against, or reconciled with, each other, and what impact institutional matters (the design of decision-making processes and the identity of decision-makers) may have on substantive decisions. As it is also clear that environmental standards

[29] N. Gunningham, 'Environment, Self-Regulation, and the Chemical Industry: Assessing Responsible Care' (1995) 17 *Law and Policy* 57–109.

[30] G. Winter, 'Perspectives for Environmental Law—Entering the Fourth Phase' (1989) 1 *Journal of Environmental Law* 38–47.

[31] At the forefront of this policy was the 'Deregulation Task Force' set up by the President of the Board of Trade in 1994. Its first Annual Report, and the government's response to it, set the general scene for developments in environmental regulation anticipated by the former UK Government, see (1996) 8 *Environmental Law and Management* 21. The position under the current labour Government may be rather different, although this remains difficult to gauge.

[32] Not least of these are issues relating to who designs the process, who participates in it, and how its effectiveness is measured. All of these are concerns within the traditional process orientation of public law, but insofar as these new systems are a sub-set of public law decision-making as it is normally understood, such concerns can clearly be extended to embrace them too.

themselves are inherently evaluative and subject to few (if any) absolutes, these factors combine to illustrate the importance of identifying both how and by whom environmental decisions are made, and the impact of public law ideas on those decision-making processes. It is to these issues that I now turn.

2. New Directions in Public Law and the Environment

The developments described immediately above represent a marked change in the nature of statutory environmental decision-making. But there are a number of trends emerging in the form of UK statutory environmental law more generally which are equally significant. They are, first, a formalization of strategic decision-making, with a consequent greater emphasis on the strategic decisions that result. Secondly, an apparently greater commitment to 'administrative transparency' involving wider public access to information and (perhaps) wider public participation in decision-making. Thirdly, a government commitment to alternative forms of environmental regulation and, in particular, to 'economic instruments'.

These directions in public law and the environment have so far been less apparent than those described above. This is partly because they have yet to resonate with the sorts of general public law concerns outlined, and with notions of openness and accountability in particular. At first glance, for example, a greater emphasis on strategic decision-making is merely an extension of existing patterns of legal decision-making processes. On closer examination, however, the implications of that emphasis take on a less familiar and (for public lawyers) less comfortable form, as explained below.

An equally significant reason for the lack of controversy attaching to these directions is that, independently, they have been enthusiastically received. In the case of economic instruments, this is complemented by limited actual experience of their use in the UK. And so a view has yet to be taken which is informed by public law, and which also considers these directions together. In adopting such a view, this account will be particularly concerned with what it reveals of the process of decision-making, and the identity of decision-makers. In this way, a more detailed picture of how process and substance relate in contemporary environmental law will begin to emerge.

National Strategic Decision-Making

Many features of the development of UK environmental law are broadly consistent with trends in environmental regulation identified elsewhere in this collection.[33] The UK version has retained a distinctive character in a number of respects

[33] In particular see Jenny Steele and Tim Jewell, 'Law in Environmental Decision-Making', Chapter 1, above, and David Robinson, 'Regulatory Evolution in Pollution Control', Chapter 2, above.

however. In particular, although providing a broad framework within which environmental decisions are made, UK statutory provisions have revealed very little of how those powers will be exercised. A particularly 'British' approach to environmental regulation has thus emerged: one in which administrative discretion has played a prominent part, fostering close collaboration with those subject to statutory controls, and resulting in essentially negotiated rule-making.[34]

Some commentators have noted more recently that this distinctive character has been subject to revision. In 1991, for example, Macrory heralded a new era of 'legal formalism' in UK environmental law with the potential to transform traditional approaches to pollution standards and objectives.[35] This was an important observation, coinciding as it did with growing environmental concern and considerable legislative and policy activity. European initiatives and certain provisions of the Environmental Protection Act 1990 clearly supported this view. The 1990 Act, for example, brought the introduction of statutory environmental quality objectives and standards in relation to the integrated pollution control regime,[36] and at around the same time limited air quality standards were articulated, along with mechanisms to introduce statutory water quality objectives.[37]

It is clearly not the case that prior to developments of this sort tactical (or site-specific) controls had been imposed with no consideration of the cumulative effects of pollution. Most obviously, new procedures for the adoption of statutory water quality objectives are clearly based on long-established non-statutory mechanisms.[38] There are also localized examples of 'tolerable limits' which are more representative of the type of informal or policy mechanisms which have developed to address strategic pollution problems. These include nuisance thresholds, trigger values in connection with land contamination, and statutory responses to major localized pollution incidents (such as the Clean Air Acts). However, in terms of the process by which such objectives are set, they hardly represent formalized mechanisms for the development and implementation of strategic policy. In pollution control at least there have thus been limited formal mechanisms within which strategic goals (including strategic environmental standards) could be set, or plans to minimize polluting emissions established. In this sense, the new formalism identified by Macrory is significant.

Whilst this evidence of formalism does remain persuasive, subsequent developments indicate that the prospect of wide-ranging transformation along these

[34] Jewell and Steele, op. cit., at 288.

[35] R. Macrory, 'Environmental Law: Shifting Discretions and the New Formalism', in O. Lomas (ed.), *Frontiers of Environmental Law* (Chichester, 1991).

[36] EPA 1990, s. 3.

[37] Air Quality Standards Regulations 1989 (SI 1989 No. 317); Water Act 1989, s. 104 (providing for the classification of waters), s. 105 (a mechanism enabling water quality objectives to be set), and s. 106 (creating a general duty to achieve and maintain objectives). Now see the Water Resources Act 1991 ('WRA 1991'), ss. 82–4.

[38] J. Seager, 'Developments in Water Quality Standards and Classification Schemes in England and Wales' (1994) 30 *Water Science Technology* 11–19.

lines has receded. Not only has progress in formulating statutory standards been slow,[39] but evidence has emerged to suggest that European measures have generally moved away from pivotal reliance on centralized numerical standards.[40] Illustrations of legal formalism of the sort identified by Macrory are also largely confined (as he recognized in 1991) to water and air pollution controls, and have not emerged in areas such as contaminated land or soil quality as might have been anticipated.[41] To this can be added a change from the 'arms length' regulatory style publicly adopted by environmental regulators in the late 1980s, and a retrenchment of the close liaison between regulators and the regulated which has historically characterized UK environmental control.[42] In place of the general formalism described by Macrory, what is now beginning to emerge is a complex interaction between some formalized standards, and certain types of formalized decision-making. This can be illustrated most clearly by reference to the making of national strategic decisions as to environmental goals.

The most general example is again provided by the land use planning system. Whilst there has long been a commitment to strategic policy preparation in planning, strategic plans themselves have quite recently been given a new emphasis. At the level of counties and metropolitan districts there is a sophisticated and well-tested process by which planning policy is developed and adopted. Strategic plans (structure plans or the first part of unitary development plans), containing 'general policies' in respect of the development and use of land, are subject to advertisement and consultation in both draft and proposal stages.[43] Local plans, which relate general policies to specific areas, are prepared in the context of strategic plans and are themselves subject to publicity and consultation.[44] The process for the adoption of both types of plan includes a public inquiry or other public hearing. Although certainly not a direct transposition of national or regional policy to sub-regional areas, development plans will be influenced by regional or strategic planning guidance issued by the Secretary of State.[45]

[39] The first eight consultation documents on proposed statutory water quality objectives were published by the National Rivers Authority in March 1996. The original intention had been to have the first statutory water quality objectives in place by spring 1993: S. Tromans and M. Grant (eds.), *Encyclopedia of Environmental Law*, para. D24–166.

[40] Compare, e.g., the technical complexity of the Bathing Waters Directive with art. 6 of the proposed Directive on Ecological Quality of Water (OJ 1994 C222), which leaves the definition of 'operational targets' to member states. Subsequent developments have led to the withdrawal of this proposal, but the principle remains. Indeed, on Han Somsen's analysis, it has become stronger: Chapter 6, below.

[41] Macrory, op. cit., at 16. Indeed, and conversely, new contaminated land provisions provide powerful evidence of the importance of the risk assessment techniques referred to above: Environment Act 1995, s. 57, introducing Part IIA into EPA 1990; Department of the Environment, *Consultation on Draft Statutory Guidance on Contaminated Land* (September 1996), ch. 2, at para. 6 et seq.

[42] Although the justifications for this may have changed, see Jewell and Steele, 'Regulatory Reform and the Pursuit of "Sustainable Development": The Environment Act 1995', above.

[43] Town and Country Planning Act 1990 (as amended) ('TCPA 1990'), ss. 31–35C; Town and Country Planning (Development Plan) Regulations 1991 (SI 1991 No. 2794). R. Duxbury, *Telling and Duxbury's Planning Law and Procedure* (10th ed., London, 1996), at 54–65.

[44] TCPA 1990, ss. 39–48. [45] Ibid., s. 31(6).

The general features of this process are quite well-established, although the strategic planning system has in fact been subject to more turbulence than this account might suggest.[46] In particular, changes made in 1991 remain controversial. The new emphasis given to plans—the so-called 'presumption in favour of the development plan'[47]—was one of the most notable changes made in 1991, and this has given rise to considerable debate. For example, the most recent work suggests that the presumption has contributed to increasing the time taken for plans' preparation, and has hence reduced their value in practice.[48] More complex is the elaborate circumscription by the Secretary of State of plan content and the consequent centralizing of policy influence which is furthered by the 1991 amendments to the process of plan preparation.[49] What is clearly uncontroversial though is the desirability of a legal process through which planning policy can find form, and then can be translated from national to sub-regional and local level.

This commitment to the adoption of strategic planning policy has not been matched historically in pollution controls. Neither does the emergence of formalized standards necessarily presuppose a new strategic emphasis. Even where such standards do appear, it has already been pointed out above that reliance on them in practice has been minimal. However, there is now an increasingly complex pattern of formalized processes for the articulation and adoption of strategic pollution policy, and the introduction of such processes is accelerating. Indeed, the pace of change is such that even before the first statutory strategic initiatives contained in the Environmental Protection Act 1990 have themselves been implemented, they have been supplemented by further measures. For example, the Environment Act 1995 makes provision for the first time for the preparation of national strategies with respect to assessment or management of air quality, and also for the recovery and disposal of waste.[50] As with the general example of environmental quality standards provided by the 1990 Act, the national air quality strategy may contain quality standards and objectives.[51] These, in turn, will become the trigger for the exercise by local authorities of powers to secure the achievement of strategic objectives, principally through 'air quality management areas' and associated 'action plans'.[52]

This trend in substantive provision for the preparation of strategic pollution policy is exacerbated by the institutional changes referred to above, and elsewhere

[46] For example, as recently as 1989 it was proposed that development plans in their present form should be replaced entirely: Department of the Environment, *The Future of Development Plans* (Cm. 560, London, 1989).

[47] TCPA 1990, s. 54A; N. Herbert-Young, 'Reflections on Section 54A and "Plan-led" Decision-Making' [1995] *JPL* 292–305.

[48] M. Wood, 'Local Plans and UDPs: Is There a Better Way?' [1996] *JPL* 807–15.

[49] Planning and Compensation Act 1991, s. 27, Sched. 4. See T. Jewell, 'Minerals and Waste: New Plan Making Powers and Procedures' (1991) 2 *Utilities Law Review* 82–7.

[50] EA 1995, ss. 80–1 and 92 respectively.

[51] Indeed, such standards form an important part of the new strategy: Department of the Environment, *The United Kingdom National Air Quality Strategy* (Cm. 3587, London, 1997), ch. 3.

[52] EA 1995, ss. 82–4.

in this book.[53] The process of integration, which includes the creation of environment agencies, involves a degree of centralization which magnifies the impact of strategic policy.[54] Specific requirements on the Environment Agency ('the Agency') to have regard to strategic policy[55] are complemented by the strategic role of the Agency (and the Secretary of State) in the formulation of that policy itself. This applies to the whole range of environmental functions exercised by the Agency, and can be contrasted with the more familiar practice of making reference to standards based not on some strategic target but rather on the capabilities of a polluter to minimize polluting emissions.[56] Clearly, whether a decision is a 'strategic' one or not depends less on the body making the decision than the purpose of the decision itself: local authorities can undertake strategic planning too. However, the centralization evident from these developments emphasizes the dominant role of the Agency in the formulation and application of that strategy.

There are a number of environmental reasons for this trend towards strategic decision-making. The internationalization of standard setting, including the influence of the European Community, has driven policy makers to seek agreed maximum limits in many areas of pollution control. This contributes an important part of the explanation for the sort of formalization of pollution standards and objectives identified in 1991. Equally significant, in the government's view at least, have been developments in our technical ability to identify environmental risks. This was given as one of the most important justifications for new air quality standards for example.[57]

It is also important to note equally influential efficiency arguments which have been proffered to support the growing role of strategic decision-making. An administrative concern to 'streamline' processes of decision-making is frequently set against the other principles which guide the design or reform of statutory decision-making processes. On one level, integrationist trends which reduce possible duplication are part of this streamlining, the aim of which is to minimize delay in actually making decisions. At another level, the addition of a strategic policy framework may also have the advantage of improving the predictability of tactical (for example, licensing) decisions, and thus of reducing wasted

[53] See, in particular, Chapter 1.

[54] Although largely a reorganization, the centralization consequent on the creation of the Agency does go some way beyond merely the more effective use of existing powers. This marks an important departure from the reasons behind the creation of Her Majesty's Inspectorate of Pollution, a predecessor of the English and Welsh Agency: A. Jordan, 'Integrated Pollution Control and the Evolving Style and Structure of Environmental Regulation in the UK' (1993) 2 *Environmental Politics* 405–27.

[55] e.g., EA 1995, s. 81.

[56] The National Air Quality Strategy recognizes the historic role of this 'rendering harmless' approach, and emphasizes the contribution to be made by the national strategy in 'address[ing] the remaining problems', op. cit., at 14.

[57] Ibid., at 3.

investment in unnecessary or abortive applications.[58] Either way, a very close link emerges between the justifications for strategic decision-making of the sort described here and competing principles of openness and accountability in decision-making, both of which necessarily complicate decision-making. This may have gone unexplored in the context of strategic environmental decision-making, but it is a link which is already familiar to public lawyers.

The environmental justifications for articulating strategic goals are linked to a particular approach to environmental standard-setting which is technically or scientifically driven, and which in the past has resulted in numerical environmental standards. A more general contribution to the legal entrenchment of strategic decision-making has been made by the broadly stated objectives or purposes for environmental laws or environmental agencies described above. These would also seem to be influencing the nature of strategic policy (that is, a move away from central reliance on statutory or quasi-statutory environmental standards) as much as the fact of that policy's preparation. These general objectives have important implications for the form and application of environmental law, and in particular for how environmental decisions are made.

Accountability and openness operate differently in different decision-making structures, and then at different levels within them. What has been identified in this section is an accelerating trend towards strategic decision-making in UK environmental law. This will not operate as a substitute for tactical decision-making, a point at which public law concerns have been well developed.

Equally, however, the role of strategic environmental policy (including pollution, conservation, and land use planning) must be to influence how those decisions are made. The emergence of processes for its formulation will change opportunities to influence that process. Equally, a move from technical standards to formalized processes of decision-making, re-establishes key concerns relating to who participates in them, and how. It reinforces concerns about process and substance, and brings us back to the familiar public law context with which this chapter began. These developments therefore indicate an important shift in the locus of decision-making under statutory environmental law in the UK.

Administrative Transparency

The reasons why openness and accountability are as a matter of principle important elements of statutory decision-making were explained above. Simply put, if the way in which decisions are made and the reasons for those decisions are visible or 'open', then decisions become susceptible to broad participation or

[58] This has long been a feature of discussions concerning planning law (see, e.g., L. Warren and V. Murray, 'PPG 9 "Nature Conservation"—A New Initiative' [1995] *JPL* 574–79) and has arisen in environmental law more widely (e.g., Department of the Environment, *Integrated Planning and the Granting of Permits in the EC* (1993), noted at (1994) 6 *Land Management and Environmental Law Report* 27).

assessment (*ex ante*), and possibly to some form of administrative or judicial review (*ex post*). Participation in decision-making in this way is likely to contribute to substantively better decisions, which take a range of interests directly into account, and which better accommodate specialist or specific knowledge or opinions. Those opinions are just as likely to emerge from groups with a particular professional interest as they are, for example, from individuals affected by a particular licensing application. A further substantive benefit is that openness may assist bodies responsible for decision-making in discharging their functions, as well as enabling the exercise of those functions to be scrutinised. Look, for example, at the importance placed by environmental regulators on public reports of pollution incidents or breaches of licensing requirements.[59]

Equally important in the case of decisions with collective implications is that openness and accountability of this sort, including an element of participation, will give decisions a particular political weight. In a sense, it will make those decisions more legitimate, and promote public confidence in both the decision-making process, and the decisions resulting from it. Given the poor prospects of securing any universal agreement, this is an important justification for procedural accountability in particular. The unusual challenge of divergent environmental philosophies brings an additional and distinctive element to this argument, as does the need to balance collective needs against local wishes in an environmental context, and the inherently evaluative character of environmental laws.[60] Openness and accountability are therefore desirable characteristics at every stage of environmental decision-making processes. One phrase which is increasingly used to emphasize this, and which provides a label here, is 'administrative transparency'. This starts from the basic need for access to information (so that what is being done can be seen), but it may also be taken to apply more broadly: it represents a principled commitment to access to decision-making too.

By way of an aside, the notion of administrative transparency can be compared to more usual references (in environmental law at least) to 'access to information'. Access to information is clearly an important part of ensuring that decision-making is open, and of fostering accountability—an importance reflected both in the following analysis and elsewhere in this book.[61] Yet whilst access to information issues must remain a starting point, there are other aspects of decision-making whose 'transparency' is equally significant. These include the knowledge

[59] The general public is an important source of information on pollution incidents, whilst *ad hoc* committees including representatives of local communities have been found to play an important part in monitoring major developers' compliance with planning restrictions, see: J. Rowan-Robinson, P. Watchman, and C. Barker, *Crime and Regulation: A Study of the Enforcement of Regulatory Codes* (1990), at 223–30; T. Jewell, *The Law and Practice of Mineral Extraction 1981–1991*, M.Phil Thesis (Leicester, 1993).

[60] The view that environmental law is evaluative is developed by David Robinson in Chapter 2 in respect of the reconciliation between environmental and 'other' goals, and by Jenny Steele in Chapter 4 in respect of the evaluation of risks.

[61] Clíona Kimber, 'Understanding Access to Environmental Information: The European Experience', Chapter 5, below.

that decisions are going to made in the first place, for example, that a strategic plan is to be prepared or a licence sought. The practical importance of this should not be underestimated despite its apparent 'obviousness'. Unfortunately, and as will become clear, empirical work has begun to highlight a number of obstacles to enabling access to decision-making even at this rudimentary level.[62] In sum, however, 'administrative transparency' is wider in practice and in principle than access to information.

It is perhaps inevitable that the attention of commentators should have focused on access to information in considering access to decision-making in general. If we are to assess the extent to which environmental decision-making as a continuum gives effect to principles of administrative transparency, however, then we must begin to explore the whole continuum. This means looking beyond access to information. In particular, a more pronounced legal hierarchy of decision-making has begun to emerge, one in which the dichotomy between the strategic and the tactical is beginning to take centre stage. In the light of this, the access to information and administrative transparency debates take on some new and unfamiliar features.

Changing Provision in Environmental Decision-Making

The established emphasis on access to information as a precursor to access to decision-making provides a starting point. Given the many uses to which information can be put once it has been obtained, no particularly clear distinction emerges from such access in itself between *ex ante* and *ex post* accountability. More elaborate provisions, designed either to enable participation before decisions are made or to enable *ex post* challenges must therefore be added. In this way a better appreciation of the whole continuum of decision-making can be gained, and of the relationships between its constituent elements. As has been suggested immediately above, certain features of contemporary environmental regulation make those relationships important.

Whilst public law principles of openness and accountability have had a wide appeal, their implementation has also been subject to general criticism. This has been most obvious in respect of central government policy-making and the limiting effects of concepts such as 'national security', but is by no means confined to this.[63] However, at least in the case of environmental licensing, there is a long history of recording and making widely available some details of decisions, and in this way of contributing to some form of transparent decision-making.

The principal method for making environmental information of this sort publicly available has been through 'registers' compiled by local authorities or

[62] Rowan-Robinson, et al, 'Public Access to Environmental Information: A Means to What End?', above, at 25 and 31–3.

[63] Generally see P. Birkinshaw, *Freedom of Information* (2nd ed., London, 1996).

statutory regulators.[64] As command-and-control licensing systems have been the dominant form of statutory response to environmental problems, so too has there been a corresponding reliance on registers as the 'key mechanism' for making associated information available.[65] In one sense it seems odd to emphasize the contribution of registers. Given that they are unashamedly concerned with site-specific licensing (or 'tactical') decisions, and contain records of decisions that have already been made, registers may be seen as representing the *end* of a decision-making process. Indeed, with the passage of time much of the information in registers will in fact be of this sort.[66]

The actual contribution of registers to *ex ante* as well as *ex post* accountability is greater then this would suggest however, for three reasons. First, an emphasis on registers reflects the incremental development of environmental licensing from origins in local solutions to what were perceived as local problems.[67] Whilst unsophisticated by modern standards, local (or tactical) licensing with a corollary record-keeping requirement is a form of public control which, in the absence of strategic (regional or national) controls, is an improvement on no controls at all. It may lack strategic direction, but it also has the potential to alleviate the most obvious or immediate health or environmental problems. The development of controls over atmospheric pollution illustrates this point well.[68] With the more recent identification or creation of environmental problems, legal controls themselves have become more extensive. That extension is evident in, if not matched by, demands for participation from interests other than regulators and the regulated, and for accountability to wider constituencies.

Secondly, the categories of information to be included in registers usually extend to licence applications. The period within which information is useful for *ex ante* purposes (for example, participating in determining that application) may be short relative to its *ex post* use (such as grounding a challenge or monitoring compliance), but this is inevitable. Thirdly, registers may form part of a process which starts before individual licensing applications are made. In the planning process, for example, strategic planning policy will have been subject to a degree of public scrutiny, and individual planning applications will have been decided in that strategic context. Registers are thus a continuation of a more elaborate process. Of course, the contribution of registers in this respect is crucially dependent on

64 Although a useful label, it should not be assumed that the term 'register' reflects a level of uniformity between different systems or ease of access to information actually kept.

65 Referred to as such by the House of Lords Select Committee on the European Communities: *Freedom of Access to Information on the Environment, Session 1989–90*, First Report (HL Paper 2).

66 Particularly so as they increasingly contain only 'current' or 'recently current' information, e.g.: EPA 1990, s. 64; Waste Management Licensing Regulations 1994 (SI 1994 No. 1056), reg. 10; and WRA 1991, s. 190.

67 G. Ashworth, *The Role of Local Government in Environmental Protection* (London, 1992).

68 Royal Commission on Environmental Pollution, Fifth Report, *Air Pollution Control: An Integrated Approach* (Cmnd. 6371, London, 1976); N. Dudley, 'Changing Public Perception of Air Pollution', in H. Bradby (ed.), *Dirty Words: Writings on the History and Culture of Pollution* (London, 1990).

what that more elaborate process is, and how transparent it is—a point returned to below.

As with strategic decision-making processes, planning law provides the best known example of registers. General planning registers are in two parts: the first comprises all applications for planning permission, the second comprises a permanent record of all applications and decisions on them. The latter will include details of conditions or limitations to which development is made subject. A separate register of certain planning enforcement activity must also be maintained.[69] Taken together, these registers are an important source of information in respect of every stage of planning decision-making *after* an application is made. In addition, the fact that an application has been made will itself be subject to publicity or advertisement,[70] and this may attract attention to the registers as a source of the relevant information.

Register provisions also apply in respect of other environmental licensing decisions or processes, many of them reflecting the planning 'model'. The lack of co-ordination in established licensing controls is reflected in rather obscure provision in respect of, for example, noise and some forms of atmospheric pollution,[71] but a more systematic approach is evident in contemporary licensing systems. Here, the use of primary legislation has resulted in the development of greater consistency across different areas of environmental law. The details required to be kept under the integrated pollution control system, for example, are if anything rather wider than planning, and extend to information obtained in pursuance of the conditions on pollution authorisations, including monitoring information collected by holders of authorisations themselves.[72] An equally broad range of information in connection with water pollution controls must also be kept and made available to the public.[73] Similar details must be collated in respect of the licensing of waste management, where a register has been maintained since the

[69] TCPA 1990, ss. 69 and 188 respectively; Town and Country Planning (General Development Procedure) Order 1995 (SI 1995 No. 419), arts. 25 and 26.

[70] This will include specific notification by the applicant for planning permission of persons with an interest in land to which an application relates, and general advertisement by the relevant planning authority: TCPA 1990, s. 65; Town and Country Planning (General Development Procedure) Order 1995, above, arts. 6 and 8.

[71] Control of Noise (Measurement and Registers) Regulations 1976 (SI 1976 No. 37), the Health and Safety (Emissions into the Atmosphere) Regulations 1983 (SI 1983 No. 943, as amended), and the Control of Industrial Air Pollution (Registration of Works) Regulations 1989 (SI 1989 No. 318).

[72] EPA 1990, s. 20; Environmental Protection (Applications, Appeals and Registers) Regulations 1991 (SI 1991 No. 507). Curiously, the marginal note to s. 20 describes that section as being concerned with 'publicity'. Given that registers are not concerned with the proactive dissemination of information this is less than accurate.

[73] WRA 1991, ss. 189–91; Water Resources (Licences) Regulations 1965 (SI 1965 No. 574) and the Control of Pollution (Applications, Appeals and Registers) Regulations 1996 (SI 1996 No. 2971). Additional trade effluent registers are kept under s. 196 of the Water Industry Act 1991. The restructuring of water legislation in 1989 and 1991 provided the opportunity to modernize register provisions dating from the Control of Pollution Act 1974 (s. 41) and the Rivers (Prevention of Pollution) Act 1951 (s. 7).

introduction of new licensing powers in 1990.[74] This trend will be continued with anticipated new powers over the remediation of contaminated land.[75] As with planning consents, applications for many (but not all) environmental licences must be advertised and made subject to consultation with specified bodies.[76]

These basic rules are subject to some qualification. Not only might requirements to advertise applications be subject to exceptions,[77] but so too is inclusion of certain information in registers. The most common statutory exceptions may be made on the grounds of national security or commercial confidentiality.[78] In such cases it is the Secretary of State who finally determines whether information is in fact confidential, and his policy in such cases is to apply the exception narrowly.[79] The emergence of more elaborate and consistent rules in respect of these exceptions reinforces the similarity between different licensing systems which has already been noted.

The established formal contribution of registers to making information available in respect of environmental licensing is clear from these illustrations. Although the rules under which registers are maintained vary, perhaps a consequence of when they were written or their subject matter, a certain consistency in basic form is apparent. In fact, that consistency is becoming more marked with the passage of time. More problematic is how register provisions tie in to stages of decision-making other that tactical licensing, and in particular how they relate to strategic decision-making processes. One initial indication of the perceived importance of openness or accountability in strategic decision-making can be discerned from the fact that in a recent commentary on access to environmental information, strategic decision-making was not considered expressly at all.[80]

[74] EPA 1990, s. 64; Waste Management Licensing Regulations 1994 (SI 1994 No. 1056), reg. 10. See also the Controlled Waste (Registration of Carriers and Seizure of Vehicles) Regulations 1991 (SI 1991 No. 1624).

[75] EA 1995, s. 78R (not in force at 1 March 1998). See EA 1995, s. 57.

[76] See, e.g., EPA 1990, Sched. 1, Pt. 1 and the Environmental Protection (Applications, Appeals and Registers) Regulations 1991, regs. 5 (advertisement) and 4 (statutory consultation), in respect of integrated pollution control; and the WRA 1991, ss. 37 and 88, and Sched. 10, in respect of water. Only consultation on waste management licence applications is provided for, not their advertisement: EPA 1990, s. 36.

[77] In particular, where (before the creation of the Environment Agency) the National Rivers Authority was of the view that a proposed discharge into water was likely to have 'no appreciable effect', then it could be exempted from advertisement: WRA 1991, Sched. 10, para. 1(5). The majority of applications were exempted in this way. New Regulations are of similar effect: The Control of Pollution (Applications, Appeals and Registers) Regulations 1996, reg. 4.

[78] See, e.g., EPA 1990, ss. 21, 22 (integrated pollution control), 65 and 66 (waste management), and s. 191A of the WRA 1991 (the latter dating from only 1995: EA 1995, Sched. 22, para. 170).

[79] In a Department of the Environment Press Release on 30 January 1990, David Trippier, then Minister for the Environment, referred to a 'presumption in favour of unrestricted access'. See R. Fairley, 'Integrated Pollution Control—Public Registers and Commercial Confidentiality' (1993) 5 *Environmental Law and Management* 111–14.

[80] W. Birtles, 'Environmental Information and Audit', in A. Boyle (ed.), *Environmental Regulation and Economic Growth* (Oxford, 1994).

It has been pointed out that a relatively open hierarchy does exist to develop planning policy in local areas, and that this extends to strategic planning policy. Certain matters are effectively reserved to central government,[81] but the policy development process is predicated on a number of elaborate mechanisms both to publicise the fact and nature of decisions being made, and the promotion of involvement in that process. Those mechanisms have themselves not gone uncriticized however. Despite the aspirations to openness represented by development plans and the process of preparing them, it has been suggested that they fail to stimulate effective public participation.[82] This may qualify the extent to which they are a reliable example to other forms of environmental decision-making. Also, national planning policy continues to coexist with plans once they are approved and to be material to planning decisions, yet in neither respect is that national policy subject to the formal consultation process applying to development plans themselves. Despite these limitations, a principled commitment to transparency in some form throughout the continuum of planning decision-making is evident.

Unlike the example provided to subsequent pollution licensing systems by planning registers, the transparency of the preparation of planning policy has not been adopted in equivalent pollution policy processes. That is not to say that there is no such provision. The extension of pollution controls has seen some increased openness, and perhaps with it accountability. In setting water quality objectives, for example, the Agency is required to consult such water undertakers and other persons as the authority considers appropriate.[83] Significantly, this does not extend to the same type of wide publicity as appears in the planning process. More generous provisions relate to the preparation of environmental quality objectives, where the Agency must advertise its proposals and make plans available for public inspection.[84] But in the case of the most recently-established strategic policy framework, the new air quality strategy, an obligation to consult only arises in respect of a restricted class of professional or commercial interests.[85] Formal opportunities to participate in developing national pollution policy are therefore very different to those under planning controls. Equally, a substantive limitation remains in that it is regulators rather than the Secretary of State or local authorities who normally translate national policy to regional, sub-regional, and local level.

[81] e.g., the general content of strategic policy (itself becoming more general, see comments on the new Planning Policy Guidance Note 1 at (1996) 8 *Environmental Law and Management* 171), and particular examples of national policy (such as determination of the need for strategic transport links: *Bushell v Secretary of State for the Environment* [1981] AC 75).

[82] M. Purdue, E. Young, and J. Rowan-Robinson, *Planning Law and Procedure* (London, 1989), at 48, and P. McAuslan, *The Ideologies of Planning Law* (Oxford, 1980).

[83] WRA 1991, ss. 82–4.

[84] EPA 1990, s. 3(5) and (7).

[85] Including the Agency, 'representatives of local authorities', 'representatives of industry', and such other bodies or persons as the Secretary of State considers appropriate: EA 1995, s. 80(1).

If *ex ante* accountability in strategic decision-making is substantively confined in this way, and the role of registers is also limited, some compensation may be found in more general provisions, such as the much-vaunted Environmental Information Regulations 1992.[86] These have been described emotively as starting 'an irresistible move to confirm the right of the citizen, pressure group, company or state agency to know much more about the environment. The concept of a "right" to environmental information is crucial because it improves environmental monitoring systems, increases the quality of environmental information which is gathered, and makes much of that information available to the public'.[87] The 1992 Regulations place a general duty on prescribed bodies and persons to make information relating to the environment available to every person requesting it.[88]

These Regulations are significant, especially because they relate to such a broad range of information that their impact reaches far beyond the main forms of legal decision-making under considerations here.[89] Where they are relied upon in decision-making however, they too would seem likely to have their greatest impact after decisions have been made.

Contribution to Openness and Accountability

It is part of my argument that certain statutory decision-making processes in UK environmental law better accommodate or aspire to public law principles of openness and accountability than others: planning controls more than pollution controls, for example; and tactical decision-making processes rather than strategic. To make some assessment of accountability in practice however, it is also important to recognize the limitations of the planning example in a pollution context, as well as the limitations of the mechanisms adopted so far.

The empirical evidence gathered suggests a number of quite fundamental practical problems with enabling effective access to information, and hence to decision-making.[90] These include difficulties with the location of registers (making them inaccessible to certain groups or individuals), problems with the mechanics of storage and presentation (making information physically difficult to find), the cost of reproducing information, the comprehensibility and sufficiency of the information actually provided, and the incompleteness of information

[86] SI 1992 No. 3240, implementing the Directive on Freedom of Access to Information on the Environment (90/313/EEC, OJ L158/56, 23.6.90). More generally see Clíona Kimber, Chapter 5, below.

[87] Birtles, op. cit., at 25.

[88] Above, reg. 3(1).

[89] They have also been criticized, particularly because of an ambiguity as to whether they apply to privatized utilities: House of Lords Select Committee on the European Communities, *Freedom of Access to Information on the Environment, Session 1996–97*, First Report (HL Paper 9), noted at (1997) 9 *Environmental Law and Management* at 25–7.

[90] T. Burton, 'Access to Environmental Information—The UK Experience of Water Registers' (1989) 1 *Journal of Environmental Law* 192–208, at 194–206, and Rowan-Robinson, et al, 'Public Access to Environmental Information: A Means to What End?', above.

resulting from irregular monitoring. Further controversy has now also arisen under the Environmental Information Regulations in respect of the impediment to access presented by the practice of charging for access. This controversy is unlikely to be dispelled by recent Parliamentary proposals to reform those Regulations.[91] In consequence, interpretations of those Regulations as conferring 'rights' are open to serious doubt.

The potential utility of mechanisms to facilitate accountability in environmental decision-making other than planning is open to more general criticism, however. First, substantive criticisms of planning processes themselves include McAuslan's influential work in the 1980s. He noted, for example, the (continuing) absence of clear legal duties to secure participation in decision-making, and extended his criticism to suggest a general official ambivalence towards encouraging participation.[92] Such criticisms apply as strongly, if not more so, to systems which incompletely adopt the planning model, as contemporary pollution controls do.

Secondly, the introduction of new mechanisms for the expression of strategic policy has important consequences for who makes environmental decisions, particularly by centralizing those decisions and giving the Agency a dominant role. Despite the fact that in many ways this was an express purpose of the reorganization undertaken in 1995, given the parallels evident with planning decision-making it is interesting to note that a similar approach has never been advocated there.[93] Equally apparent is that what planning also has which pollution control lacks is a relatively transparent intermediate level between licensing decisions and national policy: development plans. Whilst the Agency is now required to establish 'regional advisory committees',[94] and the operation of these will be interesting to observe, they are clearly not intended to be a substitute for the role of county planning authorities or regional planning guidance.

This centralizing and strategic trend also removes the substance of decisions from the immediate concerns of individuals and local communities. This has been observed in planning, where those who participate in strategic decision-making could be said to represent a far narrower range of interests (and primarily commercial and professional groups) than those who respond to individual development proposals.[95] Clearly, as the importance of strategic decisions grows, influences on its preparation will change. Given that conventional mechanisms are still employed in order to enable accountability—indeed, given that such conventional forms have even broader application in contemporary environmental law now that the planning model has been widely followed—it is not clear that reformed processes of decision-making will reflect public law aspirations to openness and

[91] House of Lords Select Committee on the European Communities, above, and the Government Response (February 1997), noted at (1997) 9 *Environmental Law and Management* 126.

[92] McAuslan, op. cit., at 15 and ch. 8.

[93] Although this conclusion is subject to rare exceptions, applying to exceptional and geographically limited areas, e.g., Enterprise Zones and the operation of Urban Development Corporations.

[94] EA 1995, s. 12.

[95] Jewell, *The Law and Practice of Mineral Extraction* 1981–1991, above.

accountability. Equally, these developments will in practice place the focus of public accountability in environmental law at the end of the decision-making continuum. Not only will this reduce the prospect of local actors being influential, but it draws attention back to the real limitations in public law of introducing substantive, rather than procedural, objections at a late stage.

Economic Instruments

A greater emphasis on strategic policy-making coupled with a higher degree of administrative transparency has been presented by some as opening up the process of statutory environmental decision-making, and as helping to expose previously hidden aspects of decision-making to public scrutiny. As such, it might be thought that it will base the fragmented corpus of environmental law more solidly in principles of public law. On my analysis, however, this view must be qualified by the centralizing of influence in decision-making which is evident in the UK, and by remaining structural and practical obstacles to 'opening up' strategic decision-making to non-commercial influence. These two trends are now exacerbated by an equally powerful third: the emergence in environmental law of economic instruments to complement traditional forms of regulatory intervention.

A government commitment in the UK to so-called 'economic instruments' is not particularly new. It found most prominent expression in the 1990 White Paper, *This Common Inheritance*, where the perceived advantages of such mechanisms were explained.[96] More recently, this commitment has been amplified into a 'presumption in favour' of economic instruments.[97] The advantages of economic instruments revolve around the desirability of giving consumers and industries clear signals about the true environmental costs of using environmental resources, and thus enable those groups, rather than regulators, to decide how best to meet environmental needs. *This Common Inheritance* also contrasted economic instruments with traditional forms of 'direct' regulation, and suggested that the total economic burden of achieving a given environmental target by direct regulation is 'generally likely to be higher than if a successful market-based instrument can be devised'.[98] The presumed advantages of economic instruments were also considered in the UK in a later report of the Royal Commission on Environmental Pollution, and have given rise to a very substantial literature, particularly in North America.[99]

These policy advantages derive from the work of economists who are concerned both with the internalization of environmental costs, and the pursuit of

[96] Cm. 1200 (London, 1990), Annex A.

[97] *This Common Inheritance: Second Year Report* (Cm. 2068, London, 1992), at 35. The Labour government has a similar view.

[98] Ibid., para. A.4.

[99] Royal Commission on Environmental Pollution, Sixteenth Report, above, at ch. 8. More generally see: T. H. Tietenberg, 'Economic Instruments for Environmental Regulation', in D. Helm (ed.), *Economic Policy Towards the Environment* (Oxford, 1991); H. Latin, 'Ideal versus Real Regulatory Efficiency: Implementation of Uniform Standards and "Fine-Tuning" Regulatory Reform' (1985) 37 *Stanford Law Review* 1267–1332; and R. Stewart, 'Regulation, Innovation and Administrative Law: A Conceptual Framework' (1981) 69 *California Law Review* 1255–1377.

more 'efficient' regulation. They argue that if the true 'social' costs of environmental harm (including, for example, those associated with the loss of global natural resources to present and future generations) are taken into account in transactions between individuals, then the markets to which those transactions give rise can secure a degree of environmental protection. If the market is working efficiently, then the degree of protection which is secured will reflect a societal 'optimum': the balance between environmental and other interests for which society is willing to pay.[100] Subject to the creation of an efficient market (a large qualification), this will also lessen the need to attribute changes in environmental quality to particular regulatory mechanisms.

Such straightforward justifications have proved a powerful influence on environmental policy in the UK and elsewhere, although concrete proposals have been very slow to emerge. Conveniently, those justifications also seem entirely consistent with the general policy commitment to de-regulation referred to above,[101] and with the resolution to make polluters pay. It is important to note, however, that along with many of the other problems faced by those seeking to introduce economic instruments, they can neither entirely replace traditional forms of environmental control, nor will they necessarily achieve deregulatory ambitions.[102] At best, economic instruments will complement existing forms of regulation. Their prominence in policy discussions suggests that they will have a limited but significant role alongside modified command-and-control approaches.

Part of the problem in introducing economic instruments is the variety of meanings given to the phrase, and the classifications that have arisen. Indeed, the Organisation for Economic Co-operation and Development (OECD) noted in 1989 that 'the confusion about what to regard as economic instruments is substantial'.[103] At a basic level, 'charges' would recover the costs of the administration of environmental regulation, although this cannot achieve environmental goals unless those charges are extended to include the environmental costs of regulated activities. There are examples of charging schemes for environmental licensing processes which are expressly intended *not* to require polluters to meet the environmental costs of their activities.[104]

'Pricing' approaches as a direct method of internalizing environmental costs within commercial decision-making could also be used more extensively than they presently are in the UK. My concern is principally with statutory mechanisms,

[100] T. Swanson, 'Economic Instruments and Environmental Regulation: A Critical Introduction' (1995) 4 *Review of European Community and International Environmental Law* 287–95.

[101] See also S. Ball and S. Bell, *Environmental Law* (3rd ed., London, 1995), at 116.

[102] Jacobs, for example, argues against crude ideological construction of economic instruments as a form of deregulation: 'both taxes and regulations operate within markets, they are both state interventions designed to influence the behaviour of otherwise autonomous firms and consumers . . .': M. Jacobs, *The Green Economy* (London, 1991), at 151. See also the Sixteenth Report of the Royal Commission on Environmental Pollution, above, at para. 8.9.

[103] OECD, *Economic Instruments for Environmental Protection* (Paris, 1989), at 13.

[104] e.g., EA 1995, ss. 41–2; D. Hughes, 'The NRA Scheme of Charges in Respect of Discharges into Controlled Waters' (1991) 3 *Land Management and Environmental Law Report* 115–17.

but the role of the common law in this respect may be of some significance.[105] Statutory mechanisms themselves might include measures ranging from industrial levies and charges on producers for environmental damage (measures focusing on polluters), to environmental charges on products (which directly impact on the consumers of those products). The former type of statutory pricing has been avoided in the UK, most controversially in the case of contaminated land where suggestions of a UK 'Superfund' have been categorically rejected.[106] The landfill tax is a good example of the second type of mechanism however, along with the more established (but smaller scale) waste recycling credit scheme.[107] The best example of a charge for a product is the lower tax duty levied on lead-free petrol.[108] These instruments enable the crude attribution of a price to environmentally harmful activity, and its allocation to those responsible for that activity. Economists' reasoning suggests that that price will, in turn, inform commercial decisions as to the creation of waste and the choice of disposal option.

The use of subsidies to encourage desirable behaviour rather than pricing to discourage undesirable behaviour is an alternative approach. The economic effects of these different mechanisms are generally regarded as being similar, but criticisms that subsidies in pollution control are especially inefficient and inequitable have inhibited their frequent use.[109] Their incidence in UK environmental law in contexts other than pollution control is not uncommon however, notably in agriculture, conservation, and forestry.[110] At the level of principle there is an important distinction between pricing and subsidies, in that a subsidy is a payment to give something up (it starts with a polluter's or landowner's rights), whereas pricing requires a payment to be made for the *use* of a resource.[111] This is one reason for criticisms of the weaknesses of current UK approaches in areas of law where subsidies predominate,[112] and begins to suggest some of the difficulties

[105] The connection between common law and 'pricing' is referred to by Jenny Steele in Chapter 4, below.

[106] In the Committee Stage of what became the EA 1995, the then Minister for the Environment and Countryside, Robert Atkins, said that 'we [the Government] have made it clear in our discussion in the consultation documents of how we intend to resolve problems of contaminated land that we would not go down the same route as the United States': *Official Report, Standing Committee B*, col. 348 (23 May 1995).

[107] Finance Act 1996, ss. 39–71, Landfill Tax Regulations 1996 (SI 1996 No. 1527, see (1996) 8 *Environmental Law and Management* 195); EPA 1990, s. 52, Environmental Protection (Waste Recycling Payments) Regulations 1992 (SI 1992 No. 462, as amended, see (1995) 7 *Environmental Law and Management* 90).

[108] Hydrocarbon Oil Duties Act 1979, s. 13A, inserted by the Finance Act 1987, s. 1.

[109] This view is recorded in *This Common Inheritance*, above, at para. A.29.

[110] e.g., Nitrate Sensitive Areas Regulations 1994 (SI 1994 No. 1729, as amended); the Set Aside Regulations 1988 (SI 1988 No. 1352, as amended); and on forestry generally see C. Reid, 'Environmental Regulation through Economic Instruments: The Example of Forestry' (1996) 8 *Environmental Law and Management* 58–64.

[111] J. Krier, 'The Pollution Problem and Legal Institutions: A Conceptual Overview' (1971) 18 *UCLA Law Review* 429–77, at 468.

[112] e.g., S. Ball, 'Reforming the Law of Habitat Protection', in C. Rodgers (ed.), *Nature Conservation and Countryside Law* (Cardiff, 1996).

of economic instruments in environmental law when viewed from a public law perspective. The fact that the choice between different types of economic instrument in itself reveals policy decisions in respect of the distribution of environmental interests is informative in the context of arguments favouring their use which rely on conventional views of economic rationality alone.

The remaining major grouping of economic instruments relates to those which seek to privatize all common resources, described as 'the most simple-minded of all simple approaches'.[113] An important reason for the introduction of economic instruments is to achieve a better indication of the 'true costs' of environmentally harmful behaviour: and unowned resources are argued to be over-exploited, such that they bear the external costs. In this way, the argument is that transferring those resources into private ownership should mean that those costs are taken into account in future. An illustration of this approach would be the creation of marketable or tradeable permits to pollute, and some such permitting schemes are now in operation.[114] Despite early indications that a similar approach might operate in the UK, no firm proposals have yet emerged.[115]

What is clear from this brief survey is that statements of a policy in favour of economic instruments have not had the radical impact that may have been anticipated. This is, firstly, because the economic controversies endure. Economists themselves are divided, for example, on such matters as the quantification of environmental costs (a precursor to the efficient operation of many instruments); the likely distributive effects of instruments, and especially taxes and charges, where lower income groups may bear a disproportionately high tax burden, for example; and the impact of economic instruments on industrial competitiveness.[116]

Secondly, the relationship between economic instruments and traditional statutory decision-making processes is also complex. On one view, by giving the responsibility for choosing the best way to control environmental costs to those generating them, economic instruments clearly obviate some of the need for extensive regulatory oversight and intervention on the command-and-control model. Indeed, the reliance they place on polluters to resolve the worst pollution in the most economically efficient manner is often presented as a key advantage of economic instruments over traditional instruments. It is equally true however that the need for institutional regulators will not disappear with the advent of new mechanisms, but will merely change. For example, judgements as to the maximum

[113] Swanson, op. cit., at 289.

[114] Notably in California: P. Park, 'The Marketable Permit Programme in California' (1996) 8 *Environmental Law and Management* 26–9.

[115] The dichotomy between aspiration and reality becomes very obvious in comparing the Department of the Environment's *The Potential Role of Market Mechanisms in the Control of Acid Rain* (London, 1992) with the *United Kingdom Air Quality Strategy* (London, 1996).

[116] Swanson, op. cit., provides an accessible introduction to many of these issues. See also OECD, *The Distributive Effects of Economic Instruments for Environmental Policy* (Paris, 1994) and European Foundation for the Improvement of Living and Working Conditions, *Environmental Taxes and Charges: National Experiences and Plans* (Dublin, 1996).

level of acceptable pollution will still need to be made, relating to the size of the market in tradeable permits for example. Such judgements bear a striking similarity to those necessary to formulate environmental quality objectives, the controversies of which have already been discussed. Permit trading itself would also have to be monitored, and compliance with emission limits ensured. However, despite the relative lack of progress towards actually introducing economic instruments in the UK, it is clear that the institutional modifications needed to ground this centralized, strategic role for regulators are in fact incrementally being made. Their reliance on the strategic context already described will be marked.

Of more central interest here is what implications economic instruments will have in public law terms. As a starting point, and as has been observed elsewhere, one consequence of their introduction is a reduction in the formal decision-making procedures required of agencies and (in consequence) of the scope of judicial review: 'even patchwork modification of the existing system would . . . involve more informal decision making procedures and a likely increase in the scope of agency discretion'.[117] It has already been argued that formal decision-making procedures are themselves undergoing change, and in particular that the emphasis is shifting from the tactical to the strategic. Economic instruments therefore seem likely to compound that trend. The particular prospect they present for greater reliance on polluters themselves in defining environmental goals represents a further move away from the realization of public law values in decision-making processes.

There also remain many obstacles to the effective operation of alternative instruments, even in economic terms. These include the absence, or uneven availability, of information on which to make decisions, as well as doubts about the supposed economic rationality of individuals. An exhaustive critique would not be appropriate here. It can be said, however, that whilst the opaqueness of economic decision-making may be no more than the opaqueness of current processes of regulatory decision-making, it is a different sort of opaqueness. It is one with which public law is unfamiliar. However, the centralizing and institutionalizing trends identified above will continue, and with them the prospect of changes in the opportunity to monitor or have access to processes of decision-making themselves.

3. Consequences and Conclusions

Certain key features of contemporary environmental decision-making under statute and their development have been identified in this chapter. This gives some impression of the balance that is now being struck between substantive environmental

[117] Stewart, op. cit., at 1375–6.

concern, and matters of legal process, in other words, how the law is coming to provide for decisions to be made which have environmental implications. The law is no less complex or disparate in consequence, but some sense of continuity or structure from a public law point of view does emerge. In particular, it does at least become more possible to assess the prospects for contemporary environmental decision-making processes, inchoate as they are, by reference to the longstanding, general principles of openness and accountability. Those principles remain central to public law in the UK, and their influence must therefore be discernible in contemporary environmental law if it is to provide decisions which are both substantively and procedurally justifiable. The application of this framework of assessment to UK environmental law enables some important features of environmental decision-making to be crystallized.

Despite their continuing prominence, widespread criticism of traditional forms of command-and-control environmental regulation have prompted major reforms. Those reforms have served to illustrate the limitations of what have, with experience, emerged to be relatively crude approaches to addressing environmental problems, without genuinely transcending them. The limitations of integrated pollution controls show this well, in particular by demonstrating the irreducibly political character of environmental decision-making. Of course, reality dictates that pollution controls must allow for pollution to be permitted. However, this also means that certain types of environmental problems (such as pollution) have been shown to be more likely to prompt an institutional solution on command-and-control lines than others (such as conservation). Further, that because of the limitations of integration within these organizational solutions, other environmental interests become merely a further consideration within decision-making processes. The process orientation here is such that there is no reasonable prospect of environmental interests being prioritized. The status of environmental factors in the land use planning process as one further 'material consideration' amongst others is a clear illustration of this.

In the sense that controls over pollution will contribute to a general environmental improvement, the conclusion immediately above may undervalue their contribution to substantive environmental protection. But it also makes those institutional solutions and the processes which they provide for decision-making the focus of public lawyers' concern. In this regard, what has also been suggested is that those processes are now increasingly likely to incorporate self-regulatory ideas, and thus to place greater reliance on polluters to address pollution themselves. This change derives partly from recognition of the weaknesses of formalized environmental standards, but it also suggests a regression from the incorporation of public law principles of accountability in environmental decision-making. This is rather ironic, given that one weakness of the standards-based approach was its contribution to obscuring the political character of environmental decisions, through their apparently apolitical nature. The decline in such approaches might therefore have been expected to lead to an improvement in accountability in decision-making. Experience with self-regulation in other contexts would suggest that this is unlikely to be the case.

Formalized standards, where they do continue to have a high profile, are now also beginning to contribute to a more explicit strategic framework within which 'environmental management systems' will operate. Even where (currently voluntary) management systems are not adopted by polluters, the preponderance of recent policy indicates the new importance of related risk assessment processes within statutory decision-making processes. Subject to that strategic framework, to the criteria defining the management system or risk assessment process itself, and to any prescriptions set out in the exercise of a regulator's discretion, those systems are likely to contribute to a process of internalizing decision-making within agencies and within commercial organizations. This trend is likely to be compounded by further reliance on innovative economic instruments. There is at present no indication (in the UK at least) that the superimposition of those systems on an otherwise familiar process of decision-making has prompted any consideration of whether they represent the 'more modern democratic institutions' which public law commentators are seeking. On my analysis they certainly do not.

The implications of the growth in strategic decision-making for both accountability and for the sorts of solutions statute is able to provide for environmental problems are both practical and institutional. On a practical level it is clearly the case that strategic decision-making is not immediately susceptible to the same level of participation, or the same sort of *ex ante* accountability, as tactical decision-making. This would be so even if the same provision was being made in respect of processes for formulating strategic environmental policy as appears in respect of land use planning at the strategic level. As I have indicated, however, new environmental laws do not even provide for this. It is true, of course, that strategic decisions are intended to pursue collective solutions in a way in which tactical decisions are not, and that the sort of accountability intended might therefore be rather different, or be expected to have a different impact. But this is not an argument against the desirability of accountability in itself.

On an institutional level, on present evidence it can be observed that *ex ante* accountability will generally be most focused on a confined range of interests, and that this can be expected to influence the content of pollution policy directly.[118] This is indicated by the combined effects of changing provision for strategic decision-making and the practical limitations of mechanisms orientated towards access to information. Interests outside that range will, for both practical and substantive reasons, have to be content with a continuing reliance on

[118] A prominent recent illustration is the 'informal' consultation undertaken in respect of the Department of Environment working paper, *Contaminated Land* (20 February 1996), with a selected group of 'representatives from a number of bodies having an interest' in the contaminated land provisions of the Environment Act 1995. That paper has provided the basis for draft statutory guidance which will define the impact of those provisions in key respects: *Consultation on Draft Statutory Guidance on Contaminated Land*, above.

ex post mechanisms of accountability. This reinforces the predominance of *ex post* accountability in UK environmental decision-making processes under statute, despite the limitations which have prompted public lawyers' expressions of strong concern.

Putative improvements in administrative transparency and the growth of strategic decision-making have important implications for shifting the locus of decision-making in UK environmental law. The new framework, whilst focusing public accountability towards the later end of the decision-making continuum, will also guide the establishment of economic instruments. Many of these trends have been presented elsewhere as both a democratizing of environmental law and more economically efficient. However, it is suggested here that, in reality, key environmental decisions will become less open, and that key environmental decision-makers will become less accountable.

4

Assessing the Past: Tort Law and Environmental Risk

JENNY STEELE

Conventionally, aspects of tort law are understood to have provided an early legal mechanism of protection for the environment.[1] A number of historical studies have assessed the extent of tort's impact in this respect, to generally critical effect.[2] By contrast, current approaches to environmental law rightly emphasize the need for more effective methods of prospective regulation, and where there is interest in civil liability this is sometimes, though not always, explained by the potential prospective benefits of liability as a deterrent or 'pricing' system.[3] Alternatively, schemes of *ex post* liability have also been proposed in order to meet the costs of remedying existing damage.

In contrast to these developments in new forms of environmental liability, this chapter will focus attention not on new liability variants, but on the common law of tort itself, and in particular on some efforts to use tort law in a reassessment of past activities.[4] The aim is not to suggest that tort ought to play any larger role in environmental law, since it is accepted that the common law suffers from many major shortcomings in this respect. In any event, UK tort law has not made great strides towards the incorporation of harm to the environment as a recognizable head of damage.[5] The 'environmental damage' referred to in the present chapter is therefore limited, and covers only damage to interests traditionally recognized by tort law. The intention is that an examination of challenges brought through tort law by affected individuals and groups, against a background which

[1] For example, *Pride of Derby v British Celanese* [1953] 1 All ER 179, 204 (Lord Denning).

[2] See for example J. P. S. McLaren, 'Nuisance Law and the Industrial Revolution—Some Lessons From Social History' (1983) 3 *OJLS* 155–221; J. F. Brenner, 'Nuisance Law and the Industrial Revolution' (1974) 3 *Journal of Legal Studies* 403–33; D. N. Dewees, 'The Efficiency of the Common Law: Sulphur Dioxide Emissions in Sudbury' (1992) 42 *University of Toronto Law Journal* 1–21.

[3] A 'pricing' system, by attaching costs to an activity without prohibiting it, would in effect be designed to deter to a particular level. That level might be predetermined by a regulatory authority; or it might be expected to emerge through the process of market exchange.

[4] See 'Nuisance, the Pale Green Tort' (in J. Conaghan and W. Mansell, *The Wrongs of Tort*, London, 1993), dealing with efforts to use tort prospectively as a means of challenging decisions relating, for example, to land use. The tort of nuisance is also capable of applying to cases of past damage, as does negligence, but in a nuisance action the questions are (in the author's view) conceived of slightly differently: J. Steele, 'Private Law and the Environment: Nuisance in Context' (1995) 15 *Legal Studies* 236–59.

[5] For analysis of attempts within various jurisdictions to make such damage actionable in tort law or in other liability schemes, see the contributions to P. Wetterstein (ed.), *Harm to the Environment* (Oxford, 1997).

has been dominated by prospective control of risk, will help raise questions which are of more general application to current environmental law developments, but which are not always explicit.

As a first step, it is important to introduce the general connections between tort law, and issues concerning prospective forms of regulation and control, in a preliminary way. Unfortunately, there is no very simple route to dividing tort as a retrospective judgment, from tort as a part of law's regulatory structure. The dual nature of tort law in this respect, and some of the problems with it, will be explored in the first section of this chapter. In the second section, some developments in regulatory thinking will be outlined. Important recent developments in regulation are examined in several chapters of this book.[6] Here, it is emphasized that such developments have, in recent years, reflected a range of theoretical approaches. Such approaches have observed and to some extent sought to explain systematically the failures of traditional, interventionist styles of regulation, and to explore alternatives, as captured for example in the notions of 'self-organization',[7] or of 'responsive regulation'.[8] Some relevant conceptual aspects of these developments are summarized, and it is suggested that the general consensus for regulatory change conceals some critical elements of disagreement in diagnosing current shortcomings and proposing a way forward.

Finally, the chapter will return to the significance of recent tort actions in reassessing risks which have been subject to regulatory control. The final section will explore some of the reasons why such cases emerge, and their distinctive character compared with earlier generations of environmental tort claims. Despite the very limited success experienced by the plaintiffs in these cases, it is explained that they raise issues relating to the evaluation of risk which are potentially of more general importance for environmental law.

1. Tort Law: Prospective and Retrospective Elements

Over the years, tort law has been understood in a variety of ways. For example, it has been attributed with a number of instrumental applications, often in opposition to the claim that it represents a morally justifiable *ex post* attribution of responsibility. These instrumental applications are of particular interest here since environmental law is concerned with controlling, managing, or reducing environmental harm.

Tort law has perhaps had distinctive 'instrumental' roles in the protection of rights such as property rights,[9] and the promotion of productive exchange through

[6] Specifically, Chapters 1, 2, and 3 above.

[7] See G. Teubner, L. Farmer, and D. Murphy (eds.), *Environmental Law and Ecological Responsibility: The Concept and Practice of Ecological Self-Organization* (Chichester, 1994).

[8] I. Ayres and J. Braithwaite, *Responsive Regulation* (Oxford, 1992).

[9] See generally P. Cane, *Tort Law and Economic Interests* (2nd ed., Oxford, 1996), especially ch. 10, 'The Province and Aims of Tort Law'.

acting as a 'pricing' mechanism.[10] Although these are distinctively associated with private law, tort is also not entirely separable from other regulatory exercises in prospective control. Tort assesses damaging behaviour and subjects it to 'standards' of (for example) reasonableness. By attempting to define certain required standards of behaviour, even retrospectively, it no doubt also pursues prospective effects, and seeks to prevent damage to some extent. Beyond this however, tort law has also had a stronger 'purposive' role in alleviating the effects of damage, in that it intervenes in order to control or distribute the damage which results from risky activities.

The relationship between these last two roles is important, but not straightforward. The two components, which could be called 'deterrence' and 'distribution', are so closely intertwined in many tort decisions, that they are hard to unravel. It may therefore be useful to provide examples which highlight the existence of each component. So, it could be said that the development of compensation or insurance systems of one sort or another has typically led to an emphasis on the loss distribution element in this distinction, perhaps at the expense of deterrence.[11] The action for breach of a statutory duty on the other hand exemplifies how the two could, in principle,[12] be regarded as compatible: the relevant statute imposes a duty to act in a particular way (prohibition/deterrence); and tort provides compensation for harm done if the duty is breached.[13]

There are various obstacles to a neat general explanation of the role of tort law along these lines. For example, failures to abide by legally-established, prospective standards constitute only a small part of the range of likely human causes of injury or damage in modern life. Damage may also result where there are no authoritative standards in place, and in some such cases tort law may apply an *ex post* judgment of unreasonableness.

For present purposes however, there is a more significant problem for any effort to describe tort law as having compatible roles in deterrence and distribution. Even though particular cases of damage may be the result of specific instances of carelessness, many such adverse outcomes can nevertheless be described as the realization of risks, and thus as part of the predictable 'side-effects' of a

[10] B. Markesinis and S. Deakin, *Tort Law* (3rd ed., Oxford, 1994), at 22. Such an approach would give tort a distinctive role in terms of the 'pricing' of environmental 'goods', where the pricing function is particularly concerned to overcome the barriers to exchange. In general, the 'pricing' of environmental goods is linked to the creation of market behaviour, where the market for a particular good did not otherwise exist.

[11] There have also been attempts to deal with this division, and to introduce deterrence elements into insurance solutions. Trebilcock, for example, has argued against 'the untenable proposition that compensating for accidents is better than preventing them': M. Trebilcock, 'Incentive Issues in the Design of "No-Fault" Compensation Schemes' (1989) 39 *University of Toronto Law Journal* 19–54.

[12] 'In principle' because the intentions of the legislature are rarely as clear as this account would imply: see generally K. Stanton, *Breach of Statutory Duty in Tort* (London, 1986).

[13] Such actions have been extensively used for example in the UK by claimants whose injuries arise from exposure to asbestos in regulated industries: W. Felstiner and S. Dingwall, *Asbestos Litigation in the United Kingdom—An Interim Report* (Oxford: Centre for Socio-Legal Studies, 1988).

relevant activity. This is partly because damage may result even where all parties are appropriately 'careful'. But also, human fallibility itself, even to the point of carelessness, can be predicted as a matter of probabilities. For both of these reasons, we know (approximately, but for sure) that a certain number of deaths and injuries will follow from many familiar activities. Thus the relationship between 'safety-assuring' standards, and mechanisms to alleviate damage, is in many instances an awkward one, because it is apparent that safety is not as such 'assured'.

These observations are certainly not new, and negligence liability as it affects road traffic provides a familiar illustration of the ambiguities involved. Here, there is an accepted or perhaps desired activity (road transport), which gives rise to behaviour and thus damage which is humanly avoidable (there is room to promote greater care on the part of road-users), but which is also in another sense inevitable once the activity is accepted (we know that even the best drivers commit errors; and we know that some less careful drivers will inevitably have access to the roads). The legal response to road traffic and the risk of harm in the form of civil liability regimes is recognised as ambivalent in the following ways.[14]

On the one hand, there is an attempt to deal with the known effects of road traffic. For this purpose, a system of compulsory third party insurance is in place which shields the immediate perpetrator from personal loss in the event of an accident, and ensures that funds are available to compensate the victim. Clearly, it is considered important that victims should be compensated. On the other hand, the standard of liability continues to be a negligence standard. Although it has again been pointed out that this standard cannot be taken to be a direct moral judgment as to the culpability of the particular defendant (there is no allowance made for example for lack of experience), this nevertheless leaves some victims to insure themselves, and will ultimately (through the rules of contributory negligence, for example, as well as the optional nature of first party personal injury insurance) leave some victims uncompensated.

Reciprocity, Risk, and Welfare

The 'side-effects' of road traffic are relatively predictable, and the law of tort (supported by liability insurance) is largely concerned with distributing those side-effects at a cost which is also relatively calculable. This situation can be described in terms of 'risk' and 'risk distribution'. In this context, the relevant risks can be seen as involving a significant degree of reciprocity,[15] and the management

[14] See generally P. Cane, *Atiyah's Accidents, Compensation and the Law* (5th ed., London, 1993).

[15] The road traffic example is sometimes seen as a special or at least a distinctive case, because it concerns 'reciprocal' risks and benefits, or an essentially 'collaborative' enterprise, where mutual participation brings 'common gains': see for example J. Finnis, *Natural Law and Natural Rights* (Oxford, 1980), at 180–1. Other writers tend to generalize from the road traffic example, or treat it as a key example of something broader. The argument below queries this generalization, at least in respect of environmental harm; and also queries whether the central case itself is as uncontroversial as it may appear.

of risk can be seen in terms of common benefit or welfare. In addition, the risks themselves have a positive as well as a negative aspect. The risk-creating activity is regarded as of mutual benefit, and only when the likely effects of the activity are understood and managed is it possible to achieve that benefit without unreasonable cost for some unlucky individuals. Arguably then, liability insurance has an important function in legitimating such risks.

If this is correct, then tort is connected with a much broader issue concerning the management and control of risks in the interests of achieving common welfare. Key features of the road traffic example include the notion of reciprocal risks; the notion of mutuality of benefit; and the idea that the overall effect—weighing the advantages against the (managed) risk—is for the common benefit. An important point of contact between controversies in tort, and controversies in regulation, can therefore be introduced, turning on these issues of welfare and reciprocity. Arguably, many forms of regulation (including tort in its distributive guise) have aimed to enhance welfare and social solidarity, whilst also depending to some extent on the possibility of consensus as to the applicable regulatory goal.

Problems With Environmental Damage: Risk Evaluation and Divided Interests

The welfare-oriented, reformist approach to tort law as a means of distributing the costs of accidents includes an appeal to mutual benefits and burdens. This approach is perhaps most powerfully represented by Atiyah's *Accidents, Compensation and the Law*.[16] Road traffic accidents are a central case for such approaches, but the point is typically generalized to a much broader range of risks. However, various features of environmental damage in particular can be picked out which would make a similar analysis problematic. If we seek to apply this approach to contemporary cases of environmental damage, then such appeals may be muted in two ways.

First, the very escalation in awareness of environmental damage and environmental risk would perhaps undermine claims to consensus in the evaluation of relevant risks. Critical debate as to the environmental effects of existing ways of living is at least more familiar, and probably more widespread, than at any previous time. The significance of this is itself disputed, of course. For example, it is unclear how far people 'really' value environmental goods, as opposed to other aspects of welfare or even convenience, and all attempts to evaluate responses

[16] Now in its fifth edition (op. cit.), but first published in 1970. William Twining has said that this classic text 'could plausibly be interpreted as a book about "the problem of compensation for accidents" viewed from the standpoint of a mildly Fabian law-reformer, who supports the welfare state in a mixed economy': W. Twining, 'Reflections on Law in Context', in P. Cane and J. Stapleton (eds.), *Essays for Patrick Atiyah* (Oxford, 1991).

to this issue have (not surprisingly) been deeply controversial.[17] In Chapter 2 above, David Robinson highlights some attempts to survey attitudes according to stated beliefs on the one hand, and actual behaviour on the other. This research illustrates an often striking difference between these two criteria for evaluation.

Despite these controversies, such developments may be illustrated even if we consider the classic case of reciprocal risks offered above, road traffic. Even this case may not be beyond question after all. In the past, it has been argued that everybody could be said to benefit from road traffic—most travel by bus, if not by car, and all benefit from the transport of goods.[18] Today, even this sense of mutual benefit from beneficial risk could be described as questionable in terms of the evaluation of the risks concerned, and of judgment as to whether current uses of road transport are appropriate. There is no indication of a change in habits among the population as a whole, but at the same time, transport and retail policy certainly fall into the recognized categories of environmental debate.

However, a second reason why appeals to mutual benefits and burdens might be problematic is that interests, as well as evaluations, are perhaps also regarded as increasingly fragmented. Though such trends can only be described in the most tentative terms, such a development would not be surprising in the light of various factors including the undermining of crucial welfare guarantees in the last one or two decades. Arguably, privatization in general, and especially privatization in traditional 'welfare' functions, brings an emphasis on individual responsibility, and makes a sense of divided interests almost inevitable.[19]

Tort law reform proposals can be used to illustrate this broad suggestion in a modest way. The new version of Patrick Atiyah's agenda for replacing tort law in respect of personal injuries commends first party insurance as the best solution.[20]

[17] In the United States, 'contingent valuation methodology surveys' have been proposed, which 'seek to measure the economic non-use value that individuals place on the environment by asking them how much they would pay to preserve a given natural resource from injury': R. B. Stewart, 'Liability for Natural Resource Injury: Beyond Tort', in R. L. Revesz and R. B. Stewart (eds.), *Analyzing Superfund* (Washington, 1995); Anonymous Note, 'Ask a Silly Question . . . Contingent Valuation of Natural Resource Damage' (1992) 105 *Harvard Law Review* 1981–2000. In the UK, the Countryside Commission's 1997 Report, 'Public Attitudes to the Countryside' (CCP 481) suggested that the public's views on the countryside 'are often wildly contradictory' (Countryside Commission Press Release 97/20, 'Schizophrenia Hits Country Views'). For example, ninety-one percent of visitors to national parks arrive by car, but seventy percent of people questioned say that driving to and around the countryside is likely to damage it. A similar pattern of responses affected (for example) the impact of home-building, and the wish to live in the countryside. The Report itself has been criticized (notably by the Ramblers' Association) for undermining arguments over access to the countryside by urban populations, and for asking questions which were virtually certain to produce conflicting responses.

[18] P. Atiyah, 'Negligence and Economic Loss' (1967) 83 *LQR* 248–96, at 272.

[19] A related but slightly different link is provided in P. Atiyah, 'Personal Injuries in the Twenty First Century: Thinking the Unthinkable', in P. Birks (ed.), *Wrongs and Remedies in the Twenty-First Century* (Oxford, 1996). There, the notion of individual culpability to be found in tort law is said to appeal to certain styles of right-wing thought at a policy level (thus explaining the persistence of tort law despite its shortcomings), rather than being described as a potential response on the part of the public to privatization.

[20] Ibid.

This would clearly separate the job of distributing the effects of risk from the job of deterrence, and it would also perhaps make the assessment of risk a private matter, placing a welfare function in the relationship between insurance company, and insured. The aim of such reforms would be to avoid complex and costly administrative systems and simultaneously to improve on the currently patchy availability of compensation.

It has been argued in response that, in (apparent) contrast to third party insurance schemes underpinned by legal liability, such reforms would also allow the accident-creating sector to avoid the costs of compensation, whilst groups who are vulnerable to the effects of accidents (for example, consumers) would be liable to bear these costs, and would take primary responsibility for doing so.[21] This set of counter-arguments clearly depends on a perception of divided interests, and refuses to regard such costs as being suffered simply in common. Accidents and compensation are not regarded as a matter of common benefits and burdens. They involve things done by one set of parties, to another. As such, this sort of thinking tends to drift towards regarding tort as a matter of judgment between two parties. Nevertheless, accidents are not entirely regarded as a matter between individual victims, and individual wrongdoers. There is an explicit reference to risk-creating, and risk-bearing, sectors or groups.

This combination of features makes the latter approach difficult to categorize as a matter of 'corrective' or 'distributive' justice. This is of some interest, because aspects of the approach may be especially pertinent in respect of environmental law, where the assessment, planning and control of risk is so central, and where the core risk-creating sector may be increasingly perceived as distinct from the groups most likely to suffer any harm which results. This is not to say that there is in fact a lack of dependence on risk-creating activities. Indeed, exactly the opposite may be argued to be the case. The point is rather that some contemporary environmental risks are diffuse in their effects, and may therefore affect a range of people whose dependence is less direct.[22] The perception of divided interests is likely to be intensified if the processes of environmental decision-making are regarded as remote from the public in general, or as favouring the interests or outlook of any particular group. This approach therefore provides further support for the argument encountered (in different forms) in Chapters 2 and 3 above, that consensus about environmental regulation is potentially threatened by those

[21] J. Stapleton, 'Tort, Insurance and Ideology' (1995) 58 *MLR* 820–43. It might be noted that the success of this argument, despite its presentation as concerned with an ideological vantage-point, does not only depend on one's conceptual approach, but also on an empirical issue concerning distribution. That is to say, the argument perhaps understates the distributive effect of liability insurance, since the burdens of tort liability do not often stay with defendants, but may themselves be widely distributed through insurance, pricing, or reduced profits. The empirical issue therefore concerns the relative distributive effects of first party and third party insurance.

[22] See the comments in section 3 below, concerning the divisions between the plaintiffs and the source of the risk in the case of many of the most recent cases of environmental damage brought in tort law.

contemporary developments which seek to take regulatory decisions closer to the heart of the risk-creating sectors.[23] In the next section, the theoretical underpinnings of some such developments are explored, with a view to considering whether the possibility of such divisions—in evaluation and interest—is given appropriate weight within these approaches.

To summarize, the question of mutual welfare as against divided interests has been a live issue in recent tort law controversies, and has been linked to a conceptual debate about the functions and philosophical structure of the subject. In terms of environmental law more broadly, the same issues might be expected to be even more central, since this is an area where there are divisions in the evaluation of risks, and a significant lack of reciprocity in the creation of those risks. However, the problems may be less clearly articulated where the main concern is one of effectiveness. In the effort to achieve 'improvement' (whether in standards, or in compliance), are issues of total general welfare treated as predominant and even unproblematic, despite the real possibility of divisions in evaluation of, and influence over, risks? This is a particular way of asking the broader question, whether 'effectiveness' of technique has become central in environmental law, at the expense of debate over goals in environmental law. In the three approaches explored below, there are fundamental differences revealed by addressing this question, despite what they seem to have in common in terms of techniques for achieving effective regulation.

2. Prospective Approaches: Locating Regulatory Goals

Many environmental lawyers have a well-established sense of the shortcomings of historical and existing methods of regulation, and of the need for effective innovations. As such, they provide a receptive audience for new approaches to regulation, and might fit naturally into the category of 'practical people who are concerned with outcomes',[24] described by Ayres and Braithwaite. There is a widespread recognition that the relationship between regulatory intervention and private ordering is a complex one, and (equally) a willingness to develop new methods of regulation in order to adapt to the intricacies of that relationship. A number of recent approaches have indeed shared a concern to transform discussions of regulation, and in particular to overcome perceived difficulties of effectiveness associated with traditional methods,[25] which are frequently regarded as ignoring the complexities of regulatory relationships. The intention here—as

[23] In Chapter 2, David Robinson expresses these concerns in terms of a 'compromise' in the Rule of Law, and for this reason regards as most promising those solutions which broaden participation to a variety of 'stakeholders'. In Chapter 3, Tim Jewell assesses similar developments through reference to concepts of 'accountability' and 'transparency'.

[24] Ayres and Braithwaite, op. cit., at 3.

[25] In general, such 'traditional' methods are associated with 'command-and-control': the application of externally-derived standards to regulated parties, backed by systems of enforcement.

explained above—is to dig beneath the practical concern with outcomes, and to locate some of the concerns identified initially through the analysis of the role of tort law in section 1.

Many recent approaches suggest that closer involvement with the regulated sector or party is an important element in achieving improvement. The obvious problem with this is that in a variety of ways, the outlook of the regulated party may become dominant. The location of decision-making is also (potentially) an important element in the perceived legitimacy of decision-making, since different social groups—and especially those who ultimately suffer the effects of risk—may not understand 'improvements' in terms of mutual benefits and burdens. Such improvements, though urgently needed, may therefore not be enough.

This section briefly considers three contemporary approaches to environmental decision-making. These are (respectively) concerned with strategies of 'self-organization'; of 'responsive regulation'; and of a category of 'sub-politics' in which law plays a part. These approaches have in common a broad belief that the 'real business' of decision-making as it affects outcomes (specifically, environmental outcomes) has, despite years of regulation, continued to go on not in the traditional political sphere, but in what may be described as the 'private' spheres of industry, commerce, or science. As such, attempts at regulation will continue to be ineffective unless they are more intimately associated with these spheres. However, the three approaches vary widely in their approach to the roles of the public, of political debate, and of the setting of regulatory goals in achieving this broad shift. The recognition of a 'critical' element in perceptions of risk might be seen as increasing with each of the variants described, though all three make some appeal to 'participation'. The intention is not to pick out any one of the three as 'correct', but to indicate some of the background issues which are important to understanding why recent environmental tort cases might be seen, despite their limited contribution to environmental protection, as conceptually significant.

The main point here is as follows. Tort developments, as suggested in section 1 above, indicate the existence of factors which undermine the sense of mutuality and reciprocity in risks and benefits. To some extent, this is illustrated by the persistence (or possibly resurgence) of notions of culpability and responsibility. In the light of this, how far do regulatory approaches suggest that centralized, authoritative statements of welfare goals and desired (or required) outcomes need to be replaced along with the traditional methods of enforcement? Are they purely involved with the attainment of improvement in the pursuit of such goals, or do they instead suggest some other process for determining what the goals of environmental regulation—rather than the techniques for attaining them—should be?[26]

[26] See also the discussion by Tim Jewell, in Chapter 3 above, of 'The Importance of Environmental Standards'.

Self-Organization

Gunther Teubner has recently advanced a positive agenda for environmental liability in particular,[27] and this aspect of his work is therefore familiar to many environmental lawyers. He proposes a shift away from an 'actor' perspective in allocating liability for environmental damage, and the development of collective forms of liability which could stimulate decision-making within broader 'networks of ecological risks'. The underlying critique of 'substantive' or 'material' law[28] is much broader, however, and these proposals for environmental liability represent one aspect of a much more general programme of 'reflexive law'. An attempt will therefore be made here to pick out some selected aspects of the general conceptual background, of particular interest given the emphases outlined above.

In common with many environmental lawyers, Teubner has suggested that the imposition of crude external 'standards' is likely to be an ineffective method of regulation. His analysis of the reasons for such ineffectiveness is deeply rooted in sociological theory,[29] and postulates the (qualified) autonomy of social subsystems including both law, and the various 'regulated' systems.[30] This autonomy causes failures of communication which cannot be overcome by traditional styles of regulation. The prognosis of ineffectiveness is, as suggested above, a familiar one in environmental law, though this explanation for it is distinctive.

However, the critique of such forms of law is not limited to doubts about effectiveness, but is also concerned with the suggested adverse social impact of the development and multiplication of interventions by substantive law, including a potential (and fruitless) disruption in the functioning of regulated 'systems'. In common with a number of writers, Teubner has described legalization, or 'juridification', as a malign—or even ugly—concept.[31] This notion of 'juridification' he traces to the idea of 'colonization of the lifeworld' developed by Habermas,[32]

[27] G. Teubner, 'The Invisible Cupola: From Causal to Collective Attribution in Ecological Liability', in Teubner, Farmer, and Murphy, op. cit. This brings into the environmental context the programme of 'reflexive law' proposed more generally: see for example G. Teubner, *Law as an Autopoietic System* (Oxford, 1993), ch. 7.

[28] 'Material' attributes of modern law are contrasted with 'formal' attributes: see for example G. Teubner, 'Juridification—Concepts, Aspects, Limits, Solutions', in Teubner (ed.), *Juridification of Social Spheres* (Berlin, 1987). The more familiar expression is perhaps 'substantive', but 'material' and 'substantive' appear to be used interchangeably: indeed, the English translation of Weber to which Teubner refers uses the word 'substantive' (M. Weber, *Economy and Society* (G. Roth and R. Whittle (eds.), California, 1978)). I am grateful to Ben Pontin for clarifying this.

[29] Teubner's work is closely related to that of Niklas Luhmann: see for example N. Luhmann, *A Sociological Theory of Law* (London, 1985). Luhmann's work is discussed in relation to public law scholarship in M. Loughlin, *Public Law and Political Theory* (Oxford, 1992), at 250–9.

[30] Teubner explains that '[t]he implementation strategy will ultimately run aground on the internal dynamics of self-referential structures of both the regulating and the regulated system'. (Teubner, 'After Legal Instrumentalism', in *Dilemmas of Law in the Welfare State* (G. Teubner (ed.), Berlin, 1988), at 309).

[31] Teubner, 'Juridification—Concepts, Aspects, Limits, Solutions', above, at 3: 'Juridification is an ugly word—as ugly as the reality which it describes'.

[32] J. Habermas, *The Theory of Communicative Action*. vol. 2, *System and Lifeworld: A Critique of Functionalist Reason* (Boston, trans. 1987).

but there are one or two very important differences. In particular, Habermas limited his notion of colonization to the effects of certain types of law (law 'as a medium', not 'as an institution'),[33] on certain types of social communication (belonging to the 'lifeworld').[34] Teubner by contrast is concerned that '[a]ny social system with a self-referential structure can be endangered by outside interference in the self-productive interaction of its elements. Even the "systems" of economy and politics can be partially paralyzed by legalization.'[35] Thus, Teubner's criticism is more general.

A key factor here concerns variations in the perception of 'democracy'. On an approach which is so involved with the diagnosis of over-legalization and its negative consequences, the removal of an external, interventionist voice can be seen as a positive step in itself. As explained in respect of the other approaches outlined below, an analysis based in the power of certain regulated sectors (rather than their vulnerability) is more likely to associate democratization with the influence of a variety of external voices.

Instead, the positive agenda for environmental liability based on 'self-organization' is concerned with devising (necessarily modest) ways of overcoming the limits of law as a mechanism of societal guidance, whilst preserving regulated systems from the effects of legalization. As explained by David Robinson in his contribution to this volume,[36] proposed shifts away from command-and-control styles of regulation are often connected with a trend away from representative styles of democracy and, by implication, with an increase in participation. But 'reflexive law' also has a distinctive approach to participation.

Participation in Self-Organization

Certainly, the reflexive law approach is based in the rejection of interventionist, substantive law, and therefore doubts the possibilities of legal interventions which, like classic command-and-control, define desired outcomes, and take full responsibility for their attainment. As explained above, this is not only because of a thesis of ineffectiveness, but also because of the adverse social impact predicted for such forms of law. In this respect, 'reflexive law' can be seen as differing fundamentally from approaches such as that of Ayres and Braithwaite (explored below) which, under the title of 'responsive regulation', nevertheless

[33] Law 'as a medium' will be broadly recognizable to lawyers as positive, instrumental law: this category is concerned with substantive goals, and depends for its validity on references to procedure and authoritative source or derivation. Norms associated with law 'as an institution' however cannot simply be justified by positivistic references to their derivation. They retain a connection with morality, and 'need substantive justification, because they belong to the legitimate orders of the lifeworld itself and . . . form the background of communicative action'; J. Habermas, 'Law as Medium and Law as Institution', in Teubner (ed.), *Dilemmas of the Welfare State*, above, at 212.

[34] The distinction here is between 'system' and 'lifeworld'. 'System' is generally thought to include the economic and political realms, whereas the 'lifeworld' incorporates social interactions.

[35] Teubner, 'After Legal Instrumentalism', op. cit., at 315.

[36] Chapter 2, above.

maintains the authoritative 'substantive' legal source in terms of the setting of goals.[37]

Furthermore, 'reflexive law' is proposed as being crucially concerned with 'participatory' elements. What needs to be more carefully examined is the nature of this reference to participation. Reflexive law aims to bring about 'regulated autonomy', and one facet of the participatory structures proposed as part of this programme is that they therefore aim at regulating the interaction of autonomous systems. This involves a concern with process-oriented structuring of institutions. As Teubner has observed, this tends to support the autonomy of social systems in reaching their own goals and solutions, in their own way, and to this extent resembles neo-liberal versions of deregulation, almost approaching faith in 'invisible hand' mechanisms.[38] 'Reflexive law' accepts that it is appropriate for law to intervene in order to influence interactions, but its influence is seen as indirect and largely procedural.

Where such procedural approaches are concerned, an immediate problem arises however in respect of environmental damage. Whereas in many contexts, one of the key techniques of 'reflexive law' is the 'equalization of power structures' (in order to allow 'participation'), environmental decision-making in many contexts involves a significant imbalance between polluters, and potentially affected groups. This effect is enhanced by the problem that environmental risks are increasingly diffuse and far-reaching, leading to problems not only in respect of inequalities in access to information and economic power, but even in identifying the potentially affected parties. Teubner himself described consumer law as perhaps lying 'on the margins' of what the procedural techniques of reflexive law could achieve, exactly because of such problems about overwhelming inequality in power structures. There is considerable overlap between environmental damage, and consumer law in this respect, and if anything the features of environmental risk isolated in section 1 above are likely to weaken further the potential of 'participation' in the sense outlined here.

A second meaning of 'participation' in reflexive law refers to internal participation, within an organization. The importance of this is that it may to some extent replace the interventionist attempt at external control which, as explained briefly above, is diagnosed as likely to be both ineffective and disruptive. Here too participation has a particular instrumental role which is not linked primarily to the welfare of the members of the organization, but to the part their participation may play in making the organization more sensitive to the external effects of its inner rationality. In both senses of participation (interaction of autonomous

[37] Indeed, it was the co-existence of substantive and reflexive elements in the theory of 'responsive law' proposed by P. Nonet and P. Selznick, *Law and Society in Transition: Toward Responsive Law* (New York, 1978), which caused Teubner to suggest that they had not isolated a stable category of law, but merely observed a stage in legal development in which components of both types of law were present: G. Teubner, 'Substantive and Reflexive Elements in Modern Law' (1983) 17 *Law and Society Review* 239–86.

[38] Ibid., at 254–5.

systems, and internal structuring of the organization) there is a concern with equalizing power structures. Nevertheless, this is explicitly not because power is regarded in a 'moralistic' fashion,[39] but because the potential of the autonomous systems needs to be seized.

Given that law is regarded within the reflexive model as essentially unable to take full responsibility for achieving proposed outcomes, perhaps it is not surprising that the proposed model of environmental liability based on self-organization described above is more fully occupied with how to structure interventions in order to trigger decision-making by relevant organizations (within networks of environmental risk), than with the goals of such liability. Presumably, the distribution of risks will fall to be decided by the organizations concerned, in response to the pattern of liability: this fits the programme of 'regulated self-regulation', and perhaps this is thought to replace the usual 'external' derivation of goals for environmental regulation. But, in order to 'trigger' such behaviour, some levels of liability must first be set.

It is interesting to note that environmental liabilities even within this model seem to be accepted as turning on the traditional goals of fairness (compensation), and efficiency.[40] These goals clearly are familiar to liability law in general, and to tort law in particular. But it has also been explained in section 1 above that there is a deep-rooted problem of ambiguity, and even incompatibility, between various goals of tort law, such as these. 'Participatory' structures in the particular sense in which they are encountered within the model of 'self-organization' are clearly intended to have some instrumental role. It must be noted though that if the law resorts to liability as a method, the liability models adopted will themselves tend either to reflect a moral judgment, or to embody some particular goal for the interventions concerned.

Responsive Regulation

Other approaches which have shared a concern with improved effectiveness by regulatory involvement 'at source' provide a contrast in that they have also considered ways of achieving public involvement in regulation. The second contemporary approach to environmental decision-making considered here is 'responsive regulation', as developed by Ayres and Braithwaite. Although their attempt to evade the impasse of the deregulation debate is said to be 'devoid of any grand theoretical aspirations',[41] their approach is nevertheless underpinned by a commitment to a 'republican' vision of democracy, and most particularly

[39] To regard power imbalances in a 'moralistic' fashion is, on Teubner's account, an error. See Teubner, 'Substantive and Reflexive Elements in Modern Law'; and, *Law as an Autopoietic System*, above, at 133.

[40] Teubner, 'The Invisible Cupola', at 24.

[41] Ayres and Braithwaite, op. cit., at 5. They therefore distance themselves from the evolutionary aspects of Nonet and Selznick's earlier work (op. cit.) adopting the same label; and also (deliberately or not) from the criticisms of it made by Teubner.

by advocacy of a positive and interventionist democracy, where the state has a role in promoting effective democratic structures by balancing power, and advancing political equality.[42]

Since Ayres and Braithwaite claim that their commitment to this form of democracy is quite independent of their proposals for regulation, it is important to consider the particular role of participation and democratization in their model. The participation of public interest groups (or 'PIGs') seems to be proposed in order to avoid a particular problem, which is the problem of 'capture' or, more generally, of under-enforcement. Strategies for avoiding the capture of the PIGs themselves are proposed, essentially through making PIG representation contestable. The key role of the participant PIG is however to gain access to the 'smoke-filled rooms' in which 'the real business of regulation is transacted'.[43] For Ayres and Braithwaite, this 'real business' essentially concerns negotiation of enforcement and compliance.

Some key features of this model can therefore be isolated from the point of view of a concern with participation. In the particular instances discussed by Ayres and Braithwaite, the proposed techniques are techniques of implementation, where the appropriate 'rules' have already been settled.[44] As such, the background assumption is that the negotiations concern the implementation of 'a good regulatory law that properly reflects the will of a democracy',[45] such that the relevant PIG is understood to fight for a public interest which the democratic will intended to be protected.

Clearly, this is designed to leave room for 'responsive regulation' to be bolted on to a variety of different democratic models of rule-making, thus increasing the chances of acceptance for the proposed innovations. However, the division of rule-making (interest determination) from implementation (negotiation) tends to separate questions about the adequacy of existing democratic structures in rule-making as such, and particularly in defining and resolving problems of environmental risk, from problems of enforcement. The issue of 'valuation' of particular risks introduced above is therefore deferred to another forum, separate from the regulatory process at the level of enforcement.

Risk and 'Crisis'

A rather different contrast can be provided by reference to the work of Ulrich Beck, which provides the third approach for consideration. Starting from the point of view that there is a critical urgency about contemporary (and especially ecological) risks, Beck has set out a particularly pessimistic account of the

[42] Ayres and Braithwaite, op. cit., at 17–18.

[43] Ibid., at 58; and generally ch. 3, 'Tripartism'.

[44] Though they also recognize that ideals of participation could be extended to rule-making, the authors clearly intend to separate rule-making from compliance.

[45] Ibid., at 81.

inadequacies of current efforts at their control.[46] Despite some apparent parallels between this account, and the prescriptions for overcoming regulatory failure examined above, there are interesting respects in which they differ fundamentally.

In particular, Beck suggests that the inadequacy of current approaches to the production, control, and distribution of risk can only be exposed and addressed by opening influential areas of specialization and expertise—where and by means of which the risk decisions are made—to scrutiny, and to critical debate. It is difficult, if not impossible, to challenge from without the specialized forms of knowledge which make up the means of producing, controlling, and authorizing environmental risk, but increasing public awareness of the power of such knowledge, and of the existence of disagreement within it, means that there are forces for change which harness (and indeed can be harnessed by) the critical possibilities of the existing fields of specialization themselves.

He therefore develops an analysis of 'sub-politics', in which the emphasis is not on centralized collective will-formation or settlement, but on the unfolding of critical developments achieved largely within the subspecialisms themselves. While Beck shares with Ayres and Braithwaite a concern for participation and universal debate in respect of risk decisions, he locates that participation quite differently: if Ayres and Braithwaite are concerned with the representation of PIGs in the 'smoke-filled rooms' of negotiation, where their concern is with the application of rules, Beck identifies the 'real' decision-making power as lying not in parliaments (nor in the negotiating room), but in the board room, or even the test tube.[47] Commercial and scientific logic are perceived as resistant to 'control', yet contestable and indeed potentially self-contesting in themselves.[48] Democratization should not be identified with putting into effect 'a' democratic will.

This last point might be said to have something in common with approaches which object to interventionist regulation on the basis that such intervention (by agents of the state) leads to the dominance of 'a' particular outlook, and is therefore undemocratic. However, the suggested solutions are, as explained, quite different. To some extent, this might reflect an idea that the 'logic' of regulated systems is fairly robust, and in no need of preservation from the interventions of the law—though Beck also considers as vitally important the potentially self-critical role of elements of that logic. But this feature also reflects the essential nature of participation in these approaches, and a difference in view as to whether 'disruptions' in the subsystems are an important adverse consequence. As explained

[46] U. Beck, *Risk Society* (London, 1992); U. Beck, *Ecological Politics in an Age of Risk* (Cambridge, 1995).

[47] 'The structuring of the future is to take place indirectly and unrecognizably in research laboratories and executive suites, not in the parliament or in political parties': U. Beck, *Risk Society*, at 223.

[48] So, 'self-confrontation' is regarded as a key feature of 'reflexive modernization' (U. Beck, A. Giddens, and S. Lash, *Reflexive Modernization*, Cambridge, 1994). Large scale hazards, for example, are perceived as contributing to the 'self-refutation' of 'the safety guarantees of the state, economic and technical authority' (Beck, *Ecological Responsibility in an Age of Risk*, op. cit., at 8; and ch. 4).

above, a 'self-organization' approach regards as desirable the self-regulation of the autonomous spheres themselves, but it is not concerned with internal democracy. Ayres and Braithwaite seek to harness the potential of participation in enforcement in particular, but separate this from debates concerning acceptable risk and the formulation of standards. Beck's approach is distinctive in seeking critical effects within the structures of specialized fields of knowledge with decision-making influence—including law.

The aim here is not to endorse Beck's view of impending ecological crisis. It is illuminating though to point to the various roles of law in his account. Law appears in a diversity of guises, and this diversity has points of contact with the analysis of tort law presented in the first section above. In particular, it is important to note that the roles of law are almost contradictory, on the one hand appearing as part of the underpinning of 'organized irresponsibility' (the sanctioning of risk such that no responsibility attaches to it); and on the other hand appearing as an element of 'sub-politics', through which critical debate may evolve—although in this role, there are particular qualifications relating to the need for a strongly independent judiciary. Beck does not in any sense offer a general analysis of law, and his expectations of what judicially-developed law is likely to be able to deliver appear hopeful out of proportion to the general pessimism of the account as a whole. Nevertheless, aspects of his description of a legally constituted, yet legally challengeable, 'risk society', may be useful to the present analysis.

On Beck's account, 'organized irresponsibility' is an effect of social structures which disallow the recognition of adverse side-effects, such that risk-creating structures have been normalized or—it might be added—legally sanctioned. As explained above, an 'insurance-based' approach to tort law does seem to have this sort of effect (or even goal), although we could also disagree with Beck about the size and acceptability—or value, to take the positive element into account—of the risks concerned. The key point, perhaps, is the very existence of disagreement on this issue.

On the other hand, certain legal forms may provide a forum in which risk structures may be questioned and responsibility for damage sought. For example, plaintiffs who claim to have suffered damage associated with nuclear power are seeking a judgment of responsibility in a context where there is in place in the UK a well-developed apparatus of prospective control, and an apparent statutory guarantee of strict liability.[49] The litigants effectively 'keep under review' the existing prospective judgment that nuclear installations are safe, by claiming to be able to establish on the balance of probabilities that in this particular instance, they were not. The role of tort law thus remains ambiguous, but the potential is there for uses which reopen or contradict apparent regulatory settlements. This effect is enhanced by the retrospective form which tort law takes. In other words,

[49] Nuclear Installations Act 1965.

such claims seek to exploit the formal reasoning of tort law, and its pattern of responsibility for foreseeable harms.

Tort Law and Risk Decisions

However, as explained above, the law of tort is by no means free from instrumental influences. Furthermore, appeals to formal patterns of responsibility are less than promising in the round, since increased recognition of the ways in which risk-creation is structured might be expected to reduce the importance of individual culpability in seeking 'solutions' to the problem of environmental damage.[50] In the section that follows, the emphasis will shift from the search for solutions in the planning of environmental risk, to instances of tort litigation raising difficult conceptual issues along these lines. Those problematic features associated above with many cases of environmental risk (lack of mutuality, differences in evaluation, privatization of decision-making) feature importantly in this account. It might be added that these features also tend to undermine approaches based in shared solutions, and they could go some way to explaining not only the persistence, but perhaps even the increasing vitality, of bi-party, corrective justice-based interpretations of tort law.[51]

Some of the most interesting conflicts in tort law, and especially as regards cases of environmental risk, are related to the connection between tort law's instrumental role (perhaps even, its role in authorizing environmental risks), and its 'other' roots in notions of autonomy, freedom, and formal justice. The strength of these latter connections is a matter for debate, but clearly their importance is undermined to the extent that the English law of tort has difficulty responding to claims involving a conflict with other relevant bodies of law or policy. This may be in direct contradiction to the intentions and hopes of some of the litigants.

The approach to tort cases which follows begins with an explanation of factors allowing these cases to emerge, which to some extent fleshes out the idea of perceived divisions in interest, and in evaluation of risks, introduced above. Importantly though, the retrospective character of tort law also opens up the problem of changing evaluations over time. The remainder is organized thematically, with reference to key tort concepts such as foreseeability. The analysis suggests that tort could in principle respond positively to some relevant cases, but that it generally does not do so. This has parallels with McLaren's account of the role of tort during the industrial revolution.[52] According to McLaren, social factors (rather than a deficiency in legal principle) were the key to tort's failure to

[50] See Tony Evans' contribution in Chapter 7 below, in which he argues that it is precisely this concern with individual instances which causes blindness to the structural causes of environmental harm.

[51] See for example E. Weinrib, 'Legal Formalism: On the Immanent Rationality of Law' (1988) 97 *Yale Law Journal* 949–1015, and many of the contributions to D. G. Owen (ed.), *The Philosophical Foundations of Tort Law* (Oxford, 1995).

[52] McLaren, op. cit.

provide compensation for those who suffered the most significant effects of environmental damage. This would be a salutary lesson in itself, since it would suggest that tort law is failing to absorb newer forms of environmental harm to individuals, much as it failed to respond to a previous generation of harms, though perhaps for rather different reasons. But it is also important to identify those reasons, and to consider whether there are lessons of more general importance for environmental law as a whole to be drawn from these cases.

3. Tort Law and Challenge

The Litigants

From the point of view of an assessment of potential challenges to risk decisions through the medium of tort law, it is useful to consider the identity of actual and potential litigants. One of the limitations of tort law as an arena for challenge has been—and, in the UK at least, still is—that it is open only to affected parties, not to 'interest groups' in any broader sense.[53] However, it is not only the distribution of harm which determines the incidence of litigation, but also the capacity of the affected parties to regard the eventual damage as arising from a legal 'wrong'.[54] There are important lessons to be learnt from a review of the parties who regard themselves as having suffered damage as a result of environmental risk, and who proceed with litigation.

Complex points of connection may arise between tort litigation, and instances of challenge by environmental groups, and this can be illustrated by cases in which pre-existing defence or interest groups are contacted by (or even seek out) legal advisers.[55] More generally however, there may also be some significance in the various senses in which these plaintiffs are distanced from the origins of the pollution itself, since such distance may help to affect the likelihood that damage will be perceived as the result of a 'wrong'. Such divisions perhaps also reflect

[53] Tort law in its classic form may therefore be contrasted with developments in (for example) the recovery of natural resource damages by certain agencies and 'trustees' in, especially, the United States. This approach seeks to combine tort law, and the protection of broader environmental interests: see T. J. Schoenbaum, 'Environmental Damages: the Emerging Law in the United States', in Wetterstein (ed.), op. cit.; and Stewart, op. cit.

[54] W. Felstiner, R. Abel, and A. Sarat, 'The Emergence and Transformation of Disputes: Naming, Blaming and Claiming' (1981) 15 *Law and Society Review* 631–54.

[55] C. Pugh and M. Day, *Pollution & Personal Injury: Toxic Torts II* (London, 1995), at 19–26, outline the role of lawyers in claimant-initiated and lawyer-initiated cases, and of victim-groups or broader environmental organizations in assisting them. In 'Shifting the Environmental Balance' (in D. Robinson and J. Dunkley (eds.), *Public Interest Perspectives in Environmental Law*, Chichester, 1995), Martyn Day has argued that access to justice by members of the public is an important component in 'public interest' approaches to environmental law. This campaigning stance on the part of certain private practitioners can be contrasted with the view expressed by J. Cooper and R. Dhavan, *Public Interest Law* (Oxford, 1986), to the effect that private practitioners may simply be expected to set up business where a market for their services exists.

aspects of the nature of contemporary environmental risks.[56] For example, the damage suffered may be well removed in time from the source of the risk: this temporal division, which is a common feature of environmental harm,[57] is illustrated by the case of *Margereson and Hancock v JW Roberts* (discussed below).[58] Environmental risks also tend to transcend spatial barriers, and as such the incidence of harm may be geographically widespread. Most of the cases of tort law challenge appear parochial when viewed on a global scale,[59] often emerging from contamination of a particular locality. Nevertheless, these cases indicate the existence of a range of potentially affected parties whose interests are outside the reach of the existing safety/compensation compromises.

A third type of division between the plaintiff and the source of the pollution is socio-economic, and this is one of the factors which marks a distinction between such cases, and earlier 'employment' risks. Although some of the cases are, as mentioned above, restricted to the effects on a given locality, the distribution of environmental risk is distinctive not only in terms of locality, but also in terms of socio-economic groups who may be affected by it.[60] Some writers have charted the decline or 'exhaustion' of traditional sources of pressure for social change, namely the social forces which gave rise to the development of welfare provision, or the (largely unionized) representation of labour interests.[61] For some, this decline or exhaustion forms the background to the development of middle-class social movements, which have been characterized as deriving from that socio-economic group best able to avoid direct economic dependence on the creators of pollution, and thus more likely to perceive their interests as separate from those sources.[62]

Historically, a number of factors, related to the observation above, have undermined the potential for tort claims to arise which challenged existing judgments of responsibility and liability. One of these has been the direct dependence of

[56] The distinctive nature of new hazards as not being delimited spatially, socially, or temporally, is proposed by U. Beck, *Ecological Politics in An Age of Risk*, op. cit., Introduction, and some of what follows here was suggested by that analysis.

[57] Hence the uncertainties over contaminated land referred to above.

[58] The cases of *Margereson v JW Roberts Ltd* and *Hancock v JW Roberts Ltd* were heard together in the High Court by Holland J, with judgment dated 27 October 1995. The defendants' appeal was dismissed by the Court of Appeal in a judgment dated 2 April 1996.

[59] Although some localized risks are of course repeated and continued on a global scale: this has been so with the risks of asbestos, for example.

[60] As such, there may be close affinities with product liability law, where early moves were made towards 'group' forms of liability: R. A. Barusch Bush, 'Between Two Worlds: The Shift From Individual to Group Responsibility in the Law of Causation of Injury' (1986) 33 *UCLA Law Review* 1473–1563.

[61] See for example Beck, *Risk Society*, at 185.

[62] See for example D. Goldblatt, *Social Theory and the Environment* (Cambridge, 1996), ch. 4, 'Social and Cultural Origins of Environmental Movements: Jurgen Habermas'. Social movements of this sort are pinpointed by Habermas as originating in particular with 'a non-productivist core of the young, middle class and well-educated' (Goldblatt, at 129). P. C. Yeager, *The Limits of Law: The Public Regulation of Private Pollution* (Cambridge, 1991), at 101–10, also stresses the affluence of those involved in the emergence of environmental movements in the US.

most of the potential victims on the risk-creating sector.[63] In the cases analysed below, the plaintiffs are in one sense or another 'neighbours' rather than employees or dependents of the polluting party. As suggested above, the most significant 'distance' between victim and polluter in the case of *Margereson and Hancock* was temporal. It was not to a great extent geographical, since the plaintiffs occupied the immediate neighbourhood. Though not employees, there was not at the time of the exposure a complete socio-economic division, since the immediate neighbourhood in question was closely identified (at least in the mind of the first instance judge, who had heard evidence from a number of local people) with the factory's workforce and families of the workforce.[64] Perhaps this case indicates therefore that attitudes to risk change over time, especially as dependence declines. However, it can be argued that in other cases, plaintiff groups regard their interests as separated from—even opposed to—those of the polluter, or those who make the decisions which create or authorize the relevant risk. Certainly, these divisions do not always match the class analysis suggested for environmental movements as such.

Key Tort Concepts in Environmental Cases

If we shift our attention away from the identity of the litigants, and back towards the internal difficulties which these cases are likely to pose for the law, a slightly different set of issues emerges. As explained above, the affected parties (the plaintiffs) are unlikely to be within the protection of established safety-assuring standards, or of established systems of compensation. It is important to recognize then that English tort law in recent years has seemed to be involved in a process of self-limitation which is captured in the idea of 'incrementalism'—although in some respects, this process is an inconsistent or sporadic one, and is also balanced (though perhaps partly also provoked) by adventurous claims from a broadening range of plaintiffs. To put it a slightly different way, appeals to 'principle' in tort law have been tempered by recognition of effects and specific 'local difficulties' affecting particular sectors to which such principles may apply.[65] In this instance, the ability of tort litigants to question the acceptability of risk-creating activity may be compromised by deference to the more general

[63] See McLaren, op. cit. It has also been argued that unions, reflecting the dependence of their members on employment, had a limited role in regulating health and safety in, for example, the asbestos industry (N. Wikeley, 'Turner & Newall: Early Organizational Responses to Litigation Risk' (1997) 24 *Journal of Law and Society* 252–75, at 268).

[64] So, for example, Holland J believed that the defendants had 'forgotten their part in achieving an equilibrium between the conduct of an asbestos factory and the interests of a community . . .'. Equally, he noted that few complaints of any sort were received from the local community during the operation of the factory, in part because the 'defendants' employees made up a significant proportion of that same community'.

[65] This is captured in the *Caparo* test, and its emphasis on established—but not fixed—categories: *Caparo Industries Ltd v Dickman plc* [1990] 2 AC 605.

policies exemplified in environmental law. Judges have appeared reluctant to develop principles, unless they are compatible with other components of the legal response to environmental risk and damage. But the search for compatibility may not be straightforward.

Foreseeability

Not surprisingly, the concept of foreseeability has been a key focus of debate. Foreseeability is a common element of all the potential 'environmental' torts,[66] so that polluters cannot be held responsible in tort for damage which they could not reasonably have foreseen at the time of the risk-creating activity.

The need to establish 'foreseeability' leads to significant problems for many plaintiffs, but it also leads to interesting questions about how we should judge past standards, and past knowledge. Although the particular structure of tort law means that these questions are asked in respect of specific defendants, similar issues could in principle arise concerning other efforts at setting acceptable levels of 'risk'. Given the practices of risk management and control, when can a risk be described as 'foreseeable'?

Recent cases of environmental mesothelioma serve as an example. In *Margereson and Hancock v JW Roberts*, the plaintiffs were not employees of the defendant company, but had been residents of the area in which the defendants' predecessors had carried out the manufacture of asbestos products: the case was therefore described as being concerned with 'environmental' exposure to asbestos dust, the consequence of which was the development of mesotheliomas, some fifty to sixty years later, by each of the plaintiffs. As non-employees, they were not within the range of people for whose protection relevant statutory duties were in place. The cases therefore reflect important features of environmental risk. It is significant that the three unpredictable elements present in the case (plaintiff, time-scale, details of the injury)[67] did not preclude a finding that the damage was 'foreseeable' in common law terms.

At first instance, the existence of regulations establishing safety requirements for the protection of employees was regarded as being of vital importance.[68] In essence, the first instance judge was of the view that the plaintiffs had been subjected to precisely the same conditions as those which had been proscribed by regulation within the factory, and that their status as non-employees did not preclude the existence of a duty in negligence owed to them. As such, the important step taken was to allow recovery for mesothelioma though the relevant

[66] *Cambridge Water v Eastern Counties Leather plc* [1994] AC 264. Foreseeability issues are not likely to arise in cases of continuing nuisances, as far as the prospective element is concerned. However foreseeability is an aspect of the tort of nuisance as it affects damage and interference already suffered.

[67] Mesothelioma was not a known condition at the time of the exposure.

[68] Asbestos Industry Regulations 1931, SI 1931 No. 1140 (the '1931 Regulations')

exposure took place at a time before the disease in question was known,[69] and was suffered by non-employees to whom no statutory duty was owed.

The decision of the Court of Appeal however was more broadly based. Rather than depending on the promulgation of regulations, and then allowing them to be effectively extended to other groups of plaintiffs, the Court of Appeal placed the relevant 'date of knowledge'—from which damage ought to have been foreseeable—before the early 1930s: indeed, virtually at the turn of the century. This was because '[t]he information which should have operated upon the Defendants' corporate mind was in existence long before Mr Margereson's birth date'.[70] In other words, the Court of Appeal regarded it as reasonable to expect the defendants to consider the dangers of exposure once the relevant knowledge could have been gathered and applied. As such, employers should not simply wait for a time when, given the existence of regulations applying to the workplace, the dangers could not have been ignored. The expectation is that industrial practice ought to outstrip, not lag behind, the development of regulatory intervention. Australian cases have come to very similar conclusions, with even clearer reasoning, seeing companies as under 'a positive obligation to seek out information and acquire knowledge and direct and modify operations and conduct to accord with safe practices'.[71]

In personal injury law, the existence of such debates over the relevant 'date of knowledge' is familiar enough. Nevertheless, the regulatory background adds an extra dimension of interest in the present context. Traditionally, regulation can be seen as an exercise whereby one group which engages in potentially damaging activity is subject to the control of an external agency (generally, a government agency). Here, the law of tort recognizes that regulatory responses can be slow, and lag behind the activities of the risk-creators; and also suggests that financial responsibility for the risks in question should in some instances nevertheless lie with the risk-creating sector, notwithstanding the slow reactions of the regulator. Up to this point, tort is perhaps compatible with some newer, 'remedial' liability variants.[72] The difference is that tort law requires a plaintiff to prove that the damage should have been foreseen, and therefore asks the very difficult question of how much a company 'ought' to do in order to ensure safety, at least for its employees and immediate neighbours. It seems that it may be expected to act more quickly than state agencies, which have to discuss, assess, and compromise relevant safety standards.

[69] The disease against which the 1931 Regulations were intended to protect employees was asbestosis; mesothelioma was not recognized as a potential effect of asbestos exposure until around 1960. See J. Steele and N. Wikeley, 'Dust on the Streets and Liability for Environmental Cancers' (1997) 60 *MLR* 265–76.

[70] Court of Appeal, above.

[71] Therefore, '[i]t was not sufficient that [the defendant companies] wait for information to be conveyed to them.' *Olson v CSR Ltd and Midalco Ltd*, Dust Diseases Tribunal of New South Wales, 24 December 1994.

[72] For example, liabilities for contaminated land introduced in the UK by the Environment Act 1995.

At first sight, this may appear inconsistent with the general environmental law emphasis on planning and prospective control, and it is certainly inconsistent with notions of 'easy' compliance, or the idea that regulators may provide a multipurpose green light for developers.[73] But it might equally be seen as a logical implication of the rapidly emerging view that 'real' decisions are made by the risk-creating sector, and that 'external' regulation is necessarily of limited effectiveness.

By contrast, from a point of view which takes a different view of the relationship between industry, its regulators, and its neighbours, the retrospective culpability judgments embodied in a case like *Margereson* can appear simply nonsensical.[74] But a close look at recent trends in environmental regulation suggests that 'welfare' approaches, which have as described above traditionally been pitted against culpability approaches, may themselves be out of step with current trends in a number of respects. In particular, the suggestion that regulation be dealt with separately from compensation, via the legislative process and above all in a prospective fashion, would appear now to be an incomplete solution. But also, the literature referred to in section 2 above concerning the multi-faceted relationship between the public and commercial interests, and particularly concerning the distinctive nature of commercial interests as resistant to public 'control', suggests that an emphasis on wealth distribution, though salutary, does not tell the full story of industry's relationship with society.

Causation

On a rather different note, the common law approach to foreseeability illustrates some interesting aspects of what lawyers mean by 'knowledge', in that companies 'ought' to have taken steps to deal with risks which were not yet authoritatively (legally) accepted as in existence. This does not however answer the question of how risk-creators 'ought' to deal with divided scientific opinion about risk. This has a significant mirror in questions of causation, where a court is asked—without the assistance of the same degree of hindsight—to interpret scientific evidence for itself. While *Margereson and Hancock* concerned the application of 'foreseeability' rules to past risks whose effects are now (and were by the time

[73] Clarity and predictability are among the key features referred to by industry, insurers, and lenders in their responses to proposals for environmental regulation and especially elements of liability. Clearly, these elements affect insurability. In addition though, licensing regimes are also judged by industry in terms of clarity and ease of compliance: see for example the Memoranda of Evidence to the House of Commons Select Committee on the Environment, of the CBI and Institute of Directors (1992 HC 55, App. 2, at 73, App. 6, at 81).

[74] Atiyah, 'Personal Injuries in the Twenty First Century', op. cit., refers (at 25, n. 46) to the mesothelioma cases against Turner and Newall to illustrate that the company's shareholders 'are paying for the misdeeds of the company's managers and directors of 40–50 years ago'. The point made is that nobody at fault is left to be 'punished'; and that the burden will fall not on 'a company', but on a group of people who are the shareholders. Arguments that companies such as T & N (who were successors in title to JW Roberts Ltd) 'ought to pay' are treated as part of a fatuous 'deep-pockets' approach. In a way, this represents a further variant of the argument that social interests are cohesive, not divided: the company's wealth is that of its employees and shareholders, and it is thus spread throughout 'ordinary' members of society.

of the trial) relatively uncontroversial, cases such as *Reay and Hope v BNF*,[75] *Merlin v BNF*,[76] *Graham v ReChem*,[77] and (arguably) *Hunter v Canary Wharf*[78] involve the contemporary interpretation of risks, and their consequences. The controversy over the definition of the risks is conducted in the trials themselves, in contrast with the definition of risks by consultation and committee which has characterized the progress of regulatory standard-setting in the UK.

Culpability

Unlike truly 'remedial' schemes, tort law generally continues not only to seek the 'causes' of damage, but also to apply tests relating to culpability. Indeed, where effects on property (and specifically land), as opposed to personal injury, are concerned, this is partly implicit in the contrast between the compensation remedy, and the remedial steps required by cleanup regimes. The *Cambridge Water* case owed its high profile partly to the fact that, in effect, it was indeed a case about the allocation of the costs of 'remedying' pollution problems. Although there was no suggestion that the plaintiffs would be 'making good' the polluted aquifer, they had nevertheless incurred expenditure in moving to a new source, in order to supply unpolluted drinking water to the local area, and these were the costs they sought to recover. The House of Lords recognized that this issue concerned the allocation of such costs on a strict liability basis; and felt that such allocation ought to be a matter for legislative rather than judicial action.[79] This again emphasizes the dominance of loss distribution (including the availability of insurance) as a policy issue in this area, and the reinterpretation of contamination and risk of damage in financial form: the central question is, who is to pay for the legal consequences?

Tort law then is still concerned with judgments as to culpability, and foreseeability is regarded as an essential factor in such judgments. The other elements of culpability do however vary from tort to tort, such that it makes sense to distinguish 'stricter' forms of liability, such as the actions in *Rylands v Fletcher* and possibly in nuisance, from negligence liability.[80] In *Margereson and Hancock*, there was no serious doubt concerning negligence in the sense of a defect in the standards observed. As such, the case (which was also argued in nuisance, and *Rylands v Fletcher*) could be decided as an issue of negligence without adversely affecting the plaintiffs' case. In *Graham v ReChem* though, it was accepted, in reliance on *Cambridge Water*, that it would be sufficient for establishing liability in nuisance if foreseeable harm had been caused by ReChem's activities, falling as they did outside the notion of 'reasonable user'.

[75] The 'Sellafield' leukaemia cases, reported at [1994] 5 *Medical LR* 1.

[76] [1990] 3 WLR 383.

[77] *Graham and Graham v ReChem International Limited* [1996] *Env LR* 158.

[78] [1997] 2 WLR 684.

[79] See in particular the comments of Lord Goff at 305.

[80] See further Steele, op. cit.

Reasonable care was not therefore an issue; and it should be noted that ReChem did not need to have been to any extent 'at fault' in their activities in order to be described as outside the 'reasonable user' category.[81]

English common law has not developed a general category of 'hazardous' activities for which liability in tort is strict.[82] Nevertheless, storing chemicals (*Cambridge Water*) and running an incinerator (*Graham v ReChem*) are activities to which stricter liability may apply. If the interpretation of *Cambridge Water* adopted in *Graham v ReChem* is correct, then both in *Rylands* (natural user) and in nuisance (reasonable user) the area of activity which is beyond the reach of 'strict' liability has been reduced. This in itself marks a slight shift away from the notion of 'public interest' which shielded industry in the past from liability in *Rylands* and in nuisance, and has interesting implications if viewed in the light of the developments outlined above. These implications are as follows.

The origins of those cases where development activities were regarded as 'natural' or 'reasonable' have been linked with the industrial revolution and the development imperative of that era.[83] Nevertheless, it would be possible to link the persistence of such limitations with the development of 'welfare' thinking in general. Responsibility according to this pattern of thought is not supposed to attach to activities which have been considered on balance beneficial, or whose operation has complied with legal limits, and a shift toward more responsibility on the part of 'innocent' polluters in this sense is only likely to follow if it is assumed that collective risk judgments can after all be mistaken; that industry can to some extent be thought responsible for the development of appropriate standards; and perhaps even that social interests are sufficiently fragmented for a 'polluter-pays' principle to be appropriately attached to environmental damage.[84] This in turn suggests that strict liability of some forms can be linked to a decline in law's ambition and perhaps ability to promote cohesion between competing social interests in a prospective way, through standard-setting and rule-making; and forms a potential link between decline in command-and-control, and increasing use of liability-like solutions.

If we were to concentrate on legal principle in the abstract, it would be possible to see traces of all these influences in the narrowing of the 'natural user' exception in *Cambridge Water*. Nevertheless, the more notable trend is that large-scale cases—cases which could be expected to have an impact on the

[81] [1996] *Env LR* 158, at 169.

[82] There is nominally a category of 'non-delegable duty' relating specifically to ultrahazardous activities; but it is very rarely invoked.

[83] See McLaren, op. cit.; M. Horwitz, *The Transformation of American Law 1780–1860* (Cambridge, Mass., 1977), at 74–5. Brenner on the other hand has suggested that it was not these influences, but the 'formal' reasoning of the judges of the day, which had most impact on the law's development: see Brenner, op. cit.

[84] The direct importance of the 'polluter-pays' principle is currently limited: see T. Jewell and J. Steele, 'UK Regulatory Reform and the Pursuit of "Sustainable Development": the Environment Act 1995' (1996) 8 *Journal of Environmental Law* 283–300.

distribution of the financial effects of environmental loss—are rarely successful. Arguably, some current approaches to environmental liability within administrative regimes are beginning to recognize the contingent nature of standard-setting and therefore to reopen the question of responsibility for risks which would, at the time of creation, have been regarded as 'normal' or legitimate.[85] Aspects of the common law actions, such as the 'natural user' defence in *Rylands v Fletcher*, can be seen as closely connected with the normalization of familiar or necessary risk, while tort actions of the type described here might equally be associated with the attempt to challenge familiar risk. Shifts in legal thinking which would tend to favour such challenge could tentatively be described as broadening responsibility judgements, and there are possible points of contact between such developments, and changes in regulatory style.

The 'Docklands' Litigation: Authorization of Risks?

Significantly, the actions brought by residents of London's 'Docklands' area have to a large extent been framed as actions not in negligence, but in private nuisance.[86] Nuisance is based in invasions of interests in property, whereas negligence is concerned with damage to other relevant interests of foreseeable victims, and with the conduct of the defendant. The injuries for which damages have been sought in the Docklands case are primarily defined at law in terms of interferences with rights over property (for example, loss of amenity with regard to television interference), and damage to property (for example, damaged carpets as a result of construction work). As such, the cases concern the effects of development on those with interests in neighbouring property, and the allegation of risks to health has played only a small part.[87] In these conditions however, where the links between plaintiffs and defendant are geographical and therefore likely to give rise to large numbers of claims which also cannot easily be fitted into established negligence categories, the basis of nuisance law in property can undoubtedly be helpful for the plaintiffs and their advisers, since it defines a recognized relationship between the parties. The House of Lords' reversal of much of the limited progress made by the plaintiffs in the Court of Appeal shows that such practical advantages can be demolished by the turns taken in the definition of legal principle.

The origins of nuisance law—as a tool for the protection of rights over land—are not necessarily in tune with the uses to which contemporary plaintiffs, in a

[85] This feature too could be attributed to the contaminated land provisions introduced by the Environment Act 1995, referred to above.

[86] Canary Wharf are sued in nuisance alone, while the London Docklands Development Corporation ('LDDC') are sued in negligence and nuisance.

[87] This reflects the fact that the property interests are easier to fit into the established common law framework. There is still an element of doubt as to whether personal injuries to occupiers are recoverable in nuisance in England, but the majority of members of the House of Lords in *Hunter* seem to have believed not. Lord Goff's judgment in particular was inconclusive on this point.

case such as *Hunter v Canary Wharf*, are likely to wish to put it. For example, not all of those who are most likely to suffer from environmental risks (notably children) are likely to have relevant interests in property, and in some senses the existence or otherwise of potential plaintiffs who qualify to bring an action in nuisance is accidental.[88] Nevertheless, there were indications in the Court of Appeal that a shift might be provoked in response to the arguments of litigants, in line with the courts' understanding of contemporary demands. In particular, there was a shift in the understanding of who should be regarded as sufficiently connected with land in order to sue in nuisance.[89] The effect was that children who occupied affected property were, according to the Court of Appeal, entitled to sue for appropriate nuisances.

This aspect of the Court of Appeal's judgment was however overruled by the House of Lords.[90] Here, the majority decided that since nuisance was a tort concerning interferences with land, it was only those who had a relevant proprietary interest in the land who would be able to sue in nuisance. This would extend for example to freeholders and lessees, but not to others merely present on the land, such as family members.

Arguably, a difference of view can be detected within the majority concerning the interferences for which these appropriate parties may claim. In particular, Lord Goff seems to have implied that the plaintiff is able to claim an amount of damages which embraces the discomfort and inconvenience of other parties on the land. Perhaps for this reason, he left open the possibility that claims for personal injuries can be brought in private nuisance. Lord Hoffmann on the other hand retreated more thoroughly from the idea that mere residents could bring an action, in that he considered that the discomfort and inconvenience of such residents would have no impact on damages. It would make no difference how many individuals experienced such discomfort. In stark contrast, damages would be increased where the plaintiff owns or leases a property distinguished by its 'size, commodiousness and value'. The distinction here is between an approach where one party's loss may be recovered, but only on the action of another (Lord Goff); and an approach where the loss of some individuals is not recoverable in nuisance at all (Lord Hoffmann). Whilst the House of Lords has been willing to clarify, in *Cambridge Water*, that nuisance as a tort is distinctive and separate from negligence, it has proved unwilling to extend this separate tort into areas of damage which are typically dealt with by negligence.

[88] As with 'test cases', lawyers may advertise for people who fit the criteria: see Pugh and Day, op. cit., at 17–26; and on test cases and the use of advertising, see C. Barnard, 'A European Litigation Strategy: the Case of the Equal Opportunities Commission', in J. Shaw and G. More (eds.), *New Legal Dynamics of European Union* (Oxford, 1995).

[89] On the authority of *Khorasandjian v Bush* [1993] QB 727, the Court of Appeal held that actions could be brought in nuisance by residents who did not have proprietory interests: *Hunter v Canary Wharf* [1996] 2 WLR 348.

[90] [1997] 2 WLR 684. See also J. Steele, 'Being There is Not Enough—The House of Lords Puts the Brakes on Nuisance in the Home' (1997) 9 *Journal of Environmental Law* 378–86.

Generally, this decision significantly reduces the likely suitability of the nuisance action for many 'toxic' tort actions. However, in the light of the comments made above about the multiple roles of law in creating and managing—as well as challenging—environmental risk, the more pertinent aspect of the Docklands litigation is perhaps the background issue of 'authorized' or 'permitted' risk, and the relationship between the litigants, and the regulatory authorities. It was suggested above that one of the roles of law is in authorizing or sanctioning risks. In some respects, this results from the very attempt to 'control' risks, since the establishment of standards can be taken to imply that behaviour which complies with those standards—despite their tendency to be revised over the years—is beyond reproach, and thus beyond the reach of judgments as to responsibility. Apart from authorization through the establishment of standards however, there is a possibly even more direct manner of authorization, which is through established planning processes. Here, specific difficulties have arisen for the application of tort law principles which link directly to the observations about the pursuit of collective welfare described above.

The Docklands case is not a typical one in terms of the applicable planning framework, but general lessons can be drawn from it. The plaintiffs' cases centred around the construction of Canary Wharf, and of the Limehouse Link Road, in particular. These are two projects among many undertaken in the course of the regeneration of Docklands, but they adequately reflect the form of development promoted in the area throughout the 1980s. The first defendants, Canary Wharf Ltd, are private developers of the sort whose investment was actively sought by the London Docklands Development Corporation ('LDDC'); the second defendant, the LDDC itself, is the relevant urban development corporation whose main role has been the preparation and marketing of development sites, and the provision of a relevant infrastructure, with the single aim of 'regeneration' of the Docklands area.[91]

The LDDC was certainly proactive throughout the early 1980s, engaging in compulsory purchase and reclamation, as well as construction work. In terms of planning however its hallmark was the relaxation of controls, most particularly in the designated enterprise zone in the Isle of Dogs, and this relaxation reflects the decision to regenerate Docklands in a way which placed principal emphasis on private investment and finance. It has been suggested, for example, in respect of the Canary Wharf development itself that 'Many were astonished that a proposal of such scale and audacity could receive planning permission without even a public inquiry',[92] and this can be perceived as just one manifestation of a more

[91] T. Brindley, Y. Rydin, and G. Stoker, *Remaking Planning* (London, 1989), ch. 6, 'Leverage Planning: the London Docklands Development Corporation'; M. Grant, *Urban Planning Law* (London, 1982), describes the LDDC as a 'single function' agency (539–43, at 540). Note that the LDDC, as one of the defendants, was not sued for having allowed the construction work, but for having carried it out: this is an important distinction from (for example) the type of case exemplified by *Anns v Merton* ([1978] 1 AC 728).

[92] Brindley, et al, op. cit., at 108.

general 'insulation from existing local government institutions and therefore from local democratic accountability'.[93] A decision was made by the Thatcher government of the early 1980s that the existing development plans for the Docklands area were inadequate because they failed to develop a property market in the area, and placed too much emphasis on the existing needs of local people. With the establishment of the LDDC, regeneration was to be pursued in the national not the local interest, and this included the development of employment patterns appropriate to a modern capital city, rather than the consolidation of existing local trade practices; and the development of a land market attractive to private finance, rather than the construction of low-cost housing.[94]

Against this background, there are three key points to be made which will link the Docklands litigation to the more general observations in this chapter, and mean that it can in a sense be used as a 'case study' for some of the points made. First, the history of the regeneration of Docklands and of the subsequent challenge via tort law can be taken to illustrate the complex relationship between the private creation of environmental degradation and risk, and public control or management of it. The creation of the LDDC and of enterprise and development zones was associated with an emphasis on less use of public control powers, though also with an era of positive public activity, including the spending of public funds in order to attract investment. This re-emphasizes the point that law cannot be seen as independent of risk-creation, nor as having a single relation to the processes which produce environmental change. There is a school of thought, largely to be found in North America, which holds that pollution is in general a creation of 'public interest' thinking, and that an emphasis on 'private' property rights will furnish the appropriate solutions.[95] Like the supposed contrast between regulation and deregulation however, simple oppositions of this type are inappropriate: the aim of public planning in the context of the LDDC has been to encourage a thriving property market, with an emphasis on property 'in action', rather than property as the subject of 'defensive' rights.[96]

[93] op. cit., at 115.

[94] As Brindley, et al, point out, the proud boast of the LDDC that it had achieved a five-fold increase in property prices in London Docklands during the 1980s is hard to reconcile with attempts to reassure local people that they too would benefit from the availability of privately owned housing; and the assumption that 'regeneration' of an area is best achieved through the development of high-cost housing and office space must be judged in light of the privatization of space which has resulted (op. cit., at 120).

[95] This view can be broadly associated with some of those writing from a 'law and economics' perspective. E. Brubaker, *Property Rights in the Defence of Nature* (London and Toronto, 1995) shares some of the sentiments. Brubaker suggests (at 19) that 'empowering those most directly affected by pollution, common law property rights protect powerfully . . . Many environmental groups prefer regulatory solutions to environmental problems. But regulations are made by remote governments who, driven by the need to create jobs or some undefined "public good," are often the least responsible stewards of natural resources.'

[96] Contrast the use of property rights as defending against environmental regulation, through 'takings' cases in the United States: here, it is the interference with rights to put property to use which is being resisted: J. Sax, 'Property Rights and the Economy of Nature' (1992) 45 *Stanford Law Review* 1433–55.

Secondly, it should be noted that the relaxation of controls in Docklands—indeed, the introduction of 'fast-track' planning—flowed from a general adoption of regeneration as being in the (national) public interest, and therefore illustrates a form of deregulation being employed in the pursuit of a supposed 'welfare' goal. This reveals a conflict between central government, and local democracy, since the objections both of local community groups, and of local borough councils, were ineffective at each stage of the development. Perhaps interestingly, the background to this case also illustrates the potentially diverse nature of opposition to development on environmental grounds. It differs from the more familiar instance of local objection to the siting of a new industrial development, in that the proposed regeneration took the form of 'cleaner', more modern, service industries, which however were generally perceived to be unlikely to result in significant employment opportunities for existing residents.[97] Although the tort litigation itself necessarily centres on protected interests—the alleged invasion of property rights, and risk of impairment to health—its history is about contests over the local environment in terms of welfare. Should we regard welfare in terms of local needs, health, and control, or in terms of wealth creation and regeneration in a national strategic sense?[98] Despite the apparent preoccupation of this case with rights over property, such issues go to the roots of an unfolding debate about the possibilities of compromise and control where environmental interests are in issue.

Finally, in the light of the comments made throughout this chapter about the relationship between prospective control and retrospective responsibility judgments, it is important to note the relationship between the relaxation of *ex ante* controls in order to achieve a public interest goal, and the possibilities for *ex post* challenge through the law of tort. *Hunter v Canary Wharf* itself confirmed the limited implications of 'planning consent' in general where such challenge is concerned. It is true that the designation of the relevant areas for 'fast track planning' was regarded by the Court of Appeal as a reason for caution: a common law court should have careful regard to an 'authoritative' decision to relax such controls, and as such there is indeed an element of authorization wrapped up in the decision not to control.[99] In general however, courts (including the Court of Appeal in *Hunter*) are beginning to make sense of the relationship between planning consents, and common law wrongs, in a more subtle way than this would suggest.

[97] Brindley, et al, op. cit., suggest that few of the jobs created by regenerating Docklands went to local people.

[98] See Law Centres Federation, 'Whose Environment is it Anyway?' (London); The Ecologist, *Whose Common Future?* (London, 1993).

[99] In apparent contrast, one member of the House of Lords considered whether the relaxation of controls was a reason for the plaintiffs' case to be given more consideration, since they had not benefited from the full protection of the planning system (Lord Hoffmann). However, it is not clear how this possibility could have had any positive impact on the plaintiffs' case, given the other general conclusions on legal principle outlined above.

In particular, it now seems clear that courts will not accept the broadest proposition yet put forward, which would have regarded the planning process as the final word, in effect, on the rights (and wrongs) of the affected parties. That is, that 'Parliament has set up a statutory framework and delegated the task of balancing the interests of the community against those of individuals and of holding the scales between individuals, to the local planning authority'.[100] The Court of Appeal in *Hunter* effectively endorsed the retreat from this broadest of statements.[101] Planning authorities are not to be regarded as receiving a power to 'weigh up' the competing interests in this definitive way—and, as a consequence, less control by the planning authority does not necessarily mean more authorization for the purposes of defending against legal challenge. The planning authority merely has the power to change the 'character of the neighbourhood', and in this sense has a limited impact on the ways in which the rules of nuisance operate.

This distinction, between 'permitting' development (even, in *Hunter*, actively encouraging, or carrying out work in order to enable it), and 'authorizing' development,[102] fits with the general suggestion above that a relaxation in control is not necessarily linked with a decline in ideas of responsibility. In this case, there are clearly competing visions of public interest, both in terms of whose interests should be served, and in terms of the competition between development, and quality of life or safety. Again, there is an interesting issue of chronology associated with such retrospective actions, which mirrors the idea of fragmented rather than cohesive interests. In terms of the legal approach to the issues, the case can be used to illustrate a decline in the idea that 'all has been resolved' through arriving at a public interest determination.

Although the particular emphasis here is on the implications of the planning process, this analysis also hints at important questions for new regulatory developments. Current policy positions in the UK emphasize, for example, the development of risk assessment processes, and the development of expertise through the new Environment Agency. At the same time, the nature of risk assessment judgments is recognized to be subjective, and expertise is recognized to be provisional. If it is right to say that definitive determinations of competing interests are currently on the decline, then there could be something of a tension between the implications of such provisional decision-making structures, and the continued existence of common law as a potential means of re-opening apparently concluded regulatory judgments.

Conclusions

Environmental issues continue to claim a significant place in the legislative agenda, to the extent that their importance—if judged by legislative activity—would appear

[100] Buckley J, *Gillingham v Medway (Chatham) Dock Co Ltd* [1992] 2 WLR 449, at 460G.

[101] This retreat was effected initially by *Wheeler v Saunders* [1995] 2 All ER 697.

[102] This distinction is introduced and explored with reference to the case of *Wheeler v Saunders* in J. Steele, 'Private Rights and Planning Consent' (1995) 2 *Web Journal of Current Legal Issues*.

to be well settled. Added to this, shared concerns about the need to improve the methods of environmental control can appear to embody an assumption of consensus. On this view, new approaches to regulation transcend the debate about regulation and deregulation, and recognize the need for ecological concerns to be 'assimilated' to risk-creating decisions, or at least for environmental interests to be represented closer to the heart of such decisions. All of this is required because of the very importance of environmental issues, and because of the limited effectiveness of traditional forms of regulation.

However, this image of consensus itself holds elements of a rather different story. Environmental lawyers have discovered—and are still discovering—that their solutions are frustrated, whether by organizational factors affecting the interaction of regulation and the regulated sphere, or because of the nature of environmental risk itself. Perhaps paradoxically then, this developing and urgent field of problems to be resolved has been closely linked with declining confidence in the role of law in achieving effective and above all definitive settlements of social interest.

Arguments in tort cases sometimes tell a parallel tale about divisions in interest, about responsibility, and about the retrospective allocation of 'blame'. This is certainly not the only kind of account of tort law which could be offered, as explained in the first section above, and an effort has been made throughout this chapter to explain why a number of instances have arisen in recent years where courts have been uneasy with plaintiffs' arguments, which are indeed more compatible with retrospective claims of wrongdoing than with a pattern of shared benefits and burdens.

Nevertheless, there are implications here for contemporary developments in environmental regulation in general. Most especially, these concern possible inconsistencies in approach between different legal frameworks, and the continued possibility that planning and standard-setting decisions will be subsequently questioned via the principles of common law, and rendered less than definitive. It has also been suggested here that there are a number of tricky 'responsibility' issues which flow in part from evolutions in regulatory technique, and in part also from changing social perceptions. One particularly problematic relationship could be picked out from this account, and that is the relationship between techniques of risk management and assessment on the one hand (which necessarily incorporate some element of knowledge that a risk exists), and the *ex post* allocation of responsibility through tort liability on the other. As techniques of risk-assessment become more explicit, the precise nature of foreseeability judgments at common law may prove to be increasingly controversial.

5

Understanding Access to Environmental Information: the European Experience

CLÍONA KIMBER

1. Introduction

There have been many developments at national and international level in recent years which aim to increase the amount of environmental information that is generally available and accessible. These have occurred not simply because of a view that information on the environment, which is the heritage of all, should be available to all, but also because the availability of environmental information plays a number of roles in improving environmental protection. In this chapter I examine the role of access to information in environmental decision-making.

Understanding the relationship between access to environmental information and environmental decision-making is an important endeavour. By understanding this relationship, more effective systems of access to information can be designed. Much of environmental law in the UK and in the EU has been adopted on a piecemeal and reactive basis with the result that legislation and legislative approaches often conflict rather than work in harmony with one another. Understanding how related areas of law fit together allows the design of more effective legislation. Redesign of information legislation is presently on the political agenda in Europe. The European Directive on Freedom of Environmental Information ('the Directive') has been in place for six years, and is being reviewed by the Commission at the time of writing.[1] An international convention on access to environmental information and public participation in environmental decision-making is also being drafted by the United Nations Economic Commission for Europe. An understanding of the relationship between environmental information and environmental decision-making would enrich this process.

For the purposes of this chapter environmental decision-making will be taken in its broadest sense, including the whole continuum of decision-making on the environment. It will include public decisions by the state, that is to say decisions across the policy process including policy formulation, policy application, and

[1] Directive 90/313/EEC of 7 June 1990, OJ L158/56, 23.6.90, at 56. Art. 8 requires the European Commission to report to the Council and Parliament on member states' experience with the operation of the Directive and make any proposals for revision which it thinks appropriate after four years from the date specified for implementation by the member states. This four year review was due to begin on 31 December 1996.

policy validation.[2] It will include decision-making by the executive and the legislature, and judicial adjudication and resolution of disputes. Decision-making in its widest sense must also include private decisions. The European Community in its Fifth Action Programme on the Environment stresses that the success of the drive towards sustainability will depend to a very considerable extent on the decisions, actions, and influence of the general public acting as citizens, consumers, and direct producers of pollution.[3] Finally, the investment and management decisions of public and private enterprises will also be included.

What then are the functions of access to environmental information and how do these relate to environmental decision-making? At a general level it is clear that information is necessary to make sense of the world around us, to judge and evaluate, and to arrive at decisions by a consideration and examination of the facts.[4] More specifically, having access to information on the environment performs a variety of informing, enabling and facilitating functions. The potential functions are varied and diffuse and are supportive rather than directly acting. It is convenient to group these functions under the following five headings.

Consciousness-raising and creation of awareness of the state of the environment

The availability of information on the environment can serve to increase public awareness. The importance of the creation of an environmental consciousness must not be underestimated. If individuals are aware that their actions as consumers or direct producers of pollution may have negative effects on the environment, this may motivate individuals to change their actions. Environmental consciousness also lays the foundation for an informed and active participation in the protection of the environment.[5] Thus the availability of information on the environment can have a profound effect on private decisions. Information is just one factor, however. Good intentions will not produce the desired results unless practical alternatives for action exist and favourable economic incentives are in place.

Facilitation of participation in the decision-making process

Without accurate, full and timely information, participation in environmental decisions becomes extremely difficult. An informed and well judged contribution cannot be made to any debate, nor can a meaningful case be put for or against a

[2] This is the classification of public decision-making adopted by G. Richardson, 'The Legal Regulation of Process', in G. Richardson and H. Genn (eds.), *Administrative Law and Government Action* (Oxford, 1994).

[3] European Community Programme of Policy and Action in relation to the Environment and Sustainable Development, *Towards Sustainability* (Fifth Action Programme) OJ C138/1 17.5.93, ch. 7.

[4] See P. Birkinshaw, *Freedom of Information: The Law, the Practice and the Ideal* (London, 1996), at ch. 1.

[5] Fifth Action Programme, op. cit., chs. 5 and 7.

contemplated decision, without access to environmental information and specific environmental data.[6]

Facilitation of accountability of government and others as regards environmental protection

Having access to information on the environment allows governments, public agencies, and all levels of state administration to be held accountable throughout the policy process. The role of freedom of access to environmental information is central here. Knowing who did what and why is the first step towards accountability. The effectiveness of such accountability is directly related to the availability of information.[7] Accountability can also extend beyond government and public bodies to industry and private bodies if information about private enterprises is available.[8] Whether this kind of extended role is possible depends on what type of information is made available, and this in turn depends on the ambit of freedom of environmental information legislation. The extent of the role of access to environmental information is essentially a political question and will be discussed in the next section of this chapter. Through the facilitation of accountability, access to environmental information has the potential to have a very marked impact on environmental decision-making. Increased scrutiny may lead decision-makers to give greater weight to environmental considerations and adhere more closely to stated environmental policy and environmental law.[9]

Promotion of public confidence in government action

The provision of information and the ending of secrecy has the potential to promote public confidence in government decision-making and also in the actions of public and private enterprises. The Royal Commission on Environmental Pollution, which in its Tenth Report argued strongly for more information on the environment, urged that secrecy serves to fuel fear and distrust.[10]

[6] This point is emphasized by many writers. See J. Rowan-Robinson, A. Ross, W. Walton, and J. Rothnie, 'Public Access to Environmental Information: A Means to What End?' (1996) 8 *Journal of Environmental Law* 19–42; Fifth Action Programme on the Environment, op. cit.; Birkinshaw, op. cit., at 14; and C. Harlow and R. Rawlings, *Law and Administration* (London, 1984) at ch. 14, 'Planning and Participation'.

[7] See D. Oliver, *Government in the United Kingdom: the Search for Accountability, Effectiveness and Citizenship* (Oxford, 1991), at 25.

[8] Industry responsibility as well as public agency accountability were two of the benefits of improved public access to information identified by A. Ross and J. Rowan-Robinson, 'Public Registers of Environmental Information: An Assessment of their Role' (1994) 37 *Journal of Environmental Planning and Management* 349–59.

[9] Ibid. See also Rowan-Robinson, et al, op. cit.

[10] Royal Commission on Environmental Pollution, *Tackling Pollution—Experience and Prospects*, Tenth Report (Cmnd. 9149, London, 1984). This is also a point stressed by Rowan-Robinson, et al, op. cit.

Enabling improved implementation and enforcement of environmental regulation[11]

The view that providing access for the public to environmental information will help in some way to reduce the implementation deficit of environmental legislation is implicit in much government (as opposed to non-governmental organization) thinking on the environment and is expressed in the principles of 'shared responsibility' and 'environmental stewardship'. In a climate of limited state resources and given the widespread nature of environmental harm there is a growing emphasis on shared responsibility and public participation in the protection of the environment.[12]

In terms of the link between access to environmental information and environmental decision-making, the role of facilitation of participation in environmental decision-making is probably the most significant. The potential functions claimed for public participation in environmental decision-making are numerous.[13] They can be grouped as follows.

Rationalization function: more rational and scientific decisions can be reached by the inclusion of all the additional perspectives and knowledge of the general public.

Integration function: integration and absorption of interested and influential sections of the community into decision-making, thereby integrating citizens and state entities and building citizen loyalty and a common society.

Legitimation function: decisions which evolve through a process of consideration and participation should reflect a broader public interest and involvement, and thus further an increased readiness to accept a decision and the authority and legitimacy of a decision.

[11] These benefits are drawn from Rowan-Robinson et al., op. cit.; Oliver, op. cit.; Birkinshaw, op. cit.

[12] In the contributions to this volume from David Robinson (Chapter 2) and Tim Jewell (Chapter 3), the growth of the new paradigm which includes ordinary citizens and ordinary citizens acting in concert with NGOs as stakeholders in pollution prevention and environmental protection is also emphasized. It is this particular aspect of freedom of environmental information which is emphasized by policy makers at European and international level. See the third recital to the Directive and recitals to the UN Economic Commission for Europe Draft Convention on Access to Environmental Information and Public Participation in Environmental Decision-making ('UNECE Draft Convention', due to be considered by the seventh session of the Working Group for the preparation of the Convention at Geneva 29 September—3 October 1997). The recent Communication to the Council of the European Union and the European Parliament by the European Commission, *Implementing Community Environmental Law* (22 October 1996), stressed implementation and enforcement through shared responsibility as one of the key elements of its strategy in ensuring implementation of Community environmental policy.

[13] These functions are drawn from the work of Richardson, op. cit., and also Harlow and Rawlings, op. cit., at ch. 14, 'Planning and Participation'. For a clear classification of these functions see U. Hellmann, *Die Öffentlichkeitsbeteiligung in vertikal gestuften Zulassungsverfahren für umweltrelevante Grossvorhaben nach deutschem und europäischen Recht* (Frankfurt am Main, 1992).

Effectivating function: this leads on from the legitimating function. An improvement of the effectiveness of administrative implementation of decisions through the avoidance of dispute and litigation is to be expected if decisions appear to be more acceptable and to have greater legitimacy.

Controlling function: through the greater transparency and publicity of decision-making processes there are increased possibilities for the public to exert a controlling influence on the decisions of public representatives.

Protection of legal rights and interests: participation in decision-making improves the possibility of ensuring that particular legal rights and interests, in particular citizens' rights to a decent environment, which may be affected by the proposed decision, will be given greater weight.[14]

Of course, access to information may have some negative effects on the decision-making process, in that it may lead to slower, more drawn out or more cautious decision-making as more parties and more perspectives are taken into account and more care is taken that a decision-maker will not be left open to political or legal challenge.

2. An Ideal System

In the introductory remarks above, I have tried to show that having access to information on the environment is intended to enable and facilitate the performance of specific functions in relation to environmental decision-making. The extent to which these functions can be performed depends in part on the effectiveness of the system of access to environmental information. In this section I will outline some criteria for assessing the effectiveness of such a system.[15] These criteria will then be used to evaluate the existing system in force in the European

[14] The recital to the UNECE Draft Convention, recognizes that every person has the right to live in an environment adequate to his (*sic*) health and well-being, and considers that in order to be able to assert this right, citizens must have access to environmental information and be entitled to participate in environmental decision-making.

[15] These criteria are drawn partly from empirical research conducted by Clíona Kimber, Meropi Voytazi, and Maria de la Torre and funded by the ESRC, as part of a project on Access to Environmental Information in the European Community (Project No. L32030000642). This research evaluated the strengths and weaknesses of the EU legislation in operation in five representative member states of the European Union; the UK, Ireland, Spain, Greece, and Germany. The range of countries chosen provides a good sample of the different types of countries within the EU, namely northern and southern countries, highly industrialized and less industrialized, federal and unitary states, and jurisdictions which are more advanced in the development of environmental law and policy and those which are less so. They are also drawn from countries which had the strongest tradition of secrecy within the EU and which would be required to make greater efforts to implement the policy of freedom of environmental information. For this reason, the conclusions drawn should be representative for the EU as a whole and should be of real interest and value in the reform process.

Community at present. Six points require particular consideration. First, setting up a system for making environmental information accessible involves, in the first place, making decisions as to what kind of information is to be made available, to whom, and on what basis. Should access be restricted to information about public bodies, or to all information held by public authorities?[16] Alternatively, should it be further extended to all information on the environment regardless of whether it is held by public or private entities? Clearly, the more information that is made available, the greater the role it will play in environmental decision-making. For this reason, there is a strong argument in favour of making accessible all information on activities which are likely to have significant effects on the environment, whether held by public or private bodies. A precedent is available here in the practice of the United States which requires public and private companies to disclose information about the release of hazardous substances into the environment.[17]

It is also clear, secondly, that legitimate rights to privacy and confidentiality must be protected and for this reason, some information may need to be kept secret.[18] The protection of business and trade secrets, for example, might justify information about production processes being withheld from the public. The balancing of interests of privacy and confidentiality on the one hand and access to information on the other is a delicate process, for if too much weight is given to the former, this could mean the destruction of the latter.

Thirdly, in designing a system it would also be important to consider the needs and capabilities of those who will use the information, and the purpose for which it will be used.[19] If we want the ordinary citizen, as well as experts and professionals, to use the system to obtain information, the system has to be clear, easy to understand, and user-friendly. This could be achieved in a number of ways, the most important of which include putting in place a straightforward and unbureaucratic method of requesting and obtaining the information, providing catalogues or databases of information held, and providing information officers to

[16] A precedent is available here in the legislation of Sweden, the Netherlands, Denmark, and France, which have legislation providing access to all information in the hands of public authorities: see R. E. Hallo (ed.), *Access to Environmental Information in Europe: the Implementation and Implications of Directive 90/313/EEC* (London, 1996), at 11 and chs. 3, 4, 10, and 16.

[17] Emergency Planning and Community Right to Know Act 42 U.S.C. §§ 11001—11050. The caution sounded by Birkinshaw, op. cit., at 22, that there is a danger in allowing information which is held by private bodies to be kept secret, supports this argument. Many such bodies exert a considerable influence in public life and may be subject to no other democratic controls.

[18] This is acknowledged by almost all writers on this subject. See in particular, Birkinshaw, op. cit., at 22; House of Lords Select Committee on the European Communities, First Report, Session 1996/97, *Freedom of Access to Information on the Environment* (HL Paper 9), at para. 60; UK Government, *Code of Practice on Access to Government Information*, Part II, 'Reasons for Confidentiality'; Hallo, op. cit.

[19] This conclusion was arrived at by the author as a result of a survey of requesters of environmental information and consultation with NGOs and other citizen-representative bodies. This survey was conducted as part of the ESRC-funded project by Kimber, Voyatzi, and de la Torre, referred to above.

assist with requests. Freedom of information legislation enacted in the US and Canada requires the publication of matters such as lists of the employees from whom, and descriptions of the methods by which, information may be obtained, registers containing descriptions of government records and their probable location, and details of procedures, rules, and policies regarding the application and interpretation of the legislation.[20]

Fourthly, an effective regime should also bear in mind the importance of making the information available in a form which is in fact useful for the purposes of the user. Individuals may request information for different reasons and the form in which the information is made available must be appropriate if it is to be useful. For example, information with which to support legal action will need to be detailed and accurate, while information with which to build the environmental consciousness of the ordinary citizen will need to be in plain language, clear, and easily understandable.

Fifthly, if the purpose of making information available is to facilitate participation in environmental decision-making, then accuracy and timeliness are of paramount importance.[21] It is very difficult to put forward convincing arguments for or against a proposed decision, or hold decision-makers accountable on the basis of information which is inaccurate, limited, or out of date.[22]

Finally, in my view, it is also important that rights of access be legally binding. The importance of a forceful assertion of citizens' rights was stressed by the House of Lords in its well-considered Report, *Freedom of Access to Information on the Environment*.[23] Anchoring a system in legislation gives strength and importance to the system, and allows for enforcement in the courts if the legislation is not applied and implemented correctly. Legislation itself is likely to be more effective if it is of good quality, clear, and unambiguous. Disputes take up time and resources, and the clearer the legislation and its central concepts, the less dispute there can be about its application. Ambiguous, unclear or complicated provisions will cause delays, problems of conformity, and problems of practical application.[24] Furthermore, ambiguity in legislation is too often used as a device to evade

[20] See Birkinshaw, op. cit., at 51–72 for a discussion of freedom of information legislation in the US and Canada.

[21] The provision of information in sufficient time is an element of the principle of good administration suggest by Justice in its 1971 Report, *Administration and Law*. The importance of obtaining information in good time was stressed by all NGOs consulted by the author.

[22] UNECE, *Guidelines on Access to Environmental Information and Public Participation in Environmental Decision-Making* (October 1995). See also W. R. Sheate and N. R. Atkinson, 'Public Participation in Environmental Decision-making: The European Dimension' (1995) 5 *Environmental Policy & Practice* 119–29, at 129 for a discussion of the importance of the quality of information.

[23] Op. cit., para. 46.

[24] These elements of good quality legislation are stressed in paras. 45–47 of the Communication of the European Commission to the Council of the European Union and the European Parliament, *Implementing Community Environmental Law*, adopted on 22 October 1996. The importance of these requirements is also emphasized in the General Guidelines on Regulatory Policy adopted by the Commission in January 1996.

its application. Thus an ideal system should set out in legislation, clearly and without ambiguity, the following matters:

(i) The scope of the legislation (who is entitled to request information, and what information may be requested);
(ii) the exceptions designed to protect legitimate interests of privacy and confidentiality;
(iii) the form in which the information is to be made available;
(iv) the appropriate administrative procedures (the time periods within which information must be provided, the scale of any costs or charges, and the practical methods by which information must be made available); and
(v) the enforcement mechanisms.

Finally, the legislation could usefully contain a clear statement of its goals and objectives, in order to assist in interpretation and application. These criteria will now be used to evaluate the existing system of access to environmental information in Europe.

3. The European Experience—Directive 90/313 on Access to Environmental Information

In the late 1980s, one of the tasks which faced the then European Economic Community was the provision of greater access to information on the environment. Demands for more openness originally came from the Green movement and their supporters. Thus, in 1985 two members of the European Parliament's Environment Committee presented a draft resolution calling for the introduction of legislation creating a right to freedom of information on the environment.[25] Positive results came slowly, however. Despite initial discussions in the Environment Committee, no action resulted. In the meantime other forces were beginning to exert an influence on community environment policy. Difficulties being experienced with enforcing community environmental policy led to a growing desire to co-opt citizens into monitoring the state of the local environment and assisting in the implementation of applicable environmental policies. Providing for access to information on the environment was seen as a way of furthering this objective. It was not surprising, therefore, when the Fourth Action Programme on the Environment in 1988 called for EC legislation on freedom of access to information on the environment.[26] This led the European Commission, finally, to present proposals for a directive in 1988. These were considered by the Parliament and the Economic and Social Committee, and following subsequent amendments,

[25] For a discussion of the history of the adoption of the Directive, see Hallo, op. cit., at 2–3, Sheate and Atkinson, op. cit., at 119, and L. Krämer, *Focus on European Environmental Law* (London, 1992), at 290–309.

[26] Fourth Environmental Action Programme, OJ C70, 18.3.87.

the Directive was adopted by the Council of Ministers in June 1990. In order to secure the assent of many reluctant member states to the adoption of the Directive, many compromises were required. The result is that the Directive produced is, in many ways, limited in its conception.

The Directive is only one of a number of developments at European level providing for more availability of information. Others include the eco-labelling and environmental impact assessment schemes,[27] a code of conduct concerning public access to Commission and Council documents,[28] and provision in other directives requiring that information be made available in specific circumstances. Nevertheless, the Directive is probably the most important of these developments. It is the only binding legal instrument which creates a general right of access to all information on the environment and which is independent of any other processes or procedures. Together with the implementing legislation adopted by the member states, it can be seen as the central instrument guaranteeing access to environmental information in Europe.

The effectiveness of this system for providing access to information in terms of the criteria outlined in section 2 above will be examined here. It is clear that in many respects the Directive has been an important step forward. Its central objective, to 'guarantee free access to information on the environment' is stated quite firmly. It sets out quite clearly who has a right to request information and establishes a corresponding duty on the part of public authorities to provide information. It then sets out the scope of the duty and defines the key concepts such as 'environmental information' and 'public authority'. The exceptions to the right to information are then elaborated, and finally the time is specified within which the information must be supplied along with the costs which may be charged. It is left to the member states to define the practical arrangements by which information is effectively made available.

There are a number of very positive points about the Directive. Of paramount importance is that it has established a legally binding right to access to information on the environment. It has the additional value that the text is written in language which is clear, direct, and relatively easy to understand. The significance of this development when compared with the pre-existing position must not be underestimated. In particular, the clarity and simplicity of the right has the potential to impact on public consciousness and lead to increased requests for information from public authorities. These requests must then lead to development of administrative practice and interpretation of the detail in the legislation. Despite its advantages, the system set up by the Directive nevertheless has a number of

[27] Regulation 880/92 of 23 March 1992, OJ L99/1, 11.4.92; Directive 85/337/EEC of 27 June 1985 on the assessment of the effects of certain public and private projects on the environment, OJ L175, 5.7.85.

[28] Declaration 93/730/EC on a Code of Conduct concerning Public Access to Council and Commission documents; Council Decision 93/731/EC of 20 December 1993 on public access to Council documents.

limitations and weaknesses which reduce its effectiveness. In evaluating the Directive against the model system identified above, the characteristics of EC directives in general must be borne in mind. That is, directives are binding as to the end to be achieved, but the choice of form and method of implementation are left to the member states. Thus, directives often do not contain the same level of specificity as national legislation and norms may require concretization in national legislation.[29]

(i) Scope

The Directive provides for access to 'information on the environment' held by 'public authorities and bodies with public responsibilities for the environment and under the control of public authorities'.[30] Thus, access to information is limited to information which is held by this group of bodies. This means that much information held or generated by purely private bodies is not subject to the access to information legislation. This includes information on manufacturing processes, products, or procedures; surveys; reports commissioned or produced by private bodies; any information or results stemming from research and development activities, together with internal communications about proposed decisions or future directions; and a whole range of private records and documents, with the exception of information which private bodies are legally obliged to supply to public or regulatory bodies.

The result is that the many enabling, facilitating, and informing functions which access to information could perform, will not be achieved where decision-making might involve or could benefit from access to these categories of information, and can only be achieved to a much more limited extent with regard to the activities and decisions of these private bodies. To give one very simple example, without information on the extent to which a manufacturing process damages the environment, consumers will not be able to hold industry accountable by making informed and environmentally-motivated consumer purchasing choices. From the very beginning, the limited scope of the Directive has a negative effect on the extent to which access to information can exert an influence on environmental decision-making.

The definition of the key concepts of 'information on the environment' and of the bodies under a duty to provide information has been criticized as being ambiguous, thus allowing disputes to arise as to their application. We have seen above, in the model system, that clarity, certainty, and the absence of ambiguity are extremely important. The concept of 'public authorities, and bodies with public responsibilities for the environment and under the control of public authorities' is particularly problematic—it is simply not clear who is included in these categories. The situation of the privatized water companies in the UK is a

[29] See S. Weatherill and P. Beaumont, *EC Law* (2nd ed., London, 1995), at 137.
[30] Arts. 2 and 3.

good example of the problems which can arise. Despite much opposition from environmental groups, these bodies have consistently argued that the Directive does not apply to them and that they have no duty to provide information.[31] Water utilities in the other member states included in the author's survey of implementation of the Directive remain firmly in the public sector, and thus, information held by them is accessible.[32]

In addition, the Directive only applies to institutions of the member states and, most surprisingly, does not apply to institutions of the European Union. Following various communications which stressed the need to make the Community more open and to improve access to documents at Community level,[33] the Council and Commission agreed a 'Code of Conduct on Public Access to Commission and Council Documents'.[34] This Code of Conduct is not legally binding, however. This failure to provide a legally binding right of access to information at Community level is a significant limitation. It severely restricts the role which can be played by citizens in environmental decision-making, and in ensuring accountability of environmental decisions taken, at European level.

The case of *WWF (UK) v Commission of the European Communities* is a good example of the difficulties which can arise.[35] In that case, NGOs and private citizens sought to challenge the allocation by the Commission of structural funds to Ireland to build an interpretative centre at Mullaghmore in the Burren, on the grounds, *inter alia*, that these funds were being used to finance a project which was damaging to the environment. The Commission refused to provide access to the documents relating to the examination of the project. The World Wide Fund for Nature ('WWF') therefore brought an action against the Commission at the Court of First Instance for access to the documents.

The Court found that the Commission had failed to give reasons for its refusal to provide the relevant information and it therefore annulled the Commission's refusal. Nevertheless, the Court did not find that the Commission was obliged to provide the relevant information. This particular case is currently subject to appeal. The WWF continues to battle for access to information which it believes necessary to mount an effective challenge to the decision, which it argues would

[31] See the written evidence of Friends of the Earth and the Campaign for Freedom of Information to the House of Lords Select Committee, op. cit., at 71.

[32] See n. 15 above. Given that activities and services which have an effect on the environment are performed in some member states by public bodies and in others by private companies, this ambiguity may lead to a disparity in the rights available between Member States. For a discussion of the system in Spain, see M. de la Torre and C. Kimber, 'Access to Information on the Environment in Spain' (1997) 6 *European Environmental Law Review* 53–62.

[33] Declaration from the Heads of State and Governments at the close of the European Council on 16 October 1992, *A Community Close to Its Citizens* (EC Bull., No. 10-1992, at 9); reaffirmed at the European Council on 12 December 1992 (EC Bull., No. 12-1992, at 7); Communication of the Commission to the Council, Parliament and the Economic and Social Committee on 5 May 1993 (93/C 156/05, OJ 1993 C156, at 5). This concluded that there was a case for developing further access to documents at Community level.

[34] Adopted 8 February 1994, OJ 1994 L46, at 58.

[35] Case T–105/95, Judgment of the Court of First Instance of 5 March 1997.

cause significant environmental harm. This case is one of a number where litigants have been hampered by restrictive rules on access to information and *locus standi* in their attempts to hold Community bodies accountable for decisions in regard to the environment.[36]

(ii) Nature and Extent of Exceptions

In the ideal model outlined above, it was accepted that certain exceptions were necessary to protect legitimate interests of privacy and confidentiality. It is fair to say that the grounds for exempting information from disclosure contained in the Directive are too numerous and too broadly drafted. In particular, the exceptions allowing information to be kept secret where it relates to matters which are *sub judice* or under inquiry, where the information is commercially confidential, where the information is supplied voluntarily to the public body, or where the supply of information would involve the supply of unfinished documents or data or internal communications, have been criticized as unnecessary and overly broad.[37] The argument has been made that the exceptions to the right to freedom of access are so numerous that the right itself is defeated.[38]

A presumption that information would be released unless its disclosure was likely to cause significant harm to the interests protected by the exceptions, would restrict the scope of these exceptions and restore a balance. A public interest override, which could specify, for example, that information in an exempt category could be disclosed if any harm or prejudice arising from disclosure is outweighed by the public interest in making information available, would also be a step forward.[39] Without these protections, there is an automatic discretion to decide to keep information secret which falls into any of the listed categories, without any examination of whether the legitimate interests to be protected really require this secrecy or this protection in every circumstance. The consequence, quite simply, is that the system of access to information is less effective.

(iii) Enforcement and Appeal Mechanisms

We have seen above, in the ideal model, the importance of a legally enforceable right in ensuring that the rights have real meaning. The Directive satisfies this criterion in that the right to have access to environmental information is expressly stated in legal form and there is a provision that a person who considers that

[36] See also *Greenpeace International and Others v Commission of the European Communities*, Order of the Court of First Instance in Case T-585/93 [1995] ECR II-2205. Reported with a comment by N. Gérard, 'Access to Justice on Environmental Matters—A Case of Double Standards?' (1996) 8 *Journal of Environmental Law* 139–57. This case was concerned with the allocation of structural funds to Spain for the building of two power stations in the Canary Islands.

[37] Hallo, op. cit., at ch. 1; House of Lords Report, op. cit., at paras. 60–7. See also the written evidence of the NGOs published with that report.

[38] G. Bakkenist, *Environmental Information: Law, Policy and Experience* (London, 1994), at 33.

[39] See Hallo, op. cit., at ch. 1. This was also one of the recommendations of the House of Lords Select Committee, op. cit., at para. 83(f).

their request has been unreasonably refused or ignored may seek judicial or administrative review of the decision in accordance with the relevant national legal system.[40] However, the national legal systems of member states may not provide appropriate review mechanisms. Judicial review in the UK, for example, is in principle limited to an examination of the fairness of the decision-making procedure, such that the merits of the substantive decision itself cannot be questioned. In addition, there is no formal procedure for administrative review.[41] The adequacy of member states' response to their obligations in this regard will be considered in the next section, but the failure of the Directive to require states to provide an appropriate mechanism for enforcement and appeal is rather an important shortcoming. Rights without adequate remedies are of little value. The consequence of lack of enforceability is that less information is accessible, and the system is less effective than it might be.

(iv) Other Weaknesses

The Directive has many other defects in terms of ambiguity and limitation of conception, not all of which can be discussed in detail. Attention must, however, be drawn to two other important areas where the Directive falls short of the ideal model. The importance of timeliness in relation to the accessing of information and the importance of considering the purpose for which information is to be used, were stressed in the model system. Quite clearly, if information is to allow citizens to participate in the formal decision-making process, they must be able to get the information in time to allow them to participate. Obtaining information after a hearing has taken place is clearly useless. Seen in this light, the provision that a response (which could include a refusal or a referral of the citizen to another source) must be given within two months allows too long a period, especially as in many cases, procedural rules regulating public participation in decision-making require completed submissions or arguments for consideration in public decision-making to be submitted within much shorter time periods.

Finally, we have the problem of costs. The Directive merely states that member states may charge a reasonable cost for supplying the information. This is ambiguous and has allowed authorities to charge high costs for information. The exact nature of the problems which have arisen will be discussed in the next section of this chapter. It is quite plain to see, however, that if the cost of obtaining the information is too high, people will not be able to afford to acquire it, and less information will be available. The adoption of the European Parliament's recommendation that only the costs of copying should be permitted to be charged would have resulted in a better system.[42] This recommendation was, however, rejected by the Commission and is not found in the final version of the Directive.

[40] Art. 4 of the Directive.

[41] See L. Bridges, G. Meszaros, and M. Sunkin, *Judicial Review in Perspective* (London, 1995).

[42] Report of the European Parliament, OJ C120, 16.5.89.

4. National Legislation on Access to Environmental Information in the Member States

Following the adoption of the Directive, the member states were then charged with its implementation. Given the fact that many had administrative and political cultures which favoured secrecy above openness, this was not likely to take place without problems. As noted above, only three member states (Denmark, France, and the Netherlands) had existing legislation which granted a positive right of access to information.[43] In the member states examined here, new legislation was necessary, because the regime providing for access to environmental information adopted by the Community was an enormous advance on what already existed. Implementation of the Directive would require great changes in the traditional political and administrative cultures of secrecy in the member states in question.[44]

As we have seen in the previous section, the system established by the Directive falls short of the ideal system in a number of respects, in particular with regard to its ambiguity and limited scope. As discussed above, directives take the form of a direction to member states of the European Union to achieve a certain result. This end result is often stated in broad or general terms. The member states are free to choose the form and method of implementation in order to achieve the required result. Thus many of the norms in a directive will need to put in more concrete form in national legislation. This is certainly true of the Directive under consideration here, as we have seen in respect of the broad and general rights set out therein. In particular, since the Directive leaves it to member states to 'define the practical arrangements under which information is effectively made available', the member states have considerable discretion in specifying how access to environmental information will be regulated. Moreover, it is also important to remember that the Directive is a floor and not a ceiling—it sketches out a system to provide a right to a minimum amount of environmental information, leaving member states free to establish a system guaranteeing a much larger amount of information if they wish.

As the member states have a considerable latitude and discretion in establishing systems of access to information on the environment, it is clear that any evaluation of the Directive would be incomplete without examining its implementation. This part will evaluate in general terms whether the systems adopted in four member states, namely the UK, Ireland, Spain, and Germany, can provide sufficient information to allow a full role to be played in environmental decision-making. By looking at more than one country, a broader picture can be drawn. The criteria for the ideal system outlined in section 2, above, will also be used to evaluate the national legislation.

[43] Ireland has since adopted a Freedom of Information Act (21 April 1997).

[44] For a discussion of the position in the UK see generally, W. Birtles, 'A Right to Know: the Environmental Information Regulations 1992' [1993] *Journal of Planning and Environment Law* 615–26. For current plans in the UK, see the white paper, *Your Right to Know—the Government's Proposals for a Freedom of Information Act*, December 1997, Cm. 3818.

The EC regime of access to information was superimposed on legal and political systems many of which were traditionally very secretive.[45] Hallo distinguishes three groups of member states in this regard. These are: those with existing general access to information legislation;[46] those where new legislation was needed and was adopted on time;[47] and those member states which have progressed most slowly.[48] In this chapter a representative sample of those in the last two categories have been examined. In all of the member states considered here, new legislation was necessary to implement the Directive. Although Article 9 of the Directive gave the member states two and a half years in which to adopt the necessary legislation (until 31 December 1992), only the UK and Ireland adopted implementing legislation on time: Germany, Greece, and Spain were significantly late.[49] It is fair to say, therefore, that the Directive and the implementing legislation mark a clear departure from pre-existing systems and have been adopted by the states in question with some degree of reluctance.

Given this background, it is not surprising that the implementation process was not without its problems and that the opportunity to bring about far-reaching changes was not taken. In general, the implementing legislation in the member states under consideration simply replicated the provisions of the Directive almost verbatim, with some adaptations, and retained a similar structure. This mirroring of the Directive is an important weakness. As pointed out above, the system established by the Directive has inherent limitations and weaknesses which reduce the extent of the right to information and thus limit the extent to which environmental information can play a full role in environmental decision-making. These weaknesses and limitations are imported directly into national legal systems. Furthermore, the necessary concretization in national legislation of the broad norms and concepts in the Directive did not take place. In particular, the requirement in Article 3 of the Directive that member states define the practical arrangements by which information is made available was not fulfilled in any of the member states. Thus the national systems fall further away from the clarity, certainty, and avoidance of ambiguity identified as necessary in the ideal model outlined above.

In addition, despite the considerable discretion and latitude allowed in the implementation process, none of the states in question went substantially beyond the terms of the Directive to adopt a more liberal regime of access to information

[45] See generally Birkinshaw, op. cit.; in Spain, see de la Torre and Kimber, op. cit.; Hallo, op. cit., contains detailed discussions of the systems in all four countries considered.

[46] Denmark, France, and the Netherlands.

[47] Belgium, Ireland, Luxembourg, and the United Kingdom.

[48] In that implementation of the Directive was substantially delayed or has still not taken place. This group comprises Germany, Portugal, Spain, Greece, and Italy.

[49] The principal pieces of implementing legislation in each country are: Environmental Information Regulations 1992 (SI 1992 No. 3240) (UK); Access to Information on the Environment Regulations, 1993 (SI 1993 No. 133), replaced by the Access to Information on the Environment Regulations, 1996 (SI 1996 No. 185) (Ireland); Ley 38/1995, de 12 diciembre, sobre el derecho de accesso a la información en materia de medio ambiente (Spain); Gesetz zur Umsetzung der Richtlinie 90/313/EWG des Rates vom 7.6.1990 über den freien Zugang zu Information über die Umwelt vom 8 Juli 1994, BGBl I 1994, p1490 (UIG) (Germany).

by, for example, reducing the amount or degree of the exceptions to disclosure permitted by the Directive, or by making them subject to a harm test, or by taking binding proactive steps to disseminate information to the general public. In other words, states implementing the Directive enacted legislation which achieved, at best, the minimum necessary for compliance.

Some of the problems which are of specific relevance to the role of information in environmental decision-making will now be examined in more detail.

Scope and Ambit of the Right

As identified in the ideal model, it is important that there is clarity and certainty in setting out the rights and duties owed and, in particular, clarity in defining who is under a duty to provide information and what information they are required to make available. We have seen in section 3 above, that in the EC regime a duty to provide information on the environment is owed by public authorities or bodies with public responsibilities for the environment and under the control of public authorities. The definitions are ambiguous and require clarification in their application. Yet we do not find that national implementing legislation goes any further in providing clear, workable definitions. In the UK, there was some discussion about including a list of public authorities with public responsibilities for the environment in an annex to the legislation. This was not done, however.[50] The implications of this failure by member states is clear: there will be much uncertainty as to the scope of the duty, and this would allow authorities or bodies who do not wish to disclose information to take advantage of the uncertainty.

The limitation of the scope of the right, confining it solely to the public sector and to information on the environment, has broader implications, however. The system adopted creates a duty on the part of the state to provide information which it has on the environment to every person who requests it. While this may seem quite broad, it is not when we compare it with the possible alternatives, and particularly with a system which makes all state information, not just information on the environment, available to the public. This provision exists for example in the US, Canada, New Zealand, Australia, and some Scandinavian countries.[51] Furthermore, as discussed above, why limit information to that held by the state or emanations of the state, in other words to the public sphere? There is a case for arguing that all information on activities which have the potential to damage the environment should be made available, as is the case with systems like the toxics release inventory in the United States which requires companies to provide information on the toxic substances they release into the environment.[52]

[50] The Guidance Document accompanying the regulations originally contained a list of more than 200 bodies covered by the regulations. This list was later omitted. The Freedom of Information Bill proposes a list system.

[51] For details of the systems in these countries, see Birkinshaw, op. cit., at ch. 2.

[52] For a discussion of the United States Emergency Planning and Community Right to Know Act, see R. Percival, A. Miller, C. Schroeder, and J. Leape, *Environmental Regulation: Law, Science and Policy* (Boston, 1996).

In other contexts there are rights of access to information which is held by private enterprises. Companies in the UK, for example, are required to make certain types of financial information available to the public under the Companies Acts. The result of the limitation of environmental information rights to publicly-held information, as discussed above in relation to the limited scope of the right contained in the Directive, is that information which is held or generated by purely private entities and which could have a role to play in public processes of environmental decision-making (as well as influencing private activities and private decision-making), can often be unavailable. Of course, a balance must be drawn between private rights on the one hand and the environmental public interest on the other, and it may be the case that there should be greater restrictions on access to private sector than public sector information. However, it is suggested that the absence of any rights to private sector information is over-restrictive.

Grounds for Exceptions to Disclosure of Information

No right is absolute, and this includes the right of access to information on the environment. As noted above, in an ideal system there must be a balance between the various legitimate interests protected. Achieving the correct balance between a right and its exceptions is difficult. If there are too many exceptions, then the right loses much of its meaning. On the other hand, legitimate interests must be protected. As discussed in section 3, the system of access to information put in place by the Directive deals with this problem by allowing member states to adopt some or all of a number of specified exceptions to the general right set out in the Directive.

However, in adopting implementing legislation, member states have by and large adopted all of the exceptions permitted, and in some instances have increased their scope. In some member states certain exceptions have nevertheless been defined more narrowly. In the Irish case, for example, the permitted exception in the Directive for information which relates to the confidentiality of the proceedings of public authorities has been removed from Irish regulations. Such narrowing of exceptions remains unusual, however.

The wide range of the exceptions is a significant problem. The number and extent of the exceptions in the EC system of access to information were already quite extensive, and have been criticized on this ground.[53] In adopting all of these exceptions and extending some, there is more scope for public bodies to refuse to disclose information. Public authorities or public servants who are unwilling to make information available to the public will be able to search among the

[53] If the exemptions in the Directive are interpreted broadly, it could allow member states to empty the Directive of substantive practical content. See Bakkenist, op. cit., at 33.

exceptions for one appropriate to their circumstances. In short, the exceptions provided for in national legislation are too numerous, and too broadly conceived. The harm test and public interest override, discussed above in relation to the Directive, would help to restore the balance between confidentiality and openness and bring the national systems of access to environmental information closer to the ideal model. These points can be illustrated with two examples.

Matters which are sub judice

It would generally be agreed that in the interests of justice, if matters are in the course of being litigated then there should be no requirement to disclose information relating to them if this would tend to interfere with the course of justice or, for example, if disclosure of information might enable one party to advance their own case unfairly or damage the case of an adversary.[54] There must be a balance, however, between the need for a fair trial, and the requirements of open justice and a legitimate public interest.[55]

It is arguable that this balance has not been correctly struck in the implementing legislation in national legal systems. The Directive allows member states to refuse a request for information where it affects 'matters which are, or have been, *sub judice*, or under enquiry (including disciplinary enquiry), or which are the subject of preliminary investigation proceedings'. This is clearly very wide as it stands, and has not been more clearly defined in national legislation. In fact the exception has been extended in the legislation adopted by UK, Germany, and Spain.[56] It is difficult to justify an exception which allows information to be kept secret simply because it *relates* to 'legal or other proceedings' without assessing whether disclosure would have any negative effects.[57] It would have been much better had national legislation included a provision which prohibited disclosure only where there was a substantial risk that legal proceedings would be seriously prejudiced. The implications of this exception are particularly important for participation in environmental decision-making. Legal or other proceedings could include the very public inquiries and licensing applications in which a person wants to participate and for which access to the related environmental information is essential for effective participation.

[54] See the discussion of contempt of court in Birkinshaw, op. cit., at 274–9.

[55] For UK judicial authority see *R v Beck, ex parte Daily Telegraph plc* [1993] 2 All ER 177, as referred to by Birkinshaw.

[56] UK Regulations, reg. 4(2)(b); Germany, UIG, §7,(1)2; Spain, AIE Act, Art. 3.1(e). The UK legislation for example, allows information to be treated as confidential if it is 'information relating to, or to anything which is or has been the subject matter of, any legal or other proceedings (whether actual or prospective)'. The shift from 'affects' to the rather broader 'relating to', and the inclusion of proceedings both actual and *prospective*, means that more information could potentially be kept secret on the basis of this exception.

[57] P. Roderick, 'The United Kingdom', in Hallo, op. cit., at 255.

Commercial or industrial confidentiality

The same need for balance is necessary as regards the protection of business and trade interests. Clearly, there are circumstances where in order to protect trade secrets or intellectual property, there is a justification for keeping information secret. This is recognized in the discretion given to member states to refuse to disclose information which affects commercial or industrial confidentiality. Again, however, national legislation does not make this exception more concrete, nor provide for guidance as to where to draw the line between protection and openness.

Instead, national legislation leaves the balance to be drawn on a case by case basis.[58] A clear definition of what constitutes a business or trade secret and clear criteria for the balancing of interests would have been more in keeping with the overall purpose of the system of access to environmental information, namely to make such information available in an easy and timeous manner. As with the *sub judice* exception, it would have been better had national legislation attempted to restrict the ambit of this exception, by adding a presumption in favour of disclosure of information unless there was a substantial risk that disclosure would seriously prejudice the trade or business interests to be protected. This is a particularly significant exception given that many environmental decisions taken by public authorities concern private enterprises and private industry. It is self-evident that participation in decisions to regulate, scrutinize or sanction such polluters is extremely difficult without the appropriate information. Thus the benefits of public participation outlined in the introduction will be lost in respect of this kind of environmental decision-making. This is a serious limitation on the effectiveness of national systems of access to environmental information.

Failure to Make Practical Arrangements

We have noted above that concretization of the general norms contained in the Directive was required in the national implementing legislation, and in particular more detailed specifications were required as to the practical arrangements by which information was effectively made available. One of the criteria of the ideal model outlined in section 2 above was that the practical arrangements, including designation and preparation of places where information may be obtained, hours of opening of public offices, provision for assistance from administrative officers and so on, should be clear, easy to understand, and user-friendly. The

[58] The German legislation gives a good example of the complexity of such a process. It provides that business or trade secrets must not unjustifiably be made available. The determination of this question is a complex two stage process which first seeks to determine whether something is in fact a business or trade secret (industry makes a claim that this is the case and may be called upon to justify its characterization), and then goes on to determine whether, notwithstanding the characterization as a business or trade secret, the information can nevertheless be disclosed. All affected parties must be heard before a ruling is made that information be disclosed (UIG §8.II 1).

practical arrangements for the exercise of a right are perhaps as important as the abstract statement of the existence of the right itself.

This criterion is not fulfilled in national legislation. In none of the states examined does the legislation define such practical arrangements, rather the bodies with a duty to provide information are left to make their own arrangements and define their own policy. In some of the member states considered there was evidence of some good practice in these areas. The Irish 'ENFO' (Environmental Information) centre, a drop-in information centre which provides a wide range of information to the general public and gives assistance with accessing more specialized information, is a model to be recommended.[59] For the most part, national legislation and practice is seriously deficient in this regard. As a result, it will be more difficult to obtain information and in particular it will be more difficult for the ordinary citizen who is not familiar with the administrative structure of the state. This limitation seriously reduces the effectiveness of the system of access to information on the environment and its ability to achieve the objective outlined above. If information on the environment is in effect inaccessible to the ordinary citizen, participation in environmental decision-making will be less easy for this group, and thus the functions of public participation in environmental decisions identified in the introduction will not be achieved.

Failure to provide for an appropriate appeal mechanism

The final criterion for an effective system of access to environmental information identified in section 2 was the need for an effective enforcement mechanism. Again, this criterion is not fulfilled in a satisfactory manner. In the UK, Germany, and Spain, no provision has been made for review mechanisms other than those which were already part of the national legal system. Existing appeal mechanisms in these countries are confined to judicial review, which is subject to many defects. In particular, it is too expensive, too time consuming, and too slow.[60] It does not provide for an effective right of appeal in practice. In Ireland, the Office of the Ombudsman has been prepared to take a proactive role in investigating complaints of refusal to disclose information. While this is a useful supplement to judicial review, the decisions are recommendatory only and non-binding.[61] The failure to provide an appropriate appeals mechanism means that there is no easy and effective method of ensuring that the legislative system is

[59] The centre includes a two-storey building with a library and adequate resources and is attended by specialized staff. Empirical work by the author in Ireland indicated general satisfaction with the centre and the way in which it is being run.

[60] For a discussion of the limitations of judicial review in the UK, see Bridges, et al, op. cit., R. Cranston, 'Reviewing Judicial Review', in Richardson and Genn, op. cit., at ch. 3. In Spain, an action for judicial review brought by Greenpeace took three years to conclude: see de la Torre and Kimber, op. cit., at 59. In interviews with the author, most NGOs emphasized that they did not have the resources to engage in judicial review in order to challenge a refusal to disclose information.

[61] See Annual Report of the Ombudsman, 1995 (Government of Ireland, 1996), at 20–4.

adhered to and that abuses of law can be remedied. The knowledge that their decisions cannot easily be challenged must impact on the practice of those deciding whether or not to keep information secret. The conclusion is that once again, the effectiveness of national systems of access to environmental information is reduced.

5. Conclusions

In this chapter I have tried to set out in specific terms the role which access to environmental information can play in environmental decision-making; to identify an ideal system which could perform this role most effectively; and then to evaluate the system established by Directive 90/313 against this ideal model. It is now appropriate to draw some conclusions.

In order to do this, we may return to the six criteria identified in this ideal model. These are: broadness of scope; a balance between privacy and confidentiality; a consideration of the needs of users; supply of the appropriate form of information; accuracy and timeliness; and a legal basis characterized by clarity and absence of ambiguity. It is clear that the Directive and national systems fall short in a number of important respects.

First, it is clear that by limiting the scope of the right of access to environmental information to public information, any role which could be played in environmental decision-making as a result of access to private information, including information of private enterprises, will now be impossible. Thus we can expect that access to environmental information will only make an impact in the public decision-making process and lack of access to information held by private concerns may reduce the effectiveness of this participation.

Secondly, the scope of the system is further limited by the fact that there is no legally binding right of access to information held by European Community institutions. This will again restrict participation in decision-making which requires access to such information and also means that participation in Community level decision-making procedures will be extremely difficult. This has already been the subject of difficulty. As mentioned above, in order to challenge the Commission decision to use EU structural funds to support the building of an interpretative centre in the environmentally sensitive area at Mullaghmore, in the Burren, Ireland, the World Wide Fund for Nature sought, and was denied, access to Commission documents. This decision is currently being challenged before the European Court.[62]

Thirdly, as described above, the system simply does not pay sufficient consideration to the needs and capabilities of the users, to the form of the information supplied, and to ensuring the accuracy and timeliness of the information. In

[62] See the discussion of the scope of the Directive in section 3, above.

addition, the lack of practical arrangements seriously affects the utility of the system.

Fourthly, when compared with the ideal model set out above, the Directive together with the implementing legislation does not deliver the desired clarity and certainty in the definition and elaboration of many of the key concepts of a system of access to information. In fact the system is characterized by ambiguity and lack of attention to necessary detail.

In conclusion, the system of access to environmental information established by Directive 90/313 falls substantially short of the ideal system put forward in section 1. As a consequence, the capacity of the system to achieve its central objective of providing access to information on the environment is much reduced. Thus the system will not enable environmental information to realise its full potential in relation to environmental decision-making. The benefits derived from consciousness-raising, from public participation in decision-making, and from accountability, including improved confidence in government action and improved implementation and enforcement of environmental regulation, will only be achieved in a half-hearted and watered down manner. This may lead to frustration and resentment. The message to the European Union and to the member states is clear. If access to environmental information is to play a full role in environmental decision-making, the legislative system must be redesigned.

6

Dynamics, Process, and Instruments of Environmental Decision-Making in the European Union

HAN SOMSEN*

1. Context

Although the birth of a discrete legal corpus designed or at least frequently applied specifically with the aim of preventing or resolving environmental problems is of recent origin,[1] law as the instrument by which society is moulded and transformed always has been a significant factor in shaping the natural and physical environment. Feudal rules on the ownership of land explain the practice of extensive (as opposed to intensive) land use and the absence of over-exploitation in the middle ages, for example,[2] whilst one result of the French Revolution was the complete liberalization of hunting, in turn leading almost overnight to the extinction of all species of game in the Republic. The substitution of metaphysics for the laws of nature, under the influence of Newtonian philosophy, underlies the emergence of laws whose prime rationale was to capitalize on the inventiveness and creativity of the human species and the full exploitation of nature by man.[3] The ensuing industrial revolution, and associated adverse health effects, heralded the birth of 'environmental law' which, under liberal ideology, only allowed a minimum degree of public intervention.[4] Fascist movements in Europe inspired some of the first wildlife protection legislation.[5] Increased acceptance and expectations

* The author should like to thank Joseph McCahery for his useful comments.

[1] G. Winter, 'Perspectives for Environmental Law—Entering the Fourth Phase' (1989) 1 *Journal of Environmental Law* 39–47. Public controls specifically designed to protect the environment first emerged by the middle of the 19th century in Britain with the adoption of the 1863 Alkali Act. Universities, on the other hand, only began teaching environmental law as a discrete legal discipline in the late 1970s. Even in the 1990s, the existence of a distinct body of 'environmental' law with its own resources and methods of law-making deriving from principles peculiar or exclusive to environmental concerns is far from universally acknowledged. See P. W. Birnie and A. E. Boyle, *International Law and the Environment* (Oxford, 1992).

[2] W. Ullmann, *Law and Politics in the Middle Ages* (New York, 1975).

[3] Surviving examples of these types of laws include patent protection, corporate law, and free-trade principles.

[4] See the Alkali Act 1863 (for the control of atmospheric pollution) and the Public Health Act 1875. Water pollution controls were contained in the Rivers Pollution Prevention Act 1863.

[5] In particular, the *Reichsnaturschutzgesetz 1935*, which in many respects set up an advanced system for the conservation of nature, and which in its first recitals explains the special relationship between Germans and nature. Hitler's regime, in particular, was infused with forms of naturalism.

of public intervention in society in the second half of this century have led to a body of environmental law heavily reliant on command-and-control forms of public regulation, the effectiveness of which has been subject more recently to considerable critical debate as a result of neo-liberal philosophy.

Clearly, in addressing the relationship between law and the environment it is not crucial to decide whether or not a discrete corpus of environmental law can be said to exist. Rather, because law is the product of socio-political and economic ideology, by way of a first axiom it is submitted that a critical study of European environmental law should take heed of this context.

The second observation also relates to possible perspectives on the study of environmental law. If environmental law is understood as the body of rules regulating the conflicting uses to which the environment is put (what can be termed an 'instrumental' perspective) the focus of study, likewise, will be instrumental. Emphasis is placed on the body of instruments normally associated with environmental law thus defined; and the study of environmental law will involve a (critical) analysis of form, substance, nature, legal effects, and the internal consistency of such instruments. The quality of environmental law is judged on the basis of internal or formal criteria: a predominantly introspective process remaining within the boundaries set by the principles underpinning the existing body of environmental law.[6]

A more functional perspective underlies the view that environmental law concerns the legal rules contributing to the prevention, reparation or reduction of environmental damage. The legal instruments themselves no longer necessarily form the boundaries of study. Rather, such instruments are assessed in the light of their function and purpose, in which external or material criteria play an important role. It follows that research should query (the effectiveness of) environmental law in relation to its function through the application of data and criteria emanating from both the natural and social sciences generally.[7] The object of environmental law—the natural and physical environment—invites consideration

His most trusted confidants, too, were under the influence of various early forms of 'greenism' whilst Walter Darré—Minister of Agriculture until 1941—idealized organic farming. It was believed that Germans possessed a capacity for harmony with nature, the antithesis of which, it was suggested, was detachment from and exploitation of the natural world. See L. Alison, 'Rival Philosophies of the Earth' (1992) 7 *The World and I* 56–72.

[6] This approach is adopted by Vandermeersch, for example, who applies four criteria to assess Community environmental law: a) continuity and internal consistency; b) effective legal instruments; c) modern and suitable law-making apparatus; and d) enforcement. See: D. Vandermeersch, 'Twintig jaar EC-milieurecht in retrospectief: van casuïstiek naar modern beleid?' (1992) 40 *Tijdschrift voor Europees en economisch recht* 532–65. Jans also relies on a mix of formal and material criteria: a) consistency; b) degree of clarity and precision of concepts used; c) extent to which legal protection is offered; and d) realization in practice of EC environmental standards: J. Jans, 'De Kwaliteit van de Europese milieuregelgeving' (1990) 38 *Tijdschrift voor Europees en economisch recht* 503–26.

[7] See L. Krämer, 'The Open Society, its Lawyers and its Environment' (1989) 1 *Journal of Environmental Law* 1–9.

of other legal and non-legal disciplines, and where possible regard should be had to such data.

A third, related, assumption is that to the extent that environmental law has matured into a discrete legal discipline, its further development should as much as possible be dictated by its constitutive elements or characterizing features. In the context of the European Union this implies that, having granted environmental goals constitutional status,[8] the Union's task is to preside over an environmental policy which revolves around these constitutive elements, rather than one which is primarily designed to compensate for the externalities associated with the internal market.[9]

A first key feature affecting environmental law is that the environment forms part of the common heritage of past, present, and future generations, and that environmental damage is usually difficult if not impossible to rectify by means of traditional legal remedies. The essence of environmental law hence becomes the prevention of harm to a *res communis,* and therefore a predominantly public rather than private concern.[10] This has numerous repercussions for the process of environmental decision-making (for example as regards its required speed, the circle of participants, access to environmental information,[11] and requirements of public accountability), the substance of the rules (for example, the extent to which private law instruments are feasible, the nature of standards—reactive, preventive, precautionary or pro-active), and requirements of the implementation and enforcement process (including the circle of participants in the process and the required nature of sanctions and remedies).[12]

[8] See, in particular, Arts. 2 and 3 in Part One of the Treaty of Rome (Principles) as well as Arts. 100r-t in Part Three (Community Policies).

[9] The Treaty itself is ambiguous in this regard, e.g., Art. 2 stipulates that it is the Community's task 'to promote throughout the Community . . . sustainable and non-inflationary growth respecting the environment', giving little credence to the autonomous character of the Community's environmental policy. The Treaty of Amsterdam appears to have freed environmental policy from its subservient position. Art. 2, as amended, would read: 'The Community shall have as its task . . . to promote throughout the Community a harmonious, balanced and sustainable development of economic activities, sustainable and non-inflationary growth, a high degree of convergence of economic performance, a high level of employment and of social protection, a high level of protection and improvement of the quality of the environment, the raising of the standard of living and quality of life, and economic and social cohesion and solidarity among Member States'.

[10] See R. B. Stewart, *Market Versus Environment* (Florence, 1995), Jean Monet Chair Papers No. 19, Robert Schuman Centre, European University Institute.

[11] This is acknowledged in both global and regional contexts. In particular, Art. 10 of the Rio Declaration underlines the importance of the participation of all concerned citizens in environmental decision-making. Special roles are attributed to women (Principle 20), youth (Principle 21), and indigenous peoples and their communities (Principle 22). At European level, *Towards Sustainability,* the Fifth Action Programme on the Environment ('Fifth Action Programme') OJ C138/1, 17.5.93, advocates greater participation of European citizens at all stages of European environmental policy-making.

[12] The Rio Declaration calls on states to give effective access to judicial and administrative proceedings, including redress and remedy. The Fifth Action Programme, ibid., stipulates that individuals

A second key feature of environmental policy and law is that, although increasingly accepted as a discrete discipline, it is 'horizontal' and therefore needs to co-exist and compete with other policy areas and legal spheres.[13] There is an inherent tension between the requirement for the evolution of environmental law to be autonomous (that is, inspired by its characterizing or constitutive features), and its horizontal nature. Hence, for the principle of integration of environmental protection requirements into other policy spheres to be realized, environmental decision-making powers must at least in part be allocated to actors whose values and goals may be at variance with—or possibly even opposed to—those underpinning the Union's environmental policy. After the coming into force of the Treaty of Amsterdam, integration of environmental policy into other policy spheres will have acquired almost constitutional status. A new Article 3d is to be inserted reading:

> Environmental protection requirements must be integrated into the definition and implementation of Community policies and activities referred to in Article 3, in particular with a view to promoting sustainable development.

Evidently, this raises complicated practical and political questions of co-ordination and the most appropriate division of powers within European public administration.

Another way in which the cross-sector nature of environmental law manifests itself (which has already been alluded to), is that at all stages of its life-cycle environmental law is heavily dependent on the availability of reliable scientific data. Environmental plan-making, standard-setting, and enforcement all require access to (scientific) environmental information. To the extent that the nature of environmental law requires public participation, as is increasingly acknowledged, this necessarily implies that such information needs to be available to the public. Finally, and importantly, as environmental problems transcend national jurisdictions, legal responses increasingly need to be initiated or co-ordinated at regional and global level. This further complicates the issues of co-ordination and division of responsibilities already mentioned.

In the remainder of this chapter the analysis of the dynamics, instruments, and processes which bear upon the present and future shape of European Community environmental decision-making will be discussed within this context.

and public interest groups should have practical access to the courts in order to ensure that their legitimate interests are protected and the prescribed environmental measures are effectively enforced.

[13] The interconnection between internal market law and environmental law is made abundantly clear in Art. 100a(3) and (4). The Community's environmental policy is drawn into the domain of other policies by virtue of Art. 130r(2) which provides that 'Environmental protection requirements must be integrated into the definition and implementation of other Community policies'. This provision is to be replaced after the coming into force of the Treaty of Amsterdam, discussed further below.

2. Environmental Regulation and Market Integration: Inter-State Dynamics

It has been suggested that a proper understanding of (European Union) environmental law requires an appreciation of its wider socio-political and economic context. The European Community, though founded in 1957 on such notions as solidarity, integration, and non-discrimination, envisaged the gradual realization of these aspirations to take place through the pursuance of a common market.[14] It is true that subsequent amendments to the Treaties in 1986 (Single European Act—'SEA'), 1992 (Treaty on European Union—'TEU'), and most recently 1997 (Treaty of Amsterdam) have provided varying degrees of impetus to existing and new non-economic goals, including those relating to the environment. However, by no means do these enjoy uniform political support compared to those directly related to the establishment of the common market. The goal of establishing and maintaining the internal market very much remains the prime ambition of the fifteen member states, and those countries which have applied for membership.

This raises the question of the extent to which a supranational organization whose prime objective it is to establish a common market is capable in principle of presiding over an environmental policy and, if so, how this policy has taken shape, and is likely to evolve in the future. How the Community has been able to overcome the constitutional hurdle formed by the absence (before 1987) of an explicit legal basis for the adoption of Community environmental law has been well-documented.[15]

The last twenty-five years have shown that it is a crude simplification to infer from the economic orientation of the Union an inherent substantive handicap to the pursuit of environmental objectives. The objective of economic integration has proved a remarkably powerful incentive for the establishment of an environmental policy. In fact, it largely explains the relatively unproblematic

[14] The terms 'common market' and 'internal market' are used interchangeably in this chapter. An early indication of the philosophy towards the establishment for the common market is found in the *Rapport des Chefs des Délégations aux Ministres des Affaires Etangères* (Secretariat of the Intergovernmental Conference, Brussels, 21 April 1956), where it is stated that '[t]he purpose of a common market must be the creation of a large area with a common economic policy, so that a powerful unit of production is formed and continuous expansion is made possible, as well as an increased stability, an accelerated increase of the standard of living, and the development of harmonious relations between the Member States' (at 13).

[15] F. Behrens, *Rechtsgrundlagen der Umweltpolitik der Europäischen Gemeinschaften* (Berlin, 1976); K. St-C. Bradley, 'The European Court and the Legal Basis of Community Legislation' (1988) 13 *European Law Review* 379–402; E. Grabitz, *Competence of the European Communities for Environmental Policy* (Berlin, 1997); G. Saggio, 'Le basi guiridiche della politica ambientale nell'ordinamento comunitario dopo d'entrata in vigore dell' Atto Unico Europeo' (1993) 33 *Rivista di Diritto Europeo* 39–50; D. Scheuning, 'Umweltschutz auf der Grundlage der Einheitlichen Europäischen Akte' (1989) 24 *Europarecht* 153–92; H. Scheuer, 'Aspects juridiques de la protection de l'environnement dans le marché commun' (1975) 109 *Revue du Marché Commun* 441–56; and A. Vorwerk, *Die Umweltpolitischen Kompetenzen der Europäischen Gemeinschaften nach Inkrafttreten der EEA* (München, 1990).

emergence of more than 100 legally-binding environmental instruments even before 1986, when the Community formally acknowledged its tasks in this field through Article 130r. Environmental product regulation in particular[16] falls squarely within the 'terms of reference' of the establishment of a common market. Regulation of industrial processes also has sufficient economic implications for the Community to justify harmonization.[17]

Nor does factual evidence bear out the popular assertion that, in conjunction with the requirement of unanimity which applied to early environmental legislation,[18] the Community's economic focus necessarily gives rise to environmental standards reflecting those of the lowest common denominator. As far as environmental decision-making procedures more generally are concerned, it appears fair to say that lawyers have exaggerated the significance of majority voting for the progression of the Community's environmental policy. A particularly powerful example of this is Directive 76/464 on pollution by dangerous substances discharged into the aquatic environment.[19] Although the requirement of unanimity was widely held responsible for disappointing progress in implementing the Directive, not a single new substance to those already controlled has been added since the introduction of qualified majority voting by Article 130s. Where environmental policy is a function of economic policy, member states with traditionally high levels of environmental protection such as Germany, the Netherlands, and Denmark may partly have viewed the Union's environmental policy as a tool to externalize (Europeanize) the costs associated with these standards.[20] In conjunction with the phenomenon of 'horse-trading' or package deals,[21] this may help to explain some of these unexpected outcomes.

The requirement—at least initially—that any environmental initiative should relate to the objective of the establishment or maintenance of the internal

[16] Arts. 30–4 EC prohibit quantitative restrictions on imports and exports and measures having equivalent effect, subject to derogations in Art. 36. See further L. Krämer, 'Environmental Protection and Article 30 EEC Treaty' (1993) 30 *Common Market Law Review* 111–43.

[17] Product standards influence domestic and foreign industries, since the import of products may be prohibited according to the national treatment principle. Process standards, on the other hand, exclusively affect domestic production because they lack extra-territorial effect. This, in turn, may lead to increased imports to compensate for domestic production loss at the expense of domestic production. Trade policy instruments such as safeguard clauses may be designed, in turn leading to 'eco-protectionism'.

[18] Arts. 100 and 235 required unanimous approval of the Council of Ministers.

[19] Directive 76/464, OJ 1976 L129/33.

[20] Art. 100a(3) is a manifestation of this concern, providing that the Commission, in its proposals envisaged in para. 1 concerning health, safety, environmental protection, and consumer protection, will take as a base a high level of protection. It should further be noted that Art. 100a(3) as originally proposed referred to 'the highest' level of protection. If this had become law, it would have placed progressive member states in a significantly stronger position. A similar provision is found in Art. 130t, which provides that member states may maintain or introduce more stringent measures than those adopted pursuant to Art. 130s, in as far as these are compatible with the Treaty. Such measures must be notified to the Commission.

[21] See E. Rehbinder and R. B. Stewart, *Environmental Protection Policy* (Berlin, 1985).

market[22] cannot even be said to have led in practice to the exclusion of environmental measures which have no such *prima facie* link. It is significant that arguably the most important piece of EC wildlife conservation legislation was adopted in 1979,[23] and that the Directive on the quality of waters used for bathing, for which the economic justification is equally tenuous, was adopted unanimously in 1976.[24]

It is therefore clear that the reality of EC environmental decision-making defeats any simple theoretical model. However, theories of jurisdictional competition do provide interesting insights into the process of Community environmental law-making, and whilst it is not practicable to examine these theories in any detail here, it is useful to present the core arguments.

At its simplest, in this field of law and economics Government is regarded as merely another producer, and law as one of its products. The general public pays for and consumes regulatory outcomes such as clean air, healthy water, and so on. In an environment of states competing for capital and taxpayers, it has long been argued that a 'race-to-the-bottom' of standards is inevitable in view of the 'prisoner's dilemma' with which these states are faced.[25] In order to prevent such a development, centralization of (environmental) regulation is necessary.

Until the late 1980s, European Community (environmental) law-making appears to have been very much inspired by the fear of a race-to-the-bottom scenario.

[22] Prior to the amendment of the Treaty following the adoption of the Single European Act, such initiatives needed to be based on Arts. 100 and 235 EC. The former empowered the institutions of the Community to take action in so far as directly affecting the establishment or functioning of the common market, the latter in 'the course of the operation of the common market'.

[23] Directive 79/409 on the conservation of wild birds, OJ 1979 L103.

[24] Directive 76/160, OJ 1976 L31.

[25] See R. Audi (ed.), *Cambridge Dictionary of Philosophy* (Cambridge, 1995). The 'prisoner's dilemma' is a problem in game theory and, more broadly, the theory of rational choice that takes its name from a familiar sort of plea bargaining situation. Two prisoners, Robin and Carol, are interrogated separately and offered the same deal. If one of them confesses ('defects') and the other does not, the defector will be given immunity from prosecution and the other will get a stiff prison sentence. If both confess, both will get moderate prison terms. If both remain silent (co-operate with each other) both will get light prison terms for a lesser offence. There are thus four possible outcomes:

(a) Robin confesses and gets immunity, while Carol is silent and gets a stiff sentence;
(b) Both are silent and get light sentences;
(c) Both confess and get moderate sentences;
(d) Robin is silent and gets a stiff sentence, while Carol confesses and gets immunity.

Assume that for Robin (a) will be the best outcome, followed by (b), (c) and (d), in that order. Assume that for Carol the best outcome is (d) followed by (b), (c) and (a). Each prisoner then reasons as follows: 'my confederate will either confess or remain silent. If she confesses, I must do likewise, in order to avoid the "sucker's pay-off" (immunity for her, a stiff sentence for me). If she remains silent, then I must confess in order to get immunity—the best outcome for me. Thus, no matter what my confederate does, I must confess'. Under those conditions, both will confess, effectively preventing each other from achieving anything better than the third best option, even though they agree that (b) is second best.

Indeed, the language commonly found in the recitals to environmental directives strongly reflects race-to-the-bottom thinking:

Whereas the disparities between the laws in force in the various member states with regard to the assessment of the environmental effects of public and private projects may create unfavourable competitive conditions and thereby directly affect the functioning of the common market; whereas, therefore, it is necessary to approximate national laws in this field pursuant to Article 100 of the Treaty . . . .[26]

However, in so far as the race-to-the-bottom theory is advanced to justify uniform EC environmental regulation at a relatively high level, critical questions have more recently been posed about the soundness of this reasoning. In the first place, the race-to-the-bottom theory ignores the advantages of environmental protection for which citizens of certain member states are prepared to pay a given price.[27] The idea that there are absolute normatively based preferences for environmental standards is largely fictitious, because where resources are scarce cost-benefit trade-offs between levels of regulation become inevitable, and no *a priori* fixed preference for any given level of regulation should be assumed. In addition, the harmonization of environmental standards may simply result in a shift of regulatory competition to other cost factors such as taxation, social programmes, and health and safety standards. It is significant that empirical data certainly do not unambiguously support the thesis that differences in levels and type of environmental protection have a major impact on competitiveness.[28]

The prisoner's dilemma analysis is therefore increasingly rejected by proponents of jurisdictional competition, and has been gradually substituted with a race-to-the-top approach. Applied to the European Union, this theory proposes that (1) member states are in fierce competition for the factors of production (in particular capital), and (2) this competition leads to an equilibrium of public goods and regulation that meets differing citizen preferences. Thus, it is argued, the adoption of uniform Community-wide standards is distorting in that it leads to inappropriately high standards in states with higher assimilative capacity, and inappropriately low standards in others, in both cases leading to a reduction in welfare by inhibiting trade without producing compensating effects.[29]

[26] Directive 85/337 on the assessment of the effects of certain public and private projects on the environment, OJ 1985 L175, second recital.

[27] See R. Revesz, 'Rehabilitating Inter State Competition: Rethinking the "Race to the Bottom" Rationale for Federal Environmental Regulation' (1992) 67 *New York University Law Review* 1210–54.

[28] See R. B. Stewart, 'Environmental Regulation and International Competitiveness' (1992) 102 *Yale Law Journal* 2061–84, at 2039. It appears that even in the most heavily regulated industrial sectors, such as the chemical industry, environmental compliance costs represent only a small percentage of manufacturing costs. See further A. B. Jaffe, S. R. Peterson, and R. N. Stavins, 'Environmental Regulation and Competitiveness of U.S. Manufacturing: What Does the Evidence Tell Us?' (1995) 33 *Journal of Economic Literature* 132–63.

[29] Stewart, op. cit.

There are fundamental differences between race-to-the-top and race-to-the-bottom theories. Both are based on the idea that competition exists between regulators which determines the nature of regulation in so far as jurisdiction to regulate the environment lies with member states. However, whereas the latter predicts that this will result in a high quality of environmental regulation in relation to citizens' preferences, the former warns of low quality regulation as a result of a prisoner's dilemma across jurisdictions. More importantly, however, whereas for the race-to-the-top to be realized decentralization is essential (as it is the very instrument which unleashes the necessary competition), the race-to-the-bottom theory views such competition as undesirable, and thus strongly favours the Europeanization of environmental law-making powers.

Both theories regard externalities as undesirable and subject to control, and justify centralization of environmental law-making so that the cost of regulation falls on those to whom it applies. For example, downstream riparian member states should not be adversely affected by local preferences of upstream riparian member states. Welfare and other distributive policies are also accepted by both schools of thought as justifying centralization of law-making. Protection of migratory birds, for example, would not be undertaken by any single member state and an initiative such as Directive 79/409 on the protection of wild birds is thus justified. It is striking that the gradual abandonment of race-to-the-bottom justifications for centralized regulation in favour of decentralized standard-setting largely runs parallel to current trends in European (environmental) law. Subsidiarity, a principle which postulates that the optimum level for standard-setting is the state, can be regarded as a political manifestation of the theory of jurisdictional competition.

Thus, Article 100a(4), which empowers member states (under strict conditions) to maintain higher national environmental standards after the adoption of a harmonizing act on the basis of Article 100a(1), is compatible with race-to-the-top thinking, and reflects a more general trend in European environmental decision-making which implicitly accepts a multi-standard Europe. It is not only provisions of primary Community law such as Articles 100a(4) and 130t which stimulate the emergence of different levels of environmental standards according to national priorities. As will be seen, recent secondary legislation is also founded on the understanding that it is both economically and environmentally desirable that different member states should be allowed to pursue varying degrees of environmental protection.[30] The provisions of the Treaty of Amsterdam to be inserted in a new title in the common provisions of the TEU concerning flexibility, allowing groups of member states to co-operate for the sake of

[30] See Stewart, op. cit. Recent examples of this can be found in the packaging directive and the proposed framework directive for water. A more established instrument allowing member states a choice in respect of the required degree of environmental protection is the 1988 directive on large combustion plants, regulating emissions of SO_2 and NO_x, which differentiates between industrialized member states and developing member states in setting emission limits.

furthering the objectives of the Union whilst others may choose to proceed at a slower pace, can be viewed as a further step towards race-to-the-top readjustment of EC environmental policy.

3. Environmental Regulation and European Integration: Institutional Dynamics

An hypothesis central to this chapter is that institutional dynamics play a role of crucial importance in providing an understanding of the Union's activities in the sphere of the environment. It is asserted that the institutions set up by the 1957 Treaty of Rome play a significant and autonomous role in moulding the Union's environmental policy. A purely intergovernmental, state-centric perspective of EC governance[31] is therefore rejected.

What separates the European Community from other regional and global organizations is its supranational institutional structure: the competence of those institutions to set agendas and to adopt binding secondary legislation by a qualified majority, and the extensive and compulsory jurisdiction of the European Court of Justice ('ECJ'). The European Parliament, the Council, the Commission, the ECJ, and the Court of Auditors are charged with carrying out the tasks of the Community.[32] In broad terms the Commission proposes and drafts environmental policy and law, has executive functions in respect of secondary legislation, supervises member states' compliance with EC environmental law, and represents the Union on the international stage. The Parliament's tasks are primarily legislative and budgetary, but include control and supervision of the Commission. The ECJ acts as an administrative court to impose judicial control on the other institutions of the Community and an international tribunal to review the compliance of member states' action with primary and secondary Community environmental law,[33] gives preliminary rulings on questions of the interpretation of Community environmental law if requested to do so by national courts, and opines on the compatibility of international agreements with the provisions of the Treaty.[34]

[31] Proponents of this perspective include G. Garrett, 'International Co-operation and Institutional Choice: The EC's Internal Market' (1992) 46 *International Organization* 533–60; A. Morvcsik, 'Negotiating the Single European Act: National Interests and Conventional Statecraft in the European Community' (1991) 45 *International Organization* 651–88; and A. Milward, *The European Rescue of the Nation-State* (Berkeley, 1992).

[32] Set out in Arts. 2 and 3 EC. Art. 4 postulates the principle of *attribution des compétences*. On the one hand this protects the preserve of the individual institutions *inter se*, at the same time its effect is that the Community takes no action other than for which it has been allocated explicit or implied powers. On the latter see C. Denys, *Impliciete Bevoegdheden in de Europeses Gemeenschap* (Antwerp, 1990).

[33] See in particular Arts. 173 and 175 EC and, on the Court: L. Brown and T. Kennedy, *The Court of Justice of the European Communities* (London, 1994); R. Barents, *Procedures voor het Hof van Justitie en het Gerecht van eerste aanleg van de EG* (Deventer, 1996); and J. Bengoetxea, *The Legal Reasoning of the European Court of Justice* (Oxford, 1993).

[34] Arts. 177 and 228(6) EC respectively.

The European Union's institutional balance is subject to a process of continuous evolution without a clear final destination, with the European Parliament, the Commission, the ECJ, and the Council of Ministers (in particular) each pursuing different and not infrequently opposing goals. Just as environmental law and policy for member states is partly an instrument of economic policy, so it also serves as a significant tool in wider institutional dynamics to shape the general direction of European integration and the respective roles of the institutions in that process. For a proper understanding of the input of the principal institutions in the Community's environmental policy, the broad aspirations of the Commission, European Parliament, and the ECJ need to be highlighted.[35] Political theory offers valuable insights in this regard. Although it is not possible to examine the extensive literature in any detail or to advance any particular theory, a short discussion of two political science theories will serve to underpin the discussion that follows. These will be functionalist theory, and economic theory.

Functionalist theory[36] explains the fact that member states have delegated such important environmental powers to these institutions in order to: facilitate environmental co-operation *inter se*; monitor compliance with common rules; identify breaches of those rules; cater for imperfect contracting;[37] and rationalize the process of negotiation.[38] Environmental agenda-setting powers have also been delegated by the governments of the member states to the Commission, to avoid endless individualistic action by member states, and to increase the credibility of regulatory agreements.[39]

A confrontation between these incentives for delegation and the responsibilities delegated in practice to the institutions of the EC *prima facie* bears out

[35] Since emphasis is being placed on the supranational institutions, no separate attention is afforded to the role of the Council of Ministers.

[36] Functionalism is based on the assumption that effect explains cause, rather than vice versa, because of the fact that actors anticipate such effects. Hence, institutional design is explained by the anticipated effects of supranational co-operation. Particularly influential has been E. B. Haas, *The Uniting of Europe* (Stanford, 1958).

[37] The institutional agreement is therefore viewed as a contract which, partly because of its complexity and partly because of the dynamics of the subject matter, will necessarily be incomplete in practice. Gap-filling and adjustment are necessary and facilitated by endowing the institutions with an autonomous role in this process. See also Garrett, op. cit., at 577.

[38] See in particular M. Polack, 'Delegation, Agency, and Agenda Setting in the European Community' (1997) 51 *International Organization* 99–134. Polack identifies four reasons for delegation to supranational agents: (a) they may monitor member state compliance with, or transgressions of, their treaty obligations; (b) they may solve problems of incomplete contracting, and hence may fill gaps and cater for unforeseen or changed circumstances; (c) authority may be delegated to them to adopt regulations which either are too complex to be considered and debated in detail by the principals or require the credibility of a genuinely independent regulator; and (d) member states will have incentives to delegate to an agent the power to initiate formal agenda-setting powers to avoid the negative result which would arise from a majoritarian system in which each individual legislator has the right to initiate proposals. This would result in an endless series of proposals from dissatisfied legislators who had been in the minority in previous votes.

[39] On the advantages of delegating regulatory powers to the Commission see G. Majone, 'Deregulation or Re-Regulation? Policy-Making in the European Community Since the Single Act', paper prepared for the research project *La Restructuration des Etats Européen*, European University Institute (Florence, 1996).

functionalism's basic predictions about the Commission and the Court. The Commission and the Court—to different degrees and in their respective roles—supervise member states' and institutions' action, amend sub-optimal contracts (through regulation and interpretation), facilitate co-operation by acting as a credible and independent negotiator, and set agendas.

Yet Polack and others have drawn attention to the fact that a functionalist approach is inclined to ignore the reality that the institutions themselves are autonomous creatures, which may reflect the preferences not only of the principals (member states) but also of themselves.[40] In economic theory this is referred to as 'agency losses'.

In the sphere of the environment as much as in any other area of Community policy, many of the rules governing the relationship between member states and the institutions are in fact designed to minimize such agency losses, or undesirable autonomous institutional activity. The principle of *attribution des compétences* in Article 4 EC and the procedures these institutions must follow, as well as the legal instruments available to them, can be regarded as a control procedure *ex ante* to avoid agency losses. In conjunction, and to the extent that these procedures fail to keep the institutions under control, a variety of *ex post* mechanisms may also bring the institutions back into the fold, including: power over appointments; comitology; judicial control; whistle-blowing by private parties; and, most dramatically, Treaty amendments. As will be seen below, the extent to which such control mechanisms are available to member states varies depending on the institution: whereas the Commission is subject to numerous controls, the European Parliament and the Court are much less inhibited, and thus perhaps can be presumed to play a more autonomous role in European environmental integration.

The Commission

The reference to 'the Commission' as a monolithic unit is deceptive, as it is made up of twenty-four separate Directorates General ('DGs') with distinctive and sometimes opposing policy-styles and objectives. DGXI has been one of the prime actors in the process of European environmental integration and has played an entrepreneurial role from 1972 onwards, not necessarily always by creating opportunities but also by exploiting those which happened to present themselves.[41] Thus, whereas the invitation to draw up an environmental action programme came from member states in 1972, the Commission fully exploited the opportunity and within

[40] Polack, op. cit. See also E. B. Haas and C. Schmitter, 'Economics and Differential Patterns of Political Integration: Projections about Unity in Latin America' (1964) 18 *International Organization* 255–76; R. O. Keohane, *After Hegemony: Cooperation and Discord in the World Political Economy* (Princeton, 1984).

[41] S. George, 'The European Commission: Opportunities Seized; Problems Unresolved', paper presented to the first UACES Research Conference (Birmingham, 1995).

a year produced a first environmental action programme which has come to dominate the agenda for EC environmental policy-making.[42] Until the mid-1980s, when oil crises, enlargement, and a general political malaise plunged other Community policies into stagnation and loss of momentum, environmental law-making continued to flourish.[43] At a time when the Common Agricultural Policy laid claim to the bulk of Community income, environmental policy, which is regulatory and hence hardly involves any Community expenditure, presented itself as a promising tool to increase the Commission's powers at little additional financial cost.[44]

The success of the internal market project is undoubtedly largely explained by the Commission's policy leadership.[45] The Commission's White Paper was largely the fruit of Jacques Delors seizing and capitalizing on ideas and opportunities presented by the European Parliament, influential businessmen, and the ECJ.[46] At a micro level too, harmonization of national environmental laws may be regarded as an entrepreneurial process, led by the Commission, of exploiting often innovative national regulatory outcomes by elevating them to Community level. It is true that the Commission's under-resourced bureaucracy is almost totally dependent on national experts and authorities at all levels of policy-making yet, as Majone points out, empirical evidence does not support the thesis that member states are actually dictating the policy process, a paradox which is explained by member states' self-interest in a strong, knowledgeable, and independent regulator which presides over a high quality environmental policy, and which can be trusted to enforce the law.[47]

As far as the Commission's enforcement powers are concerned, these are mainly found in Article 169 EC.[48] The infringement procedure embodied by this provision

[42] OJ 1973 C112.

[43] The first environmental directive was adopted in 1969 (OJ 1968 L68), ten directives were adopted in 1980, twenty in 1982, twenty-three in 1984, twenty-four in 1985, and seventeen in the first half year following adoption of the SEA: Majone, op. cit.

[44] See Majone, op. cit. This is not to say that the increase of responsibilities due to the Commission's enthusiasm to embrace new regulatory policies has been without institutional (as opposed to financial) cost. In particular, as will be seen, the prevailing implementation deficits in these areas are partly explained by the Commission's inability to secure that regulation is followed up by policy implementation.

[45] See W. Sandholtz and J. Zysman, '1992: Recasting the European Bargain', in B. F. Nelsen and A. Stubb (eds.), *The European Union: Readings on the Theory and Practice of European Integration* (London, 1994).

[46] e.g.: Altiero Spinelli's 'Crocodile Group' and the 'Kangaroo Group'; the Thorn-Davignon Commission, the Roundtable of European Industrialists, and the Union des Confédérations de l'Industrie et des Employeurs d'Europe (UNICE); and the ECJ in the form of the *Cassis de Dijon* judgment (considered below), respectively.

[47] Majone, op. cit.

[48] Which reads: 'If the Commission considers that a Member State has failed to fulfil an obligation under this Treaty, it shall deliver a reasoned opinion on the matter after giving the State concerned the opportunity to submit its observations. If the State concerned does not comply with the opinion within the period laid down by the Commission, the latter may bring the matter before the Court of Justice.' Other supervisory powers relevant in the environmental context are contained in Arts. 93 and 100a(4).

is divided into two phases: a pre-contentious or administrative phase, and a contentious or judicial phase. In the administrative phase, the Commission will seek to reach an amicable settlement with the member state(s) concerned. In the vast majority of cases this is the final outcome. Where the Commission deems it necessary to proceed to the judicial phase, it will first send an informal letter to the alleged offender inviting it to submit its observations. Where, in the minority of cases, the Commission is still not satisfied, it will send a formal letter again inviting the member state to make formal observations within a certain time. Where these observations are not received or are deemed unsatisfactory, the administrative phase is concluded with the issue of a reasoned opinion which sets the boundaries for the dispute, and which contains a final deadline enabling the member state to comply. Even where the member state does not comply with the reasoned opinion, however, the Commission enjoys total discretion in its decision whether or not to take the case to the Court.

The Commission publishes annual reports on its supervisory work which provide insights into both member states' implementing performance and the Commission's use of Article 169.[49] It should be noted that because of the discretion vested in the Commission, the infringement procedure is an important policy instrument rather than merely a legal tool.[50]

Indeed, distinctive phases in the Commission's policy as regards application of the infringement procedure can be distinguished. Whereas until the mid 1970s recourse to the procedure was regarded as *ultima ratio*, the Jenkins Commission started to pursue infringements of directives as a matter of routine: an approach which ultimately served to de-politicize the procedure, and which was justified by the rather formal nature of the infringements at issue at that time, largely involving instances of incorrect transposition.[51] The approach has recently become more controversial when cases of faulty practical implementation have arisen, which require a more detailed knowledge of the practical situation prevailing on the ground. This is politically much more sensitive, and member states therefore feel that it warrants a more balanced approach on the part of the Commission.

Unsurprisingly, member states and private organizations often exert considerable pressure on the Commission to use its discretion in certain ways. For example, it is widely asserted that the Commission's decision not to pursue the United Kingdom's alleged failure to comply with the environmental impact assessment directive even after the Commission had issued a reasoned opinion, followed explicit threats by John Major that any other decision would have jeopardized ratification of the Maastricht Treaty.[52] On the other hand, individuals are

[49] The most recent report, the thirteenth, was published as COM(96) 600.

[50] *Fifth Annual Report to the European Parliament on Commission Monitoring of the Application of Community Law* (1987), COM(88) 425 final, at 8.

[51] H. A. H. Audretsch, *Supervision in European Community Law* (Amsterdam, 1986).

[52] P. Kuznlik, 'Environmental Impact Assessment: the British Cases' (1995) 4 *European Environmental Law Review* 336–44.

actively encouraged by the Commission to 'whistle-blow' where they discover breaches of Community law, and it has designed standard complaint forms for this purpose.

The workload of DGXI far exceeds its capacity to monitor compliance with EC environmental directives effectively. Neither is the reactive and lengthy infringement procedure particularly suited to application to the enforcement of environmental law, where immediate and preventive action is often required to avoid irreparable environmental damage. The shortcomings of the infringement procedure in the sphere of the environment have been recognized by the Commission, which is now considering the establishment of minimum criteria for transferring complaints-handling and environmental investigations to member states themselves.[53]

The European Parliament

High levels of public environmental awareness and concern elevated the establishment of an EC environmental policy to one of the European Parliament's top priorities in the early 1980s. Equally influential was the realization that environmental policy provided a unique opportunity for 'heightening public awareness within member states of the need for, and commitment to, enhanced democratic control of transborder policies at EC level'.[54] It ought not to be forgotten here that the first direct elections took place in 1979.

This is not to underplay Parliament's significance in shaping EC environmental law: its influence on the adoption of the SEA, and hence the environment provisions in the Treaty, through its approval of the Draft TEU in 1984, must be acknowledged. It would be inappropriate to share the widely held view, based on the Parliament's lack of a right of initiative, that its influence is marginal. Parliament's environment committee should be commended for its productivity and the extent to which it has been able to use its relatively modest formal powers,[55] in addition to exerting considerable informal pressure, to influence both environmental agenda-setting and the initiation of environmental legislation. Parliament's role has also increased significantly since the amendment of the Treaty by the SEA and the TEU. These introduced both the co-operation and co-decision procedures,[56] and qualified majority voting for environmental policy in a substantial number of cases,[57] and thus allowed the European Parliament to propose amendments to Commission proposals.

[53] Communication to the Council of the European Union and the European Parliament, *Implementing Community Environmental Law* (October 1996), COM(96) 500.

[54] D. Judge, '"Predestined to Save the Earth": the Environment Committee of the European Parliament', in D. Judge (ed.), *A Green Dimension for the European Community: Political Issues and Processes* (London, 1992), *Environmental Politics*, Special Issue.

[55] e.g., Rules of Procedure, rr. 63 and 121.

[56] Arts. 189c and 189b EC respectively.

[57] All proposals based on Art. 100a were subject to the co-operation procedure and, following adoption of the Treaty on European Union, co-decision. Proposals based on Art. 130s are, depending on their subject matter, either subject to consultation, co-operation or co-decision.

Yet many early environmental directives which are acknowledged to be the fruit of Parliament's influence were designed to capture the imagination of the European public perhaps as much as, if not more than, to address pressing environmental problems. The best example is undoubtedly Directive 83/129 on the importation of seal pup skins. Other initiatives often followed highly-publicized incidents which Parliament effectively used to increase public awareness of its role.[58] As has been seen, this observation accords with political science and economic theory that 'the functions of supranational institutions may reflect not so much the preferences and intentions of their member state principals but rather the preferences, and the autonomous agency, of the supranational institutions themselves'.[59] Hence, institutions (agents) behave opportunistically in pursuing their own interests in as far as this is or has to be tolerated by member states (the principals) and the other institutions.

Since environmental policy was firmly embedded in the EC Treaty and Parliament's role more widely acknowledged, a more autonomous and proactive approach has become discernible. This appears in the form of Parliament's own reports on emerging issues—such as economic and fiscal instruments, eco-labelling, and the implementation of EC environmental law[60]—and marks a departure from its earlier, more public-relations inspired strategy.[61] Perhaps the clearest evidence of the importance Parliament occupies in this field derives from the intense lobbying to which it is exposed, an exercise which would be futile if Parliament did not muster considerable influence.[62]

Apart from as a vehicle to raise Parliament's profile amongst the European public, environmental policy has also served Parliament's ongoing general concern to defend and where possible extend its powers vis-à-vis the Commission and the Council of Ministers. The horizontal nature of environmental policy implies that any given Community action can be based on numerous legal bases with markedly differing implications for the role played by Parliament in the decision-making process. This became acute following the introduction of Article 100a to the Treaty, but has lost none of its importancc aftcr adoption of the TEU.[63]

[58] e.g., directives on major industrial hazards (82/501, OJ 1982 L230) and transfrontier shipment of waste (84/631, OJ 1985 L326/31), which followed the Seveso disaster in 1976, when a freak accident in a trichlorophenol production unit caused the release of a kilogram of dioxin into the atmosphere.

[59] Polack, op. cit., at 107.

[60] PE 145.367 final, 13 May 1991; PE 152.137 final, 5 November 1991; and PE 152.144 final, 28 August 1991. See also the earlier paper by Ken Collins MEP on the implementation of EC legislation relating to water: PE 116.085 final, 14 February 1988.

[61] For further examples of the European Parliament's constructive role see Judge, op. cit.

[62] See S. Mazey and J. Richardson, 'Environmental Groups and the EC: Challenges and Opportunities', in Judge, op. cit.

[63] The most important legal bases are Art. 100a EC and Art. 130s. The former provides for co-decision of the European Parliament in three readings, the latter involves consultation, co-operation or co-decision, depending on the subject matter of the proposed act. See further H. Somsen, 'The European Union and the Organisation for Economic Co-operation and Development', in J. Werksman (ed.), *Greening International Institutions* (London, 1996), and H. Somsen, 'Derecho

Environmental policy has thus frequently become the scene of (legal) confrontations between the European Parliament and Council of Ministers (in particular) and the Commission, over the appropriate legal basis for environmental legislation.[64] From the perspective of member states, the *Titanium Dioxide* case appeared significantly to extend the role of the Parliament in environmental decision-making, necessarily at the expense of member states' influence, and it thus resulted in agency loss. The elaborate and complicated amendments to the Treaty following the TEU can be viewed as an *ex post* control mechanism to stop any further erosion of member state powers over environmental decision-making, although it did not reverse the process.

Apart from agenda-setting and environmental law-making, Parliament has more recently attempted to gain control over the processes of implementation and enforcement. Its most important strategy in this regard is to watch the watchdog: the Commission. Information regarding infringements of EC environmental law reaches Parliament in different ways, one important source being complaints received by individuals (which frequently become the subject of written questions to the Commission). Parliament has also initiated its own independent reports and can claim credit for the Commission's annual reports on the monitoring of the application of Community law. The latter have brought about a degree of openness in the traditionally secretive area of the enforcement of EC environmental law, in turn enabling private individuals to influence supervision of enforcement on the part of the Commission. Member states have, perhaps paradoxically, an interest in Parliament's alertness in this field, as a control mechanism to ensure that the Commission does not act out of self-interest at the expense of their own interest. Parliament may use its discretion tactically to draw attention to individual breaches of environmental law by fellow member states.[65]

The European Court of Justice

Inherent in the nature and function of the Court is the considerable degree of independence it enjoys vis-à-vis member states. The latter cannot exercise control over the Court other than perhaps through the appointment of judges and, ultimately, a change in the Treaty rules concerning its jurisdiction.[66]

Comunitario del Medio Ambiente: Tratado, Instituciones, Procedimento de Decision e Instrumentos Juridicos', in L. P. Alfonso (ed.), *Derecho medioambiental de la Unión Europea* (Madrid, 1996). For an analysis of the use of the various procedures in the environmental context, see Judge, op. cit. Other provisions on which Community environmental action has been based include Arts. 43 (agriculture), 75 (transport), 113 (common commercial policy), 129a (consumer protection), and 228 (international policy).

[64] e.g., Case 300/89 as discussed by H. Somsen, 'Case C-300/89, *Commission v Council* (Titanium Dioxide)' (1993) 29 *Common Market Law Review* 140–51.

[65] In D. R. Kiewiet and M. D. McCubbins, *The Logic of Delegation: Congressional Parties and the Appropriation Process* (Chicago, 1991), it is argued that principals monitor their agents through the use of institutional checks.

[66] An example of this extreme control mechanism is found in Art. L.

Evidently, even the Court is limited in its freedom in a number of ways, most importantly by Community environmental law itself, which it must apply and interpret, and by the requirement that its judgments and opinions be reasoned. However, even the text of the Treaty does not constrain the Court as much as might be expected: unlike other international tribunals such as the International Court of Justice, the European Court does not feel subservient to a literal interpretation of the wording of the Treaty, nor even to the intentions and aspirations of its founding fathers.[67] Rather, it pursues a 'contextual' or 'teleological' interpretation which is designed to place the provision(s) at issue in their wider context so as to secure the realization of the dynamic and ambitious objectives spelled out in Articles 2 and 3.

It has been proposed here that, to the extent that the Court is subject to less control by member states than—in particular—the Commission, the former enjoys greater potential to play a role in shaping European environmental policy and law independent of member states. Reinforcing the Court's potential to determine the course of European environmental integration is the fact that law is often still regarded as a largely technical device distinct from politics as such. This, in turn, enables the Court to engage in environmental policy-making outside the realm of much public scrutiny.[68] This appears to be particularly true in areas of procedural environmental law such as the legal protection of individuals, where for non-lawyers the substantive implications of the Court's legal activism are shrouded in legal detail. It is particularly noteworthy that it is precisely in this area that the Court appears to be making the most innovative contributions to the development of European environmental law.[69]

Yet predictions of the Court's freedom and independence depend on the legal perspective that is adopted towards the European Court itself. A purely legalistic approach would underline the paramount importance of the text and spirit of the Treaty, and explain legal outcomes exclusively by way of constitutional teleology. If such an approach is adopted, the Court's power to operate independently from member states becomes an irrelevance (other than in cases where it

[67] Cf., Art. 31(1) of the 1969 Vienna Convention on the Law of Treaties which provides: 'A Treaty shall be interpreted in good faith in accordance with the ordinary meaning to be given to the terms of the treaty in their context and in the light of its object and purpose'. The ECJ, on the other hand, observed in *Van Gend en Loos* that 'To ascertain whether the provisions of an international treaty extend so far in their effects it is necessary to consider the spirit, the general scheme and the wording of those provisions': Case 26/62, *Van Gend en Loos* [1963] ECR 1, at 12.

[68] Similarly, A. Burley and W. Mattli, 'Europe Before the Court: A Political Theory of Legal Integration' (1993) 47 *International Organization* 41–76, note that '[the fact that] integration is most likely to occur within a domain shielded from the interplay of direct political interests leads to the paradox that actors are best able to circumvent and overcome political obstacles by acting as non-politically as possible. Thus in the legal context, judges who would advance a pro-integration "political" agenda are likely to be maximally effective only to the extent that they remain within the apparent bounds of the law' (at 57).

[69] D. Curtin and T. Heukels (eds.), *International Dynamics of European Integration*, Liber Amicorum for Henry G. Schermers (Dordrecht, 1994).

needs to assert its autonomy for the sake of protecting the spirit of the Treaty).[70] Although such legalistic approaches towards the activities of the Court are still widespread amongst lawyers, these too have begun to acknowledge that the Court is guided both by law and policy. Proponents of this school most notably include Rasmussen and Weiler.[71] Although these contextualists accept an interrelationship between the Court's judicial activities and policy, they fail to provide clear suggestions as to the precise nature and dynamics of that relationship.[72] Political scientists, on the other hand, are equally divided as to the significance of the Court in policy-making. Some emphasize the Court's subservience to member states,[73] others proclaim the Court to be an 'unsung hero' of European integration.[74] By focusing on the influence of institutions and member states in European environmental harmonization, a clearer idea might be obtained about their actual roles in this field.

4. State and Community Influence over European Community Environmental Decision-Making

The metaphor of a 'regulatory chain' to symbolize European environmental policy-making is now widely used, and has found its place in recent Community thinking. In its communication of October 1996, the Commission defines the regulatory chain as follows:

> The regulatory chain is the whole process through which legislation is designed, conceived, drafted, implemented and enforced until its efficiency is assessed. It is a methodological tool allowing for a 'holistic' approach to address instruments of environmental policy.[75]

Adapted to more commonly used language, the regulatory chain may be said to consist of five separate links: planning; ascertaining formal Community powers for proposed action; exercising formal Community powers; implementation; and enforcement.

Although in reality the policy process is much more fluid than this suggests—for example, it is artificial to maintain that the question of the legal competences for planned action and their exercise (subsidiarity) is not already taken into account at the planning stage—the regulatory chain metaphor does serve for a more systematic analysis of the institutions in the evolution of Community environmental law. It will therefore be adopted for the remainder of this chapter.

[70] For a description of such legalism see Burley and Mattli, op. cit., at 45.

[71] H. Rasmussen, *On Law and Policy in the European Court of Justice: A Comparative Study in Judicial Policymaking* (Dordrecht, 1986); J. Weiler, 'The Community System: the Dual Character of Supranationalism' (1981) 1 *Yearbook of European Law* 286–306.

[72] Burley and Mattli, op. cit., at 46. [73] Discussed in Garrett, op. cit. [74] Ibid., at 41.

[75] *Implementing Community Environmental Law* (October 1996), COM(96) 500, at 25.

Planning

From its inception, the Community's environmental policy has been plan-led; and in this respect it occupies a unique position among the Community's policies.[76] Although the initiative to conceive a first environmental action programme came from member states themselves,[77] the latter were perhaps surprised by the Commission's instant response, and subsequently showed reluctance to grant these programmes formally binding status.[78] This reaction reflects unease about elevating environmental policy to a Community level—with the associated inevitable loss of national power.[79] Always carefully avoiding the formal adoption of the action programmes *in toto*, the Council of Ministers thus sought to avoid becoming legally obliged to undertake concrete action in the areas specified in the action programmes. Unsurprisingly therefore, a comparison between the commitments made in the five environmental action programmes, and concrete practical legislative action subsequently taken, often reveals a disappointing lack of progress.

The amendments brought about by the TEU have heralded the end of this ambiguous state of affairs, since Article 130s(3) now reserves the co-decision procedure of Article 189b for general action programmes. The use of this procedure principally implies that future action programmes need to be adopted as formally binding Community acts. Thus, although Article 130s(3) states that action programmes will be adopted by 'the Council', future action programmes will in reality be adopted by the European Parliament and the Council jointly.

This signifies an important shift of power in the sphere of environmental plan-making away from member states and in favour of the European Parliament. In particular, it would seem that Parliament is now in a position to push for future environmental programmes containing clear legislative commitments tied to deadlines which the Commission is obliged to observe. Krämer rightly notes that, in conjunction with its budgetary powers, this puts Parliament in a position of considerable strength.[80] One consequence that may be expected as a result of Parliament's increased role in plan-making is the formation of new inter-institutional alliances, in particular between the Commission and the European

[76] L. Krämer, 'Um eine Umweltpolitik von innen bittend' (1994) 4 *Zeitschrift für Umweltrecht* 172–77; OJ 1973 C12/1 (First Environmental Action Programme), OJ 1977 C139/1 (second), OJ 1983 C46/1 (third), OJ 1987 C328/1 (fourth), and OJ 1993 C138/1 (fifth).

[77] EC Bull., No. 10.

[78] There appears to be a consensus, however, that these programmes do possess at least a degree of legally binding force: K. Wellens and G. Borchardt, 'Soft Law in European Community Law' (1989) 14 *European Law Review* 267–321.

[79] The first action programme was adopted as a '[d]eclaration of the Council and of the representatives of the governments of the Member States, meeting in the Council', the second and the third programmes had the status of a '[r]esolution of the Council and the representatives of the governments of the Member States, meeting in the Council', and the fourth and fifth programmes were each a '[r]esolution to the Council'.

[80] Krämer, 'Um eine Unweltpolitik von innen bittend', above, at 174.

Parliament, whose interests in furthering European environmental integration will often coincide.

The Court will now also become indirectly associated with plan-making in that it will oversee the applicability of Article 130s(3) to measures which are 'general action programmes setting out priority objectives to be attained'—which could extend to more measures than merely environmental action programmes. In addition, where future environmental action programmes come to contain clear unconditional commitments for Community action tied to concrete deadlines, failure to act may become justiciable by the European Court.[81]

Ascertaining formal powers to act

The implementation of environmental action programmes through the adoption of secondary legislation or other Community instruments is preceded by a process of locating the necessary powers to undertake the planned action and, where competing or simultaneous powers exist, ascertaining which powers should be exercised to the exclusion of others.

Locating powers

Prior to the coming into force of the SEA in 1987, the EEC Treaty lacked any explicit reference to the environment, let alone specific powers to pursue environmental objectives. This exemplifies a type of imperfection inherent in a framework treaty of unlimited duration. Not surprisingly, there is also a tool designed specifically to fill such gaps. In addition to the doctrine of implied powers which offers some gap-filling potential,[82] Article 235 anticipates situations where realization of one of the Community's objectives requires that certain action be taken, but no specific powers exist.

Significant powers to pursue environmental goals existed even prior to 1987, by virtue of Article 4, which would remain dormant unless it could be shown that their use would be needed in order to carry out 'one of the tasks' of the Community. As the EEC Treaty remained conspicuously silent on any task to protect the European environment, the real gap therefore existed not so much in the powers needed to adopt environmental legislation, as in the core tasks of the Treaty itself—spelled out in Articles 2 and 3. There is little doubt that any substantial alteration in the objectives of the Treaty could be effected only by means of the Article 236 procedure, that is the convocation of an inter-governmental conference leading to the adoption of a treaty which, after ratification of the national parliaments, amends the original Treaty.[83] Although this procedure was

[81] Art. 175 EC. [82] See Denys, op. cit.
[83] Art. 236 was repealed by Art. N of the TEU.

eventually resorted to in 1986, this was some fifteen years after the Community had started usurping environmental powers.

Whilst each institution undoubtedly had strong incentives to ensure the success of the Community's environmental policy,[84] it would be misconceived to credit any single institution with the successful expansion of the Community into this new field. As described above, member states themselves invited the institutions of the Community to elaborate an environmental action programme and, by proclaiming that economic growth was not an 'end in itself', in effect reinterpreted Article 2. In 1984, the Court ruled that environmental protection was one of the Community's 'fundamental objectives' and warranted limitations to the rules relating to the establishment of the common market. This appears merely to confirm, or at most to capitalize on, what member states themselves had already conceded.[85] Although it is true that the Court has sanctioned use of Article 100 for environmental action, it should be recalled that member states needed at that time to agree unanimously on any measure adopted under Article 100 and that, in any event, no member state has ever mounted a formal legal challenge to the use of Article 100 in this field.[86]

The fact is that the absence of unambiguous environmental goals and powers in the Treaty seems to have had hardly any impact on the evolution of the Community's environmental policy. The subsequent incorporation into the SEA of a title specifically devoted to environmental protection removed any remaining uncertainty as to the Community's objectives and powers in the sphere of the environment.

As for the environmental objectives of the Community, these were found in Article 130r(1) rather than in Article 2 and are largely consistent with those found in the action programmes.[87] More significant than the objectives and principles found in Articles 130r and 130t, which mostly reflected existing practice, was the introduction of two distinct legal bases for environmental decision-making. Article 130s, the provision in Title VII specifically relating to environmental decision-making, required unanimity, after mere 'consultation' with the European Parliament. A new Article 100a foresaw instead the adoption of measures contributing to the establishment of the internal market by means of qualified majority voting, after 'co-operation' with the European Parliament. Thus, under the so-called 'co-operation' procedure a second reading was introduced. Where Parliament proposes amendments or rejects the Council's common position in the first reading, in the second reading the Council will have to abandon the proposal

[84] See further Somsen, in Werksman (ed.), op. cit.

[85] Case 240/83, *Procureur de la République v Association de Défense des Brûleurs d'Huiles Usagées* [1985] ECR 531.

[86] The tenuous legal basis for environmental directives was raised by way of defence in the context of Art. 169 proceedings in Cases 91 and 92/79, *Commission v Italy* [1980] ECR 1099.

[87] The objectives in Art. 130r(1) were: to preserve, protect, and improve the quality of the environment; to contribute towards human health; and to ensure a prudent and rational utilization of resources.

completely, accept the amendments included by the Commission in its revised proposal by a qualified majority, or unanimously adopt a proposal other than the revised proposal.

Apart from qualified majority voting and increased democratic participation, Article 100a(4) introduced a curious but highly significant procedure designed to protect member states with high environmental preferences from the possible consequence of qualified majority voting, acknowledging for the first time the desirability of enabling member states to pursue higher environmental standards after internal market harmonization. It is true that in the sphere of the environment, minimum harmonization has been the rule since the introduction of Article 130t to the Treaty. The significance of Article 100a(4) is that it formally introduced the same principle for environmental measures which fit within the context of the establishment of the internal market.[88] This development reflects the gradual abandonment of race-to-the-bottom in favour of race-to-the-top thinking.

The TEU, adopted in 1992 and undoubtedly designed to represent a further step in the process of European integration,[89] secured a place for the Community's environmental policy in Articles 2 and 3. This needed to be more than a merely cosmetic change, as it could have signalled clearly that environmental objectives are equal in importance to the other objectives mentioned in those provisions. However, as has already been pointed out, the phrasing of Article 2 as well as the proliferation of numerous other competing policies in Article 3 still leaves considerable uncertainty as to the relative importance of environmental objectives compared to those relating to trade.

The environmental provisions were placed in Title XVI, 'Environment'. They incorporate the objectives previously found in Article 130r(1), with the addition of 'promoting measures at international level to deal with regional or world-wide problems'. As far as environmental objectives and powers are concerned, the most important change was brought about by Article 130s. This introduced new decision-making procedures for different categories of environmental measures: Article 100a, which became subject to the co-decision procedure, and Article 3b, the much debated principle of subsidiarity, which will be discussed further below.

The main novelty of the co-decision procedure—governing environmental measures falling within the ambit of the internal market—was the introduction of a third reading, and the requirement that a Conciliation Committee be convened if no agreement can be reached between the Council and the European Parliament in the second reading. This third reading is completed if, after six weeks, the Conciliation Committee approves a joint text, after which that text is referred

[88] Meanwhile, the practical importance of Art. 100a(4) should probably not be exaggerated. Minimum harmonization has been increasingly pursued in the internal market since publication of the White Paper on the Internal Market (1985), and although empirical data is not available, the limited number of cases which have arisen suggest that Art. 100a(4) has been little used.

[89] See Arts. B and C1 of the Common Provisions, which make clear that the Treaty on European Union builds upon the *acquis communautaire*.

back to the European Parliament and the Council, who then have six weeks to adopt it. If the Conciliation Committee is unable to adopt a joint text, the proposal fails unless the Council adopts the common position reached in the second reading by a qualified majority within six weeks. However, in the latter case the European Parliament has the power to reject the text adopted by the Council by an absolute majority of its members, again within six weeks. It is striking that, although the co-decision procedure has granted Parliament significant additional powers, these remain 'negative': they are powers to reject.

Article 130s, the second important legal basis for environmental acts, offers a complicated and at times confusing kaleidoscope of different decision-making procedures for different categories of environmental issues. The general rule is contained in Article 130s, which reserves the co-operation procedure for action to be taken by the Community to achieve the objectives of Article 130r. However, by way of derogation from the first paragraph, Article 130s(2) insists on the consultation procedure and hence unanimous agreement of the Council for:

(a) provisions of a fiscal nature;
(b) measures concerning town and country planning, land use with the exception of waste management and measures of a general nature, and management of water resources; and
(c) measures significantly affecting a member state's choice between different energy sources and the general structure of its energy supply.

For this more sensitive category of measures the Council may unanimously define those matters on which decisions can be taken by a qualified majority. Finally, as has been seen, general action programmes setting out priority objectives to be attained (in particular environmental action programmes) are subject to the co-decision procedure and hence to qualified majority voting with increased participation by Parliament.

This variety of decision-making procedures and the diversity of oversight procedures applicable to environmental decision-making appears to be a direct consequence of the horizontal nature of environmental policy described above. For some measures, in particular those which contribute to the establishment or maintenance of the internal market, member states are prepared to delegate significant powers to supranational agents in view of the net gains they expect to secure. Measures which do not fall within this category, and where loss of member state control is not compensated for by such benefits, are kept subject to more stringent control. This includes, in particular, those which could affect the foundations of member state sovereignty.

Determining the appropriate legal basis

It has already been observed that as a consequence of the horizontal nature of the Community's environmental policy and the principle of integration embodied in Article 130r(2), the proper legal basis for any proposed environmental measure is not self-evident. It has also been seen that different procedures involve varying degrees of member state control over regulatory outcomes, with different patterns of institutional involvement, and (in particular) democratic participation. Environmental policy is therefore a logical battlefield not only for inter-state but also for inter-institutional competition.

It is of course the Commission that proposes environmental legislation, but the Council of Ministers may alter the legal basis. *Ex post* judicial review of the Council's exercise of this power is possible by virtue of Article 173 which, following *Les Verts*[90] and the adoption of the TEU, also empowers the European Parliament to seek such review for the purpose of protecting its prerogatives. It is mostly by this route that cases involving the choice of legal basis for environmental legislation have reached the Court.

In the *Titanium Dioxide* case, which arose in the post-SEA period but prior to the adoption of the TEU, the Court was asked to determine the proper legal basis for an environmental directive after the Council had altered the legal basis from Article 100a to Article 130s.[91] The Court considered that the purpose and contents of Directive 89/428 related as much to the protection of the environment as to the elimination of disparities between national environmental laws, and the decision-making procedures under Articles 100a and 130s were fundamentally different. It was therefore not possible to base the Directive on both provisions simultaneously.

The Directive had to be based on Article 100a for the following reasons: first, in view of the principle of integration, a Community act is not dependent on Article 130s for the sole reason that it also pursues environmental objectives; secondly, Article 100a(3) indicated that the environmental objectives of Article 130r can be pursued effectively by way of harmonizing legislation based on Article 100a; and, thirdly, environmental measures which eliminate distortions of competition contribute to the establishment of the internal market and hence fall within the scope of Article 100a.

In reaching this decision, the Court implicitly rejected the argument that *lex specialis derogat lex generalis*. This had come to be accepted in the sphere of agriculture, where prior to adoption of the SEA a similar choice existed between Articles 100 and 43 of the Treaty. That choice had been decided in favour of the latter provision.[92] The Court also explicitly supported the Commission's argument that the choice of legal basis must be based on objective criteria amenable to judicial review. In other words, the Court appeared to infer from the duality of purposes of environmental directives, in conjunction with the wording of Article 100a (which accommodates environmental concerns), an *a priori* preference for

[90] Case 294/83, *Parti Ecologiste 'Les Verts' v Parliament* [1986] ECR 1339.

[91] See further Somsen, 'Case C-300/89, *Commission v Council* (Titanium Dioxide)', above.

[92] See Case 68/86, *Commission v United Kingdom* [1988] ECR 855; Case 131/86, *United Kingdom v Council* [1988] ECR 905; and Case 131/87, *Commission v Council* [1989] ECR 3743.

Article 100a. This brought considerable consequences for future environmental decision-making.

The question that ought to be addressed is whether the Court's decision was predictable and dictated by the terms of the Treaty. Could it be explained in the legalistic tradition, or was it inspired by a policy of accelerating and democratizing environmental law-making? The present writer has argued the latter, emphasizing the Court's—admittedly casual—reference to the significance of increased democratic participation of Parliament under Article 100a. Indeed, giving judgment as the TEU was being drafted offered the Court an opportunity to send a clear signal to member states that the future Treaty should introduce the co-operation procedure for environmental law-making. This argument has been countered, in particular by Barents who, technically correctly, points out that at no stage in its judgment did the Court actually base its decision on increased participation by Parliament. Rather, he argues that it is the horizontal nature of environmental policy, which the Court itself underlined, which explains why the outcome is at variance with the 'legal basis' jurisprudence in vertical policy areas such as agriculture.[93]

If we accept Barents' legalistic arguments, the Court's subsequent U-turn becomes hard to explain. This U-turn arose after a text of the Maastricht Treaty had been agreed, replacing the consultation procedure in Article 130s with the co-operation procedure. The facts of the later case were very similar to *Titanium Dioxide*. The issue concerned Directive 91/156, which again dealt with the legal basis for a waste directive.[94] Against the background of *Titanium Dioxide* and the Court's settled jurisprudence to the effect that 'waste' constituted a good within the meaning of Article 30,[95] the choice between Article 100a and 130s should have involved a straightforward application of the *Titanium Dioxide* criteria, and hence been decided in favour of the former. Instead, the Court resorted to the 'centre of gravity' test it implicitly rejected in *Titanium Dioxide*. In turn, and again not uncontroversially, this led it to the conclusion that the Directive predominantly pursued environmental objectives and hence should be based on Article 130s.[96]

Rather than a difference in facts, what appears more convincingly to explain the discrepancy of outcomes is that the Court was redressing an imbalance it had created in the earlier case for policy reasons. For this, it had been severely criticized, particularly in the face of the imminent ratification of the TEU which was

[93] R. Barents, 'The Internal Market Unlimited: Some Observations on the Legal Basis of Community Legislation' (1993) 30 *Common Market Law Review* 85–109.

[94] Case C-155/91, *Commission v Council* [1993] ECR I-939.

[95] Case C-2/90, *Commission v Belgium* [1992] ECR I-4431.

[96] The Court notes: 'However, contrary to the views of the Commission, the sole fact that the establishment or functioning of the internal market is concerned does not suffice for the application of Article 100a. It follows from the Court's jurisprudence that recourse to Article 100a is not justified if the proposed act only incidentally has the effect of harmonising the conditions of the Community's internal market' (at para. 19).

to codify its judgment.[97] Although the Court is not bound by precedent and hence is perfectly entitled boldly to change course, it is clear that these kinds of 'corrections' are not without cost. Not only does legal certainty suffer, but the Court's long-term role in the process of European integration may also be undermined. It should be borne in mind that it is precisely because it is operating under the guise of the law that it has been able so successfully to engage in judicial policy-making. U-turn decisions are bound to give rise to criticisms of overt judicial activism, in turn compromising its future position as the motor of European integration.

5. Exercising Environmental Competences: Subsidiarity

Having located the appropriate powers (or legal basis) for any planned environmental action, these must be exercised to turn that action into concrete measures. The exercise of Community powers in areas of joint member state and Community competence, which includes those relating to the environment, has become subject since 1992 to the principle of subsidiarity enshrined in Article 3b.[98]

Apart from an essential democratic principle commonly found in federations, designed to clarify the allocation of responsibilities between the Community and its member states, the principle may be viewed as an oversight procedure inserted by member states at a time when they had become increasingly alarmed about the growing level of Community involvement in existing and new policy fields. Although the extent to which it is legally enforceable remains unclear, the principle of subsidiarity constitutes a reaction to the functional spill-over which catapulted environmental policy into the European policy arena, as well as to agency losses as a result of judgments such as *Titanium Dioxide*. In this light, it is not surprising that since the signing of the TEU, the Community's environmental policy has been singled out as a candidate particularly suitable for subsidiarity.[99]

[97] e.g., U. Everling, 'Abrenzung der Rechtsangleichung zur Verwirklichung des Binnenmarktes nach Artikel 100A EWG durch den Gerichtshof' (1991) 26 *Europarecht* 179–82, and T. Schröer, 'Mehr Demokratie statt umweltpolitischer Subsidiarität?' (1991) 26 *Europarecht* 356–68.

[98] Art. 3b reads: 'The Community shall act within the limits of the powers conferred upon it by this Treaty and of the objectives assigned to it therein. In areas which do not fall within its exclusive competence, the Community shall take action, in accordance with the principle of subsidiarity, only if and in so far as the objectives of the proposed action cannot be sufficiently achieved by the Member States and can therefore, by reason of the scale and effects of the proposed action, be better achieved by the Community. Any action by the Community shall not go beyond what is necessary to achieve the objectives of this Treaty'.

[99] In 1992, Jaques Delors reportedly suggested that two areas ripe for subsidiarity were the environment and the free circulation of goods (*The Economist*, 27 June 1992, at 56). Also in 1992, the British presidency proposed a list of seventy-seven pieces of EC law to be amended, repealed or withdrawn. Of these, twenty-seven were environmental acts or proposals (*Financial Times*, 8 December 1992). See further European Parliament Document A3-038-/92 of 23.11.1992, 'The Application of the Principle of Subsidiarity to Environment and Consumer Protection Policy'.

At the same time, the emergence of subsidiarity as a constitutional principle of Community (environmental) law coincides with race-to-the-top philosophy, as it is founded on a belief in decentralization. Community policies should therefore be pursued at national level, as this is believed to result in optimum regulatory outcomes. Externalities and distributive policies, which, as has been seen in race-to-the-top philosophy, justify federal intervention, are also the types of measures which are intended to pass the subsidiarity test.

Considerable scholarly attention has been devoted to the impact of subsidiarity on the Community's environmental policy[100] and although a detailed assessment in the context of this chapter would be inappropriate, it is important briefly to explore the way in which the institutions have dealt with the principle during the first five years of its existence.

A useful starting point is the inter-institutional Agreement of 4 November 1993 in which the institutions agreed in principle how to implement Article 3b.[101] The agreement underlines the fact that subsidiarity does not call into question the *acquis communautaire* and hence leaves unaffected both the Community's powers in the sphere of the environment, and the institutional balance. It is agreed that the Commission, in its proposals for legislation, will include a justification from the perspective of subsidiarity, and that any amendment to the Commission's proposal making it more detailed or burdensome will need to be justified. The institutions will review both the content and the legal form of the instrument chosen with a view to implementing the principle. According to Part 3 of the agreement, the principle will be reviewed 'in accordance with the rules laid down in the Treaty', signalling the institutions' belief that the principle is justiciable.

The Commission has subsequently indicated that, in addition to a proportionality test, it applies a three-fold test in assessing whether Community legislation is desirable, and what form and substance it should take. It considers:

(a) the Community dimension of the problem;

(b) the most effective solution, given the means available to the Community and to member states; and

(c) the real added value of common action compared to isolated action by member states.

Although no exhaustive overview can be provided here of the proposals for environmental legislation which have so far been subject to this test, an interesting example is provided by the proposal on the ecological quality of surface waters, where six out of a total of eleven pages of the explanatory memorandum

[100] See, e.g., R. S. Axelrod, 'Subsidiarity and Environmental Policy in the European Community' (1994) 6 *International Environmental Affairs* 115–32; L. J. Brinkhorst, 'Subsidiarity and European Community Environment Policy: a Panacea or a Pandora's Box?' (1993) 2 *European Environmental Law Review* 16–24; M. Debrulle (ed.), *Future European Environmental Policy and Subsidiarity* (Brussels, 1994); and L. Lenaerts, 'The Principle of Subsidiarity and the Environment in the European Union: Keeping the Balance of Federalism' (1994) 17 *Fordham International Law Journal* 846–95.

[101] EC Bull., No. 10, at 129–30.

were devoted to the subsidiarity test.[102] The 'scale and effects' test was deemed to be satisfied because of the mere fact that 'all Member States are concerned by this action'. The 'added value' test was also fulfilled, this time by virtue of the existing body of water law with which the proposal was intrinsically linked. All in all, it appears that the subsidiarity test of Article 3b can be relatively easily satisfied.

As the inter-institutional agreement makes clear, the subsidiarity test not only applies to the question of whether the Community should exercise its powers, it also impacts on the choice of legal instruments to be employed, and their eventual content.

Choice of legal instruments

As far as the choice of instruments is concerned, Article 189 of the Treaty provides that the European Parliament, acting jointly with the Council and the Commission, shall make regulations and issue directives, take decisions, make recommendations, and deliver opinions. The characteristics of these instruments are well known. Regulations are the most powerful but also most intrusive instruments of Community environmental policy. They allow member states little or no discretion in implementation, as they contain obligations of both substance and form. In view of their characteristics, regulations have been used relatively rarely.[103] The instrument most commonly used is the directive, which is binding upon each member state to which it is addressed as to the result to be achieved, but which leaves to the national authorities the choice of form and methods for its implementation.

Article 189 is not exhaustive however, and various other instruments exist. Mention has already been made of the *sui generis* acts which were chosen for the first five environmental action programmes. In addition, there are declarations, communications, resolutions, codes of conduct, codes, guidelines, frameworks and internal instructions, and a variety of other possibilities, which are generally held to fall within the category of 'soft law'.[104] Simply put, soft law

[102] COM(93) 680 final. The proposal has recently been withdrawn in view of the proposed framework directive on water supplies. The term 'subsidiarity test' is employed here to refer to the test laid down in the second and third paragraph of Art. 3b, and hence includes the proportionality test of the third paragraph.

[103] Art. 189 provides: 'A regulation shall have general application. It shall be binding in its entirety and directly applicable in all Member States'. See Case 34/73, *Variola v Italian Finance Administration* [1973] ECR 981.

[104] On the significance of soft law in the Community see generally J. Karl, 'Zur Rechtswirkung von Protokollerklärungen in der Europäischen Gemeinschaft' (1991) 46 *Juristenzeitung* 593–9. In the Community context, soft law has been defined as: '. . . rules of conduct which find themselves on the legally non-binding level (in the sense of enforceable and sanctionable) but which according to their drafters have to be awarded a legal scope, that has to be specified at every turn and therefore do not show a uniform value of intensity with regard to their legal scope, but do have in common that they are directed at (the intention of the drafters) and have as effect (through the medium

instruments may be described as unilateral or multilateral instruments which, without possessing formal legally binding effect, are intended by their authors to have certain legal effects.

For a Community which, compared to international organizations, is characterized by its capacity to adopt binding secondary environmental instruments speedily and without the need for further ratification, the significance of soft law instruments initially comes as a surprise. However, in reality the legal as well as political significance of soft law in the European Community exceeds that in public international law. In particular, Article 5 of the Treaty, which requires member states to take all appropriate measures to fulfil Treaty obligations or resulting from action taken by the Community and to abstain from any measure which could jeopardize the attainment of the objectives of the Treaty, extends to soft law instruments. This in turn means that the Court enjoys jurisdiction to review compliance with soft law instruments.[105] Also, soft law instruments are not infrequently the first step towards a fully-fledged Community policy.

As soft law instruments do produce legal effects, and their elaboration is not subject to formal Community decision-making procedures, their attraction for the Commission becomes plain. Snyder's interpretation of Commission communications as proactive instruments, allowing it to claim its authority with regard to fundamental issues of policy while bypassing the Council and European Court, is illustrative in this regard.[106]

Soft law instruments also accord well with the subsidiarity principle because, as long as the principle of *pacta sunt servanda* is honoured, member states remain free in the choice of how to discharge their task. The Commission, in its 1992 Communication on the principle of subsidiarity (itself a soft law instrument) noted:

> The main choice where subsidiarity is concerned is between binding and non-binding measures . . . if action is needed to achieve the objectives of the Treaty, it must not be disproportionate; this implies that recourse to the most binding instrument should be used as a last resort.[107]

Subsidiarity, it will be remembered, was introduced to counter the Community's democratic deficit and lack of legitimacy more generally. Nevertheless, it leads to greater recourse to soft law instruments, the use of which inherently leads to further loss of democratic legitimacy and accountability.[108]

of the Community legal order) that they influence the conduct of Member States, institutions, undertakings and individuals, however without containing Community rights and obligations'. See F. Snyder, *Soft Law and Institutional Practice in the European Community*, European University Institute Law Working Paper No. 93/5.

[105] In Case C-322/88, *Grimaldi v Fonds des Maladies Professionelles* [1989] ECR 4407, the Court seized jurisdiction to interpret soft law instruments.

[106] op. cit.

[107] Commission of the European Communities, 'The Principle of Subsidiarity: Communication of the Commission to the Council and the European Parliament', SEC(92) 1990 final, 27 October 1992, at 14.

[108] See Snyder, op. cit., at 7.

Choice of Regulatory Technique

With the decision about the legal instrument, the Commission will also have to choose the regulatory technique embodied in those instruments. Environmental policy may be pursued through the application of a variety of regulatory techniques.[109] Where product regulation is concerned, total harmonization may be pursued in an attempt to eliminate obstacles to trade in products. Uniform Community standards come to apply to inter-Community trade in regulated products but also to purely internal situations. Their elaboration takes time, they have a stifling effect on technological innovation, and their effect is distorting in that they do not allow diversification of standards in accordance with national preferences. The practical and ideological drawbacks of this technique are now widely recognized, and it is therefore rarely used.

An alternative which is sometimes found is optional harmonization, where uniform Community standards are adopted applying to inter-Community trade but which at the request of producers may also be made applicable to the national market. No such option exists where partial harmonization is used. This involves fixing Community standards to apply to inter-Community trade but not to inter-state trade. Whilst enabling member states to elaborate national standards which reflect national environmental priorities, this technique may place national producers at a disadvantage as they are unable to benefit fully from economies of scale.

As has been seen, by far the most commonly used technique in the sphere of the environment is minimum harmonization. This involves fixing minimum Community standards, but allows member states to fix more stringent standards.[110]

Following the Court's judgment in *Cassis de Dijon* and publication of the White Paper on the Internal Market,[111] the doctrine of mutual recognition of standards has partly replaced the need for harmonization. According to this doctrine, member states should normally accept products lawfully produced and marketed in other member states, save where mandatory requirements dictate that certain proportionate and non-discriminatory protective action be taken. The technique of mutual recognition stimulates regulatory competition and hence innovation, and at the same time will significantly speed up the completion of the internal market. On the other hand, mutual recognition, an inherently reactive instrument, is difficult to reconcile with the need for the Community to pursue an autonomous and proactive environmental policy.

The mutual recognition doctrine also forms a vital ingredient of the so-called 'new approach', which involves harmonization of certain fundamental environmental requirements by private specialized standard-setting agencies, coupled with

[109] See Sevenster, *Milieubeleid en Gemeenschapsrecht*, above.

[110] H. Temmink, 'Mimimumnormen in EG Richtlijnen' (1995) 43 *Tijdschrift voor Sociaal en Economisch Recht* 79–106.

[111] Case 120/79, *Rewe-Zentrale v Bundesmonopolverwaltung für Branntwein* [1979] ECR 649 and COM(85) 310 final, respectively.

mutual recognition of national technical standards. Whereas the new approach therefore accommodates some of the criticisms levelled at the doctrine of mutual recognition, the private nature and lack of accountability of these standard-setting agencies undermines its suitability for the pursuit of environmental policy which, as has been argued earlier, should predominantly be a public concern.[112]

Choice of Regulatory Instruments

In choosing regulatory instruments, the Commission gathers advice from scientific committees in the drafting stage of legislation with a view to elaborating its eventual content. Significantly, these committees are made up of specialists proposed by member states. The Commission is also assisted by regulatory committees, consisting exclusively of government officials whose function it is to iron out political difficulties, rather than to provide scientific advice. Member state influence on environmental decision-making is therefore predominant, although the Commission also obtains scientific information and guidance by issuing open invitations to submit evidence. In a conscious attempt to limit its dependency on channels of information controlled by member states, and in view of the fact that due to its under-capacity it is unable to gain sufficient independent insights, the Commission aims to deal with interest groups which are representative of the issue under consideration and which hold considerable expertise in the field.[113] It may be expected that with the evolution of the European Environment Agency,[114] the Commission will gradually become less directly dependent on member state information.

An overview of the various regulatory instruments in the sphere of the environment reveals the multiplicity of instruments used. Sevenster has usefully categorized these into organizational, physical, and economic.[115] Examples of organizational instruments are information exchanges, co-operation between member states and the Commission or member states *inter se,* the duty to designate competent authorities to carry out certain tasks, environmental impact assessment, and inspection and reporting requirements. Physical instruments have traditionally been by far the most significant in EC environmental law. Important examples are emission standards, quality objectives, labelling and/or packaging requirements, quantitative restrictions, product norms, systems of authorization and permits, zoning, designation of areas for the purpose of the application of Community standards, recycling, sampling and testing, the elaboration of programmes, and prohibitions. Economic and fiscal instruments include Community aid for certain projects, liability, charges, and state aid.

[112] The implications of similar trends in municipal law, also partly prompted by the failings of established approaches to environmental regulation, are considered in Chapters 1 and 2.

[113] See Mazey and Richardson, op. cit.

[114] Regulation 1210/90, OJ 1990 L120.

[115] Op. cit., at 75. Sevenster mentions 'sanctions' as a fourth category. In view of its ancillary nature this will not be considered separately here.

It is difficult to explain the preference for certain legal instruments or regulatory techniques, even in individual cases. Indeed, the institutions have been criticized for failing to elaborate guidelines governing the choice even between directives and regulations.[116] The Council of Ministers has issued a resolution regarding the quality of Community law, which fails to provide any indications as regards legal instruments to be employed.[117] The Commission has published guidelines for legislative policy which address the choice of instruments as part of the proportionality test, but again without in any way articulating general criteria.[118]

Clearly, criteria relating to quality ought to play a role of predominant importance and should lead to different outcomes depending on the nature of the problem addressed. However, it is evident that precisely because the choice of instruments so directly influences their subsequent impact at national level, political and economic considerations of a general nature may actually dictate the techniques eventually preferred. A famous example is Directive 76/464 on pollution caused by certain dangerous substances discharged into the aquatic environment, where the United Kingdom's insistence on the use of quality objectives for the control of 'Black List' substances was largely inspired by economic arguments associated with the fact that quality objectives allowed it to benefit from its island status.[119]

Similarly, directives are preferred to regulations because they allow member states to assimilate Community obligations into their existing legal cultures, even though significant problems of transposition are associated with their use, which in turn have undermined their effectiveness to some extent. The shift away from precise physical and enforceable instruments such as limit values, towards open-ended standards such as BATNEEC ('best available techniques not entailing excessive cost'), as found in the directive on integrated pollution prevention and control, would at least partly appear to be inspired by similar considerations. Similarly, it is questionable whether the emerging trend to replace substantive harmonization of environmental standards with harmonization of procedures which environmental law-making at national level must satisfy, on which both the draft directive on the ecological quality of surface waters and the draft water resources framework directive are based, is dictated primarily by arguments of quality.

Environmental regulatory instruments and techniques are therefore currently subject to a process of significant change, the general thrust of which is perhaps most strikingly captured by the Conclusions of the Presidency of the Edinburgh Council of December 1992 regarding the principle of subsidiarity:

[116] Ninth Report of the House of Lords Select Committee on the European Communities, *Implementation and Enforcement of Environmental Legislation, Session 1991–92* (HL Paper 53).

[117] Resolution on the Quality of European Legislation, OJ 1993 C166. See generally T. Heukels, A. E. Kellerman, V. P. Verkruisen, and J. J. M. Sluys, *Kwaliteit Communautaire Regelgeving* (Den Haag, 1996).

[118] SEC(95) 2255/5.

[119] On the politics surrounding Directive 76/464 see Somsen, 'EC Water Directives' (1990) 1 *Water Law* 93–8.

The form of action should be as simple as possible, consistent with satisfactory achievement of the objective of the measure and the need for effective enforcement. The Community should legislate only to the extent necessary. Other things being equal, directives should be preferred to regulations and framework directives should be preferred to detailed measures. Non-binding measures such as recommendations should be preferred where appropriate. Consideration should be given where appropriate to the use of voluntary codes of conduct.[120]

Exactly how the Council's preference for framework directives and non-binding instruments is to be squared with the acknowledged need for effective enforcement is far from apparent.

Implementation

Implementation is the vehicle bridging the gap between the Community legal order and those of member states. It involves both 'transposition' (in the case of directives) and 'practical application' (in the case of directives and regulations). 'Transposition' is the incorporation into national legal orders of obligations, rights, and duties contained in Community law, whilst practical application is the incorporation of Community law into individual decisions, for instance when issuing a permit or executing a plan or programme. Because implementation is the process transforming European environmental policy into tangible action, the impact of European Community environmental policy is to an important extent a function of the faithful implementation of its (legal) instruments.

It has been seen that member states have delegated areas of environmental decision-making to supranational institutional agents which, for this purpose, dispose of a variety of regulatory competences, instruments, and techniques. For the implementation of environmental decisions, however, the roles are reversed in that it is member states which act as agents for the Community. Article 130s provides that, without prejudice to certain measures of a Community nature, the member states shall finance and implement environment policy. More generally, Article 5 enshrines the principle that while Community policy is elaborated by the institutions in accordance with the procedures laid down in the Treaty, it is member states which implement this policy. Consequently, at least as far as implementation of Community environmental policy is concerned, rather than one overarching European environmental legal culture, fifteen distinct cultures prevail, which member states are encouraged to utilize so as to employ the most cost-effective means to realize European environmental policy.

Hence, whereas decentralization of European environmental standard-setting is a phenomenon of recent origin, decentralization and jurisdictional competition were already embraced in the original Treaties for the implementation of

[120] Conclusions of the Presidency, European Council in Edinburgh, 11–12 December 1992, Part A, Annex 1, 'Overall Approach to the Application by the Council of the Subsidiarity Principle and Article 3b of the Treaty on European Union', at 9.

Community environmental policy. Directives are the embodiment of this principle and the parameters governing their implementation therefore need to be afforded particular attention.

Implementing Directives

Member states, particularly those which voted against environmental directives subsequently adopted by a qualified majority, may have significant economic or political interest in minimizing and undermining directives' impact at national level. The national authorities responsible for implementing European Community environmental law, who will not normally have participated in the decision-making process, may be reluctant to allocate scarce resources to the implementation of these obligations. Implementation gaps, which the Commission itself acknowledges are significant,[121] therefore seem almost inevitable.

At the same time, the perception that member states enjoy almost total control over the implementation process has in fact in many instances softened the latter's resistance to the adoption of environmental directives, the practical impact of which they felt they could in any event control.[122] It has been correctly observed that 'losing at the policy-making stage may not be so important if there is a second round at the implementation stage when the national government, through its bureaucracy, has an opportunity to determine what will actually happen in the policy area in that country'.[123] The use of ambiguous and vague language so often encountered in environmental directives has therefore partly been a conscious instrument initially serving both the Commission (because it allowed the adoption of environmental directives) and member states (as it appeared to allow flexibility in implementation).

This marriage of interests became increasingly unsettled when the Court, through cases instigated by the Commission, began to give concrete and relatively progressive meaning to these concepts. Paradoxically, although undoubtedly improving implementation rates, recent calls for greater clarity, transparency, and

[121] In 1995, member states had notified implementing measures for only ninety-one per cent of the Community's environmental directives, leaving as many as twenty or twenty-two directives not transposed in some member states. In the same year the Commission registered a total of 265 suspected breaches of Community environmental law, based on complaints from the public, Parliamentary questions and petitions, and cases detected by the Commission: this is over twenty per cent of all the infringements registered by the Commission in that year. In October 1996 over 600 environmental complaints and infringement cases were outstanding against member states, with eighty-five of the latter awaiting determination by the Court: Commission Communication, *Implementing Community Environmental Law*, op. cit.

[122] The best example is probably Art. 1(2)(a) of Directive 76/160 on the quality of bathing waters (OJ 1976 No. L31). See P. Bird, 'Applying EC Environmental Law on the Ground', in H. Somsen (ed.), *Protecting the European Environment* (London, 1996).

[123] G. Peters, 'Bureaucratic Politics and the Institutions of the European Community', in A. Sbragia (ed.), *Euro-Politics: Institutions and Policymaking in the 'New' European Community* (Washington D. C., 1992).

certainty in the drafting of EC environmental directives[124] may therefore lead to a less progressive European environmental policy, as it will undermine the Court's dynamic gap-filling potential.

As indicated above, many of these issues are inherently connected with the use of directives as instruments of European Community environmental policy. Traditionally, problems of transposition have been generally associated with the use of directives, whilst the implementation of regulations—which should not normally be transposed—could lead to practical implementation deficits. Although this analysis is in principle correct, it ought not to be overlooked that incorrect transposition may result in incomplete practical implementation. For example, failure correctly to transpose the exceptions to the prohibition from killing birds in Directive 79/409 on the conservation of wild birds has resulted in the granting of hunting licenses by national authorities when this should not occur.[125] Directives therefore may not only be incorrectly transposed, but they may also involve a higher risk of incorrect application in practice than regulations.

This being the case, and bearing in mind member states' possible reluctance to implement environmental directives faithfully, it is logical that the Court, whose task it is to ensure that in the interpretation and application of the Treaty the law is observed,[126] should have placed considerable constraints on member states' discretion to choose the forms and methods to implement directives. It has achieved this mostly in tandem with the Commission which, as guardian of the Treaty, may bring alleged failures in implementation to the attention of the Court. In addition, national courts may refer questions to the Court of Justice pursuant to Article 177. Although this provision, unlike Article 169, does not confer jurisdiction to pronounce on the compatibility of national implementing rules with directives, by issuing national courts with clear guidelines on the interpretation of Community environmental law, the latter are enabled to carry out this task autonomously.

It appears useful to review some of the most important principles which have arisen from the Court's case law on the implementation of environmental directives. However, the preliminary question ought first to be addressed of whether the Court accepts the premise (presented in the introduction to this chapter) that environmental law is a discrete discipline with its own distinctive characteristics and, if so, whether this has impacted on member states' discretionary powers concerning implementation. The answer to both questions appears to be 'yes'. On numerous occasions, the Court has remarked that 'as the management of

[124] e.g., *Implementing Community Environmental Law*, above, at 14.

[125] Case 247/85, *Commission v Belgium* [1987] ECR 3029; Case 262/85, *Commission v Italy* [1987] ECR 3073; Case 236/85, *Commission v Netherlands* [1987] ECR 3989; Case 412/85, *Commission v Germany* [1987] ECR 3503; Case 252/85, *Commission v France* [1988] ECR 2243; Case C-57/89, *Commission v Italy* [1991] ECR I-57; and Case C-339/87, *Commission v Netherlands* [1990] ECR I-851.

[126] Art. 164 EC.

the common heritage is entrusted to member states as regards their respective territories', the faithful transposition of Community obligations into national law becomes especially important.[127] In addition, in a number of cases the Court has accepted that 'environmental rights' are enshrined in environmental directives which individuals ought to be in a position to protect before their national courts. As will be seen, national implementing rules should therefore be such as to allow individuals to rely on them in national proceedings.[128] Additional (more stringent) requirements thus appear to apply to the implementation of environmental directives.

It has been seen that implementation consists of a process of transposition followed by practical application. Member state discretion in both areas has been substantially fettered through the Court's case law. From an analytical perspective, it is useful to divide the process of transposition into two distinct phases:[129] the duty to provide information in due time; and formal requirements relating to national implementing rules.

The duty to provide information in respect of implementing legislation is a vital pre-condition for the Commission to carry out its task under Article 155. It is also generally specified in environmental directives themselves.

Duty to provide information

Failure to provide the required information in time does not lead to the presumption that the directive has not been implemented, but is in itself a sufficiently serious breach for the Commission to initiate proceedings.[130] It appears that individuals cannot argue that implementing legislation is void on the basis that no such information has been provided by member states. This issue arose in *Cinsello Balsamo*, and was rejected in the following terms:

> It follows from the foregoing that [Article 3(2) of Directive 75/442] concerns relations between the Member States and the Commission and does not give rise to any right for individuals which might be infringed by a Member State's breach of its obligation to inform the Commission in advance of draft rules.[131]

[127] e.g., Case 236/85, *Commission v. Netherlands* [1987] ECR 3989 and Case 412/85, *Commission v Federal Republic of Germany* [1987] ECR 3503, both on Directive 79/409 (protection of wild birds).

[128] Case C-361/88, *Commission v Federal Republic of Germany* [1991] ECR I-2567 and Case C-59/89, *Commission v Germany* [1991] ECR I-2607. Also Case C-190/90, *Commission v Netherlands* [1991] ECR 3265.

[129] In Case 96/81, *Commission v Netherlands* [1982] ECR 1791, the Commission stated that it examines the implementation of environmental directives in three stages, considering: if information has been received in due time; whether the legislation is apparently satisfactory; and whether measures are taken in practice at national level.

[130] Case 96/81, *Commission v Netherlands* [1982] ECR 1791 and Case 97/81, *Commission v Netherlands* [1982] ECR 3483.

[131] Case 380/87, *Cinisello Balsamo* [1989] ECR 2491, para. 23167.

The question arises of the extent to which *Balsamo* should be distinguished from the Court's judgment in *Securitel*, which recently caused considerable commotion in the Netherlands.[132] Here the provisions at issue were Articles 8 and 9 of Directive 83/189 establishing a notification procedure for certain technical specifications. The provisions, intended to eliminate barriers to the free movement of goods caused by differing national requirements, oblige member states immediately to notify draft technical specifications for goods. Other member states are then informed and can submit observations. The Court ruled that individuals can rely on Articles 8 and 9 where no notification has taken place; in which case the national provisions are void. In the Netherlands, a large number of environmental provisions falling within the ambit of the directive were not notified and their legal status was subsequently called into question.

What appears to separate *Securitel* from *Balsamo* is the fact that Articles 8 and 9 were drafted specifically to benefit traders in certain goods to which 'technical specifications' as defined in the directive apply. Although the Court has yet to clarify the exact circle of beneficiaries of this right, it appears that only those traders can successfully invoke the directive before national courts, and not third parties (such as, for example, drivers convicted with the use of breathalysers the technical specifications of which were not notified to the Commission). General notification provisions, such as Article 3(2) of Directive 75/442, set rules which apply merely between the Commission and member states. It is noteworthy that the Court itself acknowledged in *Securitel* that its decision was partly one of policy: to introduce an element of private enforcement leading to effective preventive control that the rules are applied. Similar policy considerations do not apply to provisions such as Article 3(2) of Directive 75/442, where a right of individuals to challenge the legality of implementing legislation on the basis of a failure to notify implementing provisions would not directly lead to the realization of the Directive's environmental objectives. It therefore seems that *Securitel* has not altered the law as laid down in *Balsamo*.

Apart from the duty to provide information in due time, national implementing legislation must also satisfy a number of formal criteria. Evidently, legislation should be adopted before the expiry of the relevant deadline, although significant back-logs still exist in this regard.[133] The Court has rejected a number of justifications which were advanced by member states in the course of infringement proceedings. Unrealistic deadlines, ambiguities as to the scope of environmental directives, unforeseen national problems, existing constitutional practices lengthening the legislative process, reluctance of subordinate authorities, and the alleged direct effect of directives have all been rejected as excuses for failure to adopt legislation in time.[134]

[132] Case C-194/94, *CIA Security International v Signalson SA and Securitel SPRL* [1995] ECR I-180.

[133] See, e.g., Case 301/81, *Commission v Belgium* [1983] ECR 467.

[134] See (respectively) Cases: 301/81, above; 291/84, *Commission v Netherlands* [1987] ECR 3483; 291/84, *Commission v Netherlands* [1987] ECR 3483; 171/80, *Commission v Italy* [1981] ECR 203,

Formal requirements of national implementing rules

The Court has elaborated a number of formal criteria which national implementing legislation must satisfy, which in turn have considerably restricted member states' freedom of choice as to the form and substance of national implementing rules. Most importantly, implementation through administrative practice has consistently been rejected for reasons of legal certainty, and the protection of individual rights. In what now has become a standard formula the Court has ruled that:

> . . . the transposition of a directive into domestic law does not necessarily require that its provisions be incorporated formally and verbatim in express, specific legislation; a general legal context may, depending on the content of the directive, be adequate for the purpose provided that it does indeed guarantee the full application of the directive in a sufficiently clear and precise manner, so that, where the directive is intended to create rights for individuals, the persons concerned can ascertain the full extent of their rights and, where appropriate, rely on them before national courts.[135]

The Court's minimum standards for implementing legislation are therefore inspired by the need for individuals to enforce their rights. This had already been recognized as an important tool to secure compliance with Community law, in addition to the powers entrusted to the Commission.[136] Whereas implementation by administrative means generally falls foul of these minimum standards, the acceptability of private law instruments as flexible means to implement Community environmental standards remains shrouded in ambiguity.

Recently, the Commission has issued a soft law instrument in the form of a Communication on Environmental Agreements in which it encourages the use of agreements between industry and administrative bodies.[137] As far as their use to implement EC environmental law is concerned, however, the Commission voices caution: when directives contain rights and duties for citizens (for example, by fixing limit values), national law must contain an appropriate binding legal instrument to enable citizens to exercise their rights. On the other hand, the Communication stipulates that in respect of the implementation of environmental reduction programmes—which, as has been seen, have become increasingly apparent in EC environmental law as a consequence of the principle of subsidiarity—the adoption of environmental agreements is appropriate.

The Communication also foresees the introduction of clauses in directives which do create environmental rights, to the effect that their implementation may occur through the adoption of environmental agreements, subject to the caveat that where

1/86, *Commission v Belgium* [1987] ECR 2797, 91/79, *Commission v Italy* [1980] ECR 1099, and 71/81, *Commission v Belgium* [1982] ECR 175; 97/81, *Commission v Netherlands* [1982] ECR 1819; and 102/79, *Commission v Belgium* [1980] ECR 1473.

[135] Case C-131/88, *Commission v Germany* [1991] I ECR 825, at para. 6.

[136] Case 26/62, *Van Gend en Loos* [1963] ECR 1.

[137] COM(96) 561 final (27 November 1996). See J. C. Bongaerts, 'The Commission's Communication on Environmental Agreements' (1997) 6 *European Environmental Law Review* 84–7.

these do not lead to attainment of legally binding goals member states must resort to legislation. The Commission is evidently not empowered to overrule the Court's jurisprudence concerning formal requirements for national implementing instruments, and it remains open to debate whether the Communication accords in every respect with prevailing Community law.

Practical Implementation

Because incorporation precedes practical implementation, issues of practical implementation have only relatively recently been addressed by the Commission. Whereas issues of incorporation are of a general nature which the Commission and the Court are well capable of addressing, the same is not true of practical implementation, which requires intimate knowledge of the situation on the ground. This, the Commission manifestly lacks. In addition, where the slowness of the infringement procedure does not necessarily result in irreversible environmental damage, breaches of practical implementation ideally ought to be rectified speedily. Yet the economic and political interests at stake are particularly sensitive where practical implementation is concerned, making a speedy resolution of failures to practically implement even more illusory. To date, little use has been made of the Court's power under Article 186 to prescribe interim measures, which could be a solution to this problem.

From the perspective of member states, implementation of a judgment obliging it to alter its physical environment may be a particularly daunting task, and they may feel entitled to more flexibility on the part of the Community's institutions than they have displayed in the sphere of incorporation. A striking example is the *Marisma de Santoña* case, where Spain found itself obliged to implement a number of technically complicated and expensive changes within (perhaps) unrealistically short deadlines.[138] Yet there is little evidence to suggest that the Commission is prepared to adopt such a strategy. Thus, in respect of Britain's failure to comply with the bathing waters directive, the Court was not persuaded by the British Government's plea that it had done everything practically possible to comply. Moreover, the Commission has indicated that it will use its powers under Article 171(2) to apply for lump sum or penalty payments to be imposed on the defaulting member state. If it is to proceed with its intentions, a partial breakdown of relations between member states and the Commission would appear almost inevitable.

6. Enforcement

Enforcement manifests itself in persuasive (negotiation, conciliation, or compromise) as well as coercive (litigation or compulsion) forms or styles. It has already been

[138] Case C-355/90, *Commission v Spain* [1993] ECR I-4221.

seen that the infringement procedure of Article 169, which is determined as much by policy as by law, embodies manifestations of both techniques. Enforcement is therefore a dynamic process governed by both law and policy, involving the participation of the institutions of the Community, organs of member states, and private individuals.

Member states' preparedness to delegate substantial environmental powers to supranational institutions is conditional upon the understanding that law-breaking is vigorously pursued by an independent and trusted authority, the Commission. Hence, the Commission's enforcement task is of vital importance for the continued expansion of European integration. The importance of the Commission as an independent enforcement authority is illustrated by the virtual obsolescence of Article 170, which empowers member states to bring cases before the Court.

Community enforcement manifests itself in direct and indirect enforcement processes. The initiation of direct enforcement action pursuant to Article 169 is the responsibility of the Commission. Indirect enforcement is carried out by individuals in pursuit of their (environmental) rights before national courts, which may in turn refer preliminary questions to the Court. Under Article 177 the Court does not enjoy jurisdiction to pronounce on the compatibility of national law with Community law; however, in practice it often tailors its ruling to the facts before the national court to an extent that leaves the latter with very little discretion in deciding the case.

It has already been seen that the process embodied in Article 169 is far from tailor-made to secure compliance with Community environmental law. This is partly due to the reactive and time-consuming nature of Article 169, which does not correspond well with the need for swift enforcement action to prevent irreversible environmental harm. In addition, the key role occupied by the Commission in the process also limits its efficiency. It is well known that the Commission is dramatically under-resourced to monitor compliance with over 200 instruments of Community environmental law. In this respect, it ought to be remembered that the implementation of environmental directives is often delegated to subordinate national authorities, complicating the Commission's task of monitoring national transposition. Also, the Commission must supervise practical compliance which, in the absence of independent fact-finding powers, is a task for which it is manifestly ill-equipped. This appears to be acknowledged by the Communication of the Commission on the implementation and enforcement of Community environmental law, which foresees the introduction of national complaint procedures designed to delegate part of the Commission's responsibilities to member states.[139]

The Commission's handicaps in enforcing practical compliance are likely to be exacerbated by the increased use of instruments which leave member states

[139] COM(96) 500 final.

with considerable discretion. Use of quality objectives for example, currently celebrating something of a revival in water and air pollution control, inevitably leads to loss of Community control in the absence of comprehensive and Community-controlled monitoring networks. The enforcement of soft law instruments is also much less straightforward than the enforcement of legally binding instruments. Given the importance of the maintenance of 'fair play' for the continued vitality of the Community's environmental policy, any evidence of a widening of the enforcement gap as a result of the use of new instruments may be expected to have repercussions for member states' willingness to agree to Community environmental law in the future.

The scope for indirect enforcement of EC environmental law, although still subject to a number of significant constraints (partly to compensate for the shortcomings of direct enforcement) has been gradually increased through the activities of the Court. Thus, the requirement that national implementing provisions be of sufficient clarity and precision to enable individuals to enforce them in national courts; the direct effect of environmental directives;[140] the obligation of national courts to interpret national environmental law in a way that corresponds with the provisions of Community environmental law from which they derive;[141] and the possible liability of the state for infringements of Community environmental law,[142] have all widened the scope of public participation in the enforcement of Community environmental law. All of these are creations of the Court.

However, such increased private participation will not lead to uniform levels of enforcement of Community environmental law. This is because, as a general rule, recourse to remedies at national level for the enforcement of Community environmental law continues to be governed by national procedural laws, subject only to minimum Community standards of non-discrimination and effectiveness.[143] Differences concerning access to justice, availability, and scope of administrative review, remedies (including interim relief), powers of the court, and legal aid differ fundamentally in member states, giving rise to considerable varieties in the potential for private enforcement. The question can be asked more generally of the extent to which *ad hoc* supervision pursued through Article 177, particularly in an area where individuals normally do not have any financial self-

[140] On the direct effect of environmental directives see J. Jans, 'Legal Protection in European Environmental Law' and L. Krämer, 'Direct Effect of EC Environmental Law', in Somsen (ed.), *Protecting the European Environment*, op. cit.

[141] In particular Cases 106/77, *Simmenthall* [1978] ECR 629; 14/83, *von Colson and Kamann v Land Nordrhein Westfalen* [1984] ECR 1891; and C-213/89, *Factortame* [1990] ECR I-2433.

[142] See Cases C-6/90 and C-9/90, *Francovich and others v Italian Republic* [1990] ECR I-5357; C-392/93, *R v Her Majesty's Treasury, ex parte British Telecommunications* [1996] ECR I-1631; C-5/94, *R v Ministry of Agriculture, Fisheries and Food, ex parte Hedley Lomas* [1996] ECR I-2553; and C-179/94, *Dillenkofer v Germany*, judgment of 8 October 1996, not yet reported. For recent comments on these cases see P. Oliver (1997) 34 *Common Market Law Review* 635–80. An analysis of their implications for EC environmental law is provided by H. Somsen, '*Francovich* and its Application to EC Environmental Law', in Somsen (ed.), *Protecting the European Environment*, op. cit.

[143] Case 45/76, *Comet v Produktschap* [1976] ECR 2043 and Case 33/76, *Rewe-Zentralfinanz v Landwirtschaftskammer* [1976] ECR 1989.

interest, should be expected to lead to significant additional supervision to that entrusted to the Commission.

A number of environmental directives contain provisions concerning public participation and access to justice, a trend which may be expected to continue.[144] The Commission has also indicated that it will encourage participation of non-governmental organizations in the enforcement of Community environmental law by issuing soft law 'guidelines' on access to justice.[145] Harmonization in this area has proved most controversial as it is easily regarded as an unwarranted encroachment on national and administrative systems.[146] Moreover, harmonization measures for the sake of the protection of diffuse interests—as opposed to securing enforcement of EC environmental law, an issue which in essence revolves around national perspectives of democratic control and accountability—is difficult to reconcile with the principle of subsidiarity, and therefore arguably is not one of the tasks the Community is called upon to address.

7. Conclusion

In view of its cross-sector character, a proper insight into European Community environmental decision-making requires a contextual analysis of its dynamics, process, and instruments. In this chapter, account has been taken of the economic context within which EC environmental law operates, an understanding of which is aided by theories of jurisdictional competition. Initial centralization of environmental competences and harmonization of national environmental laws to establish uniform standards at a relatively high level, particularly relating to products, have been explained by fears of a prisoner's dilemma leading to a race-to-the-bottom in national environmental standards. The viability of this justification has become increasingly tenuous, and race-to-the-top theories are gradually becoming predominant, favouring decentralization and acceptance of differing levels of environmental regulation according to national preferences. The 1985 White Paper on the completion of the internal market may be regarded as a turning point: it embraces the concept of mutual recognition of national regulatory outcomes, and revolutionizes the Community's philosophy towards the most effective and desirable ways to achieve its goals.

The new philosophy manifests itself in different strands and at all phases of the policy process. At the level of primary Community law for example, Article 100a(4) enables individual member states to apply more stringent national environmental standards following adoption of a harmonizing directive adopted on

[144] The directive on environmental impact assessment (85/337, OJ 1985 L175) contains important provisions on public participation, see also the directive on freedom of access to information on the environment (OJ 1993 L158), and the amended proposal for a directive on civil liability for damage caused by waste (OJ 1991 C192).

[145] COM(96) 500 final, at 16.

[146] See E. Rehbinder, 'Locus Standi, Community Law and the Case for Harmonisation', in Somsen (ed.), *Protecting the European Environment*, op. cit.

the basis of Article 100a(1). Article 130s elevates minimum harmonization to a general principle of Community environmental law and Article 130r underlines that the diversity of environmental, social, and economic situations in the Community must be taken into account by the institutions in formulating environmental policy.[147] The principle of flexibility, newly inserted by the Treaty of Amsterdam, and the ensuing regionalization within the Union, is entirely consistent with trends towards greater decentralization and diversification. At the level of secondary Community law, the choice of legal instruments, regulatory techniques, and instruments has not remained unaffected either. Soft law instruments, framework directives, BATNEEC, and procedural rather than substantive harmonization all appear perfectly compatible with the conviction that allowing national regulators maximum degrees of freedom of choice will result in optimal regulatory outcomes.

In parallel with this economic context, in view of the institutions' autonomous role in shaping European environmental law, the institutional context of European environmental decision-making has been highlighted, and illustrated by political science theories. Although member states have delegated important environmental powers to the Commission, the European Court of Justice, and the European Parliament in the expectation of yielding long term gains, these not infrequently attempt to exceed their mandate: a phenomenon against which member states are armed with a variety of control mechanisms.

The institutions having been granted mandates in relation to the tasks they have been delegated, they influence the Community's environmental policy to different extents in the different phases of the policy process. Environmental planning has traditionally been largely the preserve of the Commission, which has therefore been in a strong position to influence long-term strategy, even though member states have attempted to minimize the legal status of action programmes. With the co-decision procedure now applying to environmental action programmes, however, the European Parliament will become another key player, and the legal significance of the action programmes beyond doubt.

In the debate as to the appropriate legal basis for pursuing environmental goals, all four institutions yield considerable power. The Commission enjoys the right to propose the legal basis, Parliament may suggest changes, the Council of Ministers has the power ultimately to choose, while the Court of Justice may be called upon by any of these to judge on the legality of this choice.[148] Because the issue

[147] Art. 130r(1) stipulates that 'Community policy on the environment shall . . . take into account the diversity of situations in the various regions of the Community'. Art. 130r(3) provides that, in preparing its policy on the environment, the Community shall take account of, *inter alia*, environmental conditions in the various regions of the Community, the economic and social developement of the Community as a whole, and the balanced development of its regions.

[148] Whereas member states, the Council, or the Commission may bring an action on grounds of lack of competence, infringement of an essential procedural requirement, infringement of the Treaty or of any rule relating to its application, or misuse of powers, only the European Parliament enjoys *locus standi* for the purpose of protecting its prerogatives: Art. 173 EC.

is one of interpretation, it is the Court whose position is unassailable, and it is hence not surprising that it has been the Court which has decided this debate of considerable constitutional significance.

The exercise of environmental competences is dominated by subsidiarity. In the choice of legal instruments, regulatory techniques, and instruments, this principle works to reduce Community involvement in the realization of its environmental policy to a bare minimum. Subsidiarity therefore coincides almost perfectly with race-to-the-top thinking. Yet, whereas recourse to soft law, self-regulation, and private standard-setting agencies may be desirable from a law and economics perspective, it may undermine public accountability: the very concern which served to justify the elevation of subsidiarity as a constitutional principle of Community law. This is a particularly alarming prospect in the sphere of environmental policy which, as is universally accepted and a consequence of what it seeks to protect, necessitates high levels of public participation and accountability.

Implementation of environmental directives is the responsibility of member states and a process over which the institutions of the Community exert little direct control. Implementation and law-making are intrinsically linked. The choice of legal instruments and regulatory techniques and instruments (for example, total harmonization or minimum harmonization, limit values or quality objectives) to an important degree determines the nature of the subsequent implementation process. Vice versa, member states' preparedness to agree environmental measures largely depends on the extent to which they can subsequently control implementation at national level, and hence on the instruments and techniques chosen.

An analogous relationship exists between enforcement and law-making: recourse to instruments leaving member states larger measures of discretion will inevitably complicate Community enforcement but at the same time expedite law-making. By way of response to the ensuing enforcement gap, the Court is mobilizing individuals' vigilance to uphold Community environmental law: a policy which it is able to pursue relatively unnoticed thanks to the unspectacular and technical nature of the doctrines involved. The extent to which private enforcement of Community environmental law materializes, however, will continue to depend on widely varying national provisions relating to access to justice in the sphere of the environment for the foreseeable future.

More generally, where Community environmental law consists of numerous intricate relationships between member states and the institutions of the Community, both economic and institutional contexts appear currently to be working in tandem to increase the role of the former at the expense of the latter. This will require a reorientation of the most suitable processes, tools, and instruments to secure the continued success of EC environmental law.

7

International Environmental Law and the Challenge of Globalization

TONY EVANS*

Introduction

Since the creation of the United Nations system, conventional wisdom has it that solutions to all international and global problems are found by drafting international law. This has become such an entrenched view that the discourse surrounding almost every conceivable global issue turns on a detailed examination of law creation and formal methods of implementation. The focus of such a discourse is an assumed outcome that the law is supposed to produce. Policy-makers and lawyers engaged in thinking and writing about global problems from the legal perspective rarely pay attention to the political, social, economic, and cultural contexts when conducting their analysis. Instead, they focus on legal texts, institutional processes, and organizational matters: an approach that tells us much about the abstract elegance of the law, legal processes, and organizational theory, but little about causation. John Vincent, for example, has referred to those who write about universal human rights in this vein as 'notoriously wishful thinkers', and notes how irrelevant much human rights talk is to securing the human dignity of people.[1]

However, regardless of these criticisms the legal approach to environmental questions has achieved an unquestioned acceptance by a wide range of academic disciplines. For example, in the well known edited volume *The International Politics of the Environment*, Hurrell and Kingsbury are concerned with the

> . . . processes by which inter-state agreements on the environment are negotiated; with the rules and regimes established to facilitate environmental co-operation; with the international institutions that have been, or need to be, created to implement those rules; and with the conflicting political forces on whose resolution any successful regional or global environmental initiative must depend.[2]

Thus the state is the central actor, co-operation between states the dominant process, international law the desirable outcome, and the creation of new international

* The author would like to thank Annie Taylor, Caroline Thomas, Christine Chinkin, Jenny Steele, Dave Carter, and Lisa Schuster for their helpful comments on earlier drafts of this paper.

[1] J. Vincent, *Human Rights and International Relations* (Cambridge, 1986).

[2] A. Hurrell and B. Kingsbury, *The International Politics of the Environment* (Oxford, 1992), at 1.

institutions the method of implementation. If prior questions concerned with sovereignty, the limits of international law, power, and the globalization of politics and economics are mentioned, they are framed within a conventional view of international theory, which subordinates all issues to the interests of the state and the international system.[3]

In recent years the most commonly adopted method for conducting the processes described above is the big, set-piece international conference, usually organized under the auspices of the United Nations. The United Nations Conference on Environment and Development (UNCED), held in Rio during June 1992, is the most recent example of such a conference concerning the environment. Although the creation of international law is often the outcome of such gatherings, it should not be forgotten that final agreement is reached by government representatives who are most concerned with their country's national interest, understood in terms of economic growth and development. Those who persist in the belief that international conferences are organized as a forum for articulating the interests of people living in a wider, more cosmopolitan, or global community are usually disappointed. Although the state-centric, self-interest view of international conferences is often denied—usually by pointing to the increasing numbers of international nongovernmental organizations (NGOs) invited to participate in international conferences—so far there are few signs that global interests are replacing national interests as the rationale for action.[4]

This paper argues that the failure of legal practitioners, environmental activists, and political leaders to reflect on the changing context of global political and economic relations leads to international law solutions that are a poor foundation on which to build environmental security. Important to the argument is the recent literature on globalization, which suggests that even if states had the will to develop lasting solutions to global problems, they no longer have the capacity to take decisive action. Globalization points to processes of modernity, particularly technological innovations that empower global finance and production, making state regulation less feasible. Seen from the perspective of globalization, environmental degradation is therefore a crisis of modernity and cannot be tackled by clinging to the very practices and policies that are its cause.[5] In short, globalization makes international law less relevant to a world order where categories like the state and the society of states no longer capture the full extent of global politics. At the very moment when, for the first time in history, the world boasts a global system of states, the state system seems to be less significant.

[3] For an argument that supports this type of approach see S. Smith, 'The Environment on the Periphery of International Relations: An Explanation', in C. Thomas (ed.), *Rio: Unravelling the Consequences* (Ilford, 1994), at 28–45.

[4] P. Chatterjee and M. Finger, *The Earth Brokers: Power, Politics and World Development* (London, 1994).

[5] C. Thomas, 'Beyond UNCED: An Introduction', in Thomas (ed.), op. cit., at 1–2.

The argument presented here is that international law cannot deliver the conditions for environmental security.[6] The first section will take a brief look at the Realist tradition of international political thought. This thinking prioritizes the interests of powerful hegemonic states over global environmental security. International law is therefore little more than an attempt by a hegemon to gain universal legitimacy for a set of rules and norms that support its own interests. A second section looks at the 'international society' view of international law. Although power and hegemony remain an important element in this approach, international society assumes that states do subscribe to a limited set of rules that serve their common interests. However, the international society approach to international law assumes that states are the active agents of change, with the capacity to reach and implement co-operative agreements. This view is challenged by new thinking on globalization, which is the subject of a third section. Globalization suggests that the state no longer initiates action but, instead, reacts to the changing circumstances presented to it by the continued expansion of the global economy. The final section argues that globalization requires us to re-examine and reconstruct the political and social institutions of a past era, including international law.

The Environment and the International System: the Realist Tradition

The Realist tradition of international relations begins by making a distinction between political and international theory.[7] According to this tradition, political theory is concerned with normative relationships between the institutions of government and the governed. Central to this relationship is some notion of the 'good life', which is shared by the moral community defined by the sovereign territorial state. Indeed, it is assumed that the state alone provides the only viable means for achieving the 'good life'. This requires making a further set of assumptions concerned with protecting the moral community, including ideas of self-interest, autonomy, and non-intervention. While the state may not be the most perfect form of political community, political theory assumes that it is at least perfectible. Indeed, the notion of the ideal state provides a central focus for much political theory. The task of political theory is therefore to describe existing economic, social, and political relationships and investigate alternatives.[8]

Realist international theory, on the other hand, is concerned with securing the normative order found within the state from foreign interference. The claims of

[6] This argument is presented from the perspective of the discipline of international relations. I am aware that some aspects of the characterization of international law suggested in this paper may not be accepted by some international lawyers. The purpose of the paper is to raise questions concerned with the nature of international law, however characterized, under conditions of globalization.

[7] M. Wight, 'Why is there no International Theory?', in H. Butterfield and M. Wight (eds.), *Diplomatic Investigations* (London, 1966).

[8] R. H. Jackson, 'Martin Wight, International Relations and the Good Life' (1990) 19 *Millennium: Journal of International Relations* 261–72.

autonomy, non-intervention, and self-sufficiency mean that the state must rely exclusively upon its own resources to protect its sovereignty. Since no authority exists above the state, international politics is characterized as anarchical.[9] It is an arena where states are continually engaged in issues of security, defence, and military preparedness. If political theory is concerned with normative issues, international theory is concerned with survival. International theory is therefore to do with defending the 'hard shell'[10] of the state and securing its distinctive social, political, and economic system. Put simply, the distinction between domestic and international politics can be characterized as:

> Community inside, anarchy outside; justice inside, power and, at best, order outside; effective institutions with legislative authority inside, shifting alliances and fragile balancing mechanisms outside—however normal politics is understood, interstate politics may be presented as its negation.[11]

Thus a dichotomy exists between sovereignty and anarchy, where sovereignty is defined as a culturally specific, ideal view of a moral community with shared values and purposes, while anarchy represents the rejection of this ideal.[12]

Accordingly, it is common for Realists to describe international relations as a system. It is a system because it displays regular interactions between unitary states, actions that are understood as conforming to timeless, habitual, and unchanging rules for international conduct. These rules derive from an axiomatic notion that the pursuit of military and coercive power is the best means of securing the normative order within the state.[13] International relations are therefore a sphere of politics driven by conflict, self-interest, and the need to prevail. Since power is distributed unevenly within the system, powerful hegemonic states assume responsibility for performing the necessary tasks associated with maintaining international order. This privileged position allows the hegemon to 'claim monopoly over objectivity' and proclaim its 'value-free credentials through the elevation of power to the status of self-evident truth',[14] a truth that reflects the hegemon's interests. As Richard Falk has pointed out, the 'hegemonic logic' of the system determines that even issues with global dimensions, like human rights or environmental degradation, must be subordinated to the interests of the hegemon.[15]

For the argument presented here the most important point to stress is that the Realist world is understood as abiding and unchanging. Since the abiding

[9] H. N. Bull, *The Anarchical Society* (Basingstoke, 1977).

[10] J. H. Herz, 'The Rise and Demise of the Territorial State' (1954) 9 *World Politics* 473–93.

[11] R. B. J. Walker, 'Security, Sovereignty, and the Challenge of World Politics' (1990) 15 *Alternatives* 3–27, at 15.

[12] Anarchy is used here to indicate the absence of government, not the existence of chaos.

[13] Morgenthau's assertion that '[w]e assume that statesmen (*sic*) think and act in terms of interest defined as power, and the evidence of history bears that assumption out' is the best known example of this approach. See H. J. Morganthau, *Politics Among Nations* (4th ed., New York, 1996), at 5.

[14] P. Saravanamuttu, 'Environment, Development and Security', in Thomas (ed.), op. cit., at 226.

[15] R. Falk, 'Theoretical Foundations of Human Rights', in R. P. Newburg (ed.), *The Politics of Human Rights* (New York, 1980).

principles of all international action are driven by self-interest, any manifestation of rule-governed or co-operative behaviour must be understood as subject to the shifting patterns of power relations. The creation of international law reflects these assumptions because the law is the outcome of power relationships, often conducted within international organizations, where the hegemon can use its authority to order the preferences of weaker states. As Stein has argued, the Realist understanding of international relations 'suggests that the same forces of autonomously calculated self-interest that lie at the root of the anarchic international system also lay the foundations for regimes as forms of international law'.[16] Since the Realist tradition rejects any possibility of reformulating international relations in terms of a world society—a society of people sharing a single, global history—the creation and efficacy of international law on the global environment depends upon the national interests of the hegemon coinciding with global interests.[17]

To illustrate such a coincidence the Realist might point to the Montreal Protocol on Substances that Deplete the Ozone Layer (1987),[18] designed to regulate the supply of chlorofluorocarbons (CFCs). Following the dissemination of scientific research on the depletion of the ozone layer in the 1970s, and a consequent reduction in the domestic demand for CFCs, producers in the United States had suffered a decade of falling profits. Although substitutes for CFCs were available, the potential market was inhibited by high production costs, which were between five and ten times greater than CFCs. United States producers therefore saw international regulation of CFCs as a means of achieving three aims: creating a market for substitutes; achieving market dominance as the first to produce substitutes; and securing long-term profits. Producers in the United Kingdom, on the other hand, continued to enjoy satisfactory profits and saw no advantage in investing in substitutes. By the mid-1980s, however, concerns over environmental degradation had achieved an important place on the international political agenda, which no producer could ignore. At the same time, UK producers began to understand the long-term commercial potential of turning production away from CFCs towards high profit substitutes. Thus a coincidence of economic, environmental, and national interests converged that saw powerful governments put their weight behind the Montreal Protocol.[19] As Maxwell and Weiner have observed,

> the greater reliance on international machinery and organization in addressing global environmental issues will be combined with national attempts to protect . . . commercial interests. . . . [T]he new global order will be as much about gaining a competitive advantage as about the protection of the environment.[20]

[16] A. A. Stein, 'Coordination and Collaboration: Regimes in an Anarchic World' (1982) 36 *International Organization* 299–324, at 316.

[17] Smith, op. cit. [18] Rep. 26 *ILM* 1550 (1987).

[19] The Realist might also point to the Biodiversity Convention (rep. 31 *ILM* 818 (1992)) and the UN Framework Convention on Climate Change (rep. 31 *ILM* 851 (1992)) as examples where powerful states acted to resist regulation in the name of the national interests.

[20] For a full analysis of this coincidence see J. H. Maxwell and S. L. Weiner 'Green Consciousness or Dollar Diplomacy: The British Response to the Threat of Ozone Depletion' (1993) 5 *International Environmental Affairs* 19–41.

Writing about international law in a book that is arguably the central text of traditional theory of international relations, E. H. Carr asserts that international law, 'like politics, is a meeting place for ethics and power . . . it cannot be understood independently of the *political foundations* in which it rests and of the *political interests* which it serves.'[21] The principal purpose of international law is to maintain the rules of coexistence,[22] which concerns power relationships, the conditions for order, and economic co-operation. Accordingly, the function of international law is to 'preserve the inter-state world of judicially equal members' and thus the interests of those who benefit from sustaining the international system.[23] This is the statist approach to international relations where legitimacy and sovereignty are more concerned with whether a government controls its people, than with whether it represents them. Thus, the right to a voice in creating international law is not predicated on a legitimacy derived from social representation but from the claim to sustain the principles of the current international system. Although Realists might recognize categories like international civil society and international nongovernmental organizations, all interests are subordinated to those of the state and the international system.

Edith Brown Weiss confirms this unwittingly when she writes that in 'reviewing the last forty years in international environmental law, it is apparent that countries have learned much about both the process of negotiating environmental agreements and the desirable substantive content of the agreements'.[24] For Realists, the learning referred to is the knowledge gained by state representatives that allows them to integrate environmental issues into existing political processes and policies, and the desirable outcomes are those that serve national economic interests. While it might be correct to argue that international environmental law developed over the last two decades 'reflects a community of interests',[25] the question remains which community and whose interests?

For over four decades Realist thought preoccupied the minds of both statespeople and academics. In recent years, however, Realism has come under considerable intellectual attack, largely because, in the age of interdependence and economic interconnectedness, the Realist view does not seem to capture reality. An alternative approach to Realism, which has found favour in some circles, is that of international society. This provides the focus for the next section.

The Environment and International Society

International society thinkers argue that in the modern period the autonomous state cannot perform all the tasks necessary for achieving the 'good life'. The

[21] E. H. Carr, *The Twenty Years' Crisis* (London, 1939), at 178–9. Emphasis added.

[22] Bull, op. cit., at 67–71.

[23] H. Mosler, *The International Society as a Legal Community* (Netherlands, 1980), at 5–6.

[24] E. Brown Weiss, 'International Environmental Law: Contemporary Issues and the Emergence of a New World Order' (1993) 81 *Georgetown Law Journal* 675–710, at 684.

[25] Ibid., at 710.

anarchy-society dichotomy is tempered, but not abandoned, by ideas of interdependence, particularly in the processes associated with the expansion of the global economy.[26] New phenomena, like the global division of labour, regional and national specialization, the increasing mobility of capital and finance, and the growth of multinational organizations, all contribute towards an interdependent society that places greater emphasis on co-operation between states and less on conflict, hegemony, and military power. Many of the new problems facing international society are themselves the outcome of economic interdependence, including the potential for environmental disaster. Consequently, there is a growing realization that the material well-being of people everywhere depends on social, political, and economic relationships that transcend traditional state boundaries. International relations are therefore best characterized as an international society; a community of sovereign states sharing certain common values and aspirations. An important role of international law, and the organizations associated with implementing the law, is to deter and discipline those who threaten the normative order that is the society of states.

However, because of the dichotomy between society and anarchy, international society accepts that the normative order found in the anarchical international sphere is qualitatively different from that found within domestic communities. One way of conceptualizing this has been proposed by Terry Nardin.[27] Noting that international law does provide a considerable measure of normative order that belies the moral scepticism of the Realists, Nardin begins by distinguishing between the rules of 'practical association', and those of 'purposive association'. Following the political-international theory distinction discussed above, Nardin argues that the existence of a domestic normative order presupposes a moral community possessed of a set of common values, norms, and rules. The domestic normative order therefore rests on some notion of a common purpose, or what Nardin calls 'purposive association', which is based upon the moral integrity of the individual within a culturally specific, social environment that includes a commonly held view of the 'good life'. However, because of cultural diversity and the existence of states, Nardin argues that:

> . . . it would be a mistake to regard all international relations as defined and governed by the pursuit of shared purpose . . . there is another mode of relations that is more fundamental because it exists among those pursuing divergent as well as shared purposes. Durable relations among adversaries presupposes a framework of common practices and rules capable of providing some unifying bond where shared purpose is lacking.[28]

These are the non-purposive rules of 'practical association', the most important expression of which is found in the authoritative practices and principles of international law. Such rules require no commitment to shared purposes or values,

[26] R. O. Keohane, *After Hegemony: Cooperation and Discord in the World Political Economy* (Princeton, 1984).

[27] T. Nardin, *Law, Morality, and the Relations of States* (Princeton, 1983).

[28] Ibid., at 5.

but they do provide a formal unity, an association of states, based upon restraint and accommodation. Practical association occurs when those who fail to get others to adopt their own values 'have little choice but to tolerate the existence of differences they are unable to eradicate'.[29]

Gaining an insight into the rules of practical association therefore entails an analysis of the application of rules rather than an examination of their relevance to moral purpose. To speak of justice when referring to practical association is to be concerned with the equal application of the rules rather than the consequences of their application. To revive a term that has fallen into disuse in recent times, the 'law of nations' remains the law governing relations between nations, as opposed to an alternative meaning that assumes a common purpose of humankind, or the law common to all nations, which suggests a global moral community.[30] While states may continue to seek a competitive advantage, for example by attempting to resist environmental regulation, interdependence and the existence of international law moderates self-interest. However, if the opportunity does arise for a state to exercise self-interest, the distinction between practical and purposive association offers the state an opportunity to disregard international regulation and act autonomously, free of moral compunction.

The most recent manifestation of international society might be seen in the rapidly increasing number and importance of international institutions.[31] In recent times it has become fashionable to describe these institutions as international regimes, understood as sets of principles, norms, rules, and decision-making procedures accepted by states as a guide for international action in a given issue-area of international relations.[32] Apart from overtly economic issues like trade, shipping, oil, and money, regimes have also been identified for a wide range of environmental issues.[33] Although regimes are best understood as institutions, and therefore as concerned with the customs and habits found in social life, they are often associated with international organizations charged with the task of monitoring and implementing international law.[34] According to the international society approach the reasons behind the move to build international institutions are found in the growing complexity of international life, including economic expansion, information technology, and the threat of environmental disaster. By redefining some issues as 'global commons', states tacitly acknowledge their

[29] T. Nardin, *Law, Morality, and the Relations of States* (Princeton, 1983), at 57.

[30] V. Idelson, 'The Law of Nations and the Individual', in *The Grotius Society: Transactions for the Year 1944* (London, 1962).

[31] T. Evans and P. Wilson, 'International Regimes and the English School of International Relations' (1993) 22 *Millennium: Journal of International Studies* 329–51.

[32] S. Krasner (ed.), *International Regimes* (London, 1983).

[33] See, for example, O. Young, *International Cooperation: Building Regimes for Natural Resources and the Environment* (Ithaca, 1989) and P. Haas, R. Keohane, and M. Levy (eds.), *Institutions for the Earth: Sources of Effective Environmental Protection* (Boston, Mass., 1993).

[34] An example of this would be the United Nations Commission for Sustainable Development, which oversees the implementation of Agenda 21 (United Nations Conference on Environment and Development, Agenda Item 21 (1992)).

failure to provide their citizens with security, and instead devolve responsibility to the institutions of international society.

This being said, even as members of regimes, states continue to assume the role of principal actors in world politics, resisting the claims of supra-state groups to wrest sovereignty from them. Furthermore, states remain the principal bearers of rights and duties under international law: 'they alone have the right to use force to uphold it' and 'its source lies in the consent of states expressed in custom or treaty'.[35] Thus, drawing a distinction between purposive and practical association continues to objectify the state in the same way that Realism does. If the rules of practical association are devoid of moral purpose, international society is morally problematic when trying to understand universal human rights or global environmental degradation. When problems of a global nature arise, the unquestioned starting point for seeking solutions is the state and the institutions of international society, where the rules of practical association operate.[36]

The important point to stress here is that international society, like Realism, does not offer a convincing view of history. For example, both fail to recognize that the state is not a fact of nature, but an historic solution to the problem of increasing complexity in economic, social, and political life, first recognized at the end of the seventeenth century.[37] International society is therefore a conservative approach that views all new problems through the prism of familiarity, as though we live in unchanging (indeed, unchangeable) times. It also fails to understand that the causes of new global problems are the outcome of social, economic, and political changes that have little to do with past conceptions of the sovereign state.[38] In short, lacking a theory of change, international society continues to conceptualize the state as an active policy-maker, with the capacity to manage global problems through international law and institutions.

But what if the world does undergo periods of revolutionary change, and environmental degradation is the outcome of new economic and political relationships for which international society cannot account? In the current period, for example, globalization seems a more fitting term to describe world politics. Globalization assumes that the constraints of geography on social, economic, and cultural arrangements are declining. Therefore, any approach to problem-solving that pins its hopes on regulation by objectifying the state seems unlikely to succeed.[39]

[35] Bull, op. cit., at 68.

[36] The obvious criticism of the practical/purposive distinction is that domestic law could also be viewed in the same way. Nardin's attempt to argue that rules of practical association are empty of moral content misses the obvious point that rules always advantage some groups over others, and support some interests while suppressing others. Practical rules cannot therefore be as value-free as Nardin wants us to believe. See M. Hoffman, 'States, Cosmopolitanism and Normative International Theory' (1988) 2 *Paradigms* 60–75.

[37] A. Linklater, 'The Problem of Community in International Relations' (1990) 15 *Alternatives* 135–53. See also A. Watson, *The Evolution of International Society* (London, 1992).

[38] M. C. Bateson, 'Beyond Sovereignty: An Emerging Global Community', in R. B. J. Walker and S. H. Mendlowitz (eds.), *Contesting Sovereignty: Redefining Political Community* (Boulder, 1990).

[39] R. W. Cox, 'Social Forces, Forms of States and World Orders: Beyond International Relations Theory' (1981) 10 *Millennium: Journal of International Studies* 126–55.

The objectification of the state allows a separation of the environment from the generality of global social behaviour, practice, and knowledge described by the processes of globalization. Security involves the separation of 'insiders' from 'outsiders', fundamentally contradicting the predominant themes of the modern period, which are change, interaction, and dynamism.[40] Furthermore, objectification allows particular issues to be seen as physical and scientific rather than the outcome of social relations. Rather than asking 'why' environmental degradation is occurring on such a global scale, policy-makers turn instead to questions of 'how' degradation occurs. Backed by scientific evidence, which describes a physical world divorced from social action, policy-makers overlook the possibility of finding the cause of degradation and turn instead to regulating the sites of degradation. The success or failure of this regulation is then calculated by aggregating physical outcomes following implementation. The legal process is therefore concerned with identifying miscreants and applying sanctions. It is concerned with the wilful action of human agents rather than the systemic processes and structural practices in which action takes place.

The Environment and Globalization

Interest in the notion of globalization was first aroused following the work of Immanuel Wallerstein.[41] Wallerstein argues that we live in a single world economy structured around a complex of centre-periphery relations, which places the wealthy industrial economies at the centre and the poor extraction and agrarian economies at the periphery. While governments can maintain some limited control over economic decisions, their ability to act is constrained by their country's relative power position within the wider world economy. Although the reach of this economy is global, stretching from the highest village in the Andes to the corporate office in New York,[42] its consequences are not distributed evenly. Powerful countries have a greater opportunity to influence policy outcomes than weaker countries. Nevertheless, all countries are subject to the authority of the global economy in ways that alter perceptions, values, and wants.

Globalization therefore describes something more than economic relations. It draws our attention to powerful processes of cultural, social, and political change that challenge past beliefs about the nature of sovereignty, society, and the wider international community. Consequently, globalization interrogates the old categories of international political thought, raises questions about identity and community, and confuses the distinction between domestic and international politics. Thus, globalization suggests simultaneous processes of integration and

[40] S. Dalby, 'Security, Modernity, Ecology: The Dilemma of Post-Cold War Discourse' (1992) 17 *Alternatives* 95–134.

[41] I. Wallerstein, *Historical Capitalism* (London, 1983).

[42] For an early argument of this type see A. Gunder Frank, 'The Development of Underdevelopment', *Monthly Review*, September 1966, 17–30.

disintegration: integration of global capital and economic relations, and disintegration of traditional values that define society and community.[43]

Although Wallerstein's contribution remains important, during the last decade globalization has come to mean something more than structural, centre-periphery relations based on a state-centric view of world politics. Instead, globalization implies political relationships where the social core and the social periphery cut across national boundaries,[44] creating new patterns of economic growth and consumption that are beyond the control of the state. Where in the past the state could hope to adopt national strategies for ordering the national economy—including perhaps the nationalization of key industries—the global organization of production and finance means that the state no longer initiates policy but, rather, reacts to global economic forces against which it can mount little resistance. Although globalization makes it tempting to conclude that the state is in terminal decline, such a conclusion is rejected by most writers on globalization. Instead, globalization assumes that the state continues to play an integral role as an administrative unit for creating and orchestrating the conditions for globalization. Rather than being the central actors in global politics, states are 'the authors of a regime that defines and guarantees, through international treaties and constitutional effect, the global and domestic rights of capital'.[45] Decisions made at the national level may temporarily disrupt patterns of globalization, but states cannot escape its processes.

A recent example of the close relationship between state, capital, and the environment can be seen in a policy statement published by the United States' Department of State. Under a section titled 'Advancing US Interests in Key Regions and Countries', this document states that the environmental policy of the USA is concerned with helping 'US businesses to sell their leading-edge environmental technology'. Furthermore, the environment is important because '[n]atural resource issues are critical to maintaining and advancing core US interests worldwide'. Accordingly, the Secretary of State intends to 'instruct embassies in key countries to work with NGOs and businesses to address pressing region-wide natural resource issues'.[46] Two points should be emphasized here. The first is that these statements stress the commodification of the environment and the importance of creating the conditions for trade in environmental technology.[47] The second is the

[43] S. Gill, 'Globalisation, Market Civilisation, and Disciplinary Neoliberalism' (1995) 24 *Millennium: Journal of International Studies* 399–423.

[44] R. W. Cox, 'The Crisis in World Order and the Challenge of International Organization' (1994) 29 *Conflict and Cooperation* 99–113, at 108.

[45] L. Panitch, 'Rethinking the Role of the State', in J. H. Mittelman (ed.), *Globalization: Critical Reflections* (Boulder, 1995).

[46] Department of State Environmental Initiative for the Twenty-First Century (USA), *Environmental Change and Security Report*, Issue 2, Spring 1986, at 140–1.

[47] Commodification is the result of the logic of the market. For example, it is a process that allows companies to take life forms, apply the techniques of science, patent the resulting engineered outcome, and claim ownership rights. See C. von Wetzsäcker, 'Competing Notions of Biodiversity', in W. Sachs (ed.), *Global Ecology* (London, 1993).

role of the state in ensuring that economic considerations, including the continuous supply of raw materials, take precedence over environmental protection.

Globalization acknowledges that although the development of a global economy is not a new phenomenon,[48] the introduction of technology—particularly information technology—accelerates the processes of integration and disintegration. Technology enables both production and finance to be organized on a global scale, encourages the growth of transnational (TNC) and multinational (MNC) corporations without clear national loyalties or identities, and weakens further the relationship between government and the national economy. The investment and production decisions of TNCs are determined within a global, rather than a national context to maximize profit. The global free-market in which these corporations operate is not therefore contained by traditional boundaries provided by the state. While in the past the state could hope to manage its own national economy through fiscal and interventionist policies, today a global, twenty-four hour market operates that pays no homage to national economic planning. As Held and McGrew have argued,

> . . . the internationalization of production, finance and exchange is unquestionably eroding the capacity of the individual liberal democratic state to control its own economic future. At the very least, there appears to be a diminution of state autonomy, and a disjuncture between notions of a sovereign state directing its own future and the dynamics of the contemporary world economy.[49]

Underpinning the move to a world economy is an ideology of modernity, which rests upon the twin goals of economic growth and development. The central means of achieving these goals in all countries, whether the wealthy North or the impoverished South, is strategic planning at the global level, global management, and the creation of global regimes and agreements. Ideological convergence has the effect of homogenizing and limiting the policy choices of governments. Global management requires adherence to rules that ensure all countries conform to the development model so that the 'hidden hand' of the market can operate efficiently. Consequently, responsibility for defining and implementing the rules of international action shift away from the state to international institutions. All other issues, including environmental degradation, must be subordinated to the imperative for economic development. Yet, as Stephen Gill has argued, any attempt to widen and intensify the existing patterns of accumulation and consumption currently found in the North, tends to 'deplete or destroy the eco-structure of the planet, making everyone less secure and perhaps more vulnerable to disease'.[50] The central message of modernity is therefore contradictory: it promotes global economic integration and promises economic security for all, while also threatening

[48] P. Hirst and G. Thompson, *Globalization in Question* (Cambridge, 1996).
[49] D. Held and A. McGrew, 'Globalisation and the Liberal Democratic State' (1993) 28 *Government and Opposition* 270.
[50] Gill, op. cit., at 419.

to deplete the world's resources and bring about catastrophic environmental decay for all.

The growing activities of TNCs and MNCs are perhaps the most obvious sign that the role of the state is changing. Between 1980 and 1992 the annual sales of TNCs doubled ($2.4 to $5.5 trillion) and the annual sales of many are now greater than the GDP of some states. For example, in 1992 General Motors' world-wide sales ($132.4 billion, approximately one third of which was in foreign sales) exceeded the GDP of Indonesia ($126.4 billion), Norway ($115.7 billion), Poland ($83.8 billion), and Malaysia ($57.8 billion).[51] Coupled with new technology that allows rapid movements of finance and capital, TNCs use their economic power to gain the most favourable conditions for their activities. If a state introduces environmental laws, TNCs have the capacity to seek new sites for production where regulation is less stringent. For example, the practice of exporting 'dirty' industry is well known, and finding states prepared to accept the risks is not difficult. Locked into an ideology of modernity, economic growth, and development, states become involved in a 'Dutch Auction', where countries bid against each other to offer the lowest levels of environmental, labour, and consumer regulation in the hope of attracting investment, no matter how environmentally damaging their activities might prove.[52] For the people of Bhopal, where in 1984 a leakage of toxic gas killed over 3,000 people and injured a further 200,000, the consequences of a global economy were deadly.

The changing role of the state under conditions of globalization, together with the dominance of the liberal free-market system, also brings consequences for democracy. As the state moves from being an active policy-maker to a passive unit of administration, the capacity of people to participate in defining a political agenda that expresses a genuine concern for the environment declines. For example, when a finance minister argues that the devaluation of the currency was the result of global market forces beyond his control, rather than the failure of national economic planning, as British Chancellor of the Exchequer Mr Norman Lamont did in 1992, the disjuncture between democracy and power is exposed. People begin to question what national democracy means if their government is impotent in exercising any control over economic factors that affect their daily lives. With the realization that the global rather than the national economy exercises greater influence on economic well-being, the state loses its significance as a centre of authority through which people can express their preferences. Instead, the focus turns to international institutions and organizations, which assume the task of providing the rules for action.

Although national governments continue to engage in international politics, governance is conducted by what Cox has referred to as the *Nébuleuse*,[53] a group

[51] Figures taken from United Nations Research Institute for Social Development, *States of Disarray: The Social Consequences of Globalization* (London, 1995).

[52] M. Waters, *Globalization* (London, 1995).

[53] R. W. Cox, 'A Perspective on Globalisation', in Mittelman (ed.), op. cit., at 21–30.

of formal and informal organizations without democratic pretensions. Included in the *Nébuleuse* are organizations like the World Bank, the World Trade Organization (WTO), the Trilateral Commission, and the Group of Seven (G7). These determine the norms and rules of conduct, emphasizing 'efficiency, discipline, and confidence; economic policy credibility and consistency; and limitations of democratic decision-making processes'.[54] The link between government and governed is therefore weakened, but not replaced with new forms of democracy related to global institutions.[55] As Sir Shridath Ramphal has argued,

> [m]ore and more the G7 is looking—and acting—like a self-appointed presidium. We need to convince these leaders of major western democracies that the democracy idea has a larger reach than national frontiers. Democracy at the national level but authoritarian in the global homeland—these are contradictions in terms.[56]

Over time the decline in democratic participation, coupled with the maintenance of an order in which the governed have no role, ensures that people become more accountable to remote centres of authority rather than those centres being accountable to people. This is the process of *distanciation* where 'locales are thoroughly penetrated by and shaped in terms of social influences quite distant from them'.[57] *Distanciation* ensures that the relationship between international institutions and populations is not concerned with human values, the quality of life or human dignity, but with technical issues to do with maintaining an order that supports free-market principles. For example, the debate over intellectual property rights is more concerned with rights of ownership, capital, and the commodification of the environment than with social issues concerning the moral consequences of biotechnology and the 'privatization of life forms'.[58]

This value-free, instrumental approach to international organization also raises questions about the role of scientific and economic knowledge, particularly claims to hold the truth. Since the physical world is so central to determining the environmental agenda, and science is presented as neutral and value-free, the authority of those who control scientific research is often left unquestioned. Placed in the context of a liberal free-market, which is also presented as natural, alternative values and political choices are at best marginalized and at worst simply ignored. Questions about environmental degradation are therefore questions of science, which cannot include value laden questions about alternative futures. Since growth and development represent the natural destiny of humankind, science must provide solutions to environmental problems. As Julian Saurin has pointed out, the prevailing voice in the environmental discourse is that of those who control,

[54] Gill, op. cit., at 412. See also N. Chomsky, 'World Order and its Rules: Variation on Some Themes' (1992) 20 *Journal of Law and Society* 145–65.

[55] J. Huymans, 'Post-Cold War Implosion and Globalization: Liberalism Running Past Itself' (1995) 24 *Millennium: Journal of International Studies* 471–87.

[56] Sir S. Ramphal, 'Globalism and Meaningful Peace: A New World Order Rooted in International Community' (1992) 32 *Security Dialogue* 81–7, at 82.

[57] A. Giddens, *The Consequences of Modernity* (Cambridge, 1990).

[58] Gill, op. cit., at 409.

prioritize, and enclose particular forms of knowledge. Those who hold socio-economic power derived from this particular form of enclosure determine how the environment is managed, by whom, and for whose purposes. Enclosure therefore defines the forum in which decisions are made and prioritizes some voices over others. Saurin argues:

> The notion of 'voice' itself is construed as one in which particular forms of knowledge are recognised and others are not; thus enclosure opens up the way for bureaucratization and enclosure of knowledge itself in which all conflict is settled by criteria determined by the enclosers. Finally, the enclosure of knowledge entails the replacement of discussion with measurement as a basis for decision-making.[59]

The recent epidemic of bovine spongiform-encephalopathy (BSE) in the UK offers a good example of this. The arguments over safe beef have revolved around scientific evidence presented by biologists and veterinarians. At the centre of this debate are questions about the appropriate number of cattle to slaughter in order to eradicate BSE from the national herd, and the appropriate parts of carcasses to remove before consumption. The context of these calculations is the national and international market in beef and beef products. However, globalization theory suggests that BSE is not a scientific problem. Rather, BSE is a problem of social and political values concerning the type of society in which we want to live. The government of the United Kingdom, together with the European Union, have sought to conduct the debate in the language of instrumentality and science, relying exclusively upon scientific opinion from selected experts before taking action. Other possible questions to do with the practices and procedures of industrialized agriculture, the globalization of international agribusiness, and cheap food policies, seem not to have been raised. These are social and political questions and cannot be answered by science, although government pronouncements would suggest that they can.[60] In short, since BSE is presented as a scientific problem, and therefore a problem that only those with scientific training can solve, the majority are excluded from the debate.[61]

Scientific instrumentality leads to a further point, which concerns order. Since international institutions reflect the prevailing global ideology, problem-solving becomes a technical issue concerned with the expansion of capital and maintaining the free-market. Problem-solving is therefore an exercise in dealing with the unwanted or unforeseen consequences of the dominant ideology, not with questioning it. Indeed, the force of the dominant ideology has reached such proportions that it now has the status of 'common sense' with both decision-makers

[59] J. Saurin, 'Global Environmental Degradation, Modernity and Environmental Knowledge', in C. Thomas (ed.), op. cit., Saurin draws upon the special issue of *The Ecologist*, (1992) 22, 'Whose Common Future?'.

[60] M. J. Killingsworth and J. S. Palmer, *Ecospeak: Rhetoric and Environmental Politics in America* (Carbondale, 1992).

[61] Editorial, 'BSE: Madness in the Method' (1996) 26 *The Ecologist* 45.

and academics alike.[62] Since international law is central to maintaining that order, the move from identifying a problem based on 'sound scientific evidence' to drafting law seems natural. Instead of recognizing that the prevailing order is not a given, and that 'technical fixes' can only offer partial, short-term solutions, decision-makers continue to adopt problem-solving strategies that are themselves part of the problem.

The role of international law in all this is of course to legitimate the 'technical fix' that supports particular global interests. International law is part of the problem-solving process associated with the current form of world order, an order defined by the global economy, which continues to place the state at the centre of its thinking. What globalization suggests is that we should stand aside from the familiar and attempt to take a critical, more reflective view about the nature of hegemony, power, the meaning of justice, public goods, and social change.[63] Without this element of reflection, any attempt to regulate for the environment is likely to fail. The discourse surrounding international environmental law is directed at achieving goals determined by reference to science and the familiar terms of the dominant ideology. Rather than reflecting on the potential for change, which allows the possibility of discovering a different world order, decision-makers accept the order as a given.[64]

Conclusion: Implications for International Environmental Law

The limitations of international environmental law seem clear from the above analysis. Viewed from the Realist or international society perspective, international law seems to offer only limited solutions to global environmental problems that stubbornly refuse to fit neatly into the political categories that humankind has created. When the conditions of globalization are added to the analysis, including the recognition that the authority of the state is in decline, achieving environmental security through international law seems even less possible. Indeed, globalization suggests that many established institutions, including international law, will require radical transformation as we enter the next phase of history. Even Hurrell and Kingsbury recognise this when they acknowledge that the 'increasing seriousness of many environmental problems provides one of the most intuitively plausible reasons for believing that the nation-state and the system of states may be either in crisis or heading toward crisis'.[65] Thus, our failure to acknowledge the limitations of international law, and to recognise that environmental degradation is a problem of modernity, diminishes our chances of survival. The conclusion to draw from globalization is that so long as international lawyers, academics,

[62] E. Augelli and C. Murphy, *America's Quest and the Third World* (London, 1988).

[63] Cox, 'Social Forces, Forms of States and World Orders', op. cit.

[64] M. Hoffman, 'Critical Theory and the Inter-paradigm Debate' (1987) 16 *Millennium: Journal of International Studies* 231–49.

[65] Hurrell and Kingsbury, op. cit., at 146.

and political leaders continue to behave as though environmental degradation is simply the outcome of an established and unchanging global political order, and fail to recognize that the cherished principles of the past may not provide a safe foundation for future decision-making, the environmental security of all people will remain threatened.

The reluctance to take this step can be seen in the predilection of lawyers and academics for formalism, empiricism, and written evidence. Authors who attempt to examine a particular case of environmental degradation or accident usually resort to an extensive analysis of the covenants, protocols, conventions, declarations, and procedures that are understood as international environmental law. An alternative approach would be to attempt the more difficult task of understanding the political, social, and economic context of degradation. This second approach is, of course, much more arduous and fraught with dangers. It relies upon interpretation as its methodology and opens itself to charges of value bias, epistemological confusion, or simple misunderstanding. Added to this is the problem of secrecy and the difficulty of conducting high quality research. Since governments and corporations are likely to be the objects of investigation, and openness may result in both national and international vilification, secrecy often rules. While many nongovernmental organizations have attempted to overcome the problem of secrecy, and have become adept at making public the disregard with which many governments and corporations treat environmental issues, there remains a tendency to view these organizations as self-interested, 'political' actors with little legitimacy. Faced with these difficulties, it is perhaps little wonder that many authors turn to the safety of examining legal material. But, as Michael Barkun pointed out nearly thirty years ago:

> [a] narrow concern for the assertions of documents or for the power of legally constituted organs of government mistakes appearances for reality, confuses visibility with significance and substitutes (however inadvertently) sophisticated description for explanation.[66]

For those who think and act in terms of international society in particular, the international law approach to all issues has achieved the status of 'common sense', closing the minds of decision-makers to any critical appraisal of the newly emerging world order, and leaving many questions about the efficacy of international environmental law unasked. Even when commentators do acknowledge the challenge of globalization, and tacitly recognize that the law has limited potential for achieving environmental security, the natural and normal means of problem-solving remains the creation of international law. In this way environmental security becomes a technical issue concerned with disagreements and arguments over the internal logic and elegance of the law, its coherence, extent, and meaning. More complex questions to do with efficacy, application, and obligation in particular

[66] M. Barkun, *Law Without Sanctions* (London, 1968), at 102.

social, political, and economic contexts, are therefore excluded.[67] To expect more of international law overlooks the point that international law is itself the product of traditional, state-centric thinking on global politics, and cannot therefore resolve the more damaging consequences of an alternative global order.

Although much has been made of NGO involvement in international fora, and the profile of NGOs as advisers to governments and international organizations has increased in recent times, this does not signal a radical transformation of traditional international institutions. While many NGOs have been successful at raising public consciousness over environmental security, they remain committed to the 'common sense', international law approach, and therefore tacitly accept the continuation of current forms of capital expansion and consumerism. Those that do not are never invited to participate.[68]

If the emerging order is indeed one in which the power of the state to regulate global issues is in decline, international environmental law offers little more than the impression of 'doing something' without necessarily doing anything. This is particularly serious if we accept that the capacity of globalization to generate new practices is often greater than the capacity of international society to find solutions through international regulation.[69] For example, during 1997 the number of environmental treaties under preparation strained even the most highly resourced government departments. Eileen Clausson, the United States Assistant Secretary of State for the environment, warned that 'the agenda is so full it's not even clear that a government as large as ours can handle it'.[70] Clausson goes on to argue that 'overload' and the lack of time leads to insufficient scrutiny, weak law, and implementation that fails to fulfil its promise. The need constantly to re-assess and amend existing environmental law in the light of new practices adds further to an already over-loaded agenda. Furthermore, modernization brings new generations of technology that replace the old within very short time scales. Any attempt to regulate existing practices may therefore soon become as obsolete as the practices themselves.

The existing literature reflects the growing anxiety and confusion over international environmental law and globalization. It is rare to find a writer prepared to offer an explanation of the assumed relationship between international law and a reduction in environmental degradation. This is a particularly important issue if environmental degradation owes as much to current economic and political structures and practices as it does to the self-interested, wilful individual. The international law approach to decision-making for the environment relies upon the assumption that violators can be identified, and perhaps made to answer for their actions. The 'polluter pays' principle is now well-established in both international and national law. However, the principle overlooks the fact that economic

[67] O. Young, 'The Politics of International Regime Formation' (1989) 43 *International Organization* 349–75.

[68] Chatterjee and Finger, op. cit.

[69] Bateson, op. cit., at 145–58.

[70] Quoted in 'Eco Soundings', *The Guardian* (Society section), 3 July 1996, at 4.

'[s]tructures cannot be juridical persons with intentions and capabilities', although globalization suggests that existing structures are the cause of environmental degradation.[71] The principle that the 'polluter pays' therefore confuses the *site* of environmental degradation with the *cause*, further exposing the limitations of international law.

The principle of individual responsibility for the environment is also reflected in phrases like *Our Common Future*, the title chosen for the report of the Brundtland Commission.[72] While such a phrase suggests that a world society is current, that we all share the same concerns and must therefore accept equal responsibility for saving the planet, the evidence for making such an assumption is weak. Since Brundtland was more concerned with economic development as a means of tackling poverty in less developed states, and largely ignored the consequences of increasing consumption in wealthy, technologically advanced states, the assumption of equal responsibility is questionable. As Chatterjee and Finger have pointed out, Brundtland's attempt at reinforcing a sense of global responsibility was constructed on a conceptual framework that is not universally accepted.[73] In many less developed communities, for example, economic development remains the central goal, and the notion of equal responsibility for environmental degradation, caused largely by western industrialization and over-consumption, is simply rejected.

Why then do states continue to negotiate and ratify international law on the environment? In answer to this question, public opinion and anxiety over a rapidly changing world are central issues.

The technology that supports an expansion of the global economy is also available to a wider public, which is now informed of the many threats to environmental security. Media coverage of environmental degradation is now a familiar part of our daily experience. The number and authority of environmental NGOs who undertake the task of disseminating environmental information has grown considerably during the last two decades, political parties compete with one another over which is the most 'green', and government departments are increasingly aware of the environmental consequences of the policies they develop and implement. Governments are therefore anxious to reflect the growing public concern for environmental security.

However, in an age of rapid technological and scientific change, when today's wisdom turns out to be yesterday's fad, governments are often reluctant to accept binding international agreement. When a government takes up an environmental issue, and demonstrates its concern by giving the issue political force and legitimacy through participating in regional and global conferences, it invests considerable political currency. Having done this, those governments seen to procrastinate, or who are openly obstructive or unco-operative, risk loss of status both with

[71] J. Galtung, *Human Rights in Another Key* (Cambridge, 1994).

[72] Report of the World Commission on Environment and Development, *Our Common Future* (Oxford, 1987).

[73] Chatterjee and Finger, op. cit.

domestic and international publics. Technological complexity and public opinion therefore lead governments to seek the 'lowest common denominator' that satisfies the widest possible constituency while avoiding agreement on any regulation that might act as a barrier to future action.[74] Agreeing to international environmental law therefore offers an opportunity for governments to be seen as decisive and responsible, to garner public support and reinforce traditional thinking on sovereignty and international society.

Following from this, states are aware that entering into agreements not only limits others' freedom to act, but also limits one's own freedom. For hegemonic states, who must exercise global, moral leadership by demonstrating their commitment to international law, this may prove a decisive factor when considering binding agreements. Attracting the moral status that agreeing to international law brings, while simultaneously minimizing any possible constraint on the sovereign exercise of power, or the interest of capital, preoccupies many governments. The 'common sense', international society tradition holds that security is concerned with the spatial exclusion of threat, the continuation of the domestic *status quo*, and enduring economic stability and growth. Anything that challenges this traditional notion of security is treated as a challenge to the principle of sovereignty and the international system of states. Furthermore, since the personal status and legitimacy of political leaders is derived from traditional notions of sovereignty, most are reluctant to acknowledge the challenge to globalization. To do so would entail an admission that the problem-solving capacity of political leaders is in decline, and their claim to status and legitimacy questionable.

Lastly, in the light of globalization states remain uncertain about the future of world order. This takes two forms. The first follows from the above, and concerns uncertainty over the challenge that environmental law presents to the traditional principles of the international political system. The second concerns the need to formulate a response to the emerging context of globalization. As argued earlier, with the globalization of production it is quite possible for TNCs to insist on a number of guarantees before investing in a country, including minimal trade union, health and safety, taxation, and environmental regulations. The failure of a government to provide these conditions reduces the chances of attracting investment and fulfilling the promise of economic development. Although less developed states are particularly exposed to these demands, global competition over investment means that even wealthy countries remain reluctant to promote environmental standards (national or international) that may reduce the chances of foreign investment, or risk the withdrawal of existing investments.[75]

The political energy consumed in creating international law should be evidence enough that the environment is now well established as a significant addition to

[74] M. A. Kaplan and N. B. Katzenbach, *The Politics and Foundations of International Law* (London, 1961).

[75] T. Evans, 'Universal Human Rights: Imposing Values', in C. Thomas and P. Wilkin (eds.), *Globalization and the South* (Basingstoke, 1997).

the international political agenda. However, environmental questions are, and will remain, political. Economic globalization brings social, cultural, and political changes to communities throughout the world, raising questions about the future world in which we want to live. Globalization theory argues that existing institutions no longer have the capacity to deliver whatever vision of the future we might choose. Focusing so singularly on international law elevates the legal approach beyond its potential, offers a distorted view of progress, and overlooks the inconvenient fact that international law is politically motivated. International environmental law is particularly political because it cannot avoid threatening traditional thinking on world order. The distinction between the politics of law and the technique of the law is rarely recognized and continues to cloud much writing on international law.

None of this is to argue that problem-solving for the environment through law is of no consequence. However, under conditions of globalization it is not self-evident that international law governing relations between states is the appropriate kind of law for a future world. The state system cannot be separated from international law. There are not two systems with international law taking the dominant role, although the literature often seems to suggest that this is the case. This is inconvenient for those who adopt the international law approach to decision-making for the environment, but no amount of academic or legal industry will alter the relationship. While a transnational system of law capable of regulating the behaviour of a wide range of actors, including states, TNCs, and international financial corporations may be desirable, it does not yet exist.

The argument set out in this chapter is not simply that international law is incapable of protecting the planet from further environmental degradation, but that it acts as a barrier to achieving such a goal. To focus so singularly on international law offers an illusion of orderliness that deflects attention from wide-ranging, fundamental disagreements when thinking about the environment. It also deflects attention from questions to do with the continuing role of the state under conditions of globalization. Furthermore, it deflects attention from the purpose of the environmental discourse, which is to create the conditions for environmental security.

8

International Environmental Law in Evolution

CHRISTINE CHINKIN*

1. International Law and the Environment

A common theme of the essays in this book is that they examine the extent to which law can provide answers to environmental questions. This issue is especially pertinent in the context of international environmental regulation. International environmental law is still in its infancy with its origin often dated from the 1972 Stockholm Declaration.[1] Despite this short existence, it is now recognized that the primary goal of the international legal order, the maintenance of international peace and security, can only be achieved by a broad understanding of the causes of global insecurity including decline in the quality and quantity of accessible natural resources and all forms of environmental degradation.[2] Growing realization of the threats presented by environmental ruination to global stability has provided the impetus for legal regulation, but this in turn has exposed the inadequacies of the contemporary international legal order in providing an effective regime for the preservation of the environment.[3]

This chapter will examine how states have used and developed established legal techniques in response to the challenges presented by the need for international regulation and prohibitions for environmental protection that transcends borders. It will first discuss the tensions within the international legal system that impede the formulation of international regulatory standards and uncover the inadequacies of formal law-making. This highlights the importance of decision-making[4]

* The author thanks Shaki Sanusi for her excellent research assistance and encouragement in the writing of this chapter.

[1] Stockholm Declaration on the Human Environment, adopted by the United Nations Conference on the Human Environment, UN Doc. A/Conf.48/14 and Corr. 1 (1972) rep. 11 *ILM* 1416 (1972) (hereinafter Stockholm Declaration). See further O. Schachter, 'The Emergence of International Environmental Law' (1991) 44 *Journal of International Affairs* 457–93.

[2] As the Secretary-General of the United Nations expressed it, 'A porous ozone shield could pose a greater threat to an exposed population than a hostile army.' B. Bhoutros-Ghali, *An Agenda for Peace, Preventive Diplomacy, Peacemaking and Peace-keeping*, Report of the Secretary-General pursuant to the Statement adopted by the Summit Meeting of the Security Council on 31 January 1992, 17 June 1992, A/47/277 para. 13. See also paras. 5, 17, 22, and 26, and United Nations Conference on Environment and Development, Agenda Item 21, UN Doc. A/Conf.151/PC/100/Add. 1 (1992) (hereinafter Agenda 21).

[3] A. Springer, *The International Law of Pollution—Protecting the Global Environment in a World of Sovereign States* (Westport, Conn., 1983).

[4] This chapter uses the concept of decision-making in a broad sense that encompasses authoritative constitutive decisions by a range of actors (including judges, arbitrators, national government officials, international governmental organization personnel, and international conferences) and public

through techniques for dispute containment and resolution, but these too are restricted by procedural constraints and lack of effective implementation. The chapter concludes that although states have reacted to the pressing demands for environmental guarantees by the multiple articulation of standards through traditional law-making and by evolving newer methods, such apparent consensus often conceals continuing substantive and political differences between states. The formulation of new processes deflects attention from the lack of clearly defined and enforced implementation measures that are applicable to all relevant players and defers the time for context-specific decision-making.[5] Continued deference to state sovereignty weakens the authority of third party decision-makers and excludes other participants from law-making and resolution. The appearance of order and progress is thereby created without the substance of real transformation. The rhetoric of legal regulation remains unfulfilled without either political will or economic incentive for compliance. It must be questioned whether the current structures and processes of international law are capable of meeting the challenges presented by the need for rational global environmental decision-making.

2. Conflicting Interests and International Environmental Law

The International Context of Environmental Decision-Making

International environmental standard-setting and implementation operate within the current legal system constructed upon the doctrine of the sovereign equality of states. This legal order develops in the context of the complex 'international political forces that work to complicate the negotiation and implementation of rational environmental policies between states . . .'.[6] In order to construct an effective international regulatory regime, states need to take a realistic view of the capacity for environmental degradation to undermine their long-term interests. The potential for environmental disputes to escalate into conflict and the worldwide consequences of such phenomena as climate change, depletion of the ozone layer, the reduction of biodiversity, pollution of vital water supplies, deforestation, and desertification demand global mechanisms for long-term containment, management, and resolution of environmental issues that might be at variance with short-term national gain. States act to protect their national sovereign interests

order decisions. In a decentralized legal system lacking legislative authority, the legal process evolves through such decision-making. See R. Higgins, '. . . international law is a continuing process of authoritative decisions' (R. Higgins, *Problems and Process: International Law and How We Use It* (Oxford, 1994), at 2); H. Lasswell and M. McDougal, *Jurisprudence for a Free Society: Studies in Law, Science and Policy* (Dordrecht, 1992), vol. 1, 191–2.

[5] See M. Koskenniemi, 'The Future of Statehood' (1991) 32 *Harv ILJ* 397–410.

[6] A. Hurrell and B. Kingsbury, 'The International Politics of the Environment: An Introduction', in A. Hurrell and B. Kingsbury (eds.), *The International Politics of the Environment* (Oxford, 1992), at 1.

and, at least within a democratic framework, need domestic support. Global, as opposed to national, survival however demands international policies directed at sound environmental management based on co-operation, restraint, and concerted and directed action. International regulation can provide a framework for such action by promoting stability and predictability through the creation of legitimate expectations for compliance, but only political will can lead to the achievement of 'sustainable' environmental standards.[7]

The generation of such political will is especially difficult where interests are polarized as for example between developed and developing states. The latter may see the environmental standards of the former as too costly and as prejudicial to their own national economic growth. The failure at the United Nations Conference on the Environment and Development (UNCED) to achieve a comprehensive 'Earth Charter' with far-reaching provisions on all aspects of the environment demonstrates the differing priorities and agendas of states in the North and those of the South.[8] At UNCED, states from the North focused upon particular 'global environmental issues' while the primary concerns of those from the South that suffer worst from the environmental degradation caused by extreme poverty were development issues in a general sense.[9] This representation of polarized views between the North and South is itself too simplistic with diverse interests driving the policies of different states within this categorization.[10] Nevertheless these conflicting views are perhaps epitomized by the absence at UNCED of any binding agreement on forests. Conservation of the world's remaining forests can be viewed alternatively as a global environmental necessity or as an inhibition on a state's right to exploit its natural resources in pursuit of its national economic development. All that could be agreed on forests at UNCED was the

[7] 'Sustainable development' was defined by the World Commission on Environment and Development Experts Group on Environmental Law, *Our Common Future* (Oxford, 1987), at 43, as 'development that meets the needs of the present without compromising the ability of future generations to meet their own needs.' The nature of sustainable development and its influence in domestic law are discussed in respect of the UK by Jenny Steele and Tim Jewell in Chapter 1 above, and more generally by David Robinson, in Chapter 2.

[8] The timing of UNCED after the collapse of the former Soviet Union and the end of the cold war meant that issues were raised there in a North-South axis rather than the East-West axis that had dominated international agendas since 1945; see I. Rowlands, 'The International Politics of Environment and Development: The Post-UNCED Agenda' (1992) 21 *Millenium: Journal of International Studies* 209–26.

[9] Ibid. These respective viewpoints are epitomized in the inclusion of references to development throughout the Declaration on Environment and Development, Rio de Janeiro, 14 June 1992 rep. 31 *ILM* 876 (1992) (hereinafter Rio Declaration), in contrast with the Stockholm Declaration. The Rio Declaration (Principle 1) refers first to concerns for sustainable development.

[10] e.g., in the negotiations for the UN Framework Convention on Climate Change, 1992 rep. 31 *ILM* (1992) 851 (hereinafter Climate Change Convention) there were 'conflicts related to energy production and consumption patterns, levels of technological development in the use and conservation of energy and resources and the specific vulnerability of certain countries which may be significantly affected by climate change.' See S. Murase, 'Perspectives from International Economic Law on Transnational Environmental Issues' (1995) 253 *Hague Receuil* 287–431, at 315, citing P. Sands, *Principles of International Environmental Law* (Manchester, 1995, vol. 1), at 273.

Statement of Principles for a Global Consensus on the Management, Conservation and Sustainable Development of All Types of Forest.[11] This reasserts the sovereign right of states to utilize, develop, and manage their forests in accordance with their own development needs and levels of social and economic development while 'urging' the management of forest resources in conformity with the needs of current and future generations and recognition of the vital role forests play in protecting fragile ecosystems. The opposing starting points lead to diverse claims such as those by developing states for compensation and other financial incentives from developed states (or international institutions) for any accepted constraints on their development intended to enhance global sustainable development.[12] Formulation of such claims leads to separate, not joint law-making strategies.[13]

Contradictory scientific expert opinion impedes full acceptance of the precautionary principle and creates difficulties in reaching agreement on targets, for example for timely reduction of harmful carbon dioxide emissions.[14] Demands for economic development within the framework of sovereign equality and free trade principles allow for individualized national standards and targets,[15] and compromise solutions, such as that for the sale of CFC quotas to those unwilling or unable to reduce their own emissions, as allowed by the Montreal Protocol.[16] While this accords with market principles and may facilitate overall compliance by providing a solution for over-quota states, it does not reflect any urgency for global reduction.

The legal norm of state sovereignty also disguises the reality that states are no longer the only, or perhaps even the major, players. The activities of transnational corporations (TNCs) must be subject to international legal scrutiny, but

[11] A Non-legally Binding Authoritative Statement of Principles for a Global Consensus on the Management, Conservation and Sustainable Development of All Types of Forest, 13 June 1992, rep. 31 *ILM* 881 (1992).

[12] Some such claims have met with a positive response, for example the experimental Global Environmental Facility and Global Environment Trust Fund in the World Bank; International Bank for Reconstruction and Development Resolution 91–5, 1991, rep. 30 *ILM* 1758 (1991). This was transformed into a permanent financial mechanism by the Instrument for the Establishment of the Restructured Global Environment Facility, 1994, rep. 33 *ILM* 1273 (1994). It provides a source of financial assistance in four areas: climate change, destruction of biological diversity, pollution of international waters, and ozone depletion.

[13] Birnie and Boyle give the example of the proposal that charges be levied for the use by developed states of the biological resources found in developing states: P. Birnie and A. Boyle, *International Law and the Environment* (Oxford, 1992), at 7.

[14] Rio Declaration, Principle 15, encapsulates the precautionary principle: in order to protect the environment, the precautionary approach shall be widely applied by states according to their capabilities. Where there are threats of serious or irreversible damage, lack of full scientific certainty shall not be used as a reason for postponing cost-effective measures to prevent environmental degradation.

[15] Rio Declaration, Principle 11, states that '[s]tandards applied by some countries may be inappropriate and of unwarranted economic and social costs to other countries, in particular developing countries'.

[16] The Montreal Protocol on Substances that Deplete the Ozone Layer, with Annex A, 19 September 1987, rep. 26 *ILM* 1550 (1987) (hereinafter Montreal Protocol), Art. 2(5).

are outside the structures of accountability that have been developed on the assumption of state jurisdiction and control.[17] Environmental harm caused by the activities of TNCs, for example the escape of gas from the Union Carbide factory at Bhopal and the Exxon oil pollution in Alaska, has given rise to prolonged litigation and settlement processes within domestic arenas.[18] Neither the substance nor the processes of international law can accommodate such claims, but this means there is no authoritative international legal statement of standards or liability. Even codes of conduct for TNCs, which are non-binding in character, have had only limited success.[19] States' need for foreign investment to compete in the global economy and the drive to maximize corporate profits work against internationally observed environmentally-sound operating practices. The globalization of the economy and the liberalization of international trade limit the relevance of state-made international law, even where there is governmental will for compliance. International legal objectives of stability, international peace and security and sustainable development can only be attained through acceptance of these realities and the recognition of the practical limitations upon state sovereignty that they entail. This is the new paradigm of international environmental law,[20] and suggests the need for an evolving international legal order.[21]

Tensions within Principles of International Law

Despite its apparent newness, much of international environmental law is based upon long-standing principles of international law, such as those relating to state responsibility for actions committed within territory under a state's jurisdiction and control that harm another state,[22] the obligation to perform treaties,[23] and reparations for breach of international legal standards.[24] Alongside these traditional

[17] State responsibility only attaches for acts of non-state actors that can be imputed to the state. This doctrine is problematic with respect to the actions of TNCs.

[18] C. Abraham and S. Abraham, 'The Bhopal Case and the Development of Environmental Law in India' (1991) 40 *ICLQ* 334–65.

[19] e.g., United Nations Draft Code on Conduct of Transnational Corporations rep. 23 *ILM* 626 (1984).

[20] N. Robinson, 'Universal and National Trends in International Environmental Law' (1993) *Environmental Policy and Law* 148–54. See also: '[t]oday what we need is a new paradigm based on the understanding that the Earth's biosphere and the processes taking place in it form an indivisible whole very closely connected with the processes taking place in human society.' S. Vinogradov, 'International Environmental Security: The Concept and Implementation', in A. Carty and G. Danilenko (eds.), *Perestroika and International Law: Current Anglo-Soviet Approaches to International Law* (Edinburgh, 1990), at 196–7.

[21] E. Brown Weiss, 'International Environmental Law: Contemporary Issues and the Emergence of a New World Order' (1993) 81 *Georgetown LJ* 675–710.

[22] These principles were expounded in the *Trail Smelter Arbitration* (*United States v Canada*) 3 *RIAA* (1941) 1907, *Corfu Channel Case* (*United Kingdom v Albania*) Merits 1949 *ICJ Rep*. 4 (Judgment of 9 April).

[23] Vienna Convention on the Law of Treaties, 23 May 1969, 1155 *UNTS* 331, Art. 26.

[24] *Factory at Chorzów* (Claim for Indemnity) (*Germany v Poland*) (Merits) 1928 *PCIJ* Ser. A No. 17.

principles are emergent norms with specific environmental import.[25] In turn these principles and norms intersect with other doctrines of contemporary international law such as those relating to state sovereignty, territorial jurisdiction and control, the right to self-determination, including permanent sovereignty over natural resources, protection of fundamental human rights, and international economic law.

Environmental provisions may be forcefully resisted in order to protect claims to territory or to access to resources that rest upon established principles of international law such as boundary delimitation and jurisdictional zones. For example, on 28 March 1995 Spain commenced proceedings against Canada in the International Court of Justice (ICJ) in respect of a dispute relating to the Canadian Coastal Fisheries Protection Act 1985, as amended May 1994, and measures taken by Canada under that Act.[26] The application claimed that on 9 March 1995 Canadian authorities had boarded a fishing boat flying the Spanish flag on the high seas beyond the Canadian exclusive economic zone. Spain asserted that Canada was attempting to impose its conservation and management measures upon all states fishing in the Northwest Atlantic Fisheries Organization area contrary to the freedom of high seas fishing.[27] The case focuses upon the uncertain situation of access to straddling fish stocks and highly migratory species. It requires judicial evaluation of the competing interests of coastal states and long-range fishing states within the contexts of traditional freedom of fishing on the high seas, coastal state environmental and conservation measures justified by declining fishing resources, and regional arrangements for access to maritime zones.[28]

International Environmental Regulation versus National Security

Like human rights law, environmental regulation goes to the heart of the domestic jurisdiction exception to international intervention,[29] for example through the perception of environmental policies as threatening to individual state security. Claims of state sovereignty are especially forceful when security interests are alleged to be at risk and countervailing environmental arguments may simply be denied by states. For example in the *Nuclear Tests* cases, France denied the jurisdiction of the ICJ to hear the application brought by New Zealand and Australia on the basis of its reservation to acceptance of the jurisdiction of the Court. The second exception to the French Declaration under Article 36(2) of the Statute of

[25] For example, the International Law Commission's (ILC's) reference on International Liability for Injurious Consequences arising out of Acts not Prohibited by International Law has focused primarily on environmental harm.

[26] International Court of Justice Communique, No. 95/8, 29 March 1995.

[27] Geneva Convention on the High Seas, 1958, 450 *UNTS* 82, Art. 2; United Nations Convention on the Law of the Sea, Montego Bay, 10 December 1982, rep. 21 *ILM* 1261 (1982), Art. 87.

[28] The Court will have to decide this dispute in light of existing international law before the Agreement for the Implementation of the Provisions of the United Nations Convention on the Law of the Sea of 10 December 1982 Relating to the Conservation and Management of Straddling Fish Stocks and Highly Migratory Species, 4 August 1995, rep. 34 *ILM* 1542 (1995).

[29] United Nations Charter, Art. 2(7).

the ICJ, excluded 'disputes concerning questions which, according to international law, are exclusively within domestic jurisdiction'.[30] New Zealand and Australia sought a declaration that French atmospheric nuclear testing in the South Pacific was not consistent with international law.[31] In their pleadings the applicant states supported their submission by drawing upon the environmental consequences of nuclear testing.[32] France denied the Court's jurisdiction claiming its nuclear policy to be essential to its national defence and therefore exclusively a matter of domestic concern.[33] The further dispute with New Zealand arising out of the sinking of the *Rainbow Warrior* in Auckland Harbour in 1985 focused upon similar issues. France claimed state immunity from the exercise of New Zealand's criminal jurisdiction over the acts of its agents operating in New Zealand territory to support its defence programme.[34] On the other side of the coin, the United States perceived its security interests to be threatened by New Zealand's domestic legislation banning vessels that were either nuclear powered or carrying nuclear matter from its ports. The United States took unilateral measures against New Zealand thereby asserting that the latter's obligations under the collective defence treaty, ANZUS,[35] took priority over environmental concerns.[36]

Conflict between environmental protection and national, and even international security, was especially evident in the aftermath of the 1991 Gulf War. Acting in response to the breach of international peace and security caused by Iraq's aggression against Kuwait,[37] the Security Council used its powers under Chapter VII of the United Nations Charter to authorize the use of 'all necessary means' to liberate Kuwait from Iraqi occupation.[38] Such broad authorization presents two separate environmental concerns. First, does 'all necessary means' legitimate measures that are destructive of the environment, including even the use of nuclear weapons?[39] Second, where does responsibility lie for the environmental damage caused by conflict? The Security Council has affirmed the liability of Iraq for

[30] Under Art. 36(2) states parties may 'at any time declare that they recognise as compulsory *ipso facto* and without special agreement, in relation to any other state accepting the same obligation, the jurisdiction of the Court in all legal disputes . . .'. The French reservation was made 20 May 1966 (1972–3) *YBICJ* 60.

[31] *Nuclear Tests (Australia v France; New Zealand v France)* 1974 *ICJ Rep.* 253; 1974 *ICJ Rep.* 457.

[32] *Nuclear Tests cases*, Pleadings, Oral Arguments and Documents, vol. 1, at 9.

[33] The Court avoided ruling on jurisdiction by finding the case to be inadmissible on other grounds; 1974 *ICJ Rep.* 253 at para. 59. In 1974 France terminated its acceptance of the jurisdiction of the Court.

[34] Report of the *Rainbow Warrior* Affair, 74 *ILR* 241.

[35] Pacific Security Treaty (ANZUS Treaty), 1 September 1951, 131 *UNTS* 83. The parties are the United States, Australia, and New Zealand.

[36] C. Chinkin, 'Suspension of Treaty Relationships: The ANZUS Alliance' (1990) 7 *UCLA Pacific Basin LJ* 114–57.

[37] United Nations Charter, Art. 39.

[38] SC Res. 678, 28 November 1990.

[39] Legality of the Threat or Use of Nuclear Weapons, 1996 *ICJ Rep.* (Adv. Op. 8 July), rep. 35 *ILM* 809 (1996), see below text to nn. 159–73. The ICJ did not consider the use of nuclear weapons in pursuance of Security Council objectives.

all direct damage, including environmental damage, caused by its illegal acts.[40] The claims covered include loss suffered as a result of 'Military operations . . . by either side during the period 2 August 1990 to 2 March 1991'.[41] However allocation of liability for environmental harm (including that for cleansing and restoration measures) to Iraq in this instance does not resolve the wider tension between the objectives of international environmental law, the international use of force, and Security Council powers under the United Nations Charter.[42]

International Environmental Law versus Human Rights Approaches

The traditional basis of international law as regulating inter-state behaviour has been challenged by the recognition of the international legal personality of other actors, most notably that of international organizations[43] and individuals through the development of human rights law and international criminal law. Environmental disputes highlight some of the dilemmas facing decision-makers caused by tensions inherent in the international legal doctrines themselves, in particular that between state sovereignty on the one hand and individual and communal interests on the other. Protection of the environment has become the concern of individuals. The right to a clean and healthy environment has been claimed, somewhat controversially and variably, in the language of human rights.[44] This may have localized application, for example for access to clean water supplies; be regionalized as between riparian, adjacent or opposite coastal states; or internationalized as in the claims of atmospheric and marine pollution caused through nuclear testing. The highly publicized actions of Greenpeace, an international non-governmental organization (NGO), against French nuclear testing in the Pacific and against Shell in its proposed disposal of the Brent Spar oil rig demonstrate the growing prominence of non-state actors in the international environmental arena. NGO actions can result in international law claims, for example the damage Greenpeace suffered through the death of a crew member of the *Rainbow Warrior* and destruction of its property was settled through separate (private) arbitration proceedings with France.

[40] SC Res. 687, 3 April 1991, para. 16 affirms that Iraq 'is liable under international law for any direct loss, damage, including environmental damage and the depletion of natural resources, . . . as a result of Iraq's unlawful invasion and occupation of Kuwait.'

[41] Decisions Adopted by the Governing Council, 22 July 1991–26 June 1992, Decision 7 rep. 31 *ILM* 1045 (1992).

[42] Rio Declaration, Principle 24, requires only that states 'respect international law providing protection for the environment in times of armed conflict and cooperate in its further development'. See also, Protection of the Environment in Times of Armed Conflict, GA Res. 47/37, 25 November 1992.

[43] Reparation for Injuries Suffered in the Service of the United Nations 1949 *ICJ Rep*. 174 (Adv. Op. 11 April).

[44] e.g., Stockholm Declaration, Principle 1; African Charter on Human Rights and Peoples Rights, 27 June 1981, rep. 21 *ILM* 58 (1982), Art. 24 (hereinafter African Charter); European Social Charter, 1961, 529 *UNTS* 89, Art. 11; Additional Protocol to the Inter American Convention on Human Rights, 1989, Art. 11, rep. 28 *ILM* 156 (1989); GA Res. 45/94, 1990.

The human rights approach to international environmental law has been the subject of debate and uncertainty.[45] As Boyle points out, it is noticeable that the Rio Declaration has eschewed the language of rights stating only that 'human beings are at the centre of concerns for sustainable development. They are entitled to a healthy and productive life in harmony with nature'.[46]

Conceiving environmental law in human rights terms has a number of consequences.[47] The framework becomes that of claims brought by individuals or NGOs against their treatment by their own state, rather than that of inter-state relations. This may facilitate proceedings before domestic courts where human rights obligations have been incorporated within national law. The language of rights is empowering for individuals and to some extent allows environmental claims to trump non-rights based claims. Such an approach would 'recognise the vital character of the environment as a basic condition of life, indispensable to the promotion of human dignity and welfare, and to the fulfilment of other human rights.'[48] Internationally, such claims would come within the jurisdictional competence of the United Nations human rights and regional treaty bodies,[49] including the right of individual petition, where applicable.[50]

However there are also practical and conceptual difficulties.[51] The precise content of a right to a clean or adequate environment is unclear, allowing states considerable discretion in defining their obligations. Is the required standard subject to regional or economic variation? Claims based on environmental human rights might conflict with other human rights necessitating value choices as to priorities and generating confrontation. To whom is a right to a clean environment owed and against whom can it be claimed? Is it an individual or a group right? Still more complex is the concept of inter-generational equity, that is the obligation upon the current generation to preserve an adequate environment for future

[45] A. Boyle, 'The Role of International Human Rights Law in the Protection of the Environment', in A. Boyle and M. Anderson (eds.), *Human Rights Approaches to Environmental Protection* (New York, 1996).

[46] Principle 1. See D. Shelton, 'What Happened in Rio to Human Rights?' (1992) 3 *YBIEL* 75–93, at 82.

[47] Boyle, op. cit., at 45. Boyle discusses the Final Report of the Sub-Commission on the Prevention of Discrimination and Protection of Minorities, UN Doc. E/CN.4/Sub.2/1994/9, which proposes a Declaration on Human Rights and the Environment.

[48] Ibid., at 49.

[49] For example the Human Rights Committee established under the International Covenant on Civil and Political Rights, 16 December 1966, 999 *UNTS* 171, Art. 28; the Commission and Court established by the European Convention for the Protection of Human Rights and Fundamental Freedoms, 4 November 1950, *ETS* No. 5, Art. 19 (hereinafter European Convention); the similar organs under the American Convention on Human Rights, 22 November 1969, *OAS TS* No. 36, Art. 33 (hereinafter American Convention). Protocol No. 11 to the Convention for the Protection of Human Rights and Fundamental Freedoms, Restructuring the Control Machinery Established Thereby, 11 May 1994 rep. 33 *ILM* 943 (1994), Art. 1 will replace Art. s 19–66 of the Convention.

[50] European Convention, Art. 25; American Convention, Art. 44; International Covenant on Civil and Political Rights, First Optional Protocol, 16 December 1966.

[51] Boyle, op. cit., at 48–57.

generations.[52] Who can legitimately claim such a right?[53] A focus upon human rights also supports the anthropocentric view that preservation of the environment is only for the benefit of humanity rather than a recognition of the 'intrinsic or inherent value of other species and the environment in general'.[54] Finally it must also be admitted that despite assertions of human rights norms as peremptory norms of international law (*jus cogens*),[55] compliance and implementation remain as problematic as in other areas of international law. There can be no expectation that the conjunction of environmental law with human rights law would promote conforming behaviour.

International Environmental Law versus the Right to Development

The emergent right to development has been controversial in human rights law and presents particular conflicts with simultaneously emergent environmental norms.[56] Like the right to self-determination with which it is closely associated, the right to development has been expressed as a peoples', or collective, right.[57] This formulation provides scope for potential conflict both with the claims of states and of individuals. For individuals the right to development might imply adequate living conditions that foster personal growth and achievement,[58] while states focus upon national economic demands.[59] Principles of 'good governance' that demand governmental openness and accountability have been one way of attempting to reconcile individual human rights with policies for economic

[52] Stockholm Declaration, Principle 1, asserts the 'solemn responsibility to protect and improve the environment for present and future generations.' Rio Declaration, Principle 3, states 'The right to development must be fulfilled so as to equitably meet developmental and environmental needs of present and future generations.'

[53] E. Brown Weiss, *In Fairness to Future Generations* (New York, 1989). See also, Legality of the Threat or Use of Nuclear Weapons, 1996 *ICJ Rep.* para. 29, rep. 35 *ILM* 888 (1996) (diss. op. Judge Weeramantry).

[54] Boyle, op. cit., at 51.

[55] A rule of *jus cogens* is a peremptory norm of international law from which no derogation is allowed: Vienna Convention on the Law of Treaties, 1969, Art. 53. Art. 64 provides that a treaty that conflicts with a rule of *jus cogens* is void.

[56] There is a huge literature on the right to development. See especially P. Alston, 'Making Space for New Human Rights: The Case of the Right to Development' (1988) 1 *Harvard Human Rights Yearbook* 3; P. Alston, 'Revitalising United Nations Work on Human Rights and Development' (1991) 18 *Melb ULR* 216–57; M. Bedjaoui, 'The Right to Develoment', in M. Bedjaoui (ed.), *International Law: Achievements and Prospects* (Paris and London, 1991). For a summary of its possible content see J. Paul, 'The United Nations and the Creation of an International Law of Development' (1995) 36 *Harv ILJ* 307–28.

[57] Declaration on the Right to Development, GA Res. 41/128, 4 December 1986; African Charter, Art. 22. On the parallels between sustainable development and self-determination see D. McGoldrick, 'Sustainable Development and Human Rights' (1996) 45 *ICLQ* 796–818, at 801–3.

[58] For example, International Covenant on Economic, Social and Cultural Rights, 16 December 1966, 993 *UNTS* 3, Art. 11.

[59] International Covenant on Civil and Political Rights and International Covenant on Economic, Social and Cultural Rights, common Art. 1 states: 'All peoples have the right to self-determination. By virtue of that right they . . . freely pursue their economic, social and cultural development'.

growth,[60] for example through policies of the international and regional development banks. This has been summarized by the World Bank in the following terms:

> Popular participation is the process by which people, especially disadvantaged people, influence the decisions that affect them. . . . 'Participation' means influence on development decisions, not simply involvement in the implementation or benefits of a development activity . . .[61]

Accordingly loans agreements include requirements for local and NGO participation. The concept of sustainable development can be used to integrate and balance the considerations of adequate human rights guarantees, economic growth, and environmental protection.[62] Thus following on from Rio Declaration, Principle 1, Principle 4 states that: 'In order to achieve sustainable development, environmental protection shall constitute an integral part of the development process and cannot be considered in isolation from it'.

Nevertheless, practical achievement of this balance remains problematic. The dispute over the construction of the Sardar Sarovar Dam on the Narmada river in India demonstrates the tensions caused by the competing demands of the right to development, the human rights of those living in the construction area, and environmental awareness. The domestic enterprise for the advancement of agriculture and standards of living through improved water supplies was internationalized by the early financial participation of Japan and the World Bank.[63] There were also multi-party domestic interests at stake: for example those of central and regional state governments, landowners, villagers in the affected areas, oustees/squatters, construction workers, labour unions, and investment corporations. The Indian government failed to comply with its own environmental report,[64] or with regulations for consultation, resettlement, and payment of compensation. Demonstrations against forced resettlement and environmental harm in turn generated serious violations of civil and political rights such as the violent break-up of protest movements, arrests, and ill-treatment under detention. Concerns about the environmental and social impact of the proposed construction led to the World Bank imposing deadlines for compliance with resettlement and rehabilitation policies and carrying out on-site inspections and reports before eventually withdrawing from the project. Questions and debates within the US

[60] Good governance incorporates the rights of those affected to be consulted and to participate. It has its human rights roots in International Covenant on Civil and Political Rights, Art. 25.

[61] Cited in Asia Watch, *Before the Deluge: Human Rights Abuses at India's Narmada Dam* (1992), at 30.

[62] McGoldrick, op. cit.

[63] In 1985 the World Bank approved a loan of US$450 million for the construction of the dam. Its conditions included fulfilment of environmental impact assessment and rehabilitation. Japan withdrew its Official Development Assistance Funding in 1990; Asia Watch, op. cit.

[64] Ministry of Environment and Forests, *Environmental Aspects of Narmada Sagar and Sardar Sarovar Multi-Purpose Projects* (1987) found the project did not satisfy environmental requirements. Nevertheless the Ministry gave clearance in 1987 for the project to go ahead.

Congress also demonstrate how those resisting massive development projects that fail to satisfy environmental demands can arouse international support.

In response to such outbursts the World Bank introduced an innovative inspection procedure in 1993. Affected people in a project area of a World Bank-financed project can request inspection by a three-person panel to determine compliance with Bank practices and procedures, including those relating to the environment.[65] This mechanism allows intended beneficiaries to put forward their concerns about a project, but the Panel can only present its findings to the Board of the Bank, which determines its response. As of July 1997, only one such request has resulted in an inspection, raising doubts as to the Bank's commitment to independent evaluation of its projects.[66]

International Environmental Law versus International Trade

There may also be conflict between international trade law and the imperatives of international environmental law.[67] Environmental measures may be discounted by states where they conflict with the exigencies of international trade. Conflicting demands are generated between states' needs for continuing access to resources and the competitive edge that is unfairly gained by states that do not comply with regional or international environmental regulation. These tensions were recognized at Rio where it was agreed that:

> States should co-operate to promote a supportive and open international economic system that would lead to economic growth and sustainable development in all countries, to better address the problems of environmental degradation. Trade policy measures for environmental purposes should not constitute a means of arbitrary or unjustifiable discrimination or a disguised restriction on international trade. Unilateral measures to deal with environmental challenges outside the jurisdiction of the importing country should be avoided . . .[68]

Trade agreements may make provision for environmental protection. Exception (b) to Article XX of the General Agreement on Tariffs and Trade (GATT) allows restrictive measures 'necessary to protect human, animal or plant life or health.'[69] In 1947 explicitly environmental concerns were not envisaged, but a

[65] The Inspection Panel, International Bank for Reconstruction and Development, Report, August 1 1994 to July 31 1996. The Asian Development Bank and the Inter-American Development Bank have instituted similar procedures.

[66] The Arun III project in Nepal. Other inspection requests are pending.

[67] See T. Schoenbaum, 'Free International Trade and Protection of the Environment: Irreconcilable Conflict' (1992) 86 *AJIL* 700–27.

[68] Rio Declaration, Principle 12. Agenda 21, Chapter 2 calls upon the international community to ensure that 'environmental and trade policies are mutually supportive, with a view to achieving sustainable development'.

[69] 55 *UNTS* 308. Art. XX(g) excepts measures 'relating to the conservation of exhaustible natural resources if such measures are made effective in conjunction with restrictions on domestic production or consumption.'

broad interpretation can be given that extends the phrase to a range of actions for environmental protection.[70]

However the GATT/WTO is an institution for the liberalization of international trade that deals only peripherally with other concerns such as environmental protection. Trade sanctions imposed for failure to observe environmental standards may be deemed contrary to the requirements of GATT, especially when imposed unilaterally to further one state's particular agenda as accepted in Principle 12. These tensions are well illustrated by the GATT Panel decisions in the Tuna/Dolphin fishing disputes.[71] In the first case the Dispute Settlement Panel reported that the US embargo of Mexican-caught tuna, imposed because of the latter's non-compliance with US rules for the reduction of dolphin mortality in tuna fishing, was incompatible with GATT and was not justified by Article XX.[72] In the second case a further embargo against states that imported tuna from states subject to the primary embargo was also ruled contrary to GATT.[73]

The US use of domestic legislation to impose its own dolphin-friendly standards upon foreign states was motivated by the demands of environmental lobbyists to enforce its Marine Mammal Protection Act 1972. Simultaneously the US protected its own tuna industry. This stance contrasts with its rejection of New Zealand's domestic standards with respect to shipping that could not be confirmed as neither nuclear powered nor carrying nuclear weapons. Unlike the US in the tuna example, New Zealand was only imposing its nuclear-free requirements upon other states to the extent that it was barring such ships from its ports. However, the US resisted New Zealand's stand as conflicting with its security interests. The two examples show both the power of domestic audiences in formulating external environmental policies and that environmental issues cannot be isolated from other state objectives. Internationally, the GATT regime for trade liberalization provided Mexico with a forum in which to challenge successfully the actions taken against it, an option that was not open to New Zealand. A permanent committee on trade and environment issues has now been established within the GATT/WTO.[74]

[70] Murase explains that environmental concerns were confined in 1947 to 'the very limited area of sanitary and phytosanitary measures for the protection of human health, animals and plants.' Murase, op. cit., at 328.

[71] This account draws heavily upon the outstanding discussion by B. Kingsbury, 'The Tuna-Dolphin Controversy, The World Trade Organization, and the Liberal Project to Reconceptualize International Law' (1994) 5 *YBIEL* 1–40. See also Murase, op. cit., at 322–48.

[72] United States Restrictions on Imports of Tuna (*Mexico v United States*) rep. 30 *ILM* 1598 (1991).

[73] United States Restrictions on Imports of Tuna (*EEC and the Netherlands v United States*) rep. 33 *ILM* 839 (1994).

[74] The Committee on Trade and Environment was established as part of the WTO to work on recommendations 'to enhance the positive interaction between trade and environment'. Its predecessor, the GATT Working Group on Environmental Measures and International Trade, did not meet for many years. The Committee reported to the Singapore Ministerial Conference, December 1996. See T. Schoenbaum, 'International Trade and Protection of the Environment: the Continuing Search for Reconciliation' (1997) 91 *AJIL* 268–313.

An attempt to accommodate trade and environmental interests has been made in the North American Free Trade Agreement (NAFTA). The Preamble includes a commitment to achieve its objectives 'in a manner consistent with environmental protection and conservation'.[75] This was fleshed out by the North American Agreement on Environmental Co-operation passed to 'support the environmental goals and objectives of the NAFTA'.[76] Institutional weight was provided through the establishment of the North American Commission on Environmental Co-operation with its own Council and Secretariat. *Inter alia* it has some supervisory powers over national environmental laws, provides a forum for environmental co-operation, acts as a point of inquiry and for receipt of comments from NGOs, and has dispute resolution functions.[77] Article 6 provides the important interface between domestic and international law by providing that parties 'shall ensure that interested persons may request the Party's competent authorities to investigate alleged violations of its environmental laws and regulations and shall give such requests due consideration in accordance with law'.

Another potential tension between environmental concerns and free market principles lies in demands for free exchange between states of the results of research and the latest scientific information and technology that are instrumental in developing appropriate global approaches to environmental protection. In the 1970s, demands for a New International Economic Order (NIEO) included preferential treatment for developing states in the free transfer of technology.[78] The motivation was not environmental, but to advance the economic development of all states. The rejection of many of the aspirations upon which the NIEO was constructed is illustrated by the fate of the original Part XI of the United Nations Convention on the Law of the Sea (UNCLOS).[79] This provided for acquisition of technology and scientific knowledge by the International Sea-Bed Authority and the promotion of its transfer to developing states for the benefit of all states.[80] The long deadlock caused by the rejection of Part XI by Northern states was ended by the successful negotiation of an amended Part XI. This requires enterprises and developing states wishing to obtain technology to seek to obtain it 'on fair and reasonable commercial terms . . . on the open market' or through joint venture arrangements.[81]

[75] Canada-Mexico-United States, North American Free Trade Agreement, Washington, Ottawa and Mexico City, December 1992 rep. 32 *ILM* 289 (1993).

[76] Canada-Mexico-United States, North American Agreement on Environmental Cooperation, Washington, Ottawa and Mexico City, September 1993 rep. 32 *ILM* 1480 (1993), Art. 1(d).

[77] Canada-Mexico-United States, North American Agreement on Environmental Cooperation, Arts. 8–16. See K. Patton, 'Dispute Resolution under the North American Commission on Environmental Co-operation' (1994) 15 *Duke JCIL* 87–116; and 'R. Steinberg, Trade-Environment Negotiations in the EU, NAFTA and WTO: Regional Trajectories of Rule Development' (1997) 91 *AJIL* 231–67.

[78] Resolution on the Charter of Economic Rights and Duties of States, GA Res. 3281 1974 (XXIX).

[79] S. Chatterjee, 'The Charter of Economic Rights and Duties of States: An Evaluation after 15 Years' (1989) 40 *ICLQ* 669–84.

[80] United Nations Convention on the Law of the Sea, 1982, Art. 144.

[81] Agreement Relating to the Implementation of Part XI of the United Nations Convention on the Law of the Sea, 1982, rep. 33 *ILM* 1309 (1994), Annex, Section 5(1)(a).

3. International Environmental Decision-Making: Prescription

The decentralized international legal system lacks formal mechanisms for law and policy-making. International environmental law has therefore been elaborated in the same ways as other areas of international law, primarily through treaties and customary international law.[82] Governing principles of environmental law have evolved as custom,[83] but the content of customary principles is uncertain, and the requirement of uniform, consistent state practice makes customary international law inherently ineffective as a tool of social change.[84]

Since Stockholm there has been a considerable increase in international environmental regulations and prohibitions through treaty law.[85] International standards have been formulated in bilateral and multilateral treaties at the regional and international levels.[86] Treaties have been agreed that are limited to particular issues, while others have been drafted more widely. In response to greater environmental knowledge, treaties have become detailed, specific, and operational.[87] Different treaty models have been used.[88] One model is the creation of environmental regimes.[89] The network of mutual rights and obligations is one of the benefits of treaty regimes over simple standard-setting treaties and is perceived as promoting compliance.[90] Factors thought to have a role in facilitating (or impeding) viable treaty regimes include reliable scientific consensus and data, the public perception of risk, costs of control and prohibitions, including non-monetary costs, perceptions of fairness, short term political benefits and risks, the number and interests of relevant players, previous agreements, the inclusion of monitoring

[82] Statute of the International Court of Justice, Art. 38(1). The two elements of customary international law are state practice and *opinio juris*.

[83] I. Brownlie, 'A Survey of International Customary Rules of Environmental Protection' (1973) 13 *Natural Resources Journal* 179–89; Birnie and Boyle, op. cit., at ch. 3.

[84] Springer gives the example of the principle of 'reasonable use' of shared resources and points out that '[W]hat constitutes reasonable use as derived from past practice may be the very activity that has given rise to the present environmental threat . . .': Springer, op. cit.

[85] R. Hahn and K. Richards, 'The Internationalization of Environmental Regulation' (1989) 30 *Harv ILJ* 421–46, at 423.

[86] In 1972 there were fewer than three dozen multilateral treaties in international environmental law: today there are nearly nine hundred agreements that contain important environmental provisions. E. Brown Weiss, above n. 21, at 675.

[87] Ibid., at 686.

[88] Murase identifies four models of treaty-making: the UNCLOS model of comprehensive regulation; the framework model; the GATT model of successive negotiation rounds; and the OECD 'pledge and review' model; Murase, op. cit., at 316–21.

[89] Regime theory has been developed within international relations rather than international law. A definition that makes apparent its relevance to international law is 'sets of implicit or explicit principles, norms, rules and decision-making procedures around which actors' expectations converge in a given area of international relations' (Hurrell and Kingsbury, op. cit., at 12). In Case Concerning Gabcíkovo-Nagymaros Project (*Hungary-Slovakia*) 1997 *ICJ Rep.* (Judgment of 25 September), the ICJ considered treaty arrangements for the construction and operation of locks onto the Danube not only to be a joint investment programme, but to establish a regime.

[90] Hurrell and Kingsbury, op. cit., at 22–30.

and implementation procedures, the negotiation forum, and the scope of the potential impact of the agreement.[91]

Another law-making model is the use of framework conventions with accompanying (or subsequent) detailed protocol(s) allowing for flexibility, adaptability, and amendment as circumstances require. A framework convention provides a structure for further co-operation in developing effective monitoring procedures, exchanging information, and facilitating scientific research, while protocols provide greater specificity in complex regulation and facilitate response to changed scientific knowledge.[92]

Despite the increase in the number of environmental agreements, their more sophisticated structure and their greater substantive breadth, there are disadvantages to environmental decision-making by treaty. Negotiation can be slow,[93] ratifications may be delayed preventing the treaty coming into force,[94] ratification by dissentient states is unlikely,[95] and amendment remains difficult. Negotiated texts are frequently indeterminate and imprecise, especially where adopted by consensus. The very number of treaties with environmental implications entered into since 1972 with overlapping, duplicating, and sometimes conflicting provisions makes it difficult to specify the obligations a state has incurred. Apart from the uncertain limitations of the doctrine of *jus cogens*, states may by agreement abrogate rules of general international law.

Further, there is no international institution with overall responsibility for developing environmental norms equivalent to the role played for example by the United Nations Human Rights Commission. Environmental issues arise within the work of many of the specialized agencies and there is a lack of cohesion and coherence between them. The United Nations Environment Programme (UNEP) was created by General Assembly resolution in 1972 to serve 'as a catalyst in developing and coordinating an environmental focus in the programmes of other organizations rather than initiating or mandating environmental programmes on its own account'.[96] Formulation of legal standards was not included within UNEP's first

[91] E. Hahn and Richards, op. cit.

[92] Brown Weiss, above n. 21, at 688. Examples of framework conventions are the Vienna Convention for the Protection of the Ozone Layer, 22 March 1985, rep. 26 *ILM* 1529 (1987) with the subsequent Montreal Protocol and the Adjustments to the Montreal Protocol on Substances that Deplete the Ozone Layer, 29 June 1990, rep. 30 *ILM* 537 (1991); the Climate Change Convention; and the Convention on Biodiversity, June 1992, rep. 31 *ILM* 818 (1992) (hereinafter Biodiversity Convention).

[93] For example, negotiations for the United Nations Convention on the Law of the Sea lasted from 1973 to 1982. On the other hand the Convention on Early Notification of a Nuclear Accident, Vienna, 1986, rep. 25 *ILM* 1370 (1986) was agreed only months after the Chernobyl disaster had highlighted the need.

[94] The United Nations Convention on the Law of the Sea did not come into force until November 1994, twelve years after it was opened for ratification and accession.

[95] Vienna Convention on the Law of Treaties 1969, Art. 34: a treaty does not create either obligations or rights for a third State without its consent.

[96] Birnie and Boyle, op. cit., at 42. UNEP was established by GA Res. 2997, 1972. Unlike the specialized agencies it has no express or implied treaty powers from which to develop its competency to fulfil its functions.

priorities, although it has evolved an increasingly 'vigorous role' in doing this.[97] The creation of the UN Commission on Sustainable Development after demands at UNCED for a more powerful international environmental institution to monitor implementation of Agenda 21 has not significantly changed the situation.

The traditional sources of international law have been described as 'slow, cumbersome, expensive, uncoordinated and uncertain'.[98] The work of the International Law Commission (ILC) on Injurious Consequences of Acts Not Prohibited by International Law illustrates these shortcomings. The reference has been worked on over two decades. It falls within the function of 'progressive development', rather than 'codification', since state practice does not favour liability for lawful acts.[99] The ILC is uniquely placed to attune emergent environmental principles with general international law, but strongly held opinions on the potential scope of the reference to inhibit lawful activities on a state's own territory have impeded agreement on even draft texts. The realization that the reference is unlikely to lead to any binding agreement is a sobering reflection of the difficulties in creating new environmental law.

The drawbacks of treaty law and custom have led to the search for new methods of law-making,[100] most notably through so-called 'soft law' techniques, for example General Assembly resolutions, institutional codes, and guidelines.[101] Unlike treaties, such instruments create no formal obligations. They also generally lack linguistic precision and implementation procedures. Nevertheless their conclusion is not without value.[102] Their texts reflect a political consensus that may be morally difficult for states to repudiate. The fact that an instrument is formally non-binding may foster flexibility and adaptation. The formulation of principles has been described as the first step in the law-making process, in that it directs attention towards the substance of the potential rule.[103] The agenda for change contained in many soft law instruments may harden into binding legal obligation through the generation of sufficient state practice for the creation of a rule of customary law, or by facilitating negotiation of a subsequent treaty. Thus principles contained in the non-binding Stockholm Declaration have become pivotal in determining principles of customary international law. While reiteration

[97] Ibid., at 42–3.

[98] G. Palmer, 'New Ways to Make Environmental Law' (1992) 86 *AJIL* 259–283.

[99] United Nations Charter, Art. 13 provides for the functions of 'codification and progressive development' of international law.

[100] There have been academic proposals for the recognition of new methods of international law-making. See, e.g., Palmer, op. cit., and I. Gunning, 'Modernizing Customary International Law: The Challenge of Human Rights' (1991) 31 *VJIL* 211–47.

[101] Examples of soft environmental instruments include both the Stockholm Declaration and the Rio Declaration; the World Charter for Nature, 1982, rep. 23 *ILM* 455 (1983); and the Hague Declaration on the Environment, 1989 rep. 28 *ILM* 1308 (1989).

[102] See P.-M. Dupuy, 'Soft Law and International Law of the Environment' (1991) 12 *Mich JIL* 420–35; C. Chinkin, 'The Challenge of Soft Law: Development and Change in International Law' (1989) 38 *ICLQ* 850–66.

[103] H. Meijers, 'How is International Law Made? The Stages of Growth of International Law and the Use of Customary Rules' (1978) 9 *Neths YBIL* 3–26.

(for example in the Rio Declaration) cannot of itself give binding effect to a non-binding statement, it may be an indication of acceptance as custom. Principles that have evolved, been radically changed or newly introduced provide evidence of directions and trends that cannot be easily disregarded. For example, Rio Declaration, Principle 2, reiterates the two strands of the Stockholm Declaration, Principle 21. This confirms the centrality of state sovereignty over natural resources, and of state responsibility to ensure that activities within its jurisdiction and control do not cause damage to the environment of other states or in areas beyond national jurisdiction. The addition of development policies in Rio Declaration, Principle 2, indicates the growing acceptance of the right to development as customary international law.

However the uncertainty and unpredictability of state compliance with international environmental treaties (as well as other treaties) makes the distinction between 'hard' and 'soft' instruments more one of degree than form. The supremacy accorded to states' interests in international law-making (through both hard and soft law instruments) impedes systematic and effective environmental law-making. It is state practice that constitutes customary international law and only states can conclude international treaties.[104] Since states also comprise the membership of the General Assembly and the specialized agencies, resolutions of those bodies also primarily promote states' interests. The lack of a specialist environmental agency within the UN system has impeded the development of a separate institutional and bureaucratic expertise that might develop its own agenda and become a driving force for change.

It might appear that the dominance of states in legal prescription has been lessened through the intrusion of nongovernmental entities. The increase in number and influence of international environmental NGOs has been dramatic. In particular, NGOs were highly visible participants at UNCED especially through the parallel NGO Forum that has become a feature of United Nations global conferences. NGOs have become proficient at accessing governments and making their concerns known by engaging in such activities as attending regional preparatory meetings, lobbying governments, preparing draft texts, commenting upon and amending draft texts, disseminating information locally and regionally, and raising and educating public opinion. The Rio Declaration indirectly recognizes the scope of NGO activity but it is nevertheless easy to overstate their impact.[105] States still control the agenda, procedures, and final statements of international conferences. Influence therefore rests upon the contact and co-operation governments allow between themselves and NGOs. Although Conferences such as UNCED have a high popular profile as a means of international law-making, in reality they are less important than bilateral and multilateral treaty negotiation

[104] Vienna Convention on the Law of Treaties, 1969, Art. 2.

[105] Rio Declaration, Principle 27 requires 'States and people' to co-operate in good faith 'and in a spirit of partnership in the fulfilment of the principles'.

processes, including those provided for within certain treaties for update and appraisal.[106]

4. Decision-Making Through Mechanisms for Compliance and Dispute Prevention

The deficiencies of general international law-making mean that international and national decision-makers may find they have no precise governing law to apply and must fall back on broad, open-ended legal principles.[107] The exercise of sovereign discretion is facilitated where treaty language is indeterminate and capable of subjective application. These inadequacies mean that the corpus and practice of law must be fleshed out through treaty performance. An advantage of treaty-making is that provision can be made for ongoing communications between the parties, including mechanisms for monitoring, exchanging information, and sharing research. Such arrangements in turn constitute evolving state practice. Where disputes or differences develop between the parties to even a bilateral treaty, the processes attempted for their resolution and the outcome have practical precedential effect in that they exemplify state practice and create expectations as to future conduct, both between the parties and with respect to non-parties. The limitations of international prescription accentuate the importance of decision-making through dispute prevention, management, containment, and resolution processes whereby substantive legal principles for future application may be derived.

Formalized methods for treaty compliance include regular monitoring of the treaty standards and prohibitions. This presumes ongoing co-ordination of states' policies and their collective understanding of their legal rights and duties. It also requires institutional supervision, monitoring, and resolution of actual and potential disputes and differences.[108] Where a treaty has been negotiated, future relations between states parties and other international actors follow a constant pattern of action and reaction, claim and counter-claim. Potential disputes may be pre-empted by early consultation systems and ongoing exchanges between all participants. Such co-operation requires the consent of states and a political willingness to comply with formal and informal agreements worked out within the treaty framework. The maintenance of communications throughout the life of an

[106] e.g., The Protocol on Environmental Protection to Antarctica, 1991 rep. 30 *ILM* 1455 (1991) requires parties to negotiate an Annex on liability for environmental damage there. Even though the Protocol has not entered into force discussions on a liability Annex are underway.

[107] Such principles include the duty to co-operate (or good neighbourliness), the duty to prevent foreseeable harm, and the precautionary principle. The status and substance of these principles are disputed: see Birnie and Boyle, op. cit., at ch. 3.

[108] 'The main consequence of this concern for collective interests is the prominence of intergovernmental commissions, "meetings of parties", and other institutions both in developing international regulation and in ensuring compliance and resolving conflicts of interest by diplomatic or political means.' Ibid., at 86.

agreement can minimize the eruption of a dispute that threatens its continued existence and the formal abandonment of the principles earlier agreed.

Treaties requiring regular inter-state communications, reporting systems,[109] or systems for ensuring concerns are brought to the attention of the other parties, are important for this reason. So too are institutional arrangements for locating and managing disputes within the framework of global and regional organizations, for example through consultative meetings and supervision of treaty performance.[110] Such arrangements may include a standing body as a form of negotiation forum, provision for consultations in light of latest scientific and technical information, arrangements for expert advice on a shared basis available to all treaty parties, and dispute resolution mechanisms.[111] Multilateral framework conventions such as those on the ozone layer, climate change, and biodiversity provide for meetings of the parties that keep implementation under periodic review, receive reports and information, and evaluate amendments.[112] An innovation in environmental treaties has been the formulation of non-compliance, or non-performance, procedures that allow an especially designated Implementation Committee to seek an 'amicable solution' between an allegedly non-performing party and an 'involved state' that has raised the matter.[113] Subsidiary bodies to the general meeting of the parties are also used to provide timely advice, for example on scientific and technological matters.[114] Supervisory mechanisms need not be limited to states parties and the benefits of including non-state perspectives through regular informal meetings with, for example, independent environmental experts, regional and local enforcement agencies, or representatives from industry are becoming realized and NGO observer status might be accorded. While the formalization of these decision-making processes within a treaty regularizes their position, their effectiveness rests, as ever, upon the political will of the parties to make them fully operational.

[109] Such treaties draw upon the monitoring processes of human rights law. However their effectiveness in securing compliance to human rights has been questioned and the same concerns are relevant here: A. Bayefsky, 'Making the Human Rights Treaties Work', in L. Henkin and J. Hargrove (eds.), *Human Rights: An Agenda for the Next Century* (Washington, 1994).

[110] Cf. Koskenniemi, op. cit., at 402.

[111] Examples of treaties with regional institutional mechanisms are the South Pacific Nuclear Free Zone Treaty, Raratonga, Cook Islands, 6 August 1985, Annex 4; and the South Pacific Convention for the Protection of the Natural Resources and Environment of the South Pacific Region, Noumea, Protocol for the Prevention of Pollution of the South Pacific Region by Dumping and Protocol Concerning Co-operation in Combating Pollution Emergencies in the South Pacific Region, rep. 26 *ILM* 38 (1987). In the performance of all these treaties the South Pacific Forum plays a major role.

[112] e.g., Montreal Protocol, Art. 11; Biodiversity Convention, Art. 23; Climate Change Convention, Art. 7 (Conference of the Parties).

[113] e.g., Montreal Protocol, Art. 8. For the relationship between procedures for non-compliance and those for dispute resolution, see M. Koskenniemi, 'Breach of Treaty or Non-Compliance? Reflections on the Enforcement of the Montreal Protocol' (1992) 3 *YBIEL* 123–62. See also G. Handl, 'Compliance Control Mechanisms and International Environmental Obligations' (1997) 5 *Tulane Journal of International and Comparative Law* 29–49.

[114] Biodiversity Convention, Art. 25; Climate Change Convention, Arts. 9 and 10.

However, elaborate structural devices may conceal the underlying weaknesses of the substantive obligations. Further, they may not strengthen the parties' commitment to treaty performance. The possibility remains that even negotiated implementation processes between the parties will lead to compromises and accepted practices that weaken the treaty text. Offering incentives for compliance might appear to reward non-performance. Further, negotiations over environmental regimes occur within the context of a range of other political and economic agendas that bear upon their outcome. There is no guarantee that environmental obligations will prevail. Political desire to avoid confrontation or disputes (especially between states with regional or political alliances) may encourage dilution of the treaty requirements and create an attitude of disrespect or indifference towards its terms.

5. Decision-Making Through International Adjudication

Public and Private Dispute Resolution Processes

Disputes inevitably do erupt. Higher international standards and greater specificity may encourage claims by states that compliance is not possible, or give rise to interpretative differences where there are competing interests that prevent compromise. Gaps and indeterminacy also generate disputes. Global inequalities spawn claims for special consideration that are legitimated by treaty provisions for equitable solution and references to inherent notions of fairness.[115] States have an obligation to resolve their disputes through peaceful means.[116] The United Nations Charter provides a non-exhaustive list of processes: negotiation, enquiry, conciliation, mediation, arbitration, and adjudication.[117] The principle of state sovereignty means that all these processes, including adjudication, are consensual.[118] Ideally, effective international dispute resolution mechanisms must have procedural integrity, and be economic to users, non-coercive, open to all interested parties, and fair. To promote durable solutions their use and outcomes must not offend feelings of national pride and honour. While the frequency of use of a particular process may be an indicator of its viability, effectiveness will be judged by the outcome in specific cases. A preferred outcome is one that accommodates the paramount interests of the parties, does not undermine the interests of other actors, and upholds international community values.[119]

[115] J. Schulkin and P. Kleindorfer, 'Equity Decisions: Economic Development and Environmental Prudence' (1995) 17 *Human Rights Quarterly* 382–97.

[116] United Nations Charter, Art. 2(3).

[117] United Nations Charter, Art. 33.

[118] Statute of the International Court of Justice, Art. 36.

[119] For discussion of a 'wise' outcome see R. Fisher and W. Ury, *Getting to Yes, Negotiating Agreement Without Giving In* (Boston, Mass., 1981); C. Menkel-Meadow, 'Towards Another View of Legal Negotiation: The Structure of Problem-Solving' (1983–4) 31 *UCLA Law Review* 754–832.

In the decentralized international legal system where state practice is a constitutive element of customary international law, the objective of consistency in both process and outcome acquires considerable significance. International law is a system of public law in its regulation of the conduct of states, although diplomacy frequently depends upon secrecy. Processes conducted in private such as negotiation and third party assisted negotiations (mediation and conciliation) may be thought to be especially suitable for international environmental disputes.[120] Their procedural flexibility, the control the parties retain over the process and outcome, the scope for the parties to explore their underlying interests and for the third party to assist in crafting an agreement tailor-made for the dispute and disputants all support this viewpoint. However these processes are screened from public scrutiny and the conformity (or otherwise) of the outcome with legal requirements may not be apparent. International arbitration proceedings and awards are also confidential unless the parties agree to publication.[121] Even in democratic societies details of negotiated processes need not be made public. Concerns about ordering through private decision-making processes may be even more pertinent in international than domestic law because of the concealment of state practice it involves.[122]

The ICJ and International Environmental Law

Reported adjudicative proceedings are therefore especially important both for providing a model of international environmental decision-making and for moulding principles of international law.[123] However as with international law-making, international adjudication suffers from major limitations that restrict its effectiveness in performing these tasks. In domestic law environmental regulations are subject to judicial interpretation and application, hence developing an emergent body of jurisprudence in public and private law. The role of adjudication within the international legal system, in particular the lack of compulsory jurisdiction, limits its potential to develop an equivalent body of international environmental law.

Some cases with a substantial environmental element have been decided by the ICJ and have been instrumental in crystallizing principles of customary international law. For example in the *Corfu Channel* case, the ICJ expounded underlying principles of state liability for harm caused from territory under a state's jurisdiction and control.[124] As a consequence of the UNCED, and in recognition

[120] e.g., H. Gregorczsk, 'The Appropriateness of Mediation in International Environmental Disputes' (1996) 7 *Australian Dispute Resolution Journal* 47–60.

[121] Published arbitral awards can become influential sources of international environmental law, e.g., the *Trail Smelter Arbitration* (*United States v Canada*) 3 *RIAA* (1941) 1907; *Lac Lanoux Arbitration* (*France v Spain*) 24 *ILR* 101.

[122] See R. Abel, *The Politics of Informal Justice* (New York, 1982).

[123] See M. Fitzmaurice, 'Environmental Protection and the International Court of Justice', in V. Lowe and M. Fitzmaurice (eds.), *Fifty Years of the International Court of Justice* (Cambridge, 1996).

[124] *Corfu Channel Case* (*United Kingdom v Albania*) Merits 1949 *ICJ Rep.* 4 (Judgment of 9 April).

of the growing number of applications with environmental significance, the ICJ created in July 1993 the first specialist Chamber for the resolution of environmental disputes.[125]

No case has yet been submitted to the environmental chamber, although there are a number of pending and recent cases with environmental components. States may be reluctant to identify a dispute as primarily environmental and prefer to present it as a point of general international law such as treaty interpretation. Uncertainty as to the weight the Court might give to arguments based upon emergent principles of environmental law might encourage states to minimize such claims and to rely upon more established areas of law.[126]

An example of a dispute recently decided by the Court that might well be labelled environmental is that arising out of the Gabcíkovo-Nagymaros Project between Hungary and Slovakia.[127] The dispute concerns the suspension by Hungary of a project for the construction of a dam and locking system on the Danube and the consequent diversion of waters. Agreement for a joint investment venture on this project was reached in the Budapest Treaty of 16 September 1977 on the Construction and Operation of the Gabcíkovo-Nagymaros Barrage System between Hungary and the predecessor state to Slovakia, Czechoslovakia.[128] Hungary unilaterally purported to terminate the Treaty in 1989 and the Czech and Slovak Federal Republics proceeded with a provisional solution that involved damming part of the Danube. Steps were taken to resolve this dispute through the European Commission where the parties agreed to establish a working group of experts to examine options for resolution. Failure to reach a settlement led Hungary in October 1992 to file an application before the ICJ for a ruling on the legality of its actions in terminating the Treaty. By a Special Agreement signed at Brussels on 7 April 1993 the two states submitted to the Court certain specific issues that centred on the implementation, interpretation and termination of the 1977 Treaty. Hungary also included arguments based upon environmental principles to justify its unilateral denunciation of the Treaty. It alleged, *inter alia*, that the envisaged construction will cause water pollution, including contamination of drinking water in Hungary, and growth of destructive algae. The judges deciding the case visited the site of the dispute to enhance their understanding of the potential impact. This is the first time the ICJ has used its powers of on-site inspection.

In deciding that Hungary had not, in 1992, legally terminated the 1977 Treaty, the Court noted that newly developed norms of environmental law were, by the terms of the Treaty itself, relevant to its future implementation. Articles 15, 19, and 20 require the parties in performing the Treaty to ensure the water quality

[125] Statute of the International Court of Justice, Art. 27.

[126] The *Spain v Canada* dispute referred to earlier raises precisely such a tension. It has not been submitted to the Environmental Chamber.

[127] Case concerning Gabcíkovo-Nagymaros Project (*Hungary v. Slovakia*) 1997 *ICJ Rep.* (Judgment of 25 September).

[128] 48 *YBICJ* 204 (1993–4).

of the Danube, and to protect nature. Indeed, since awareness of environmental concerns has increased since 1977, and there is now realization of the need for on-going assessment of environmental risks, these Articles have acquired a greater significance than when they were agreed, and allow the Treaty to be adapted accordingly. In looking towards future performance, the parties should examine afresh the environmental impact of the Gabcíkovo power plant in the light of new environmental norms and standards. The Court advised that third party facilitation might be helpful in doing this, provided each party is prepared to be flexible in its position. The Court thus integrated environmental issues into its rulings upon aspects of treaty law and state responsibility. Without perceiving the dispute primarily in environmental terms, it recognized the need for international obligations to be performed in a way that takes due account of developing environmental standards.

Such issues are significant, since the labelling of a dispute as environmental rather than as one of general international law may have consequences perceived as undesirable by the parties. For example it might force acknowledgment of the legitimacy of non-party interests, including those of non-state entities. Not doing so allows parties to the dispute to minimize other interests and to maintain control over its parameters by presentation in the terms they choose. But many conflicting interests are typically at stake in international environmental disputes. The effective exclusion of non-party interests from ICJ proceedings except as mediated through state presentations is a considerable limitation on its effectiveness in environmental decision-making.[129]

Procedural Limitations in Contentious Cases before the ICJ

Only states may be parties in contentious proceedings before the ICJ,[130] and participation by non-parties, even those whose interests are adversely affected, is strictly limited, even for states. The Court's Statute and Rules of Procedure give only limited provision for third party state input into cases before it and non-state interests are accorded even less consideration. The Court has been careful to preserve the autonomy of states parties through the preservation of a strictly bilateral model of adjudication and a restrictive interpretation of third party procedures.

The Statute of the ICJ provides for the third party procedure of intervention.[131] Article 62 allows a third party state to request intervention into existing proceedings where it considers it has 'an interest of a legal nature that may be affected by the decision in the case'. Article 63 provides for the different situation where the Court must consider the construction of a convention to which other states not before the Court are also parties. Such states have the right to intervene in

[129] See further C. Chinkin, *Third Parties in International Law* (Oxford, 1993), especially Part II.
[130] Statute of the International Court of Justice, Art. 34.
[131] Ibid., Arts. 62 and 63.

the proceedings. The growing number of multilateral environmental treaties might be expected to make this procedure regularly invoked. However to date there has been little effective use of either Article 62 or Article 63.

Requests under Article 62 have been most frequent in the context of boundary (especially maritime boundary) disputes and only once has such a request been granted.[132] A successful request to intervene is perhaps even less probable where the third party interest takes the form of feared or actual environmental damage which may be difficult to substantiate or quantify. The proceedings in the contentious cases with respect to French nuclear testing in the Pacific illustrate both the barriers to establishing appropriate applicant states to challenge such actions and the dilemma facing other concerned parties.

In the first round of cases relating to French nuclear testing in the Pacific in 1974, territories in the Pacific region had not yet attained statehood and consequently had no standing before the Court. Fiji, the only Pacific Island state then independent, requested to intervene on the side of New Zealand and Australia against France.[133] The Court found the case to be inadmissible on the grounds that statements by the French government that the current round of atmospheric testing would be its last meant that the applicants' objective had been accomplished and there was no longer a dispute between the parties upon which to give judgment.[134] Fiji's request to intervene was therefore not considered. The Court left open the possibility of reopening the case if France failed to abide by its commitment. In 1995 New Zealand did just this.[135] Samoa, the Solomon Islands, the Marshall Islands, and the Federated States of Micronesia, all Pacific Island states that regarded themselves as having a direct interest in the adverse consequences of nuclear testing, requested intervention under Articles 62 and 63.[136] Their purpose under Article 62 was 'to protect their interests under general international law . . .' and 'to affirm the collective character of the obligations involved.' Samoa, for example, argued that it has a legal interest 'in the prevention of any

[132] On intervention under Art. 62 see *Case Concerning the Continental Shelf* (*Tunisia/Libya Arab Jamahiriya*), Application by Malta to Intervene, 1981 *ICJ Rep.* 3 (Judgment of 14 April); *Case Concerning the Continental Shelf* (*Libya Arab Jamahiriya/Malta*), Application by Italy to Intervene, 1984 *ICJ Rep.* 3 (Judgment of 21 March); *Land, Island and Maritime Frontier Dispute* (*El Salvador/Honduras*), Application by Nicaragua to Intervene, 1990 *ICJ Rep.* 92 (Judgment of 13 September). On intervention under Art. 63 see Military and Paramilitary Activities in and against Nicaragua (*Nicaragua v United States*), Declaration of Intervention, 1984 *ICJ Rep.* 215 (Order of 4 October). Nicaragua's request to intervene in the *Land, Island and Maritime Frontier Dispute* was the first successful request under Art. 62.

[133] *Nuclear Tests*, Application by Fiji for Permission to Intervene, 1974 *ICJ Rep.* 530; 1974 *ICJ Rep.* 535 (Order of 20 December).

[134] *Nuclear Tests*, (*Australia v France*) 1974 *ICJ Rep.* 253 at para. 59. A similar finding was made in the case commenced by New Zealand.

[135] New Zealand's Request for an Examination of the Situation in accordance with para. 63 of the Court's 1974 Judgment concerning *Nuclear Tests* (*New Zealand v France*), 1995 *ICJ Rep.* 306 (Order of 22 September).

[136] Although Australia had been an applicant in the 1974 *Nuclear Tests* cases, in 1995 it requested intervention alongside the states listed.

unlawful introduction into the marine environment of radio-active material'. It did not allege that it would suffer particular damage, although it asserted that the proposed tests would 'upset the status quo in the region and had the potential to cause serious, possibly irreparable harm to the marine environment', including harm to the culture, traditions, and well-being of peoples. This last claim indicates the difficulties of quantifying actual or potential environmental damage and some of the complexities that face an international decision-maker required to assess it.

The Pacific Island states also claimed intervention as of right under Article 63, invoking the Convention for the Protection of the Natural Resources and Environment of the South Pacific Region.[137] New Zealand asked the Court to declare that it would be unlawful for France to conduct nuclear tests in the Pacific without first carrying out an environmental impact assessment in accordance with international standards and as is required by Article 16 of the above Convention.[138] Although the Court highlighted that its conclusion 'was without prejudice to the obligations of States to respect and protect the natural environment' it avoided responding to these claims.[139] It ruled that it lacked jurisdiction because New Zealand's application did not fall within paragraph 63 of its 1974 decision. This had envisaged reopening the earlier case only if France were to recommence atmospheric nuclear testing. This had not occurred. Consequently, like Fiji's request in 1974, the validity of the requests to intervene was not even considered. In dissenting opinions, Judges Weeramantry and Palmer (the *ad hoc* Judge selected by New Zealand) discussed emergent principles of environmental law more fully, in particular those of inter-generational equity and the precautionary principle. These they thought to be relevant to an assessment of New Zealand's claim for reconsideration of the 1974 ruling.[140] Although the substantive issues were not ruled upon, presentation of written and oral arguments by the Pacific Island states created a forum for public expression of their hostility to the testing that gained considerable media attention.

In the 1974 Nuclear Tests cases the Court also avoided ruling upon whether Australia and New Zealand had standing to bring the claim. Only a few years earlier in the 1966 *South West Africa* cases the Court had restricted standing to states with a specific legal interest in the claim.[141] In that case the Court rejected the introduction of an *actio popularis* by denying standing to a state that has no

[137] Noumea, 24 November 1986, rep. 26 *ILM* 38 (1987).

[138] This provision is an example of the adoption of the 'precautionary approach' to international environmental matters. New Zealand claimed that all parties to the Convention shared an interest in its implementation.

[139] New Zealand's Request for an Examination of the Situation in accordance with Paragraph 63 of the Court's 1974 Judgment concerning *Nuclear Tests* (*New Zealand v France*), 1995 *ICJ Rep.* 306 at para. 64.

[140] M. Craven, 'New Zealand's Request for an Examination of the Situation in accordance with Paragraph 63 of the Court's 1974 Judgment concerning Nuclear Tests (*New Zealand v France*), Order of 22 September' (1996) 45 *ICLQ* 725–34.

[141] *South West Africa Cases* (*Ethiopia v South Africa*; *Liberia v South Africa*), Second Phase, 1966 *ICJ Rep.* 4 (Judgment of 18 July). The Court held that '[t]o generate legal rights and obligations, it must be given juridical expression and be clothed in legal form.' Ibid., at 34.

greater interest in a matter than that shared by every other member of the international community. This rejects the concept of public interest litigation, that has been so important in bringing environmental matters into domestic courts, in the international arena. In 1970 there was perhaps some retreat by the Court from this strict requirement for an applicant state to have a direct legal interest in the claim. In the *Barcelona Traction* case it stated that:

> . . . an essential distinction should be drawn between the obligations of a state towards the international community as a whole, and those arising vis à vis another State in the field of diplomatic protection. By their very nature the former are the concern of all States. In view of the importance of the rights involved, all states can be held to have a legal interest in their protection; they are obligations *erga omnes*.[142]

It can be argued that environmental duties come within the 'obligations of a state towards the international community as a whole' and that consequently any state should be able to commence proceedings claiming breach of such duties. This proposition was argued by Australia in the first *Nuclear Tests* cases, although it also claimed that radioactive fall-out violated its own territorial sovereignty. Judge *ad hoc* Barwick pointed out that '[Australia] does not claim an individual right exclusive to itself . . . it puts the obligation not to test nuclear weapons as owed by each State to every other State in the international community: . . . each State can be held to have a legal interest in the maintenance of a prohibition against the testing of nuclear weapons'.[143]

Judge Barwick agreed that acceptance of the proposition that the duty not to test nuclear weapons is owed to all members of the international community would imply that the applicant states (and all other states) had the requisite legal interest to bring the claim. However he thought that this was not a preliminary question but one that needed full argument on the merits. The dismissal of the proceedings meant that this did not occur. In the 1995 case, New Zealand argued that French nuclear testing violated the rights of all members of the international community and that no nuclear tests giving rise to radioactive fall-out should be conducted. The obligations correlative to these rights were characterized by New Zealand as owed *erga omnes*, but again the Court provided no guidance on this issue.

It remains uncertain whether the requirement of a direct legal interest remains if a state is to be able to commence proceedings before the ICJ. The *South West Africa* cases concerned human rights abuses by South Africa through its violation of the Mandate Agreement between itself and the League of Nations. Mandate arrangements also made possible exploitation of the natural resources of mandated territories without regard to environmental degradation.[144] The *South*

[142] *Barcelona Traction Light and Power Company Case* (*Belgium v Spain*) New Application, 1970 *ICJ Rep*. 3, 32 (Order of 5 February).

[143] *Nuclear Tests Cases*, 1974 *ICJ Rep*. 253, at 436 (Diss. Op. Judge Barwick).

[144] See the facts of *Certain Phosphate Lands in Nauru* (*Nauru v Australia*), Preliminary Objections, 1992 *ICJ Rep*. 240 (Judgment of 26 June).

West Africa ruling suggests that no other state has sufficient legal interest to challenge such behaviour. This might appear of historic interest only with the termination of the mandate/trusteeship system, but states can still cause environmental damage in the territory of another state.

One such situation is damage caused by military forces legitimately in the territory of another state. A third state would not apparently have standing to seek a declaration that unlawful environmental harm had been caused through their actions.[145] In another scenario, suppose a state party proposed the commercial development of a world heritage area in contravention of its obligations under the World Heritage Convention. Could another state party claim breach of the treaty?[146] Through entering into such treaties states undertake international obligations to observe standards with respect to matters that were previously within domestic jurisdiction. Human rights treaties have established monitoring committees and in some cases the right of inter-state complaint of non-compliance. This model has been followed in some environmental treaties, but it leaves open whether treaty parties have standing to commence proceedings for breach before the ICJ. Article 36 of the Court's Statute would seem to answer this in the affirmative and in the 1995 proceedings New Zealand (and the intervening states) claimed violation by France of the Noumea Convention.[147] However the lack of any ruling on the substance of the claim meant that the question of standing was not considered.

Another limitation to the prospect of adjudication is the so-called '*Monetary Gold* principle' that requires the dismissal of a case because of the absence from the Court of a third state whose interests form the very subject matter of the case.[148] This principle has been argued in two cases with environmental significance. First, in *Certain Phosphate Lands in Nauru*, Australia raised a preliminary objection to the Court's determining the application brought against it by Nauru in a case that presented important questions about state liability for environmental harm.[149] Australia, in conjunction with New Zealand and the United Kingdom, was first the mandate, and subsequently the trusteeship, authority in Nauru. During this period intensive mining of phosphates was carried out, primarily for the benefit of the mandate/trusteeship powers. After independence Nauru brought proceedings against Australia claiming, *inter alia*, that there is a general obligation

[145] The legal position of UN peacekeeping forces might present such questions. The state in which they are located might not want to claim for any environmental damage caused, especially if it had requested their presence. A third state might consider this to be a matter of general international concern but have no legal basis for raising it.

[146] Convention for the Protection of World Cultural and Natural Heritage, 23 November 1972, 1037 *UNTS* 151.

[147] Art. 36(2) bestows jurisdiction 'in all legal disputes concerning: (a) the interpretation of a treaty . . .'

[148] *Case of the Monetary Gold Removed from Rome in 1943* (*Italy v France, United Kingdom and United States*) Preliminary Question 1954 *ICJ Rep*. 32 (Order of 15 June).

[149] *Certain Phosphate Lands in Nauru* (*Nauru v Australia*), Preliminary Objections, 1992 *ICJ Rep*. 240 (Judgment of 26 June).

under international law that a state responsible for the administration of territory should not bring about changes to the condition of the territory that will cause irreparable damage to it. In particular, it claimed that Australia's administration of its territory had violated that principle through the intensive phosphate mining that had destroyed the land for any other usage and by failing to take measures for rehabilitation. Australia contended that the case could not be decided in the absence of indispensable third parties, namely the other mandate/trustee states, New Zealand and the United Kingdom. The Court rejected this argument holding that a determination of the responsibility of New Zealand and the United Kingdom was not a pre-requisite for a determination with respect to whether Australia was in breach of its obligations.[150]

The Court's finding of jurisdiction encouraged a negotiated settlement between Nauru and Australia and the removal of the proceedings from the Court.[151] This private agreement forestalled an international judicial ruling on the international responsibility of states for the environmental despoliation of territories placed under their control through the international mandate and trusteeship systems, or on how the 'sacred trust of civilisation' translates into environmental duties owed to the inhabitants of such territories.[152] Private negotiations conducted outside any regulatory framework may terminate the immediate dispute, but they ignore the broader implications of the legal principles at stake and the desirability of authoritative legal statements.

Although in the *Nauru* case, the court limited the *Monetary Gold* principle with respect to indispensable third parties, it was argued again in the *East Timor* case.[153] Prior to 1975 Portugal was the undisputed colonial power in East Timor. Subsequent to the invasion in that year by Indonesia, Portugal has had no physical presence in the territory. The UN has not recognized Indonesia's annexation of East Timor and deems the territory as non-self-governing with Portugal retaining legal authority. In 1991 Australia and Indonesia concluded the Timor Gap Treaty establishing a regime for the allocation and exploitation of resources, notably the potentially valuable hydrocarbon deposits, in the maritime areas between the southern coast of East Timor and Australia.[154] Portugal claimed that Australia had violated its sovereign rights by negotiating the Timor Gap Treaty with Indonesia. Lying behind this presenting issue were the claims of the people of East Timor to self-determination, including permanent sovereignty over their natural resources. The Court held that it had no jurisdiction in the absence of Indonesia, the alleged wrongdoing state. It could not determine the validity of Portugal's claim without judging the actions of Indonesia and to

[150] Ibid., para. 55.

[151] Australia-Republic of Nauru: Settlement of the Case in the International Court of Justice Concerning Certain Phosphate Lands in Nauru, 10 August 1993 rep. 32 *ILM* 1471 (1993).

[152] Covenant of the League of Nations, 1919, Art. 22.

[153] *East Timor* (*Portugal v Australia*) 1995 *ICJ Rep.* 90 (Judgment of 30 June).

[154] Indonesia has not made a Declaration accepting the Court's jurisdiction under Art. 36(2) of the Statute of the International Court of Justice as have Portugal and Australia.

do this in its absence would be contrary to the principle of consent to the jurisdiction of the ICJ. The Court therefore indirectly affirmed the legitimacy of the Treaty.[155] Although the Court reaffirmed the East Timorese right of self-determination, it gave no substance to this right and in particular gave no guidance as to its application in respect of conservation of natural resources.

Non-state entities have no access to the Court either as parties or as intervenors. There is no procedure through which the East Timorese could present their case to the Court except as mediated through the applicant state, Portugal.[156] Where there is no state willing to commence proceedings on behalf of a non-state entity, or where there is no suitable respondent state that has accepted the Court's jurisdiction, even this limited prospect of a hearing is denied.

In its contentious jurisdiction the Court has not favoured the submission of third party (whether state or non-state) arguments through any form of amicus brief. Under Article 50 of its Statute, the Court may entrust any selected individual, body, bureau, or commission with the task of making an enquiry, or giving an expert opinion. This competence could be usefully exercised, for example in the proceedings commenced by Spain against Canada. It can be expected that the competing claims of distance fishing fleets to have unrestricted high seas access to fishing resources, and those of coastal states to be able to impose measures for conservation and management of stocks, will be presented by the parties. In an adversarial process each party argues its strongest possible case and presents evidence accordingly. In such a case it could be helpful to the Court to receive opinions from non-party, independent experts about the need (or otherwise) for environmental regulation. The Court has not however availed itself of this opportunity, and has only occasionally heard evidence from third parties.[157]

The ICJ's limitations on standing, its denial of jurisdiction where the interests of an indispensable third party form the subject matter of the case, and its restrictions on third party access diminish significantly the potential for environmental concerns to be considered and decided by the Court. This reduces the development of judicial expertise in environmental matters and prevents the clarification of environmental norms. The inadequacy of third party participation in judicial proceedings lowers the Court's credibility where there are multilateral interests at stake and lessens its relevance for other actors in the international arena. The ICJ Rules of Procedure have changed remarkably little since the creation of its predecessor, the Permanent Court of International Justice, in 1920. The Court

[155] Treaty between Australia and the Republic of Indonesia on the Zone of Co-operation in an Area between the Indonesian Province of East Timor and Northern Australia, Timor Sea, 11 December 1989, in force 9 February 1991, Aust. TS No. 9, 1991. W. Martin and D. Pickersgill, 'The Timor Gap Treaty' (1991) 32 *Harv ILJ* 566–82.

[156] Italy's attempt to do this through intervention was rejected as an 'improper purpose of intervention'. *Case Concerning the Continental Shelf* (*Libya Arab Jamahiriya/Malta*), Application by Italy to Intervene, 1984 *ICJ Rep*. 3.

[157] e.g., in the *Corfu Channel Case*, the UK called a witness to testify that the mines had been laid by Yugoslavia.

has paid no heed to the pressing demands of international civil society for participation that have been acknowledged elsewhere in the international legal system, albeit to a limited extent. NGOs are playing an increasingly active role in the formulation of international environmental standards, may be invited to consultations on treaty performance, but are excluded from participation in state-controlled dispute resolution processes, most notably adjudication by the ICJ. For example, the World Heritage Convention recognizes the contribution made by NGOs to the development of environmental law by bestowing official status upon three NGOs and authorizing the World Heritage Committee to call upon these bodies 'for the implementation of its programmes and projects'. Other treaty regimes accord NGOs observer status, as has the UN Commission on Sustainable Development. NGOs are less able to be effective across the spectrum of environmental activities where participation in formal dispute resolution processes is denied. However there is little indication of any willingness on the part of the ICJ to allow such procedural innovation to further development of substantive law.

Advisory Jurisdiction

The ICJ also has jurisdiction to give advisory opinions on legal questions when asked to do so by the General Assembly or Security Council, or by other organs of the United Nations on questions arising within the scope of their activities.[158] This would seem to be an effective way of seeking guidance from the ICJ on general principles, for example of environmental law. A request for an advisory opinion does not depend upon the existence of a dispute between states and is framed in terms of seeking guidance on a point of international law. This jurisdiction would appear especially appropriate where there is no relevant treaty, inconsistent state practice, and uncertainty as to the legal position. However there are also limitations upon the effectiveness of the strategy of seeking an advisory opinion, as well as doubts about the willingness of the Court to give guidance on crucial environmental issues. These can be illustrated by the recent advisory opinions relating to nuclear weapons. In 1993 the World Health Organization (WHO) requested an advisory opinion on the following question:

> In view of the health and environmental effects would the use of nuclear weapons by a State in war or other armed conflict be a breach of its obligations under international law, including the WHO Constitution?[159]

This request was motivated by campaigning by an NGO 'umbrella' organization, the World Court Project, whose membership included the International Association of Lawyers against Nuclear Arms and International Physicians for the Prevention of Nuclear War. Their success demonstrates that where NGOs

[158] United Nations Charter, Art. 96.

[159] Legality of the Use by a State of Nuclear Weapons in Armed Conflict, 1996 *ICJ Rep*. (Adv. Op. 8 July).

are sufficiently mobilized and informed they can influence the actions of intergovernmental specialized agencies to access procedures barred to themselves. The Court advised however that specialized agencies are only competent to request opinions within the 'scope of their activities'. The WHO is authorized to examine the effects on health of the use of nuclear weapons (and other hazardous activities) and to urge preventive measures to protect the health of peoples at risk. The question put to the Court did not pertain to the health and environmental effects of nuclear weapons, but to the legality or otherwise of their use in light of those effects. The competence of WHO does not depend upon the prior legality of the actions in question. Indeed questions of legality fall within the competence of other parts of the United Nations system upon which the WHO cannot encroach. The Court therefore found it had no jurisdiction to give an opinion. This rejection of jurisdiction is a narrow and legalistic construction of the Charter requirement that the request appertain to the activities of the requesting body.

The WHO request was followed by a similar, but not identical, request from the General Assembly. In 1994 the General Assembly asked the following question: 'Is the threat or use of nuclear weapons in any circumstances permitted under international law?'[160]

Unlike that posed by the WHO, this question was not explicitly directed at the environmental consequences of nuclear weapons. However it indirectly presents precisely the central dilemma discussed above. On the one hand are issues of state sovereignty, and the right of states to pursue their security interests, on the other are the demands for global security free from the environmental damage that use of such weapons would incur. Since there are no explicit principles of either customary or treaty law that authorize or prohibit the use of nuclear weapons, the Court was required to evaluate these conflicting tensions. The Court responded strongly and positively to the environmental arguments put to it:

> The Court recognizes that the environment is under daily threat and that the use of nuclear weapons could constitute a catastrophe for the environment. The Court also recognizes that the environment is not an abstraction but represents the living space, the quality of life and the very health of human beings, including generations unborn. The existence of the general obligation of States to ensure that activities within their jurisdiction and control respect the environment of other States or of areas beyond national control is now part of the corpus of international law relating to the environment.[161]

Despite this affirmation, the Court considered that the crucial question was whether obligations for environmental protection demand total restraint during military conflict. It asserted that threat or use of force by nuclear weapons contrary to Article 2(4) of the Charter is unlawful,[162] and any such threat or use must also

[160] Legality of the Threat or Use of Nuclear Weapons, 1996 *ICJ Rep.* (Adv. Op. 8 July) rep. 35 *ILM* 809 (1996).

[161] Ibid., at para. 29.

[162] United Nations Charter, Art. 2(4) requires member states to refrain from 'the threat or use of force against the territorial integrity or political independence of any state, or in any other manner inconsistent with the Charter of the United Nations'.

be compatible with the requirements of international law applicable in armed conflict, including principles of international humanitarian law[163] and environmental obligations. Thus, '[r]espect for the environment is one of the elements that go to assessing whether an action is in conformity with the principles of necessity and proportionality.'[164] However by seven votes to seven, with the casting vote of the President, the Court opined that:

> . . . in view of the current state of international law, and of the elements of fact at its disposal, the Court cannot conclude definitively whether the threat or use of nuclear weapons would be lawful or unlawful in an extreme circumstance of self-defence in which the very survival of a State would be at stake.

The Court was unwilling to pronounce that states' right to self-defence in extreme circumstances is ultimately limited by the illegality of nuclear weapons. Although 'important environmental factors are properly to be taken into account', in the end the imperatives of state sovereignty and survival were accorded higher priority than the interests of peoples not to be subject to the personal and environmental consequences of nuclear weapons.[165]

Argument before the Court was restricted to states. Although the wording that allows the submission of information by international organizations in advisory proceedings is not restricted to intergovernmental organizations,[166] the Court has rejected requests to make submissions from NGOs and interested individuals.[167] Written and oral statements were made by the largest number of states ever in an advisory hearing.[168] As an inter-governmental organization the WHO also entered submissions but none were allowed from NGOs, although some associated with the World Court Project had requested to be allowed to do so. Thus expert opinions from, for example, scientists, physicians and environmentalists, were not put directly to the Court but were included only in so far as states used them.[169] States remain dominant within advisory proceedings even when the opinion is sought in the name of an inter-governmental organization responding to NGO pressure.

[163] These are contained primarily in the 1949 Geneva Conventions and 1977 Protocols.

[164] Legality of the Threat or Use of Nuclear Weapons, 1996 *ICJ Rep.* at para. 30.

[165] United Nations Charter, Art. 51 preserves the inherent right of states to use force in self defence 'if an armed attack occurs'.

[166] Statute of the International Court of Justice, Art. 66(2) requires the Registrar of the Court to notify states 'entitled to appear before the Court' and international organizations 'considered by the Court . . . as likely to be able to furnish information' that they may submit written or oral statements.

[167] In the WHO advisory opinion the requests of the International Physicians for the Prevention of Nuclear War and the International Peace Bureau to make submissions to the Court were refused; 48 *YBICJ* 208–9 (1993–4).

[168] Thirty-five states filed written statements in the WHO request; twenty-eight in the General Assembly request (although Nauru subsequently withdrew its request). Twenty-two states made oral submissions in a single round of combined hearings; Legality of the Threat or Use of Nuclear Weapons, 1996 *ICJ Rep.* at paras. 5–10.

[169] Included among those who appeared before the ICJ were the mayors of Hiroshima and Nagasaki, who gave factual and statistical evidence on the fate of their cities, and a Council Member, Rongelap Atoll Local Government, Marshall Islands. These individuals appeared on behalf of Japan and the Marshall Islands, respectively.

The largely unsuccessful attempts by members of the international community to gain a definitive statement from the ICJ on the legality of nuclear weapons illustrate the obstacles to effective international decision-making on such questions. Indeed it was argued in the advisory opinion on the legality of nuclear weapons that the Court should not give an opinion because of the political nature of the question, its vagueness, abstract nature, and complexity.[170] Another argument advanced as to why the Court should decline to give an opinion was the possible disruption to the negotiations for disarmament and test banning. This approach favours diplomacy and treaty negotiation as the appropriate decision-making processes in controversial areas of international relations, despite their slowness and their potential to being derailed by a single state.[171]

To its credit, the Court affirmed its responsibilities as 'the principal judicial organ of the United Nations'.[172] Only 'compelling reasons' could justify refusing to give an opinion and the political context of the question did not detract from its legal content. However the legal content was problematic. Where there is no applicable treaty, the Court must extrapolate from state practice to determine whether there is an applicable rule of customary international law or general principles of law upon which to base its decision.[173] The Court was in a 'no-win' situation where any decision was likely to be rejected by key states according to their nuclear capability. An opinion confirming illegality would be likely to be denounced by nuclear states on the grounds that it amounted to law-making rather than applying existing law, and was as such outside the authority of the Court.[174] On the other hand, a categorical statement of legality would be open to criticism for failing to give sufficient weight to emergent environmental law. Nevertheless in highly charged political contexts, the Court must attempt to preserve its own legitimacy and credibility with all member states of the UN, a role that appears unsustainable in light of such intensely held differing opinions on many aspects of international law. Perhaps from the perspective of the Court, an equivocal opinion that entwines the diverse strands of human rights, international humanitarian law, environmental law, and the use of force was the best option.

[170] Legality of the Threat or Use of Nuclear Weapons, 1996 *ICJ Rep.* at paras. 15–18.

[171] The Comprehensive Nuclear Test Ban Treaty, adopted by the General Assembly, September 1996, cannot come into force without signature by India which is currently rejecting it.

[172] United Nations Charter, Art. 92. Another view, that the legitimacy of the use of nuclear weapons is a question of fundamental moral values that is not suited to adjudication, was convincingly made by M. Koskenniemi, 'The Post-Adjudicative Phase: Commentary', in C. Peck and R. Lee (eds.), *Increasing the Effectiveness of the International Court of Justice* (The Hague, 1997).

[173] Statute of the International Court of Justice, Art. 38(1)(c). In the *Corfu Channel Case* the Court referred to 'certain general and well-recognized principles, namely elementary considerations of humanity, even more exacting in peace than in war; . . .' 1949 *ICJ Rep.* 4. This could be a good starting point for environmental questions.

[174] The Court's task is to determine 'any question of international law.' Statute of the International Court of Justice, Art. 36(2)(a). Art. 59 states that 'The decision of the Court has no binding force except between the parties and in respect of that particular case.' Judges Weeramantry and Koroma regretted the Court's refusal to take an active approach in developing the law.

Decision-Making by the ICJ

The lack of compulsory jurisdiction also limits the Court's availability for decision-making. Even where states have accepted the jurisdiction of the Court by making a declaration under Article 36(2) of the Statute, sensitive environmental issues can be excluded by reservation. Declarations can also be withdrawn, as was the case with France after the 1974 *Nuclear Tests* cases. The trend towards regional treaties on nuclear prohibitions has provided some certainty and built an interlocking network of legal obligations that has not been possible through judicial decision-making.[175] But, in turn, other environmental treaties have sought to encourage recourse to the Court. Compulsory dispute resolution clauses that include the option of reference to the ICJ are one distinguishing feature between treaties and soft law instruments. A favoured technique is to provide maximum flexibility by allowing parties to specify a form of dispute settlement, but to require submission to a named process should they fail to do so. Part XV of the Law of the Sea Convention provides a model. Where parties fail to agree on a dispute resolution process, or the process leads to no successful outcome, they shall 'proceed expeditiously to an exchange of views . . . by negotiation or other peaceful means'.[176] If there is no settlement the compulsory procedures culminating in a binding decision are activated. Parties to the Convention may make a declaration accepting the compulsory jurisdiction of one or more of the following dispute resolution institutions: the International Tribunal for the Law of the Sea; the ICJ; a general arbitral tribunal; or the special arbitral tribunal constituted under Annex VIII for the categories of dispute specified therein. If both parties to a dispute have accepted the same forum it will be submitted to that forum. If they have not, or if a party has made no declaration, the dispute will be submitted to general arbitration under Annex VII. Somewhat similarly, the 1985 Convention for the Protection of the Ozone Layer allows parties to declare in advance that they accept the compulsory jurisdiction of the ICJ or compulsory recourse to arbitration. If attempts at settlement through negotiation or mediation fail, and no common compulsory process has been accepted, there is an obligation to submit to conciliation.[177] It remains to be seen whether treaty clauses of this type encourage the submission of environmental disputes to public third party decision-making, but it must be acknowledged that the portents are not good.

The absence of authoritative judicial decision-making at the international level means that the decisions of domestic courts may carry greater weight. In states where treaties are self-executing, or where treaty obligations have been

[175] e.g., Treaty for the Prohibition of Nuclear Weapons in Latin America (Tlatelolco), 1967, 634 *UNTS* 281; South Pacific Nuclear Free Zone Treaty; Treaty on the South East Asia Nuclear Weapon Free Zone, 15 December 1995, rep. 35 *ILM* 635 (1996); and African Nuclear Weapon Free Zone Treaty, Addis Ababa, 21–3 June 1995, rep. 35 *ILM* 698 (1996).

[176] United Nations Convention on the Law of the Sea, Art. 283.

[177] Biodiversity Convention, Art. 27; Climate Change Convention, Art. 14. Procedures are fleshed out through Annexes or by the Conference of the Parties.

implemented by legislation, claims may in some circumstances be brought in national courts for the implementation of such obligations.[178] However this results in international instruments being construed by domestic decision-makers who may have different foreign and domestic policy priorities, or who may defer to the notion of national interest. There can be no guarantee of consistency in the interpretation of shared obligations by courts in different states, and this undermines still further the objective of common international standards.

6. Conclusions

The expansion of international regulation since the creation of the UN in 1945 into areas previously considered within domestic jurisdiction has been dramatic. The experiences gained and techniques used in other contexts have been adapted in attempts to provide a rational framework for international legal environmental regulation. Unlike domestic legal systems, there is no international legislature. International law-making goes through a number of stages, the first of which is the formulation of principles that direct attention towards the substance of a potential rule. This is followed by the articulation of the rule in either soft or hard law form.[179] Agreement in soft law form more readily promotes the necessary consensus for legitimacy but lacks the force of binding obligation.

Considerable progress has been made in these stages of environmental law-making but much less in the subsequent ones of implementation, monitoring, and enhancing compliance. In many ways the progress of environmental law has mirrored that of human rights. Human rights standards were mainly formulated in the 60s and 70s drawing upon the framework provided by the Universal Declaration of Human Rights.[180] In the 90s the challenge has been to make more effective the mechanisms for implementation developed within the United Nations and regional bodies. Similarly the need with environmental law is to facilitate compliance with the standards adopted, whether through incentives, coercive strategies, collective action, or some combination of approaches. However it is uncertain whether the leisurely pace of the growth of human rights law can be afforded for environmental protection. While time is of the essence for individuals threatened by specific government abuse, this is more evidently the case where global environmental survival is at stake, especially as ever advancing scientific knowledge demands constant evaluation of the standards agreed and refinements as appropriate. Institutionally, the Commission on Human Rights was given the explicit mandate in 1946 of furthering the legal protection of human rights within the UN

[178] e.g., *Commonwealth of Australia v State of Tasmania* (1983) 158 CLR 1, H. Ct. of Australia (*Tasmanian Dams Case*).

[179] H. Meijers, op. cit.

[180] GA Res. 217 A (III), 10 December 1948.

system.[181] It has evolved a range of procedures including the network of thematic and country special rapporteurs, complaints procedures, working groups, naming of violators, and most recently the establishment of the post of UN Commissioner for Human Rights. While none of these procedures is sufficient, the cumulative effect is much greater. The lack of any parallel body for the international protection of the environment inhibits holistic and coherent development of the law.

Attempts have been made to adapt international law to the exigencies of environmental demands, for example by innovative techniques of law-making, through institutional creativity, by facilitating dispute resolution and non-compliance processes, and by some acknowledgment of the functions which can be performed by NGOs in the overall picture. But these responses remain at the peripheries in that they provide no fundamental challenge to the current state-oriented structure of the international legal system. The development of an adequate international environmental law is restrained by doctrines of state sovereignty, consent, and non-intervention.

One consequence is the lack of any centralized law-making process coupled with the historical fragmentation of international standard-setting and dispute resolution through duplication between the specialized agencies and other bodies, each with their own emphases, techniques, and agendas. Duplication and lacunae are both encountered in international regulation. Another consequence is the democratic deficit in participation in international institutional decision-making, including judicial decision-making. The indeterminacy of negotiated treaty language and the context-specific outcomes of dispute resolution processes that reduce their precedential value are further obstacles to a coherent body of international environmental law. Indeed these inadequacies challenge the structural basis of the international legal system in the political independence and territorial integrity of states, and the role of inter-governmental organizations as functional extensions of the states that comprise their membership.[182]

[181] P. Alston, 'The Commission on Human Rights', in P. Alston (ed.), *The United Nations and Human Rights: A Critical Appraisal* (Oxford, 1992).

[182] Cf., Hurrell and Kingsbury, op. cit., at 3.

Bibliography

Abel, R., *The Politics of Informal Justice* (New York, 1982).

Abraham, C., and Abraham, S., 'The Bhopal Case and the Development of Environmental Law in India' (1991) 40 *International and Comparative Law Quarterly* 334–65.

Ackerman, B. A., and Stewart, R. B., 'Reforming Environmental Law: The Democratic Case for Market Incentives' (1988) 13 *Columbia Journal of Environmental Law* 171–99.

Alfonso, L. P. (ed.), *Derecho medioambiental de la Unión Europea* (Madrid, 1996).

Alison, L., 'Rival Philosophies of the Earth' (1992) 7 *The World and I* (journal produced by the Washington Times) 56–72.

Alston, P., 'Making Space for New Human Rights: The Case of the Right to Development' (1988) 1 *Harvard Human Rights Yearbook* 3–40.

—— 'Revitalising United Nations Work on Human Rights and Development' (1991) 18 *Melbourne University Law Review* 216–57.

—— 'The Commission on Human Rights', in Alston (ed.), *The United Nations and Human Rights: A Critical Appraisal* (1992).

—— (ed.), *The United Nations and Human Rights: A Critical Appraisal* (Oxford, 1992).

Anderson, J. L., 'The Environment Revolution at Twenty-Five' (1995) 26 *Rutgers Law Journal* 395–430.

Anon., 'Ask a Silly Question . . . Contingent Valuation of Natural Resource Damage' (1992) 105 *Harvard Law Review* 1981–2000.

Arnstein, S., 'A Ladder of Citizen Participation' (1969) 35 *Journal of the American Institute of Planners* 216–24.

Ashworth, G., *The Role of Local Government in Environmental Protection* (London, 1992).

Asia Watch, *Before the Deluge: Human Rights Abuses at India's Narmada Dam* (1992).

Atiyah, P., 'Negligence and Economic Loss' (1967) 83 *Law Quarterly Review* 248–96.

—— *Accidents, Compensation and the Law* (London, 1970).

—— 'Personal Injuries in the Twenty-First Century: Thinking the Unthinkable', in Birks (ed.), *Wrongs and Remedies in the Twenty-First Century* (1996).

Audi, R. (ed.), *Cambridge Dictionary of Philosophy* (Cambridge, 1995).

Audretsch, H. A. H., *Supervision in European Community Law* (Amsterdam, 1986).

Augelli, E., and Murphy, C., *America's Quest and the Third World* (London, 1988).

Axelrod, R. S., 'Sudsidiarity and Environmental Policy in the European Community' (1994) 6 *International Environmental Affairs* 115–32.

Ayres, I., and Braithwaite, J., *Responsive Regulation* (Oxford, 1992).

Bakkenist, G., *Environmental Information, Law, Policy and Experience* (London, 1994).

Balkenborg, D., 'Bargaining Power and the Impact of Lender Liability for Environmental Damages', Southampton Discussion Paper in Economics and Econometrics No. 9709 (Southampton, 1997).

Ball, S., 'Reforming the Law of Habitat Regulation', in Rodgers (ed.), *Nature Conservation and Countryside Law* (1996).

—— and Bell, S., *Environmental Law* (3rd ed., London, 1995).

Barents, R., 'The Internal Market Unlimited: Some Observations on the Legal Basis of Community Legislation' (1993) 30 *Common Market Law Review* 85–109.

—— *Procedures voor het Hof van Justitie en het Gerecht van eerste aanlag van de EG* (Deventer, 1996).

Barker, A. (ed.), *Quangos in Britain: Government and the Networks of Public Policy-Making* (London, 1982).

Barkun, M., *Law Without Sanctions* (London, 1968).

Barnard, C., 'A European Litigation Strategy: the Case of the Equal Opportunities Commission', in Shaw and More (eds.), *New Legal Dynamics of European Union* (1995).

Barusch Bush, R. A., 'Between Two Worlds: The Shift From Individual to Group Responsibility in the Law of Causation of Injury' (1986) 33 *UCLA Law Review* 1473–563.

Bateson, M. C., 'Beyond Sovereignty: An Emerging Global Community', in Walker and Mendlowitz (eds.), *Contesting Sovereignty: Redefining Political Community* (1990).

Bayefsky, A., 'Making the Human Rights Treaties Work', in Henkin and Hargrove (eds.), *Human Rights: An Agenda for the Next Century* (1994).

Beck, U., *Risk Society* (trans., London, 1992).

—— *Ecological Responsibility in an Age of Risk* (trans., Cambridge, 1995).

—— Giddens, A., and Lash, S., *Reflexive Modernization* (Cambridge, 1994).

Beder, S., *Toxic Fish and Sewer Surfing* (Sydney, 1989).

Bedjaoui, M., 'The Right to Development', in Bedjaoui (ed.), *International Law: Achievements and Prospects* (1991).

—— *International Law: Achievements and Prospects* (Paris and London, 1991).

Behrens, F., *Rechtsgrundlagen der Umweltpolitik der Europäischen Gemeinschaften* (Berlin, 1976).

Bengoetxea, J., *The Legal Reasoning of the European Court of Justice* (Oxford, 1993).

Bhoutros-Ghali, B., *An Agenda for Peace: The Report of the Secretary-General Pursuant to the Statement Adopted by the Summit Meeting of the Security Council on 31 January 1992* (New York, 1992).

Bird, P., 'Applying EC Environmental Law on the Ground', in Somsen (ed.), *Protecting the European Environment* (1996).

Birkinshaw, P., *Freedom of Information: the Law, the Practice and the Ideal* (2nd ed., London, 1996).

Birks, P. (ed.), *Wrongs and Remedies in the Twenty-First Century* (Oxford, 1996).

Birnie, P. W., and Boyle, A. E., *International Law and the Environment* (London, 1992).

Birtles, W., 'A Right to Know: the Environmental Information Regulations 1992' [1993] *Journal of Planning and Environment Law* 615–26.

—— 'Environmental Information and Audit', in Boyle (ed.), *Environmental Regulation and Economic Growth* (1994).

Bongaerts, J. C., 'The Commission's Communication on Environmental Agreements' (1997) 6 *European Environmental Law Review* 84–7.

Bonyhady, T. (ed.), *Environmental Protection and Legal Change* (Sydney, 1992).

Boyer, M., and Laffont, J. -J., 'Environmental Risks and Bank Liability', Paper presented to the Workshop on Designing Environmental Policy for Management of Natural Resources and the Environment, Crete, 1994.

Boyle, A. (ed.), *Environmental Regulation and Economic Growth* (Oxford, 1994).

—— 'The Role of International Human Rights Law in the Protection of the Environment', in Boyle and Anderson (eds.), *Human Rights Approaches to Environmental Protection* (1996).

—— and Anderson, M. (eds.), *Human Rights Approaches to Environmental Protection* (Oxford, 1996).

Bradby, H. (ed.), *Dirty Words: Writings on the History and Culture of Pollution* (London, 1990).

Bradley, K., St-C., 'The European Court and the Legal Basis of Community Legislation' (1988) 13 *European Law Review* 379–420.

Braithwaite, J., 'Enforced Self Regulation: A New Strategy for Corporate Crime Control' (1982) 80 *Michigan Law Review* 1466–1587.

Brenner, J. F., 'Nuisance Law and the Industrial Revolution' (1974) 3 *Journal of Legal Studies* 403–33.

Bridges, L., Meszaros, G., and Sunkin, M., *Judicial Review in Perspective* (London, 1995).

Brindley, T., Rydin, Y., and Stoker, G., *Remaking Planning* (London, 1989).

Brinkhorst, L. J., 'Subsidiarity and European Community Environment Policy: A Panacea or a Pandora's Box?' (1993) 2 *European Environmental Law Review* 16–24.

Brown Weiss, E., *In Fairness to Future Generations: International Law, Common Patrimony, and Intergenerational Equity* (New York, 1989).

—— 'International Environmental Law: Contemporary Issues and the Emergence of a New World Order' (1993) 81 *Georgetown Law Journal* 675–710.

Brown, L., and Kennedy, T., *The Court of Justice of the European Communities* (London, 1994).

Brownlie, I., 'A Survey of International Customary Rules of Environmental Protection' (1973) 13 *Natural Resources Journal* 179–89.

Brubaker, E., *Property Rights in the Defence of Nature* (London and Toronto, 1995).

Bull, H., *The Anarchical Society* (Basingstoke, 1977).

Burley, A., and Mattli, W., 'Europe Before the Court: A Political Theory of Legal Integration' (1993) 47 *International Organization* 41–76.

Burton, T., 'Access to Environmental Information—The UK Experience of Water Registers' (1989) 1 *Journal of Environmental Law* 192–208.

Butterfield, H., and Wight, M. (eds.), *Diplomatic Investigations* (London, 1966).

Calabresi, G., and Melamed, A. D., 'Property Rules, Liability Rules and Inalienability: One View of the Cathedral' (1972) 85 *Harvard Law Review* 1089–1128.

Cane, P., *Atiyah's Accidents, Compensation and the Law* (5th ed., London, 1993).

—— *Tort Law and Economic Interests* (2nd ed., Oxford, 1996).

—— and Stapleton, J. (eds.), *Essays for Patrick Atiyah* (Oxford, 1991).

Carr, E. H., *The Twenty Years' Crisis* (London, 1939).

Carty, A., and Danilenko, G. (eds.), *Perestroika and International Law: Current Anglo-Soviet Approaches to International Law* (Edinburgh, 1990).

Chappell, D., and Moore, R. D., *The Use of Criminal Penalties for Pollution of the Environment: A Selective and Annotated Bibliography of the Literature*, Studies in Regulation and Compliance, Department of Justice, Canada, 1988.

Chatterjee, P., and Finger, M., *The Earth Brokers: Power, Politics and World Development* (London, 1994).

Chatterjee, S., 'The Charter of Economic Rights and Duties of States: An Evaluation after 15 Years' (1989) 40 *International and Comparative Law Quarterly* 669–84.

Chinkin, C., 'The Challenge of Soft Law: Development and Change in International Law' (1989) 38 *International and Comparative Law Quarterly* 850–66.

—— 'Suspension of Treaty Relationships: The ANZUS Alliance' (1990) 7 *UCLA Pacific Basin Law Journal* 114–57.

—— *Third Parties in International Law* (Oxford, 1993).

Chomsky, N., 'World Order and Its Rules: Variation on Some Themes' (1992) 20 *Journal of Law and Society* 145–65.

Churchill, R., Warren, L., and Gibson, J. (eds.), *Law, Policy and the Environment* (London, 1991), *Journal of Law and Society*, Special Issue.

Conaghan, J., and Mansell, W., *The Wrongs of Tort* (London, 1993).

Cooper, J., and Dhavan, R. (eds.), *Public Interest Law* (Oxford, 1986).

Cotterrell, R., *Law's Community* (Oxford, 1995).

Countryside Commission (UK), *Public Attitudes to the Countryside* (CCP 481, 1997).

Cox, R. W., 'Social Forces, Forms of States and World Orders: Beyond International Relations Theory' (1981) 10 *Millenium: Journal of International Studies* 126–55.

—— 'The Crisis in World Order and the Challenge of International Organisation' (1994) 29 *Conflict and Cooperation* 99–113.

—— 'A Perspective on Globalisation', in Mittelman (ed.), *Globalization: Critical Reflections* (1995).

Cranston, R., 'Reviewing Judicial Review', in Richardson and Genn (eds.), *Administrative Law and Government Action* (1994).

Craven, M., 'New Zealand's Request for an Examination of the Situation in accordance with Paragraph 63 of the Court's 1974 Judgment concerning Nuclear Tests (*New Zealand v. France*), Order of 22 September' (1996) 45 *International and Comparative Law Quarterly* 725–34.

Curtin, D., and Heukels, T. (eds.), *International Dynamics of European Integration* (Dordrecht, 1994).

Dalby, S., 'Security, Modernity, Ecology: The Dilemma of Post-Cold War Discourse' (1992) 17 *Alternatives* 95–134.

Day, M., 'Shifting the Environmental Balance', in Robinson and Dunkley (eds.), *Public Interest Perspectives in Environmental Law* (1995).

de la Torre, M., and Kimber, C., 'Access to Information on the Environment in Spain' (1997) 6 *European Environmental Law Review* 53–62.

Debrulle, M., (ed.), *Future European Environmental Policy and Subsidiarity* (Brussels, 1994).

Denys, C., *Impliciete Bevoegdheden in de Europeses Gemeenschap* (Antwerp, 1990).

Department of State Environmental Initiative for the Twenty-First Century (USA), *Environmental Change and Security Report*, Issue 2, Spring 1986.

Department of the Environment, *The Future of Development Plans* (Cm. 569, London, 1989).

—— *This Common Inheritance* (Cm. 1200, London, 1990).

—— *Improving Environmental Quality: The Government's Proposals for a New, Independent Environment Agency* (London, 1991).

—— *The Potential Role of Market Mechanisms in the Control of Acid Rain* (London, 1992).

—— *This Common Inheritance: Second Year Report* (Cm. 2068, London, 1992).

—— *Integrated Planning and the Granting of Permits in the EC* (London, 1993).

—— *Sustainable Development: The UK Strategy* (Cm. 2426, London, 1994).

—— *Community Involvement in Planning and Development Processes* (London, 1995).

—— *Guide To Risk Assessment and Risk Management* (London, 1995).

—— *The United Kingdom National Air Quality Strategy* (Cm. 3587, London, 1997).

—— *Your Right to Know—the Government's Proposals for a Freedom of Information Act* (Cm. 3818, London, 1997).

Dewees, D. N., 'The Efficiency of the Common Law: Sulphur Dioxide Emissions in Sudbury' (1992) 42 *University of Toronto Law Journal* 1–21.

Dovers, S., 'Information, Sustainability, and Policy' (1995) 2 *Australian Journal of Environmental Management* 142–56.

Downing, P., 'Cross-National Comparisons in Environmental Protection: Introduction to the Issues' (1982–3) 11 *Policy Studies Journal* 39–43.

—— and Kimball, J., 'Enforcing Pollution Control Laws in the US: Introduction to the Issues' (1982/3) 11 *Policy Studies Journal* 55–65.

Dudley, N., 'Changing Perception of Air Pollution', in Bradby (ed.), *Dirty Words: Writings on the History and Culture of Pollution* (1990).

Dupuy, P.-M., 'Soft Law and the International Law of the Environment' (1991) 12 *Michigan Journal of International Law* 420–35.

Duxbury, R., *Telling and Duxbury's Planning Law and Procedure* (10th ed., London, 1996).

Ehlermann, C.-D., 'The Internal Market following the Single European Act' (1987) 24 *Common Market Law Review* 361–409.

Environment Protection Authority (NSW), *Annual Report 1994–95* (Sydney, 1995).

—— *Protection of the Environment Operations Bill 1996: Impact Analysis of the Draft Schedule of EPA-Licensed Activities*, 1996.

Environment Protection Authority (Victoria), *The Environmental Protection Act 1970: 25 Years of Making a Difference* (Melbourne, 1996).

Environmental Protection Agency (USA), *Permits Improvement Team Concept Paper on Environmental Permitting and Task Force Recommendations—Draft,* May 1996.

European Foundation for the Improvement of Living and Working Conditions, *Environmental Taxes and Charges: National Experience and Plans* (Dublin, 1996).

Evans, T., 'Human Rights: Imposing Values', in Thomas and Wilkin (eds.), *Globalization and the South* (1997).

—— and Wilson, P., 'International Regimes and the English School of International Relations' (1993) 22 *Millennium: Journal of International Studies* 329–51.

Everlung, U., 'Abrenzung der Rechtsangleichung zur Verwirklichung des Binnenmarktes nach Artikel 100A EWG durch den Gerichtshof' (1991) 26 *Europarecht* 179–82.

Fairley, R., 'Integrated Pollution Control—Public Registers and Commercial Confidentiality' (1993) 5 *Environmental Law and Management* 111–14.

Falk, R., 'Theoretical Foundations of Human Rights', in Newburg (ed.), *The Politics of Human Rights* (1980).

Farrier, D., 'In Search of Real Criminal Law', in Bonyhady (ed.), *Environmental Protection and Legal Change* (1992).

Felstiner, W., and Dingwall, S., *Asbestos Litigation in the United Kingdom—An Interim Report* (Oxford, 1988).

—— Abel, R., and Sarat, A., 'The Emergence and Transformation of Disputes: Naming, Blaming and Claiming' (1981) 15 *Law and Society Review* 631–54.

Finkle, P. Z. R., 'Canadian Environmental Law in the Eighties: Problems and Perspectives' (1983) 7 *Dalhousie Law Journal* 257–76.

Finnis, J., *Natural Law and Natural Rights* (Oxford, 1980).

Fisher, R., and Ury, W., *Getting to Yes, Negotiating Agreement Without Giving In* (Boston, Mass., 1981).

Fitzmaurice, M., 'Environmental Protection and the International Court of Justice', in Lowe and Fitzmaurice (eds.), *Fifty Years of the International Court of Justice* (1996).

Flynn, J., 'How Will Article 100a(4) Work? A Comparison with Article 93' (1987) 24 *Common Market Law Review* 689–707.

Franklin, N., 'Environmental Pollution Control: The Limits of Criminal Law' (1990) 2 *Current Issues in Criminal Justice* 81–94.

Garrett, G., 'International Co-operation and Institutional Choice: The EC's Internal Market' (1992) 46 *International Organization* 533–60.

George, S., 'The European Commission: Opportunities Seized; Problems Unresolved', Paper Delivered to the First UACES Research Conference (Birmingham, 1995).

Gérard, N., 'Access to Justice on Environmental Matters—A Case of Double Standards?' (1996) 8 *Journal of Environmental Law* 149–57.

Gibbs, W. W., 'The Treaty that Worked—Almost', September 1995, *Scientific American* 18–20.

Gibson, J., 'The Integration of Pollution Control', in Churchill, Warren, and Gibson (eds.), *Law, Policy and the Environment* (1991).

Giddens, A., *The Consequences of Modernity* (Cambridge, 1990).

Gill, S., 'Globalisation, Market Civilisation, and Disciplinary Neoliberalism' (1995) 24 *Millenium: Journal of International Studies* 399–423.

Goldblatt, D., *Social Theory and the Environment* (Cambridge, 1996).

Grabitz, E., *Competence of the European Communities for Environmental Policy* (Berlin, 1977).

Graham, C., 'Self Regulation', in Richardson and Genn (eds.), *Administrative Law and Government Action* (1994).

—— and Prosser, T., *Privatizing Public Enterprises: Constitutions, the State, and Regulation in Comparative Perspective* (Oxford, 1991).

Grant, M., *Urban Planning Law* (London, 1982).

Gregorczsk, H., 'The Appropriateness of Mediation in International Environmental Disputes' (1996) 7 *Australian Dispute Resolution Journal* 47–60.

Groth, A., and Wade, L. (eds.), *Public Policy Across Nations: Social Welfare in Industrial Settings* (Greenwich, 1985).

Gunder Frank, A., 'The Development of Underdevelopment', September 1966, *Monthly Review* 17–30.

Gunning, I., 'Modernizing Customary International Law: The Challenge of Human Rights' (1991) 31 *Virginia Journal of International Law* 211–47.

Gunningham, N., *Pollution, Social Interest and the Law* (London, 1974).

—— 'Environment, Self-Regulation, and the Chemical Industry: Assessing Responsible Care' (1995) 17 *Law and Policy* 57–109.

—— 'From Adversarialism to Partnership? ISO 14000 and Regulation', Paper Delivered at the Australian Centre for Environmental Law (Canberra, 1996).

Haas, E. B., *The Uniting of Europe* (Stanford, 1958).

—— and Schmitter, C., 'Economics and Differential Patterns of Political Integration: Projections about Unity in Latin America' (1964) 18 *International Organization* 255–76.

Haas, P., Keohane, R., and Levy, M. (eds.), *Institutions for the Earth: Sources of Effective Environental Protection* (Cambridge, Mass., 1993).

Habermas, J., *The Theory of Communicative Action, Vol. 2. System and Lifeworld: A Critique of Functionalist Reason* (Boston, trans. 1987).

—— 'Law as Medium and Law as Institution', in Teubner (ed.), *Dilemmas of Law in the Welfare State* (1988).

Hadfield, B. (ed.), *Judicial Review: A Thematic Approach* (Dublin, 1995).
Hahn, R., and Richards, K., 'The Internationalization of Environmental Regulation' (1989) 30 *Harvard International Law Journal* 421–46.
Haigh, N., and Irwin, F. (eds), *Integrated Pollution Control in Europe and North America* (Washington D. C., 1990).
Hajer, M. A., '"Verinnerlijking" (Internalization): The Limits to a Positive Management Approach', in Teubner, Farmer, and Murphy (eds.), *Environmental Law and Ecological Responsibility: The Concept and Practice of Ecological Self-Organization* (1994).
Haley, J. O., 'Sheathing the Sword of Justice in Japan: An Essay on Law Without Sanctions' (1982) 8 *Journal of Japanese Studies* 265–81.
Hallo, R. E. (ed.), *Access to Environmental Information in Europe: the Implementation and Implications of Directive 90/313/EEC* (London, 1996).
Handl, G., 'Compliance Control Mechanisms and International Environmental Obligations' (1997) 5 *Tulane Journal of International and Comparative Law* 29–49.
Hardin, G., 'The Tragedy of the Commons' (1968) 162 *Science* 1243–8.
Harding, R., and Fischer, L. (eds.), *Proceedings of Precautionary Principle Conference* (University of New South Wales, 1993).
Harlow, C., and Rawlings, R., *Law and Administration* (London, 1984).
Hart, H. L. A., *The Concept of Law* (Oxford, 1969).
Hawkins, K., *Environment and Enforcement: Regulation and the Social Definition of Pollution* (Oxford, 1984).
Hellmann, U., *Die Öffentlichkeitsbeteiligung in vertikal gestuften Zulassungsverfahren für umweltrelevante Grossvorhaben nach deutschem und europäischen Recht* (Frankfurt am Main, 1992).
Helm, D. (ed.), *Economic Policy Towards the Environment* (Oxford, 1991).
Henkin, L., and Hargrove, J. (eds.), *Human Rights: An Agenda for the Next Century* (Washington, 1994).
Her Majesty's Treasury, *Spending Public Money: Governance and Audit Issues* (Cm. 3179, London, 1996).
Herbert-Young, N., 'Reflections on Section 54A and "Plan-led" Decision-Making' [1995] *Journal of Planning and Environment Law* 292–305.
Herz, J. H., 'The Rise and Demise of the Territorial State' (1954) 9 *World Politics* 473–93.
Heukels, T., Kellerman, A. E., Verkruisen, V. P., and Sluys, J. J. M., *Kwaliteit Communautaire Regelgeving* (Den Haag, 1996).
Higgins, R., *Problems and Process: International Law and How We Use It* (Oxford, 1994).
Hirschorn, J., Jackson, T., and Baas, L., 'Towards Prevention—the Emerging Environmental Management Paradigm', in Jackson (ed.), *Clean Production Strategies: Developing Preventive Environmental Management in the Industrial Economy* (1993).
Hirst, P., and Thompson, G., *Globalization in Question* (Cambridge, 1996).
Hoffmann, M., 'Critical Theory and the Inter-Paradigm Debate' (1987) 16 *Millenium: Journal of International Studies* 231–49.
—— 'States, Cosmopolitanism and Normative International Theory' (1988) 2 *Paradigms* 60–75.
Horwitz, M., *The Transformation of American Law* 1780–1860 (Cambridge, Mass., 1977).
House of Lords Select Committee on Sustainable Development, *Report from the Select Committee on Sustainable Development, Session 1994–95* (HL Paper 72).

House of Lords Select Committee on the European Communities, *Freedom of Access to Information on the Environment, Session 1996–97*, First Report (HL Paper 9).
Hughes, D., *Environmental Law* (1st ed., London, 1986).
—— 'The NRA Scheme of Charges in Respect of Discharges into Controlled Waters' (1991) 3 *Land Mangement and Environmental Law Report* 115–17.
—— *Environmental Law* (3rd ed., London, 1996).
Hurrell, A., and Kingsbury, B. (eds.), *The International Politics of the Environment* (Oxford, 1992).
—— and Kingsbury, B., 'The International Politics of the Environment: An Introduction', in Hurrell and Kingsbury (eds.), *The International Politics of the Environment* (1992).
Hutchinson, A., 'Sault Ste Marie, *Mens Rea,* and the Halfway House: Public Welfare Offences Get a Home of Their Own' (1979) 17 *Osgoode Hall Law Journal* 415–44.
Hutter, B., *The Reasonable Arm of the Law? The Law Enforcement Procedures of Environmental Health Officers* (Oxford, 1988).
Huymans, J., 'Post-Cold War Implosion and Globalization: Liberalism Running Past Itself' (1995) 24 *Millenium: Journal of International Studies* 471–87.
Idelson, V., 'The Law of Nations and the Individual', in *The Grotius Society: Transactions for the Year 1944* (London, 1962).
Irwin, F. H., 'An Integrated Framework for Preventing Pollution and Protecting the Environment' (1991) 22 *Environmental Law* 1–76.
Jackson, R. H., 'Martin Wight, International Relations and the Good Life' (1990) 19 *Millenium: Journal of International Studies* 261–72.
Jackson, T. (ed.), *Clean Production Strategies: Developing Preventive Environmental Management in the Industrial Economy* (Stockholm, 1993).
Jacobs, M., *The Green Economy* (London, 1991).
Jaffe, A. B., Peterson, S. R., and Stavins, R. N., 'Environmental Regulation and Competitiveness of U.S. Manufacturing: What Does the Evidence Tell Us?' (1995) 33 *Journal of Economic Literature* 132–63.
Jans, J., 'De Kwaliteit van de Europese milieuregelgeving' (1990) 38 *Tijdschrift voor Europees en economisch recht* 503–26.
—— 'Legal Protection in European Environmental Law', in Somsen (ed.), *Protecting the European Environment* (1996).
Jewell, T., 'Minerals and Waste: New Plan Making Powers and Procedures' (1991) 2 *Utilities Law Review* 82–7.
—— 'Planning Regulation and Environmental Consciousness: Some Lessons From Minerals?' [1995] *Journal of Planning and Environment Law* 482–98.
—— and Steele, J., 'UK Regulatory Reform and the Pursuit of "Sustainable Development": The Environment Act 1995' (1996) 8 *Journal of Environmental Law* 283–300.
Johnson, N., 'Accountability, Control and Complexity: Moving Beyond Ministerial Responsibility', in Barker (ed.), *Quangos in Britain: Government and the Networks of Public Policy-Making* (1982).
Jordan, A., 'Integrated Pollution Control and the Evolving Style and Structure of Environmental Regulation in the UK' (1993) 2 *Environmental Politics* 405–27.
Jowell, J., 'The Rule of Law Today', in Jowell and Oliver (eds.), *The Changing Constitution* (1989).
—— and Oliver, D. (eds.), *The Changing Constitution* (2nd ed., Oxford, 1989).
—— and Oliver, D. (eds.), *The Changing Constitution* (3rd ed., Oxford, 1994).

Judge, D. (ed.), *A Green Dimension for the European Community: Political Issues and Processes* (London, 1992), *Environmental Politics*, Special Issue.

—— '"Predestined to Save the Earth": the Environment Committee of the European Parliament', in Judge (ed.), *A Green Dimension for the European Community: Political Issues and Processes* (1992), *Environmental Politics*, Special Issue.

Kaplan, M. A., and Katzenbach, N. B., *The Politics and Foundations of International Law* (London, 1961).

Karl, J., 'Zur Rechtswirkung von Protokollerklärungen in der Europäischen Gemeinschaft' (1991) 46 *Juristenzeitung* 593–9.

Kee, D., 'Sooty Skies and Burning Rivers No Longer Dragons to Slay', November 1995: 1 *Environmental Manager* 19–21.

Keohane, R. O., *After Hegemony: Cooperation and Discord in the World Political Economy* (Princeton, 1984).

Kiewiet, D. R., and McCubbins, M. D., *The Logic of Delegation: Congressional Parties and the Appropriation Process* (Chicago, 1991).

Killingsworth, A. J., and Palmer, J. S., *Ecospeak: Rhetoric and Environmental Politics in America* (Carbondale, 1992).

Kingsbury, B., 'The Tuna-Dolphin Controversy, The World Trade Organization, and the Liberal Project to Reconceptualize International Law' (1994) 5 *Yearbook of International Environmental Law* 1–40.

Koppen, I., 'Ecological Covenants: Regulatory Informality in Dutch Waste Reduction Policy', in Teubner, Farmer, and Murphy (eds.), *Environmental Law and Ecological Responsibility: the Concept and Practice of Ecological Self-Organization* (1994).

Koskenniemi, M., 'The Future of Statehood' (1991) 32 *Harvard International Law Journal* 397–410.

—— 'Breach of Treaty or Non-Compliance? Reflections on the Enforcement of the Montreal Protocol' (1992) 3 *Yearbook of International Environmental Law* 123–62.

—— 'The Post-Adjudicative Phase: Commentary', in Peck and Lee (eds.), *Increasing the Effectiveness of the International Court of Justice* (1997).

Krämer, L., 'The Open Society, its Lawyers and its Environment' (1989) 1 *Journal of Environmental Law* 1–9.

—— *EEC Treaty and Environmental Protection* (London, 1990).

—— *Focus on European Environmental Law* (London, 1992).

—— 'Environmental Protection and Article 30 EEC Treaty' (1993) *Common Market Law Review* 111–43.

—— 'Um eine Unweltpolitik von innen bittend' (1994) 4 *Zeitschrift für Umweltrecht* 172–7.

—— 'Direct Effect of EC Environmental Law', in Somsen (ed.), *Protecting the European Environment* (1996).

Krasner, S. (ed.), *International Regimes* (London, 1983).

Krier, J., 'The Pollution Problem and Legal Institutions: A Conceptual Overview' (1971) 18 *UCLA Law Review* 429–77.

Kuznlik, P., 'Environmental Impact Assessment: the British Cases' (1995) 4 *European Environmental Law Review* 336–44.

Landy, M. K., Roberts, M. J., and Thomas, S. R., *The Environment Protection Agency: Asking the Wrong Questions from Nixon to Clinton* (New York, 1994).

Lasswell, H., and McDougal, M., *Jurisprudence for a Free Society: Studies in Law, Science and Policy* vol. 1. (Dordrecht, 1992).

Latin, H., 'Ideal versus Real Regulatory Efficiency: Implementation of Uniform Standards and "Fine-Tuning" Regulatory Reform' (1985) 37 *Stanford Law Review* 1267–1332.

—— 'Regulatory Failure, Administrative Incentives, and the New Clean Air Act' (1991) 21 *Environmental Law* 1647–1720.

Law Centres Federation (UK), *Whose Environment is it Anyway?*

Law Reform Commission (Canada), *Our Criminal Law*, 1976.

—— *Crimes Against the Environment*, Working Paper 44, 1985.

—— *Recodifying Criminal Law*, Report 31, 1987.

Lenaerts, L., 'The Principle of Subsidiarity and the Environment in the European Union: Keeping the Balance of Federalism' (1994) 17 *Fordham International Law Journal* 846–95.

Lewis, N., 'Regulating Non-Government Bodies: Privatization, Accountability, and the Public-Private Divide', in Jowell and Oliver (eds.), *The Changing Constitution* (1989).

Lewis, R., 'Contaminated Land: The New Regime of the Environment Act 1995' [1995] *Journal of Planning and Environment Law* 1087–96.

Linklater, A., 'The Problem of Community in International Relations' (1990) 15 *Alternatives* 135–53.

Lipman, Z., and Roots, L., 'Protecting the Environment through Criminal Sanctions: The Environmental Offences and Penalties Act 1989 (NSW)' (1995) 12 *Environmental and Planning Law Journal* 16–36.

Lomas, O. (ed.), *Frontiers of Environmental Law* (Chichester, 1991).

Loughlin, M., *Public Law and Political Theory* (Oxford, 1992).

Lowe, I., 'Implementing the Precautionary Principle', in Harding and Fischer (eds.), *Proceedings of Precautionary Principle Conference* (1993).

Lowe, V., and Fitzmaurice, M. (eds.), *Fifty Years of the International Court of Justice* (Cambridge, 1996).

Luhmann, N., *A Sociological Theory of Law* (London, 1985).

McAuslan, P., *The Ideologies of Planning Law* (Oxford, 1980).

McAuslan, P., and McEldowney, J. (eds.), *Law, Legitimacy and the Constitution* (London, 1985).

McDougal, M. S., 'Law as a Process of Decision: A Policy-Oriented Approach to Legal Study' (1956) 1 *Natural Law Forum* 53–72.

McGoldrick, D., 'Sustainable Development and Human Rights' (1996) 45 *International and Comparative Law Quarterly* 796–818.

MacKenzie, D., 'Ozone's Future is Up in the Air', 16 December 1995, *New Scientist* 14–15.

McLaren, J. P. S., 'Nuisance Law and the Industrial Revolution—Some Lessons From Social History' (1983) 3 *Oxford Journal of Legal Studies* 155–221.

McLeod, G., 'Do We Need an Environmental Court in Britain', in Robinson and Dunkley (eds.), *Public Interest Perspectives in Environmental Law* (1995).

Macrory, R., 'Environmental Law: Shifting Discretions and the New Formalism', in Lomas (ed.), *Frontiers of Environmental Law* (1991).

Majone, G., 'Deregulation or Re-Regulation? Policy-Making in the European Community Since the Single Act', paper prepared for European University Institute research project, *La Restructuration des Etats Européen* (Florence, 1996).

Markesinis, B., and Deakin, S., *Tort Law* (3rd ed., Oxford, 1994).

Martin, W., and Pickersgill, D., 'The Timor Gap Treaty' (1991) 32 *Harvard International Law Journal* 566–82.

Maxwell, J. H., and Weiner, S. L., 'Green Consciousness or Dollar Diplomacy: The British Response to the Threat of Ozone Depletion' (1993) 5 *International Environmental Affairs* 19–41.

Mazey, S., and Richardson, J., 'Environmental Groups and the EC: Challenges and Opportunities', in Judge (ed.), *A Green Dimension for the European Community: Political Issues and Processes* (1992), *Environmental Politics*, Special Issue.

Meijers, H., 'How is International Law Made? The Stages of Growth of International Law and the Use of Customary Rules' (1978) 9 *Netherlands Yearbook of International Law* 3–26.

Menkel-Meadow, C., 'Towards Another View of Legal Negotiation: The Structure of Problem-Solving' (1983–4) 31 *UCLA Law Review* 754–832.

Millichap, D., 'Sustainability: A Long-Established Concern of Planning' [1993] *Journal of Planning and Environment Law* 1111–19.

Milward, A., *The European Rescue of the Nation-State* (Berkeley, 1992).

Ministry of the Environment and Forests (India), *Environmental Aspects of Narmada Sugar and Sardar Sarovar Multi-Purpose Projects* (1987).

Mittelman, J. H. (ed.), *Globalization: Critical Reflections* (Boulder, 1995).

Morganthau, H. J., *Politics Amongst Nations* (4th ed., New York, 1996).

Morvcsik, A., 'Negotiating the Single European Act: National Interests and Traditional Statecraft in the European Community' (1991) 45 *International Organization* 651–88.

Mosler, H., *The International Society as a Legal Community* (Netherlands, 1980).

Murase, S., 'Perspectives from International Economic Law on Transnational Environmental Issues' (1995) 253 *Hague Receuil* 287–431.

Nardin, T., *Law, Morality, and the Relations of States* (Princeton, 1983).

Nelson, B. F., and Stubb, A. (eds.), *The European Union: Readings on the Theory and Practice of European Integration* (London, 1994).

Newburg, P. (ed.), *The Politics of Human Rights* (New York, 1980).

Nonet, P., and Selznick, P., *Law and Society in Transition: Towards Responsive Law* (New York, 1978).

Ogus, A., *Regulation: Legal Form and Economic Theory* (Oxford, 1994).

—— and Richardson, G., 'Economics and the Environment—A Study in Private Nuisance' (1977) 36 *Cambridge Law Journal* 284–325.

Oliver, D., *Government in the United Kingdom: the Search for Accountability, Effectiveness, and Citizenship* (Oxford, 1991).

Organisation for Economic Co-operation and Development, *Economic Instruments for Environmental Protection* (Paris, 1989).

—— 'Recommendation of the Council on Integrated Pollution Control', C(90)164 final, 31 January 1991.

—— *The Distributive Effects of Economic Instruments for Environmental Protection* (Paris, 1994).

—— *Reducing Environmental Pollution: Looking Back, Thinking Ahead. An Examination of OECD Member Country Progress, Trends and Opportunities for Accelerated Pollution Reduction in the 1990s and Beyond* (Paris, 1994).

Osborne, D., and Gaebler, T., *Reinventing Government: How the Entrepreneurial Spirit is Transforming the Public Sector* (Reading, 1992).

Ostrom, E., *Governing the Commons: The Evolution of Institutions for Collective Action* (Cambridge, 1991).

Owen, D. G. (ed.), *The Philosophical Foundations of Tort Law* (Oxford, 1995).

Palmer, G., 'New Ways to Make Environmental Law' (1992) 86 *American Journal of International Law* 259–83.

Panitch, L., 'Rethinking the Role of the State', in Mittelman (ed.), *Globalization: Critical Reflections* (1995).

Park, P., 'The Marketable Permit Programme in California' (1996) 8 *Environmental Law and Management* 26–9.

Patton, K., 'Dispute Resolution under the North American Commission on Environmental Cooperation' (1994) 15 *Duke Journal of Comparative and International Law* 87–116.

Paul, J., 'The United Nations and the Creation of an International Law of Development' (1995) 36 *Harvard International Law Journal* 307–28.

Peck, C., and Lee, R. (eds.), *Increasing the Effectiveness of the International Court of Justice* (The Hague, 1997).

Percival, R., Miller, A., Schroeder, C., and Leape, J., *Environmental Regulation: Law, Science and Policy* (Boston, 1996).

Peters, G., 'Bureaucratic Politics and the Institutions of the European Community', in Sbragia (ed.), *Euro-Politics: Institutions and Policymaking in the 'New' European Community* (1992).

Peterson, M., and Wade, L., 'Environmental Pollution Policy in Japan: A Public Choice Hypothesis', in Groth and Wade (eds.), *Public Policy Across Nations: Social Welfare in Industrial Settings* (1985).

Pitchford, R., 'How Liable Should a Lender Be? The Case of Judgement-Proof Firms and Environmental Risk' (1995) 85 *American Economic Review* 1171–85.

Polack, M., 'Delegation, Agency, and Agenda Setting in the European Community' (1997) 51 *International Organization* 99–134.

Prosser, T., 'Democratisation, Accountability and Institutional Design: Reflections on Public Law', in McAuslan and McEldowney (eds.), *Law, Legitimacy and the Constitution* (1985).

Pugh, C., and Day, M., *Pollution and Personal Injury: Toxic Torts II* (London, 1995).

Purdue, M., 'Integrated Pollution Control in the Environmental Protection Act 1990: A Coming of Age of Environmental Law?' (1991) 54 *Modern Law Review* 534–51.

—— Young, E., and Rowan-Robinson, J., *Planning Law and Procedure* (London, 1989).

Ramphal, S., 'Globalism and Meaningful Peace: A New World Order Rooted in International Community' (1992) 32 *Security Dialogue* 81–7.

Rankin, M., and Finkle, P., 'The Enforcement of Environmental Law: Taking the Environment Seriously' (1983) 17 *University of British Columbia Law Review* 35–7.

Raphael, A., *Ultimate Risk* (London, 1994).

Rasmussen, H., *On Law and Policy in the European Court of Justice: A Comparative Study in Judicial Policymaking* (Dordrecht, 1986).

Rehbinder, E., 'Locus Standi, Community Law and the Case for Harmonisation', in Somsen (ed.), *Protecting the European Environment* (1996).

—— and Stewart, R., *Environmental Protection Policy* (Berlin, 1985).

Reich, R. B., 'Public Administration and Public Deliberation: An Interpretive Essay' (1985) 94 *Yale Law Journal* 1617–40.

Reid, C., 'Judicial Review and the Environment', in Hadfield (ed.), *Judicial Review: A Thematic Approach* (1995).

—— 'Environmental Regulation through Economic Instruments: The Example of Forestry' (1996) 8 *Environmental Law and Management* 56–64.

Resource and Conservation Assessment Council (NSW), *Draft Interim Forest Assessment Report*, June 1996.

Revesz, R., 'Rehabilitating Inter State Competition: Rethinking the "Race to the Bottom" Rationale for Federal Environmental Regulation' (1992) 67 *New York University Law Review* 1210–54.

—— and Stewart, R. B. (eds.), *Analyzing Superfund* (Washington, 1995).

Richardson, G., 'Policing Pollution: The Enforcement Process' (1982/3) 11 *Policy Studies Journal* 153–64.

—— 'The Legal Regulation of Process', in Richardson and Genn (eds.), *Administrative Law and Government Action* (1994).

—— and Genn, H. (eds.), *Administrative Law and Government Action* (Oxford, 1994).

Robbins, D. H., 'Public Interest Environment Litigation in the United States', in Robinson and Dunkley (eds.), *Public Interest Perspectives in Environmental Law* (1995).

Robinson, B., 'ISO 14000: Eagle or Albatross', paper delivered to 'ISO 14000—Regulation, Trade, and Environment', Conference of the Australian Centre for Environmental Law, Australian National University, Canberra, 2 July 1996.

Robinson, D., 'Public Participation in Environmental Decision-Making' (1993) 10 *Environmental and Planning Law Journal* 320–40.

—— 'Public Interest Environmental Law Firms in the United States', in Robinson and Dunkley (eds.), *Public Interest Perspectives in Environmental Law* (1995).

—— and Dunkley, J. (eds.), *Public Interest Perspectives in Environmental Law* (Chichester, 1995).

Robinson, N. (ed.), *Agenda 21: Earth's Action Plan* (New York, 1993).

—— 'Universal and National Trends in International Environmental Law' (1993) *Environmental Policy and Law* 148–54.

Roderick, P., 'The United Kingdom', in Hallo (ed.), *Access to Environmental Information in Europe: the Implementation and Implications of Directive 90/313/EEC* (1996).

Rodgers, C. (ed.), *Nature Conservation and Countryside Law* (Cardiff, 1996).

Rose-Ackerman, S., *Controlling Environmental Policy: The Limits of Public Law in Germany and the United States of America* (New Haven, 1995).

Ross, A., and Rowan-Robinson, J., 'Public Registers of Environmental Information: An Assessment of their Role' (1994) 37 *Journal of Environmental Management and Planning* 349–59.

Rowan-Robinson, J., Watchman, P., and Barker, C., *Crime and Regulation: A Study of the Enforcement of Regulatory Codes* (Edinburgh, 1990).

—— Theron, C., and Ross, A., 'Policing Pollution: Private Regulation and the Role of Lenders' [1996] *Environmental Liability* 114–18.

—— Ross, A., Walton., W., and Rothnie, J., 'Public Access to Environmental Information: A Means to What End?' (1996) 8 *Journal of Environmental Law* 19–42.

Rowlands, I., 'The International Politics of Environment and Development: The Post-UNCED Agenda' (1992) 21 *Millenium: Journal of International Studies* 209–24.

Royal Commission on Environmental Pollution, *Air Pollution Control: An Integrated Approach*, Fifth Report (Cm. 6371, London, 1976).

—— *Tackling Pollution—Experience and Prospects* (Cmnd. 9149, London, 1984).

—— *Best Practicable Environmental Option*, Twelfth Report (Cm. 310, London, 1988).
—— *Freshwater Quality*, Sixteenth Report (Cm. 1966, London, 1992).

Ruckelshaus, W., First Administrator of the EPA, Address 'Stopping the Pendulum', to the Environmental Law Institute, Washington D. C., 18 August 1995.

Sachs, W. (ed.), *Global Ecology* (London, 1993).

Saggio, G., 'Le basi guiridiche della politica ambientale nell'ordinamento comunitario dopo d'entrata in vigore dell'Atto Unico Europeo' (1993) 33 *Rivista di Diritto Europeo* 39–50.

Sandholtz, W., and Zysman, J., '1992: Recasting the European Bargain', in Nelson and Stubb (eds.), *The European Union: Readings on the Theory and Practice of European Integration* (1994).

Sands, P., *Principles of International Environmental Law*, vol. 1 (Manchester, 1995).

Saravanamuttu, P., 'Environment, Development and Security', in Thomas (ed.), *Rio: Unravelling the Consequences* (1994).

Saurin, J., 'Global Environmental Degradation, Modernity and Environmental Knowledge', in Thomas (ed.), *Rio: Unravelling the Consequences* (1994).

Sax, J., 'Property Rights and the Economy of Nature: Understanding *Lucas v South Carolina Coastal Council*' (1992) 45 *Stanford Law Review* 1433–55.

Sbragia, A. (ed.), *Euro-Politics: Institutions and Policymaking in the 'New' European Community* (Washington D. C., 1992).

Schachter, O., 'The Emergence of International Environmental Law' (1991) 44 *Journal of International Affairs* 457–93.

Scheuer, H., 'Aspects juridiques de la protection de l'environnement dans le marché commun' (1975) 109 *Revue du Marché Commun* 441–56.

Scheuning, D., 'Unweltschutz auf der Grundlage der Einheitlichen Europäischen Akte' (1989) 24 *Europarecht* 153–92.

Schoenbaum, T., 'Free International Trade and Protection of the Environment: Irreconcilable Conflict' (1992) 86 *American Journal of International Law* 700–27.

—— 'Environmental Damages: the Emerging Law in the United States', in Wetterstein (ed.), *Harm to the Environment* (1997).

——'International Trade and Protection of the Environment: the Continuing Search for Reconciliation' (1997) 91 *American Journal of International Law* 268–313.

Schröer, T., 'Mehr Demokratie statt umweltpolitischer Subsidiarität' (1991) 26 *Europarecht* 356–68.

Schulkin, J., and Kleindorfer, P., 'Equity Decisions: Economic Development and Environmental Prudence' (1995) 17 *Human Rights Quarterly* 382–97.

Seager, J., 'Developments in Water Quality Standards and Classification Schemes in England and Wales' (1994) 30 *Water Science Technology* 11–19.

Sevenster, H., *Milieubeleid en Gemeenschapstrecht* (Deventer, 1992).

Sharratt, P. (ed.), *Environmental Management Systems* (Rugby, 1995).

Shaw, J., and More, G. (eds.), *New Legal Dynamics of European Union* (Oxford, 1995).

Sheate, W. R., and Atkinson, N. R., 'Public Participation in Environmental Decision Making: The European Dimension' (1995) 5 *Environmental Policy & Practice* 119–29.

Sheldon, C., 'BS 7750 and Certification—A Developmental History', in Sharratt (ed.), *Environmental Management Systems* (1995).

Shelton, D., 'What Happened in Rio to Human Rights?' (1992) 3 *Yearbook of International Environmental Law* 75–93.

Smith, S., 'The Environment on the Periphery of International Relations: An Explanation', in Thomas (ed.), *Rio: Unravelling the Consequences* (1994).

Snyder, F., *Soft Law and Institutional Practice in the European Community*, European University Institute Law Working Paper No. 93/5 (Florence, 1993).

Somsen, H., 'EC Water Directives' (1990) 1 *Water Law* 93–8.

—— 'Derecho Comunitario del Medio Ambiente: Tratado, Instituciones, Procedimento de Decision e Instrumentos Juridicos', in Alfonso (ed.), *Derecho medioambiental de la Unión Europea* (1996).

—— 'The European Union and the Organisation for Economic Co-operation and Development', in Werksman (ed.), *Greening International Institutions* (1996).

—— '*Francovich* and its Application to EC Environmental Law', in Somsen (ed.), *Protecting the European Environment* (1996).

—— (ed.), *Protecting the European Environment* (London, 1996).

Springer, A., *The International Law of Pollution—Protecting the Global Environment in a World of Sovereign States* (Westport, Conn., 1983).

Stanton, K., *Breach of Statutory Duty in Tort* (London, 1986).

Stapleton, J., 'Tort, Insurance and Ideology' (1995) 58 *Modern Law Review* 820–43.

State Pollution Control Commission, *Annual Report*, 1990–91.

Steele, J., 'Private Law and the Environment: Nuisance in Context' (1995) 15 *Legal Studies* 236–59.

—— 'Private Rights and Planning Consent' (1995) 2 *Web Journal of Current Legal Issues.*

—— 'Being There is Not Enough—The House of Lords Puts the Brakes on Nuisance in the Home' (1997) 9 *Journal of Environmental Law* 378–86.

—— and Wikeley, N., 'Dust on the Streets and Liability for Environmental Cancers' (1997) 60 *Modern Law Review* 265–76.

Stein, A. A., 'Coordination and Collaboration: Regimes in an Anarchic World' (1982) 36 *International Organization* 299–324.

Steinberg, R., 'Trade-Environment Negotiations in the EU, NAFTA and WTO: Regional Trajectories of Rule Development' (1997) 91 *American Journal of International Law* 231–67.

Stenzel, P. L., 'Right to Know Provisions of California's Proposition 65: The Naivete of the Delaney Clause Revisited' (1991) 15 *Harvard Environmental Law Review* 493–527.

Stewart, D., and McColl, G., 'The Resource Assessment Commission: An Inside Assessment' (1994) 1 *Australian Journal of Environmental Management* 12–23.

Stewart, R. B., 'Regulation, Innovation and Administrative Law: A Conceptual Framework' (1981) 69 *California Law Review* 1255–1377.

—— 'Environmental Regulation and International Competitiveness' (1992) 102 *Yale Law Journal* 2061–84.

—— 'Liability for Natural Resource Damage: Beyond Tort', in Revesz and Stewart (eds.), *Analyzing Superfund* (1995).

—— *Market Versus Environment*, Jean Monet Chair Papers No. 19, European University Institute (Florence, 1995).

Swanson, T., 'Economic Instruments and Environmental Regulation: A Critical Introduction' (1995) 4 *Review of European Community and International Environmental Law* 287–95.

Temmink, H., 'Mimimumnormen in EG Richtlijnen' (1995) 43 *Tijdschrift voor Sociaal en Economisch Recht* 79–106.

Teubner, G., 'Substantive and Reflexive Elements in Modern Law' (1983) 17 *Law and Society Review* 239–86.

—— 'Juridification—Concepts, Aspects, Limits, Solutions', in Teubner (ed.), *Juridification of Social Spheres* (1987).

—— (ed.), *Juridification of Social Spheres* (Berlin, 1987).

—— 'After Legal Instrumentalism', in Teubner (ed.), *Dilemmas of Law in the Welfare State* (1988).

—— (ed.), *Dilemmas of Law in the Welfare State* (Berlin, 1988).

—— *Law as an Autopoietic System* (Oxford, 1993).

—— 'The Invisible Cupola: From Causal to Collective Attribution in Ecological Liability', in Teubner, Farmer, and Murphy (eds.), *Environmental Law and Ecological Responsibility: The Concept and Practice of Ecological Self-Organization* (1994).

—— Farmer, L. and Murphy, D. (eds.), *Environmental Law and Ecological Responsibility: The Concept and Practice of Ecological Self-Organization* (Chichester, 1994).

Thomas, C., 'Beyond UNCED: An Introduction', in Thomas (ed.), *Rio: Unravelling the Consequences* (1994).

—— (ed.), *Rio: Unravelling the Consequences* (Ilford, 1994).

—— and Wilkin, P., *Globalization and the South* (Basingstoke, 1997).

Tietenberg, T. H., 'Economic Instruments for Environmental Regulation', in Helm (ed.), *Economic Policy Towards the Environment* (1991).

Trebilcock, M., 'Incentive Issues in the Design of "No-Fault" Compensation Schemes' (1989) 39 *University of Toronto Law Journal* 19–54.

Tromans, S., and Grant, M. (eds.), *Encyclopedia of Environmental Law* (London, 1993).

Twining, W., 'Reflections on Law in Context', in Cane and Stapleton (eds.), *Essays for Patrick Atiyah* (1991).

Ullman, A., 'The Implementation of Air Pollution Control in German Industry' (1982–3) 11 *Policy Studies Journal* 141–52.

Ullmann, W., *Law and Politics in the Middle Ages* (New York, 1975).

United Nations Economic Commission for Europe, *Guidelines on Access to Environmental Information and Public Participation in Environmental Decision-Making* (1995).

United Nations Environment Programme—Industry and Environment, 'Vienna Plus Ten. The Vienna Convention—10 Years of Achievement', November 1995: *OzoneAction Special Supplement*.

United Nations Research Institute for Social Development, *States of Disarray: The Social Consequences of Globalization* (London, 1995).

United Nations/World Commission on Environment, 'Development Proposals for International Environmental Law Developments Toward the Year 2000' (1986) 16 *Environmental Policy and Law* 90–6.

Vandermeersch, D., 'Twintig jaar EC-milieurecht in retrospectief: van casuïstiek naar modern beleid?' (1992) 40 *Tijdschrift voor Europees en economisch recht* 532–65.

Vincent, J., *Human Rights and International Relations* (Cambridge, 1986).

Vinogradov, S., 'International Environmental Security: The Concept and Implementation', in Carty and Danilenko (eds.), *Perestroika and International Law: Current Anglo-Soviet Approaches to International Law* (1990).

Vogel, D., *National Styles of Regulation: Environmental Policy in Great Britain and the United States* (Ithaca, 1986).
von Moltke, K., *The Vorsorgeprinzip in West German Environmental Policy* (London, 1987).
von Wetzsäcker, C., 'Competing Notions of Biodiversity', in Sachs (ed.), *Global Ecology* (1993).
Vorwerk, A., *Die Umweltpolitischen Kompetenzen der Europäischen Gemeinschaften nach Inkrafttreten der EEA* (München, 1990).
Walker, R. B. J., 'Security, Sovereignty, and the Challenge of World Politics' (1990) 15 *Alternatives* 3–27.
—— and Mendlowitz, S. H., *Contesting Sovereignty: Redefining Political Community* (Boulder, 1990).
Wallerstein, I., *Historical Capitalism* (London, 1983).
Warren, L., and Murray, V., 'PPG 9 "Nature Conservation"—A New Initiative' [1995] *Journal of Planning and Environment Law* 574–9.
Waters, M., *Globalisation* (London, 1995).
Watson, A., *The Evolution of International Society* (London, 1992).
Watson, J. S., 'Legal Theory, Efficacy and Validity in the Development of Human Rights International Law' (1979) 3 *University of Illinois Law Forum* 609–41.
Weale, A., *The New Politics of Pollution* (Manchester, 1992).
Weatherill, S., and Beaumont, P., *EC Law* (2nd ed., London, 1995).
Weber, M., *Economy and Society* (Roth, G., and Whittle, R., eds., California, 1978).
Weiler, J., 'The Community System: the Dual Character of Supranationalism' (1981) 1 *Yearbook of European Law* 286–306.
Weinrib, E., 'Legal Formalism: On the Immanent Rationality of Law' (1988) 97 *Yale Law Journal* 949–1015.
Wellens, K., and Borchardt, G., 'Soft Law in European Community Law' (1989) 14 *European Law Review* 267–321.
Werksman, J. (ed.), *Greening International Institutions* (London, 1996).
Wetterstein, P. (ed.), *Harm to the Environment* (Oxford, 1997).
Wight, M., 'Why Is There No International Theory?', in Butterfield and Wight (eds.), *Diplomatic Investigations* (1966).
Wikeley, N., 'Turner and Newall: Early Organizational Responses to Litigation Risk' (1997) 24 *Journal of Law and Society* 252–75.
Winter, G., 'Perspectives for Environmental Law—Entering the Fourth Phase' (1989) 1 *Journal of Environmental Law* 38–47.
Wood, M., 'Local Plans and UDPs: Is There a Better Way?' [1996] *Journal of Planning and Environment Law* 807–15.
World Commission on Environment and Development, *Proposed Legal Principles for Environmental Protection and Sustainable Development: Our Common Future* (Oxford, 1987).
Yeager, P. C., *The Limits of Law: The Public Regulation of Private Pollution* (Cambridge, Mass., 1991).
Young, O., *International Cooperation: Building Regimes for Natural Resources and the Environment* (Ithaca, 1989).
—— 'The Politics of International Regime Formation' (1989) 43 *International Organisation* 349–75.

Index

Abel, 124, 250
Abraham, 233
access to information (*see also* information legislation), 15, 17, 52–62, 72, 76, 91–6, 104, 139–60, 164
  charging, 97, 151
  development in EU, 146
  functions, 140–3
  ideal system, 143–6
access to justice, 2, 202, 205
accountability (*see also* public law), 27, 141, 190, 203, 205, 220
  criticism of mechanisms, 97–8
  ex ante, 76, 91–2, 96, 104
  ex post, 77, 91–2, 105
Ackerman, 11, 34–5, 49
adaptive management, 69–70, 72
administrative law, 44
administrative transparency (*see also* public law, principles of openness and accountability), 89–98
  compared with access to information, 90–1
Alaska, 233
Alfonso, 177
Alison, 162
Alston, 238, 265
ambiguous language, 160, 195
Anderson, 35, 47, 68, 237
Arnold, 42
Arnstein, 54
Asarco copper smelter, 59
Ashworth, 92
assimilation, 21, 25, 78–81, 83, 138, 192
  explained, 79–80
Atiyah, 24, 111–12, 129
Atkins, 100
Atkinson, 145–6
atmospheric controls, 5–6
Audi, 167
Audretsch, 174
Augelli, 222
Australia (*see also* New South Wales, Victoria), 54, 60, 128, 234–5, 253, 256–7
  forestry industry policy, 61
  Resource Assessment Commission, 61
Ayres, 108, 114, 117, 119–21, 122
Axelrod, 188

Baas, 43
Bakkenist, 150, 155
Balkenborg, 16
Ball, 99–100
Barents, 170, 186
Barker, 74, 90
Barkun, 223
Barnard, 133
Barwick, 255
Bateson, 215, 224
BATNEEC (*see also* best), 193
Bayefsky, 248
Beaumont, 148
Beck, 120–2, 125
Beder, 42
Bedjaoui, 238
Behrens, 165
Bell, 99
Bengoetxea, 170
best (*see also* BATNEEC)
  available control technology, 34
  practicable environmental option, 81
  practicable means, 35
Bhopal, 219, 233
Bhoutros-Ghali, 229
biosphere, 33
Bird, 195
Birkinshaw, 91, 140–2, 144–5, 153–4, 156
Birks, 24, 112
Birnie, 161, 232, 243–4, 247
Birtles, 94, 152
board room, 121
Bonyhady, 47
Borchardt, 180
Boyer, 16
Boyle, 161, 232, 237–8, 243–4, 247
Bradby, 34, 92
Bradley, 165
Braithwaite, 23, 108, 114, 117, 119–22
Brenner, 107, 131
Bridges, 151, 158
Brindley, 134–6
Brinkhorst, 188
British Standard specification, 64–5
Brown, 170
Brownlie, 243
Brown Weiss, 212, 233, 238, 243–4
Brubaker, 135
Brundtland Commission, 225
BSE, 221
Bull, 210
Burley, 178–9

Burrows, 20
Burton, 96
Bush, 125
Butterfield, 209

Calabresi, 16
Campaign for Freedom of Information, 149
Canada, 234
  Law Reform Commission, 48
Cane, 108, 110–11
Carr, 212
Carson, 40
Carty, 233
CFCs, 211, 232
Chappell, 30, 32, 37, 47–8, 52
Chatterjee, 208, 224–5, 242
Chinkin, 1–4, 9, 18, 27, 235, 245, 252
Chomsky, 220
Churchill, 81
Clausson, 224
collective liability, 68–9
Collins, 176
command-and-control, 11–16, 23, 28–9, 32, 33–9, 42–9, 72, 78, 92, 99, 101, 103, 117, 131, 162
commodification, 25, 220
common heritage, 163
common law, 8, 16, 100, 107, 129, 132, 136–8
communicative informality, 13, 65
comparative legal study, 33
competing visions of public interest, 137
Conaghan, 107
concealment of state practice, 250
conservation, 7
consultation
  with confined range of interests, 104
consumer lifestyles, 47–8
contract, 24
control (*see also* command-and-control), 9–16, 21, 27, 121, 129, 193
  ex ante, 136
  ex post, 136
  integrated controls (*see also* integration), 11
Cooper, 124
cost-benefit analysis, 8
Countryside Commission, 112
Cox, 215, 217, 219, 222
Cranston, 158
Craven, 254
criminal law, 33–5, 47–9, 68, 236
  a blunt tool, 49
  public welfare offences, 48
  sentencing options, 68
Crocodile Group, 173
Curtin, 178

Dalby, 216
Danilenko, 233
Darré, 162
Day, 124, 133
DDT, 13, 35–6
Deakin, 109
Debrulle, 188
decision-making, 2, 17, 22, 26, 50, 53, 72, 84, 93–4, 98, 115, 159–60, 163–4, 167, 179–205, 223, 227, 229–30
  and access to information, 139–60
  centralizing of influence, 98
  environmentally better decisions, 78–9
  identity of decision-makers, 77
  in international environmental law, 243–64
  institutional context, 204
  international context, 230–3
  opening to critical debate, 121–2
  political nature, 61, 103
  remote, 113–14
  statutory processes, 74–105
  strategic, 86–9, 104, 180
deep pockets liability, 23, 26, 129
de la Torre, 143–4, 149, 153, 158
Delors, 173, 187
Denys, 181
democracy (*see also* participation), 1, 27, 38, 54, 72, 77, 104–5, 117, 119–21, 175, 183, 185–6, 190, 203, 219–20, 231, 250
  democratic deficit, 265
  participatory, 1
  representative, 1
  republican vision, 119
Denmark, 64
Denning, 107
Denys, 170
development, 20
  and environmental protection, 9, 21
Dewees, 107
Dhavan, 124
Dicey, 54
diffusion, 3–9, 12, 15, 20, 81
  explained, 4
Dingwall, 109
discretion, 67, 72
disintegration of traditional values, 217
distantiation, 220
divided interests, 111–14, 123, 129, 131, 137–8, 164, 239
  developed/developing states, 231, 242
  EU institutions/member states, 205
  national/local, 135–6
Docklands litigation, 132–7
Dovers, 31, 53, 60
Downing, 37, 47
Dudley, 92
Dunkley, 44, 53, 78, 124

Dupuy, 245
Duxbury, 86

Earth Charter, 231
East Timor, 257–8
EC(EU) directives, 148, 152
  minimizing impact, 195–200
ecological concerns (*see also* sustainable development), 138
ecological covenants, 66
ecological degradation (*see also* environmental degradation), 25
ecological problems, 2
ecological risks, 120
economic instruments, 62–3, 104, 192
  and public law, 102
  UK commitment, 98–102
  variety of meanings, 99–101
economic theory, 172
education, 58–9
end-of-pipe approaches, 12, 14, 28, 34–5, 42
enforcement gap (*see also* implementation deficit), 202
Enlightenment, 23
environmental damage, 20, 107–8, 131, 175
environmental degradation, 27, 49, 210, 215–16, 218, 220, 224–5, 227, 229–30, 240
  as crisis of modernity, 208, 222
environmental discourse, 227
environmental issues, 137–8
environmental law (*see also* EU/UK/US environmental law, international law), 21, 26, 28
  as aspect of public law, 26–7
  development, 3–4, 6, 8, 20–1, 143, 161–4, 196, 229, 264
  instrumental/functional perspective, 162
environmental management systems, 64–5, 69, 104
environmental regimes, 243
environmental risks
  nature of, 125
environmental security, 209, 223
environmental standards, 81–2, 8
  inherently evaluative, 84
  technical measurability, 82
environmental stewardship, 81, 142
environmental treaties, 224
EU (*see also* EC(EU) directives), 221
  Commission, 172–5, 180, 183, 185, 188–93, 195–201, 203–4, 251
  Conciliation Committee, 183–4
  Council, 180, 182–5, 189–90, 193–4, 204
  DGXI, 172, 175
  enforcement, 200–3
  European Court of Justice, 18, 177–9, 181–2, 185–7, 190–1, 195–202, 204–5
  European Environment Agency, 192
  European Parliament, 175–7, 180–6, 189, 204
  Fifth Action Programme on the Environment, 140
  relations between institutions and member states, 170, 172, 179, 205
  supranational institutional structure, 170–2, 176
EU environmental law, 2, 4–5, 8, 15, 17–19, 24–5, 64, 86, 88, 139–60, 163–205
  and internal market, 163–70, 184–5, 191
  choice of instruments, 189–90
  choice of regulatory instruments, 192–4
  choice of regulatory technique, 191–2
  economic context, 203–5
  implementation, 194–200
  implementing directives, 195–200
  formal powers, 181–7
  new philosophy, 203–5
  planning, 180–1
  practical implementation, 200
  regulatory chain, 179–205
  subsidiarity, 187–90, 193, 199, 203, 205
Europe, 34
Evans, 1–2, 18–19, 23–5, 27, 123, 214, 226
Everling, 187
exploiting uncertainty, 154
exporting dirty industry, 219

Fabian, 111
Fairley, 94
Falk, 210
Farmer, 13, 49, 108, 116
Farrier, 47–8
Felstiner, 109, 124
Fiji, 253
Finger, 208, 224–5
Finkle, 30, 32, 52
Finnis, 110
Fischer, 61
Fisher, 249
Fitzmaurice, 250
forests, 61, 231–2
framework conventions, 244
France, 64, 234–5, 253–6
Franklin, 48
French Revolution, 161
Friends of the Earth, 80, 149
functionalist theory, 171–2

G7, 220
Gaebler, 47
Galtung, 225
Garrett, 170–1, 179

GATT, 63–4, 240–1
General Motors, 219
Genn, 76, 140, 158
George, 172
Gérard, 150
Germany, 35
Gibson, 81
Giddens, 121, 220
Gill, 217–18, 220
global commons, 214
global environmental change, 27
global environmental resources, 20
global environmental security, 3
global free-market, 218
globalization, 1–2, 24–5, 164, 208–9, 233
global survival, 27
Goff, 130, 132–3
Goldblatt, 125
government failure, 22, 25
Grabitz, 165
Graham, 11, 76–7
Grant, 86, 134
Green Alliance, 80
Green movement, 146
Greenpeace, 55, 236
Gregorczsk, 250
Groth, 33
Gulf War, 235
Gunder Frank, 215
Gunning, 245
Gunningham, 13, 20, 23, 65, 83

Haas (E), 171–2
Haas (P), 214
Habermas, 116–17, 125
Hadfield, 74
Hahn, 243–4
Haigh, 80–1
Hajer, 49
Haley, 33
Hallo, 144, 146, 150, 153, 156
Handl, 248
Hardin, 32, 61
Hargrove, 248
Harlow, 141–2
Hawkins, 14, 20, 32, 39, 47
Held, 218
Hellmann, 142
Helm, 98
Henkin, 248
Herbert-Young, 87
Herz, 210
Heukels, 178, 193
Higgins, 230
Hiroshima, 261
Hirschorn, 43
Hirst, 218
Hitler, 161
Hoffmann, 133, 136, 215, 222
holistic approach, 5, 29–33, 50, 71, 179, 265
horizontal/vertical policy, 186
Horwitz, 131
Hughes, 6, 34, 99
Hungary, 251
Hurrell, 207, 222, 230, 243, 265
Hutchinson, 48
Hutter, 20
Huymans, 220

ICI, 55
Idelson, 214
idioms of analysis, 23, 37–41
  institutional idiom, 38–9, 55, 62
  policy discourse idiom, 38, 62
  political economics idiom, 38
  rational choice idiom, 37, 70
Iles, 69
impact auditing, 59–60
implementation deficit (*see also* enforcement gap), 36, 142, 173
Indonesia, 257
information-based strategies, 25
information legislation
  Australia, 154
  Belgium, 153
  Canada, 145, 154
  Denmark, 144, 152–3
  EU, 139, 146–60
  France, 144, 152–3
  Germany, 152–9
  Greece, 152–9
  Ireland, 152–9
  Italy, 153
  Luxembourg, 153
  Netherlands, 144, 152–3
  New Zealand, 154
  Portugal, 153
  Scandinavia, 154
  Spain, 152–9
  Sweden, 144
  UK, 152–9
  US, 145, 154
information technology, 218
innovative approaches, 12–17, 19, 67–70, 114, 120, 173, 204, 245, 265
institutional dynamics, 170–9
insurance, 23–4, 109–13, 130
  third party, 24
integrated pollution control system, 81
integration, 3–7, 11, 29–33, 50, 67–8, 71–2, 78–81, 83, 88, 142, 164, 178, 184, 193, 217
  explained, 4, 79, 81
  organizational, 6–7

inter-disciplinary approach, 50
International Court of Justice, 4, 250–64
  advisory opinions, 259–62
  amicus brief, 258
  environmental chamber, 251
  exclusion of non-party interests, 252
  lack of compulsory jurisdiction, 263–4
  only states as parties, 252
  standing, 254–6
  third party state, 252–3, 256–8
international institutions, 214–15, 219, 221, 236
international law, 2, 4–5, 18–20, 24, 27, 207–27, 229–65
  adjudication, 249–59, 263–4
  and globalization, 216–27
  characterizations, 209
  compliance, 247–9
  dispute resolution, 247–9
  failings of international environmental law, 265
  international society view, 212–16
  legitimating role, 222
  limitations, 222–7, 229–30
  primary goal, 229
  realist tradition, 209–12
  sources, 243–7
  tensions within principles, 233–42
International Law Commission, 245
International Organization for Standardisation, 64–5
international relations, 209–27
international trade (*see also* GATT), 240–2
Iraq, 235–6
Ireland, 64
  ENFO, 158
  Office of the Ombudsman, 158
Irwin, 50, 80–1
Israel, 64

Jacobs, 99
Jackson (R), 209
Jackson (T), 43
Jaffe, 168
Jans, 162, 202
Japan, 33, 239
Jenkins, 174
Jewell, 1, 3, 7, 9, 16, 26, 62, 79, 84–7, 90, 114–15, 131, 142, 231
Johnson, 74
Jordan, 88
Jowell, 74–5
Judge, 175, 177
judicial activism, 187
judicial review, 151, 158, 185
  defects, 158
  resources barrier, 158
juridification
  as ugly concept, 116

Kangaroo Group, 173
Kaplan, 226
Karl, 189
Katzenbach, 226
Kee, 36
Kellerman, 193
Kennedy, 170
Keohane, 172, 213–14
key questions, 71–2
Kiewiet, 177
Killingsworth, 221
Kimball, 37
Kimber, 1–2, 10, 15, 17, 25, 90, 96, 143–4, 149, 153, 158
Kingsbury, 207, 222, 230, 241, 243, 265
Kleindorfer, 249
Koppen, 13, 55
Koroma, 262
Koskenniemi, 230, 248, 262
Krämer, 146, 162, 166, 180, 202
Krasner, 214
Krier, 100
Kuwait, 235
Kuznlik, 174

Laffont, 16
Lamont, 219
Landy, 58
Lash, 121
Lasswell, 230
Latin, 35, 37, 39, 47, 54, 69–70, 98
law and economics, 16, 135, 167, 205
Leape, 154
Lee, 262
Lenaerts, 188
lenders, 23
legal disciplines, 21–2
legal techniques, 3, 11–17, 21–2
lenders, 16
Levy, 214
Lewis (N), 74
Lewis (R), 78
Linklater, 215
Lipman, 48, 68
logging operations, 45
Lomas, 85
loss distribution, 130, 132
Loughlin, 75, 116
Lowe, 61, 250
Luhmann, 116

MacKenzie, 68
Macrory, 85–6

Majone, 171, 173
Major, 174
Mansell, 107
Margereson, 128
Markesinis, 109
market, 99, 102, 109, 135, 163–4, 218–20, 232, 242
market failure, 22
market research techniques, 57
Martin, 258
Mattli, 178–9
Maxwell, 211
Mazey, 176, 192
McAuslan, 77, 95, 97
McColl, 61
McCubbins, 177
McDougal, 30, 230
McEldowney, 77
McGoldrick, 238–9
McGrew, 218
McLaren, 107, 123, 126
McLeod, 78
Meijers, 245, 264
Melamed, 16
Mendlowitz, 215
Menkel-Meadow, 249
Meszaros, 151
Miller, 154
Millichap, 79
Milward, 170
Mittelman, 217, 219
modernity, 208, 218–19, 222
Moltke, 8
Moore, 30, 32, 37, 47–8, 52
moral judgment, 119
More, 133
Morgenthau, 210
Morvcsik, 170
Mosler, 212
multinational corporations, 24–5, 213, 218–19, 226–7, 232–3
Murase, 231, 241, 243
Murphy, 13, 49, 108, 116, 222
Murray, 89

NAFTA, 242
Nagasaki, 261
Nardin, 213–15
national security, 234–6
Nauru, 256–7
Nébeleuse, 219–20
negligence, 110
Nelsen, 173
Netherlands, 64, 198
Newall, 129
Newburg, 210
New International Economic Order, 242
New South Wales, 34, 42, 44–6, 51, 53, 56–7, 60–2
  EPA, 56
  Interim Forest Assessment Process, 61
  litter control, 66
Newton, 161
New Zealand, 234–5, 241, 253, 256–7
NGOs, 142, 149, 158, 203, 208, 217, 223–5, 236–7, 239, 246, 248, 259, 261, 265
Nixon, 10
Nonet, 118–19
normative principles of law, 75
North America, 34
nuclear testing, 253–5
nuclear waste, 18, 48
nuclear weapons, 259–62
nuisance, 85,
  common law, 16, 127, 130–4, 137
  statutory, 6

OECD countries, 50, 99
Ogus, 12, 16, 20, 73
Oliver, 74–5, 141
organised irresponsibility, 122
Organization for Economic Cooperation and Development, 62
Osborne, 47
Ostram, 32
other voices, 14
Owen, 123
ozone-depleting substances, 68, 263

Pacific Island States, 253
Palmer, 221, 245, 254
Panitch, 217
paradigm shifts
  international environmental law, 233
  pollution control, 51
  waste management, 43
Park, 101
participation (*see also* democracy), 14–15, 17, 28, 54–5, 60, 66, 71, 77, 95, 117–20, 140–3, 151, 156, 159–60, 163–4, 185–6, 202–3, 205, 239
  official ambivalence, 97
Patton, 242
Paul, 238
Peck, 262
Percival, 154
Peters, 195
Peterson, 33, 168
philosophical perspective
  eco-philosophy, 38
  ideology of modernity, 218
  individualist, 23–4
  liberal, 23, 70, 219–20

neo-liberal, 23, 162
neo-Marxist, 38
Pickersgill, 258
Pitchford, 16
planning, 26, 49, 79, 86, 93, 95, 134, 138, 184
fast-track, 136
relationship with common law, 136–7
Polack, 171–2, 176
political transformation, 19
polluter-pays principle, 8–9, 37, 70, 131, 224–5
pollution
characterizations, 41
control, 2, 7, 15, 29–72, 81, 85, 87, 95, 100, 103
empires, 37
perceptions of, 52
respectable, 47
shift, 42
ways of controlling, 31
Pontin, 116
Portugal, 257–8
practical/purposive association, 213–15
precautionary principle, 8
preventive principle, 8
prisoner's dilemma, 167–9
private spheres, 115
privatization, 1, 22–6, 101, 112, 135, 220
privatized water companies, 148
procedural/substantive relationship, 73, 77–8, 84, 202
process approach to law, 30–2
process-oriented responses, 28
process-related, 65
product ban, 13
property—*see* rights
Prosser, 11, 77
public attitudes
brown bombers, 57
grudging greens, 57
lip service greens, 57
living green, 57
public awareness, 52–62, 140
public interest groups, 120
public law, 1, 73–105
constitutional view of, 75
explained 73–5
fair process, 75–6
principles of openness and accountability, 76–7, 89–90, 96–8, 103
procedural character, 73–4, 77
state of, 78
traditional role of, 80
public participation—*see* participation
public/private relationship, 16–17, 19, 26, 74, 135, 155
public relations exercise, 54, 56, 176, 226
Pugh, 124, 133
Purdue, 5, 8, 95

race-to-the bottom, 17, 24, 167–9, 183
race-to-the top, 24, 168–70, 183, 188, 205
Rainbow Warrior, 235–6
Ramphal, 220
Rankin, 32, 52
Raphael, 23
Rasmussen, 179
Rawlings, 141–2
ReChem, 130–1
reciprocity, 110–11
undermined (*see also* divided interests), 115
Rehbinder, 166, 203
Reich, 59
Reid, 74, 100
reflexive law, 65, 67, 116–18
equalization of power structures, 118–19
participation, 118–19
regulated autonomy, 118–19
registers, 91–6
regulation, 20
regulatory failure, 24
research laboratories, 121
respectable polluters, 47
respect for the environment, 261
responsive regulation, 119–20
Revesz, 112, 168
rhetoric, 45, 230
Richards, 243–4
Richardson, 16, 20, 32, 39, 47, 76, 140, 158, 176, 192
rights
environmental, 197, 237
human rights, 207, 210, 215, 236–9, 255–6, 262
importance of certainty, 154
intellectual property, 220
inter-generational rights, 237–8
landowner's, 100
of access to information, 15, 147, 149–50, 155–7, 159
of ownership, 220
of the citizen, 96–7
participation rights, 54
polluter's, 100
practical/abstract, 158
property rights, 108, 132, 135–6
to a decent environment, 143
to a voice, 212
to development, 2, 9, 238–40, 246
to exploit natural resources, 231
to information, 25, 53, 145, 153
to international trade, 2
to privacy and confidentiality, 144

rights (*cont.*):
  to self-defence, 261
  to self-determination, 238
  transposition of EU rights, 194–7, 199
  without adequate remedies, 151
Rio Declaration, 9, 49, 79, 163, 208, 231, 237–40, 246
risk
  assessment, 8, 21, 60, 86, 104, 115, 137–8
  creating and bearing, 113
  creating sector, 128–9
  distribution, 110, 119, 121
  management, 11, 16, 26, 58, 69, 111, 127, 138
  realization, 109–10
Robbins, 44
Roberts, 58
Robinson (B), 34–5, 50
Robinson (D), 1–3, 5, 10, 12–14, 16, 23, 25, 28, 44–5, 53–4, 60, 73, 78, 82, 84, 90, 112, 114, 117, 124, 142, 231
Robinson (N), 79, 233
Roderick, 156
Rodgers, 100
roles of law, 122, 138
Roots, 48, 68
Rose-Ackerman, 10
Ross, 22, 81, 141–2
Roth, 116
Rothnie, 81, 141
Roundtable of European Industrialists, 173
Rowan-Robinson, 22, 81, 91, 95–6, 141–2
Rowlands, 231
Ruckelshaus, 60, 67
rule of law, 13, 75
Rydin, 134

Sachs, 217
Saggio, 165
Sandholtz, 173
Sandman, 55, 60
Sands, 231
Santon, 109
Sarat, 124
Saravanamuttu, 210
Sardar Sarovan Dam, 239
Saurin, 220–1
Sax, 135
Sbragia, 195
Schachter, 229
Sched, 87, 94
Schermers, 178
Scheuer, 165
Scheuning, 165
Schmitter, 172
Schoenbaum, 124, 240–1
Schroeder, 154
Schröer, 187
Schulkin, 249
Seager, 85
self-interested individuals, 37
  NIMBY, 37
self organization, 117–18
self-regulation, 13, 22–3, 30, 63–7, 82–3, 103–4
  modified self-regulation, 65–7
Selznick, 118–19
Sevenster, 191–2
Seveso disaster, 176
shared responsibility, 8
Shaw, 133
Sheate, 145–6
Sheldon, 64
Shelton, 237
Slovakia, 251
Sluys, 193
Smith, 208, 211
smoke-filled rooms, 120–1
Snyder, 190
soft law, 189–90, 199, 202, 245, 263–4
Somsen, 1–5, 17–18, 23–4, 86, 176–7, 182, 185, 193, 195, 202–3
sound scientific evidence, 222
South-Africa, 64
sovereignty, 184, 209–10, 212, 216, 226, 232, 234, 246, 265
Spain, 200, 234
Spinelli, 173
Springer, 229, 243
Stapleton, 111, 113
state (*see also* sovereignty), 229–65
  as central actor, 207–8, 212, 215
  as historical phenomenon, 215
  as principal source of law, 47
  as subject, 18
  changing role, 1, 5
  conceptions of, 22
  incapacity of, 24–5
  interests of, 19, 246
  lesser significance, 208
  passive role, 217–19
  self-defence, 261
  self-interest of, 210–11, 214
Stavins, 168
Steele, 1, 7, 9, 12, 15, 23, 28, 67, 84–6, 90, 100, 107, 128, 130–1, 133, 231
Stein, 211
Stenzel, 59
Stewart (D), 61
Stewart (R), 11, 34–5, 49, 98, 102, 112, 124, 163, 166, 168–9
Stockholm Declaration, 231, 238, 243, 245–6
Stoker, 134
strategic/tactical distinction, 104
Stubb, 173

sub judice, 156
Sunkin, 151
sustainability, 3, 140
sustainable development, 6–9, 11, 25–7, 39–41, 49, 51, 81, 163–4, 231, 239–40
sustainable growth, 25
Swanson, 99, 101
Sweden, 35
Sydney's surfing beaches, 62
systems approach, 32

technique/goal distinction, 114
techniques, 8, 19–20
teleological interpretation, 178
Temmink, 191
Teubner, 13, 49, 55, 65, 67, 69, 108, 116–19
Thatcher, 135
Theron, 22
Thietenberg, 98
third parties, 44, 65–6
Thomas, 58, 208, 210, 221, 226
Thompson, 218
Thorn-Davignon, 173
tort law, 1, 24, 107–38
  ambiguous role, 122–3
  causation, 129–30
  contrast with regulation, 128–9
  culpability, 130–2
  deterrence, 109
  distribution, 109
  foreseeability, 127–30, 138
  instrumental application, 108–9, 119
  litigants, 124–6
  plaintiff/polluter relationship, 125–6
  social factors as basis of failure, 123–4
trade secrets, 157
transnational corporations—*see* multinational corporations
Trebilcock, 109
Trilateral Commission, 220
Trippier, 94
Tromans, 86
tuna, 241
Turner, 129
Twining, 111

UK, 35, 38, 50, 53, 56, 60, 81, 139, 211, 221, 256–7, 264
  adoption of strategic planning, 86–9
  bathing waters, 200
  Department of the Environment, 54
  Environment Agency, 88, 137
  negotiated rule-making, 85
  new formalism, 85
  regional advisory committees, 97
  Royal Comission on Environmental Pollution, 141
UK environmental law, 3–12, 14, 84–9
Ullmann (A), 52
Ullman (W), 161
UN, 18, 207–8, 237, 246, 262
  Charter, 249
  Commission on Human Rights, 264–5
  Commission on Sustainable Development, 214, 245, 259
  Convention on the Law of the Sea, 242, 263
  Economic Commission for Europe, 139, 141–2
  Environmental Programme, 244
  General Assembly, 260
  peacekeeping forces, 256
  Security Council, 235–6
UNICE, 173
Ury, 249
US, 26, 30, 33–5, 38, 44–7, 56, 71, 144, 211, 235, 241
  Congress, 239–40
  Department of State, 217
  EPA, 10, 44–5, 58–60, 71
US environmental law, 10–11

Vandermeersch, 162
vehicle emissions, 36, 39–41, 47, 49, 52, 59
Verkruisen, 193
Victoria, 51, 60, 67, 70
  EPA, 64
Vincent, 207
Vogel, 38
voices, 212, 221
von Wetzsäcker, 217
Vorwerk, 165
Voyatzi, 143–4

Wade, 33
Walker, 210, 215
Wallerstein, 216–17
Walton, 141
Warren, 81, 89
watching the watchdog, 177
Watchman, 90
water quality, 39–41, 45, 59, 63, 85–6, 93, 95, 166–7, 169, 176, 184, 189, 192, 230, 236, 251
Waters, 219
Watson, 215
Weale, 34–5, 37, 42
wealth distribution, 129
Weatherill, 148
Weber, 116
Weeramantry, 254, 262
Weiler, 179
Weiner, 211

Weinrib, 123
welfare, 12–13, 16, 50, 111–12, 115, 125, 129, 131, 168–9
  contests, 136
Wellens, 180
Werksman, 176, 182
Wetterstein, 102, 124
whistle blowing, 175
Whittle, 116
Wight, 209
Wikeley, 126, 128
Wilkin, 226
Wilson, 214
Winter, 21, 83, 161
Wood, 87
World Bank, 220, 239–40
World Court Project, 259, 261
World Health Organization, 259–61
World Heritage Committee, 259
World Trade Organization, 220
World Wide Fund for Nature, 149

Yeager, 38, 125
Young, 95, 214, 224

Zysman, 173